THE

VIRGINIA REPORT

OF

1799—1800,

TOUCHING THE

ALIEN AND SEDITION LAWS;

TOGETHER WITH THE

VIRGINIA RESOLUTIONS

OF DECEMBER 21, 1798,

THE DEBATE AND PROCEEDINGS THEREON

IN THE

HOUSE OF DELEGATES OF VIRGINIA,

AND

SEVERAL OTHER DOCUMENTS

ILLUSTRATIVE OF

THE REPORT AND RESOLUTIONS.

THE LAWBOOK EXCHANGE, LTD.
Clark, New Jersey

ISBN 978-1-58477-374-0

Lawbook Exchange edition 2003, 2018

The quality of this reprint is equivalent to the quality of the original work.

THE LAWBOOK EXCHANGE, LTD.
33 Terminal Avenue
Clark, New Jersey 07066-1321

*Please see our website for a selection of our other publications
and fine facsimile reprints of classic works of legal history:*
www.lawbookexchange.com

Library of Congress Cataloging-in-Publication Data

Virginia. General Assembly. House of Delegates.
　　The Virginia report of 1799-1800, touching the Alien and Sedition laws: together
with the Virginia resolutions of December 21, 1798, the debate and proceedings thereon
in the House of Delegates of Virginia, and several other documents illustrative of
the report and resolutions.
　　　　p. cm.
　　Originally published: Richmond : J.W. Randolph, 1850.
　　Includes bibliographical references and index.
　　ISBN 1-58477-374-X (cloth: acid-free paper)
　　　　1. Alien and Sedition laws, 1798. 2. Kentucky and Virginia resolutions of
　　1798. I.
　　Madison, James, 1751-1836. II. Title.

KF9397.V572003
345.73'0231—dc21   2003052759

Printed in the United States of America on acid-free paper

THE

VIRGINIA REPORT

OF

1799—1800,

TOUCHING THE

ALIEN AND SEDITION LAWS;

TOGETHER WITH THE

VIRGINIA RESOLUTIONS

OF DECEMBER 21, 1798,

THE DEBATE AND PROCEEDINGS THEREON

IN THE

HOUSE OF DELEGATES OF VIRGINIA.

AND

SEVERAL OTHER DOCUMENTS

ILLUSTRATIVE OF

THE REPORT AND RESOLUTIONS.

———

RICHMOND:

J. W. RANDOLPH, 121 MAIN STREET,

ALSO FOR SALE BY FRANCK TAYLOR, WASHINGTON; CUSHING AND BROTHER,
BALTIMORE; AND T. AND J. W. JOHNSON, PHILADELPHIA.

1850.

PHILADELPHIA:
C. SHERMAN, PRINTER.

PREFACE.

THE design of this pamphlet, an edition of which was printed at Richmond some years ago, is to convey to the public the "Virginia Report of 1799," a state paper which, having wrought a great effect upon the political parties of its day, is still,—though more praised than read,—highly esteemed as a commentary on the Federal Constitution. The other papers which go along with the " Report," are intended, like this preface, only to illustrate it.

After the lapse of so many years, the reader, it is hoped, will not take it amiss that his memory is refreshed as to some of the incidents of the period that gave birth to this document ; a period perhaps the most critical in our national annals.

The present Federal Constitution, succeeding to the "Articles of Confederation," having been ratified by eleven states, commenced its operation, *nominally*, on the 4th of March, 1789, under the auspices of WASHINGTON, as the first President. In his Cabinet, and in the first Congress, were organized the parties afterwards known as " Federalists" and " Republicans." The former, under the sagacious lead of Alexander Hamilton, the Secretary of the Treasury, fearful of a recurrence of that anarchy which had overtaken the country under the imbecile government of the " Confederation," were inclined to a vigorous exercise of the federal power, and consequently adopted a liberal construction of the Federal Constitution. The Republicans, on the other side, headed by Mr. Jefferson, were apprehensive of a gradual absorption, by the central government, of the powers reserved to the states and to the people. Consolidation was their great terror, as the absence of all government was the terror of their opponents ; and consolidation they viewed, justly, as the forerunner not of monarchy only, but of despotism.

Mr. Hamilton, being a declared admirer of the English Constitution in the abstract, gave occasion to many of the opposite party to impute to him, and to his political associates, sentiments unfavourable to the existing institutions of the country; in short, a proclivity to monarchy. This suspicion, undoubtedly unjust as regards the great mass of the Federalists, was fortified. by their avowed opinions touching the necessity of what, in the phrase of the time, was called a *strong government.*

The occurrence of the French Revolution affected these parties with different emotions. The Republicans looked on in trusting faith that it would result in giving to France institutions modelled after our own, calculated to insure rational freedom, but affording no encouragement to licentiousness. The Federalists were less sanguine. They feared that the French people neither appreciated the blessings of liberty founded on law, nor were capable of attaining them, and they conceived all their conclusions confirmed by the succession of tragic scenes which accompanied the progress of the Revolution. Thenceforward sympathy with France constituted a prominent point of difference between their adversaries and themselves.

In 1793, upon the execution of Louis XVI., a war broke out between France and England, which, as it was characterized by unusual animosity between the contending parties, led to an emulous violation by both of the rights of neutral commerce. From these outrages no country suffered more than the United States, the citizens of which, instead of uniting to require indemnity from both belligerents, allowed their partisan feelings to array them as the apologists, or the denouncers, of one or the other, as previous tendencies disposed them. The Republicans favoured France, influenced as well by a natural sympathy for a great people struggling, as they supposed, for freedom, as by gratitude for the assistance so recently received in the war of our Revolution, and animated by a hostility, not yet extinct, towards our former enemy, Great Britain. The Federalists leaned towards England as the champion of conservatism, and the bulwark against that pernicious license everywhere propagated by French writers and emissaries.

The Republicans identified France with liberty, and cherished its cause with proportionate ardour. The Federalists saw in it only irreligion, private profligacy, bloody excess, and, in the end, the despotism of the sword, and abhorred it as a combination of all that was hateful to their reason, and their habits.

On the other hand, England was to the Federalists the embodiment of a government at once vigorous and free; not insensible to the opinions of its people, but impassive to their prejudices and passions ; and the regard due to those qualities, was extended to the country. To the Republicans, England was a monarchy, and their late oppressor, and now appeared to be a reluctant and surly friend, in each and all of which characters, it was alike odious.

The war had not been long in progress, when many Americans, stimu- lated by French agents, and the thirst of gain, and relying upon the pre- possessions of their countrymen, hastened to fit out armed vessels in several of our ports, to cruise under French commissions, against the enemies of France. England remonstrated, and there was issued, in consequence, General Washington's famous proclamation of neutrality, which, with the instructions founded upon it, rigorously interdicted such enterprises for the future. This led to a correspondence between Mr. Jefferson, then Secretary of State, and Genet, the French minister, resident here, in which the latter, confiding in the supposed popular partiality for France, crowned a series of impertinences by threatening to appeal from the government to the people of America, and was in consequence, by the request of the President, recalled.

Genet's recall,—his successor being a man of more moderation,—had the effect to restore those cordial feelings for France to which the former's indefensible conduct had given a shock. Meanwhile our commerce was suffering much from the depredations of both belligerents. In 1794, Mr. Jay, the Chief Justice of the United States, having been despatched as a special envoy to England, to adjust the numerous differences which had been accumulating with that country since the peace of 1783, the jealousy of France blazed fiercely out ; and when, the next year, the treaty nego- tiated by Mr. Jay was ratified by our government, the indignation of the Directory knew no bounds. Spoliations of our commerce were committed with as little reserve as if actual war existed, and the conduct of the French government was marked by every circumstance of contumely.

Jay's treaty, meanwhile, was received in America with a severity of reprehension which bespoke the decided Anti-Anglican dispositions of our people. It must be admitted, indeed, to have involved a painful sacrifice of the rights of our country, in more than one particular. It had the effect, however, to postpone a war with England until we were better able to bear it, and,—our Union preserved,—we shall probably never again be subjected to a like humiliation. The manifestations of popular feeling in- duced, in the French Directory, the conceit that the government of Ame- rica might be separated from its citizens. Acting upon this delusion, they took leave of Mr. Monroe, then our representative at Paris, with warm professions of regard for the people of America, and of undisguised hostility to the administration, and refused, with studied indignity, to receive Mr. Pinckney, who had been sent out as Mr. Monroe's successor.

Parties in the United States were thus situated when General Washington, at the end of his second term, resigned the reins of power to Mr. Adams, who was himself a Federalist, and chose his cabinet from those of kindred sentiments. Very soon after his accession, Mr. Adams made an effort to compose our misunderstanding with France by sending thither a solemn embassy, consisting of Mr. Charles C. Pinckney of South Carolina, Mr. Marshall of Virginia, and Mr. Gerry of Massachusetts. The joint appointment of gentlemen so distinguished ought to have evinced to France the strong desire of our government to conciliate her. They were treated, however, with an insolence inconceivable, were not admitted to an audience, and were subjected to the mortification of being approached by certain agents of Talleyrand, the minister for public affairs, with proposals as degrading as they were direct, for a bribe. The proposition was, that £50,000 sterling should be distributed amongst certain members of the Directory, as the necessary price of entering upon the negotiation. The envoys having peremptorily refused to buy, in any way, the privilege of presenting the just demands of their country, Messrs. Pinckney and Marshall were dismissed; Mr. Gerry, who, as belonging to the Republican party, was insultingly supposed to be more pliable, being requested to remain.

The envoys having communicated these transactions to their government, the correspondence was laid before Congress, and printed, the names of Talleyrand's brokers being veiled under the respective letters X. Y. Z. and W. The publication, like an electric shock, awakened all the dormant fires of patriotism in America. As one man the people stood forward prepared to vindicate the insulted honour and violated rights of their country. The President, anticipating the national spirit, in his message of 21st June, 1798, communicating the return of Mr. Marshall to the United States, peremptorily declared that he would " never send another minister to France without assurances that he would be received, respected, and honoured, as the representative of a great, free, powerful, and independent nation."

So strong was the general irritation under what was called " the X. Y. Z. excitement," that party lines were in a degree obliterated, and the administration of Mr. Adams was, for a brief period, lifted to a great height of popularity, whence, however, it was very soon precipitated into irretrievable disgrace.

The Federalists, elated at the spring-tide of favour setting in upon the administration, resolved to avail themselves of it to the utmost. With this view they proceeded vigorously with preparations for a war with France, and determined to take decisive steps to expel from the country all aliens who might be supposed hostile or dangerous to its institutions. Thus they hoped to keep up the excitement of anger against France, and of jealousy against her apologists amongst our own people, whilst they got rid of the French propagandists, and unquiet English and Irish agitators, who were employed too much in preaching license, under the name of liberty. The Alien Act was accordingly passed 25th June, 1798, being especially aimed, it was thought, at Volney, Collot, Priestley, and a few others. Then they essayed to curb what they called the licentiousness of the press by the Sedition Act, which received the assent of the President on the 14th July, 1798.

These two laws, but especially the last, were fatal to the party which originated them. The Alien Act alone, as being directed against comparatively few persons, and those strangers, might not have been so obnoxious, but the Sedition Law, trespassing, as it seemed to do, upon the freedom of the press, so cherished by the Anglo-Saxon race, raised a storm, before which all the recent popularity of Mr. Adams's administration vanished like morning mist.

Suspicions of the darkest ultimate designs were entertained and disseminated. "For my own part," says Mr. Jefferson, addressing a friend, "I consider those laws as merely an experiment on the American mind, to see how it will bear an avowed violation of the Constitution. If this goes down, we shall immediately see attempted another act of Congress, declaring that the President shall continue in office during life, reserving to another occasion the transfer of the succession to his heirs, and the establishment of the Senate for life !"

To these suspicions a deeper tinge was imparted by the preparations for the impending war with France. These, however indispensable, exposed the administration to misconstruction, and to complaints both loud and deep. An additional army, first of 10,000 and afterwards of 30,000 men was authorized to be raised in the event of a declaration of war, or an actual invasion, or imminent danger thereof, and the President was besides, authorized to accept the services of an indefinite number of volunteers. A navy was also begun on a liberal scale. To meet the expense of these measures, besides duties on imports, and a loan of $5,000,000, a direct tax of $2,000,000, (whereof the quota of Virginia was $345,488 66,) was laid on dwelling-houses, lands, and slaves. These burdens predispos-

ing the people to murmur, they hearkened readily to the vehement accu-
sations with which the press, the hustings, and even conversation teemed.

The Alien and Sedition Laws, the army and navy bills, and the large
sums placed within reach of the President, were represented as parts of
the same plan to perpetuate and enlarge his power.

In proportion as ideas like these gained ground, the Alien and Sedition
Laws became more odious. The zeal of the opposite party rising with
the prospect of success, and stimulated by a sense of the importance of
the principles supposed to be invaded, they addressed themselves, with
renewed ardour, to the task of overthrowing the administration. Nor
were its supporters idle or indifferent. The New England and the Middle
States were generally favourable to the party in power; the Southern
and Western States were for the most part Republican. But minorities
imposing in numbers and in character existed on either side. Both parties hastened to call into action all the political machinery available for
them respectively, of which the most efficient consisted in the solemn declarations of the several state legislatures touching the obnoxious laws.

Important as the crisis really was, it was factitiously exaggerated by
the partisanship on both sides. The advocates of administration, in order
to maintain the constitutionality of the Sedition Act, amongst other arguments, insisted that the offence denounced by it was an offence at *common
law,* and was therefore punishable in the courts of the United States, in-
dependently of the statute. The statute, it was said, was even more
favourable to the accused than the common law. The assumption involved in this argument, that the common law constituted part of the
federal jurisprudence, created more alarm than the main topics of complaint, the Alien and Sedition Laws themselves. It was regarded as an
accumulation, at one stroke, of all authority in the hands of the Federal
Government, there being no subject, legislative, executive, or judicial,
which the common law did not embrace; and it was anxiously urged
that the effect would be an annihilation of state sovereignty, and the
erection of a government consolidated, and therefore despotic. " Other
assumptions of ungiven power," said Mr. Jefferson, " have been in detail.
The bank law, the treaty doctrine, the sedition act, alien act, the undertaking to change the state laws of evidence in the state courts, by certain
parts of the stamp act, &c., &c., have been solitary, unconsequential,
timid things, in comparison with the audacious, bare-faced, and sweeping
pretension to a system of law for the United States, without the adoption
of their legislature, and so infinitely beyond their power to adopt."

The legislatures of the several states prepared to bear their parts in the drama. That of Virginia, which assembled in December, 1798, was looked to by both parties with peculiar interest. The plan of opposition to be pursued there was probably arranged by Mr. Jefferson and Mr. Madison, though neither was a member. The plan was to resolve that the Alien and Sedition Laws were unconstitutional and merely *void*, (which latter phrase, however, was ultimately struck out of the resolutions, as actually adopted,) and to address the other states, to obtain similar declarations. It was not contemplated to commit the commonwealth to any foreshadowed course of action, but to reserve the power to shape future measures by the events which should happen. Mr. Jefferson drew the resolutions for Kentucky,* which was ready to act consentaneously with Virginia, (and did, in fact, act before her,) and they were proposed in her legislature by Mr. Breckenridge. The Virginia resolutions,† submitted and ably defended by Mr. John Taylor, of Caroline, were from the pen of Mr. Madison.

The Virginia resolutions, having been officially communicated to the legislatures of all the other states, encountered from some of them a disapproval so decided as to make it necessary to sustain the propriety of them by argument. Accordingly, during the whole summer of 1799, the state was agitated with preparations for the approaching conflict. The Republicans possessed a decided majority in the legislature, and amongst the people, but the minority, besides being respectable for numbers, comprehended many individuals eminent for public and private virtue, for capacity, and for services rendered their country, and were sustained also by the august name of WASHINGTON.

The General Assembly, which convened in December, 1799, contained an unusual weight of ability and experience. Virginia mustered for the occasion her strongest men. The author of the resolutions was chosen for the county of Orange, and against him was marshalled no less a champion than PATRICK HENRY, who was elected from the county of Charlotte, but died before taking his seat.

To that General Assembly was submitted from a committee, at the head of which was Mr. Madison, that dignified and lucid report vindicatory of the resolutions of the previous year, ever since known in Virginia, as "Madison's Report," and out of it, as "the Virginia Report of 1799." It assisted materially in perfecting the victory already, in effect, achieved

---

* See them, *post*, p. 163. The authorship of these resolutions has lately been claimed for the distinguished gentleman who offered them.

† *Post*, p. 22.

by the Republican party. In the ensuing autumn, or rather winter, Mr. Jefferson was elected President, and the Alien and Sedition Laws having expired by their own limitation, no thought was entertained of renewing them, and their policy was abandoned, probably for ever.

This pamphlet, as remarked in the beginning, contains, besides the "Report," certain other publications calculated to illustrate it. The whole is arranged in the following order, viz. :

I. The Alien and Sedition Acts, 17 to 21.
II. Resolutions of Virginia of 21st December, 1798, with the debate thereon, 22 to 161.
III. Resolutions of Kentucky of 10th November, 1798, 162 to 167. .
IV. Counter-resolutions of several states in response to those of Virginia, 168 to 177.
V. Report of 1799, preceded by an analysis thereof, 178 to 237.
VI. Instructions to Virginia senators of January, 1800, and votes thereon, 238 to 248.
VII. Appendix: containing
    1. A letter from Mr. Madison to Mr. Everett, touching the construction of the first resolution of 1798, 249 to 256.
    2. A letter from the same to Mr. Ingersoll, relative to the Bank question, 257.
    3. A letter from the same to the same, on the same subject, 258 to 260.

In conclusion, it is proper to observe that this edition is intended especially for the use of students, and that the learned reader must expect to find in the notes, and in the analysis prefixed to the report, much with which *he* could dispense.

THE VIRGINIA REPORT,

ETC. ÉTC.

I. THE ALÍEN AND SEDITION ACTS.

AN ACT CONCERNING ALIENS.

[Approved June 25, 1798.]

ABSTRACT.

SECTION I. Confers power on the President to *order* aliens to *depart*.
1. What aliens.
   Such as the President shall judge dangerous to the peace and
   safety of the United States, or shall have reasonable grounds to
   suspect of treasonable or secret machinations against the government.
2. How proceeded against.
   By the President's order to depart, served by the marshal or other
   person. But the President may grant a license to remain on
   proof *by the alien*, that he is not dangerous; and may require
   bond and security of such person.
3. Consequences of disobedience.
   Imprisonment, on conviction, not exceeding three years, and perpetual disability to become a citizen.
SECTION II. Confers on the President power to *remove* aliens.
1. What aliens.
   Such as are above described, who are
   1. In prison, in pursuance of this Act.
   2. Dangerous, and proper to be speedily removed.
2. Consequences of returning without President's permission.
   Imprisonment, on conviction, as long as the President thinks the
   public safety requires it.
SECTION III. Requires masters of ships to report to officers of customs, all
   aliens on board.

2

SECTION IV. Gives the District and Circuit Courts of the United States
cognizance of all offences against this Act; and requires
marshals, and other officers of the United States to execute the President's orders under it.
SECTION V. Allows alien to remove his effects.
SECTION VI. Continues act in force for two years.

  ' SECTION 1. *Be it enacted by the Senate and House of Representatives*
of the United States of America, in Congress assembled, That it shall be
lawful for the President of the United States, at any time during the continuance of this act, to *order* all such *aliens* as he shall judge dangerous
to the peace and safety of the United States, or shall have reasonable
grounds to suspect are concerned in any treasonable or secret machinations against the government thereof, to depart out of the territory of the
United States within such time as shall be expressed in such order; which
order shall be served on such alien, by delivering him a copy thereof, or
leaving the same at his usual abode, and returned to the office of the
Secretary of State, by the marshal, or other person, to whom the same
shall be directed. And in case any alien, so ordered to depart, shall be
found at large within the United States after the time limited in such order
for his departure, and not having obtained a *license* from the President to
reside therein, or having obtained such *license,* shall not have conformed
thereto, every such alien shall, on conviction thereof, be imprisoned for a
term not exceeding three years, and shall never after be admitted to become a citizen of the United States : *Provided always, and be it further
enacted,* That if any alien so ordered to depart shall prove, to the satisfaction of the President, by evidence, to be taken before such person or persons as the President shall direct, who are for that purpose hereby authorized to administer oaths, that no injury or danger to the United States will
arise from suffering such alien to reside therein, the President may grant
a *license* to such alien to remain within the United States for such time as
he shall judge proper, and at such place as he may designate. And the
President may also require of such alien to enter into a bond to the United
States, in such penal sum as he may direct, with one or more sufficient
sureties, to the satisfaction of the person authorized by the President to
take the same, conditioned for the good behaviour of such alien during his
residence in the United States, and not violating his license, which license
the President may revoke whenever he shall think proper.

  SECT. 2. *And be it further enacted,* That it shall be lawful for the
President of the United States, whenever he may deem it necessary for
the public safety, to order to be removed out of the territory thereof any
alien who may or shall be in prison in pursuance of this act; and to
cause to be arrested and sent out of the United States such of those aliens
as shall have been ordered to depart therefrom, and shall not have obtained
a license as aforesaid, in all cases where, in the opinion of the President,
the public safety requires a speedy removal. And if any alien so removed
or sent out of the United States by the President shall voluntarily return
thereto, unless by permission of the President of the United States, such
alien, on conviction thereof, shall be imprisoned so long as, in the opinion
of the President, the public safety may require.

SECT. 3. *And be it further enacted,* That every master or commander of any ship or vessel which shall come into any port of the United States after the first day of July next shall, immediately on his arrival, make report in writing to the collector or other chief officer of the customs of such port, of all aliens, if any on board his vessel, specifying their names, age, the place of nativity, the country from which they shall have come, the nation to which they belong and owe allegiance, their occupation, and a description of their persons, as far as he shall be informed thereof, and on failure, every such master and commander shall forfeit and pay three hundred dollars, for the payment whereof, on default of such master or commander, such vessel shall also be holden, and may by such collector or other officer of the customs be detained. And it shall be the duty of such collector or other officer of the customs, forthwith to transmit to the office of the Department of State true copies of all such returns.

SECT. 4. *And be it further enacted,* That the Circuit and District Courts of the United States shall respectively have cognizance of all crimes and offences against this act. And all marshals and other officers of the United States are required to execute all precepts and orders of the President of the United States, issued in pursuance or by virtue of this act.

SECT. 5. *And be it further enacted,* That it shall be lawful for any alien who may be ordered to be removed from the United States, by virtue of this act, to take with him such part of his goods, chattels, or other property, as he may find convenient; and all property left in the United States, by any alien who may be removed as aforesaid, shall be and remain subject to his order and disposal, in the same manner as if this act had not been passed.

SECT. 6. *And be it further enacted,* That this act shall continue and be in force for and during the term of two years from the passing thereof.

SEDITION ACT.

An act in addition to the act intituled, " An act for the punishment of certain crimes against the United States."

[Approved July 14, 1798.]

ABSTRACT.

SECTION I. Punishes combinations against United States government.
1. Definition of offence:
Unlawfully to combine or conspire together to oppose any measure of the government of the United States, &c.
This section was not complained of.

2. Grade of offence:
> A high misdemeanour.

3. Punishment:
> Fine not exceeding $5000, and imprisonment six months to five years.

SECTION II. Punishes *seditious writings.*

1. Definition of offence:
> To write, print, utter or publish, or cause it to be done, or assist in it, any false, scandalous, and malicious writing against the government of the United States, or either House of Congress, or the President, with intent to defame, or bring either into contempt or disrepute, or to excite against either the hatred of the people of the United States, or to stir up sedition, or to excite unlawful combinations against the government, or to resist it, or to aid or encourage hostile designs of foreign nations.

2. Grade of offence:
> A misdemeanour.

3. Punishment:
> Fine not exceeding $2000, and imprisonment not exceeding two years.

SECTION III. Allows accused to give in evidence the truth of the matter charged as libellous.

SECTION IV. Continues the Act to 3d March, 1801.

SECTION 1. *Be it enacted by the Senate and House of Representatives of the United States of America, in Congress assembled,* That if any persons shall unlawfully combine or conspire together, with intent to oppose any measure or measures of the government of the United States, which are or shall be directed by proper authority, or to impede the operation of any law of the United States, or to intimidate or prevent any person holding a place or office in or under the government of the United States, from undertaking, performing, or executing his trust or duty: and if any person or persons, with intent as aforesaid, shall counsel, advise, or attempt to procure any insurrection, riot, unlawful assembly, or combination, whether such conspiracy, threatening, counsel, advice, or attempt shall have the proposed effect or not, he or they shall be deemed guilty of a high misdemeanour, and on conviction before any court of the United States having jurisdiction thereof, shall be punished by a fine not exceeding five thousand dollars, and by imprisonment during a term of not less than six months, nor exceeding five years; and further, at the discretion of the court, may be holden to find sureties for his good behaviour, in such sum, and for such time, as the said court may direct.

SECT. 2. *And be it further enacted,* That if any person shall write, print, utter, or publish, or shall cause or procure to be written, printed, uttered, or published, or shall knowingly and willingly assist or aid in writing, printing, uttering, or publishing any false, scandalous and malicious writing or writings against the government of the United States, or either House of the Congress of the United States, or the President of the United States, with intent to defame the said government, or either House of the said Congress, or the said President, or to bring them, or either of them, into contempt or disrepute; or to excite against them, or either or any of them, the hatred of the good people of the United States, or to stir up sedition within the United States; or to excite any unlawful combinations therein, for opposing or resisting any law of the United States, or any act of the President of the United States, done in pursuance of any such law, or of the powers in him vested by the Constitution of the United States; or to resist, oppose, or defeat any such law or act; or to aid, encourage or abet any hostile designs of any foreign nation against the United States, their people or government, then such person, being thereof convicted before any court of the United States having jurisdiction thereof, shall be punished by a fine not exceeding two thousand dollars, and by imprisonment not exceeding two years.

SECT. 3. *And be it further enacted and declared,* That if any person shall be prosecuted under this act for the writing or publishing any libel aforesaid, it shall be lawful for the defendant, upon the trial of the cause, to give in evidence in his defence, the truth of the matter contained in the publication charged as a libel. And the jury who shall try the cause shall have a right to determine the law and the fact, under the direction of the court, as in other cases.

SECT. 4. *And be it further enacted,* That this act shall continue and be in force until the third day of March, one thousand eight hundred and one, and no longer: *Provided,* That the expiration of the act shall not prevent or defeat a prosecution and punishment of any offence against the law, during the time it shall be in force.

II. RESOLUTIONS OF VIRGINIA

OF DECEMBER 21, 1798,

AND DEBATE AND VOTE THEREON.

RESOLUTIONS AS ADOPTED BY BOTH HOUSES OF ASSEMBLY.

1. *Resolved,* That the General Assembly of Virginia doth unequivocally express a firm resolution to maintain and defend the Constitution of the United States, and the Constitution of this State, against every aggression, either foreign or domestic, and that it will support the government of the United States in all measures warranted by the former.

2. That this Assembly most solemnly declares a warm attachment to the union of the States, to maintain which, it pledges all its powers; and that for this end it is its duty to watch over and oppose every infraction of those principles, which constitute the only basis of that union, because a faithful observance of them can alone secure its existence, and the public happiness.

3. That this Assembly doth explicitly and peremptorily declare that it views the powers of the Federal Government as resulting from the compact, to which the States are parties, as limited by the plain sense and intention of the instrument constituting that compact; as no further valid than they are authorized by the grants enumerated in that compact; and that in case of a deliberate, palpable, and dangerous exercise of other powers not granted by the said compact, the States, who are the parties thereto, have the right, and are in duty bound, to interpose for arresting the progress of the evil, and for maintaining within their respective limits, the authorities, rights, and liberties appertaining to them.

4. That the General Assembly doth also express its deep regret that a spirit has in sundry instances been manifested by the Federal Government, to enlarge its powers by forced constructions of the constitutional charter which defines them; and that indications have appeared of a design to expound certain general phrases (which, having been copied from the very limited grant of powers in the former articles of confederation, were the less liable to be misconstrued), so as to destroy the meaning and effect of the particular enumeration, which necessarily explains and limits the general phrases, and so as to consolidate the States by degrees into one sovereignty, the obvious tendency and inevitable result of which would be to

transform the present republican system of the United States into an absolute, or at best, a mixed monarchy.

5. That the General Assembly doth particularly protest against the palpable and alarming infractions of the Constitution, in the two late cases of the "alien and sedition acts," passed at the last session of Congress, the first of which exercises a power nowhere delegated to the Federal Government; and which by uniting legislative and judicial powers to those of executive, subverts the general principles of free government, as well as the particular organization and positive provisions of the federal Constitution; and the other of which acts exercises in like manner a power not delegated by the Constitution, but on the contrary expressly and positively forbidden by one of the amendments thereto; a power which more than any other ought to produce universal alarm, because it is levelled against that right of freely examining public characters and measures, and of free communication among the people thereon, which has ever been justly deemed the only effectual guardian of every other right.

6. That this State having by its convention which ratified the federal Constitution, expressly declared, "that among other essential rights, the liberty of conscience and of the press cannot be cancelled, abridged, restrained, or modified by any authority of the United States," and from its extreme anxiety to guard these rights from every possible attack of sophistry or ambition, having with other States recommended an amendment for that purpose, which amendment was in due time annexed to the Constitution, it would mark a reproachful inconsistency and criminal degeneracy, if an indifference were now shown to the most palpable violation of one of the rights thus declared and secured, and to the establishment of a precedent which may be fatal to the other.

7. That the good people of this commonwealth having ever felt, and continuing to feel the most sincere affection to their brethren of the other States, the truest anxiety for establishing and perpetuating the union of all, and the most scrupulous fidelity to that Constitution which is the pledge of mutual friendship, and the instrument of mutual happiness, the General Assembly doth solemnly appeal to the like dispositions of the other States, in confidence that they will concur with this commonwealth in declaring, as it does hereby declare, that the acts aforesaid are unconstitutional, and that the necessary and proper measure will be taken by each, for co-operating with this State in maintaining unimpaired the authorities, rights, and liberties reserved to the States respectively, or to the people.

8. That the Governor be desired to transmit a copy of the foregoing resolutions to the executive authority of each of the other States, with a request that the same may be communicated to the legislature thereof. And that a copy be furnished to each of the senators and representatives representing this state in the Congress of the United States.

☞ The original resolutions offered by Mr. John Taylor to the House of Delegates may be seen, *post*, p. 148.

DEBATE IN THE HOUSE OF DELEGATES ON THE
FOREGOING RESOLUTIONS.

Thursday, December 13, 1798.

The House resolved itself into a committee of the whole House, on the state of the commonwealth, Mr. *Brackenridge* in the chair; when the resolutions presented to the House by Mr. *John Taylor*, and referred to the committee, being taken up for its consideration—

Mr. JOHN TAYLOR began, by expressing great regret at the occasion which brought him forward. He conceived it to be an awful one. That liberty was in danger, and as that rested on the foundation of responsibility, every effort should be made to repel attempts to subvert it. He could assure them, that his feeble efforts should be used for that purpose. He said that two subjects were contemplated ·by the resolutions before them, to which he should chiefly confine his observations. He should consider the constitutionality of the laws referred to in the resolutions, and their correspondence with human rights, natural and civil. He compared the executive of Great Britain with the Congress of the United States. The prerogatives of the first, were limited and defined by the constitution of England, as were the powers of the latter by the Constitution of the United States; and if the king at any time overleaped his boundaries, it was always certainly opposed, and met with correction. He stated the case of ship-money imposed by Charles I. What was the consequence of that measure? It was opposed. He applied that case to the Congress of the United States. The powers of Congress, by the Constitution, were defined, as clearly as were those prerogatives. That, in Great Britain, where the prerogatives were limited, wherever the executive overleaped their bounds, other organized bodies would always control and check it. So, if Congress overleaped their bounds, some organized body should certainly oppose it. Concluding the general government to be limited in its powers, he proceeded to inquire if Congress, in passing the alien and sedition laws, had overleaped its bounds. He mentioned a law, which Congress had passed at the same session, respecting alien enemies, as it had been suggested that the one particularly called the alien law was justifiable on account of danger to be apprehended from foreigners. This alien enemy law passed by Congress, as well as a law of Virginia, upon that subject, were made in favour of aliens. They were necessary, and found to be the usage of all nations. A contrary usage would be cruel and inhuman. Such laws as these were attended with mutual advantages to the nations at war. They constituted a mutual assurance that the persons and property of its own citizens would be safe in the country of the other. This was not the object of the law in contemplation. The other laws were sufficient for every purpose. That aliens, when arrested and made prisoners, were not dangerous. He said he would ask the question whether alien friends possessed any rights. If so, they might be secured by the Constitution. Then, if they were infringed, the Constitution was broken. If Congress could infringe the rights of those people, they might infringe the rights of others. One usurpation begat another. We ourselves might as well be the victims as others. He said, that alien friends, by the common law, had the rights of life, liberty, and property; and that these common law rights were secured by the Constitution; to prove which, he quoted that clause of the Constitution by which those rights are secured, which Constitution literally reached aliens, by using in all places the term "persons," not "natives." He then put the case of our population being increased by a considerable emigration of foreigners to this country, who might be disposed to retain their foreign citizenship : we should then have amongst us a body of men, of whom the President would be the despot : they would be entirely in his power. He further observed that, suppose government (never an enemy to power) should strengthen its hands by corruption, by patronage, by standing armies, by a system of fears, (he would not say that our government had done so, but in case a government should do so,) that in such case, this body of emigrants, thus dependent upon government, would be a proper instrument in the hands of the executive, to effect its purposes : that executive power was the greatest enemy which republican principles had. He asked, if any one would then assert that to strengthen executive power in this way, wholly unforeseen by those who formed the Constitution, so as to extend beyond their intention, could be agreeable to the Constitution : that republican principles were the great end of the Constitution. Then, if he had proved this law inimical to those principles, he said that he had attained the great end at which he aimed.

He next observed, that the Constitution cautiously attempted to distribute its powers. It was nothing more than a deed of trust made by the people to the government. The government, then, had no right to outstrip its powers. Were they not defined? Had the Constitution given any power to deprive any *person* of trial by jury? That if once we were to permit executive power to overleap its limits, where was it to stop? And, if the executive branch exercised powers not bestowed, it overleaped the Constitution. He asked if we had arrived to that situation, that the powers which the people possessed were to be surrendered. Were we approaching the system of Divine right. He proceeded to construe the alien law, and said that the precedent established by it was dangerous, both as it affected individuals, and as it affected states. That a power inclined to usurpation, to the injury of aliens, would be inclined to usurp, in the construction of the Constitution, to the injury of states; and that the precedent in the one case, would soon ripen into a law, for justifying the other.

He next read the sedition law, and proceeded to comment upon the words of it, especially the words *counsel or advise*. He asked how he could counsel or advise another, without speaking to him; consequently these words extended to words spoken. He put the case of his counselling his neighbour to withstand the two laws of Congress before mentioned. That, by the construction of the last-mentioned law, words were reached, and duties prevented : so that, if he should advise his neighbour in regard to those laws, the latter one enacted a punishment. He then asked, what was the case of a representative in State Legislatures. He had taken an oath to oppose unconstitutional laws. What was he to do? On one hand was perjury, on the other a prison. Suppose a law were to infringe the guarantee made by the Constitution, of a republican form of government. What was a representative to do? Was he not to withstand it? If such law should tend to destroy that guarantee, were we to wait until the enemy's detachments closed us in on every side? This sedition law said yes. In the construction of this law we were placed in the hands of lawyers. The judge would construe the law. There were two kinds of construction, a strict construction, and a liberal construction. The judge might put upon it a liberal construction. He stated an historical fact. That sedition was forbidden by the common law. That the law of England respecting treason, went no farther in describing that offence, than our law does in describing sedition. He then cited the case of Algernon Sidney. That Algernon Sidney wrote a book in answer to Filmer, to prove "that the authority of kings was not of divine original (a thing in those days deemed necessary to be proved). He wished a necessity might never appear for a new edition of this book. For this he was prosecuted and tried, condemned and executed. And this was a liberal construction of the law. He thought that this case might well be applied in an argument on the subject of this law of ours. However, the law was said to be harmless. That to bring themselves within it, men must unlawfully combine, they must conspire, they must lie, for that they might still tell truth without danger. But this could never satisfy him that it was not dangerous, when he recollected that the best patriots had been sacrificed by sedition laws, with the help of construction.

He then said that another distinction had been set up, that this law was not to restrain the freedom, but the licentiousness of speech. This, he observed, was an epithet which might be applied to any attempt to restrain usurpation. Men find no difficulty in pronouncing opinions to be both false and licentious, which differ from their own. That this same distinction (if it was just) would empower Congress to regulate religion, the freedom of which is secured by the same article which secures the freedom of speech. They might in the end be induced to regulate the mode of petitioning, that it might be performed orderly, and not licentiously, as it is in some countries, by crawling on the belly towards a throne, and licking the dust. He then observed, that a power to restrain treason, was more necessary in a government, than to regulate sedition: that our Constitution had yet limited the power over treason to a few cases, which he stated. However, Congress might still regulate the punishment in case of treason; and it was possible, that they might establish in such case a punishment short of death; a punishment even inferior to that for sedition. What then would result? Treason was the genus; sedition a species. If the first were limited, and the second not, what security had we? He then read the third article of the amendments to the Constitution, concerning freedom of speech, &c., and asked in what sense this clause was understood at the time of adoption? Could it then have been contemplated by any one, that such a law as this would ever have been passed? The adoption of the Constitution by this state was accompanied by a condition containing a reservation of these very rights: so that they must have been understood in a very different sense then, than when these laws of Congress passed. He read the ratification of the Constitution by the convention of this state, and said that the same ought to be looked upon as a contemporaneous exposition of the part of the Constitution referred to. He then asked, if the sedition law did in no respect cancel, restrain, or infringe the liberty of the press! And concluded his observations upon the first of the two subjects, to which he had before mentioned he should confine them, by saying that, if he had proved the laws spoken of to be unconstitutional, the objection to them on that ground was strong; and by asking further, could they then be justified upon the ground of necessity, or that they were harmless?

He began his observations upon the second subject, by asking if those laws were correspondent with human rights? Those rights, he said, were, freedom of speech, freedom of person, a right to justice, and to a fair trial. If an alien possessed those rights, he asked, could he avail himself of them under the present law? Could a citizen, under the sedition law, exercise the freedom of speech, or of religion, which last, a few days before, he had heard called a social right? It was not so. It was either a natural duty, or a natural right. Was it possible that at this day, religious worship could be restrained by law? The right of opinion, he said, should be held sacred. It ought never to be given up in any one instance. Religion was only a branch of opinion. With what propriety could that range of thought, bestowed by the Creator upon the human mind, be controlled by law. He deemed it a sacrilege for government to undertake to regulate the mind of man. It was a subject by no means within its powers. What would be the consequence of such a measure? Universal ignorance amongst the people. He then asked, if ignorance was a desirable thing? And were the free exercise of the faculties of the human mind, to be once restrained and shut up, he would ask them, then, what was man? He was therefore opposed to those laws, as being destructive of the most essential human rights. He again asked, if such laws were ever contemplated at the time of the adoption of the Constitution, and what would be the consequence of the destruction of those essential human rights, of which he had spoken? What would be the probable effects of those laws? They would establish executive influence, and executive influence would produce a revolution. There was great danger in throwing too great weight in any one scale. · He then proceeded to inquire whether those laws would increase executive influence, and concluded that they would. That they would by begetting fear. If public opinion were to be directed by government, by means of fines, penalties and punishments, on the one hand, and patronage on the other, public opinion itself would be made the stepping stone for usurpation. If Congress should undertake to regulate public opinion, they would be sure to regulate it so as to detach the people from the state governments, and attach them to the general government. But, he said, the most dangerous effect of those laws would be, the abolition of the right to examine public servants. He again referred to Sidney's case, and recited the doctrine of Filmer, to illustrate this subject. To bring about such a measure as this, he said, it would be necessary for Congress, in the first place, to establish the point, that they were the masters, and not the servants, of the people. He said, government might do wrong. Could a criminal be ever brought to justice, who had a power to regulate the mode of his own examination? And is it not criminal in a government to oppress a people? If its acts were wrong, they would produce discontent: discontent was the only road to redress. But redress could never be obtained, because the sedition law prohibited the only mode of obtaining it, by punishing that very matter of exciting discontent. He asked what was despotism? He defined it to be, a concentration of powers in one man, or in a body of men. The manner of concentrating them was unimportant: the end was the same. Individuals and states were equally affected by such concentration of power. The concentration of it in an individual, would enslave other individuals; a concentration of it in Congress, would operate to the destruction of the state governments; and that, if the balance of power which the state governments ought to hold against Congress, were once lost, we must be precipitated into a revolution. He adverted to the vast power concentrated in the Senate of the United States. This had been seriously viewed at the time of the adoption of the Constitution, and since. That, at the time of framing the Constitution, mutual concessions were made between the states, which he believed to be the sole reason for admitting the small states to an equal share of power in that body, with the large, the real counterbalance of which concession, was the existence of state governments. Thence he concluded, that being thus situated, if the balance which the states ought to hold, should happen to be lost, the small Senate of the United States, might govern America. He further said, that although he had read in pamphlets and newspapers, and also had heard it reported, that such principles as he held, led to commotion, still he would assert that it was more likely to happen that a majority of small states might adopt, measures which would oppress the rest, although they should contain the greatest number of citizens: and that the result of this would be a civil war. The many would not submit to the few, and all history would show, that a majority armed with power, would never yield it without a struggle. He said that *oppression* was the road to civil war. To prove which, he asked what produced the war between Britain and America? Oppression. What produced the revolution of France? Oppression. What produced the revolt of the United Provinces from Spain? Oppression. He said, the way to keep a nation quiet, was to make it happy: that oppression goaded it on to civil war. In justification of which opinion, he stated that the people of the United States were at this time under the pressure of certain grievances. The way then to stop civil war, would be to stop oppression. But, said gentlemen, we must not disunite. To this he would answer, remove oppression, and union would take place. He had observed it asserted in a pamphlet circulated at this place, that these late measures of the government might be justified on the ground of self-defence. Under such a pretence as that, he said, Congress might pass any law whatever. This never could have been the object of the Constitution. He said, that the old instrument of confederation contained the same language, but no such power as that contended for was ever claimed. Had it ever possessed it, its want of energy would not have suggested the present Constitution. (He then read the preamble of the articles of confederation, reciting that the same was entered into for the public good, &c.)

By adopting a different construction from that made by himself, he said the propriety of no law which Congress should ever pass could be denied. He then concluded by saying, that our rights were the offspring of pangs and peril. Let them never then be wrested from us. It was the custom in some countries, for the prince to send for the first born child of every subject, to have him trained as a soldier for his army. In that case, could the distressed parent be assured that by surrendering his first-born, he would secure the rest? The first-born of American rights, was the free examination of public servants. Were we to surrender that, could we be certain that the rest would be secured? That these rights were the fruit of victory, and recompense of blood. We had defended them against the arms of Britain. Never then let us surrender them to the arts of sophistry and ambition.

Mr. *George K. Taylor* moved that the committee might rise, in order to give time to himself and the other members to consider well the subject before them. He said, it was an important one, as the object of inquiry seemed to be, to impeach with unconstitutionality, two laws passed by both Houses of Congress, and by them declared to be constitutional.

Mr. *Foushee* made a few remarks in opposition to those of Mr. *George K. Taylor* in regard to the probable constitutionality of the laws, by reason of their having passed both Houses of Congress.

Mr. *Nicholas* hoped that the gentleman from Prince George did not intend, by moving to rise, to preclude from speaking any person then disposed to speak.

Mr. *George K. Taylor* said that he did not; but (after waiting some time and no member rising to speak) he renewed his motion for the committee's rising.

The committee rose accordingly, reported progress, and had leave to sit again.

IN THE HOUSE OF DELEGATES,

Friday, December 14, 1798.

The House resolved itself into a committee of the whole House, on the state of the Commonwealth, Mr. *Brackenridge* in the chair, when, Mr. *John Taylor's* resolutions being still under consideration, Mr. *Magill* said, if he were in order, he would move that the resolutions should be read.

The chairman declared the same to be in order, and the resolutions were read accordingly by the clerk. Whereupon,

Mr. GEORGE K. TAYLOR arose, and said that he never felt himself impressed with more awe than on that occasion. The subject was of itself sufficiently momentous; but the resolutions before them rendered it still more so. They contained a declaration, not of opinion, but of fact. They declared the acts of Congress, called the alien and sedition laws, to be unconstitutional, and not law. These laws, he said, had been passed by both houses of Congress. One of those houses was formed of the immediate representatives of the whole American people, the other of members chosen by the state legislatures. These two houses thus formed, and thus representing the whole people, and the respective state sovereignties, had passed those laws after solemn deliberation and discussion, and declared them to be constitutional. In such case, he conceived, the Legislature of Virginia, the representative of a part only of the American people, ought to deliberate seriously before they undertook to give an opinion upon them; and if their opinion should be such as the resolutions stated, they should still endeavour to couch that opinion in different language; for, by those resolutions, as they then stood, the people were encouraged most openly to make resistance. He compared the two legislative bodies, Congress and the Assembly of Virginia, together. He presumed the former to be as wise, as watchful of the public interests, as the latter. He then called the attention of the committee to what had been the determination of the legistatures of the other states. All which had taken these laws under their consideration, had given them their decided approbation, either by way of resolution, or address to the President. It could not be denied but that they had some wisdom, and that it was not exclusively confined to the Legislature of Virginia. As the legislatures then, of so many states, had concurred in the approbation of them, he thought it necessary for the Legislature of this state to hesitate in expressing its opinion of their unconstitutionality, especially when they reflected on the consequence attending it. For if these laws were unconstitutional, the resolutions made it the duty of the people to defend themselves against them. He said he would then proceed to show to the committee, that those laws were not unconstitutional. In that attempt he was not certain whether or not he should succeed. He possibly might bring them to doubt, and should he do that, he should feel in some measure satisfied. On the other hand, they might be assured that the consequences of pursuing the advice of the resolutions, would be insurrection, confusion, and anarchy. The business upon which they were acting, he said, was of an extensive nature. The gentleman from Caroline had spoken upon both laws. He should confine himself to the alien law only. He conceived that would be as much as he could perform. For in doing that, he should fatigue himself, and he expected the committee also.

He proceeded then to examine the situation of aliens coming into this country. He said, they had no more rights here, than they had elsewhere. He asked upon what footing aliens came into any country? By *right*, or by *permission?* Still it was said, that their *rights* were to be affected by this law of Congress. He then cited and read Vattel, page 157, section 94, to show that a nation may prohibit foreigners from entering its territory; and from that authority concluded, that their admission into a country was by no means a matter of right, but of favour. He said, the alien did not come within the scope of the general laws of the country into which he came. During his stay therein, he was to be *protected* indeed by those laws; but was not the *object* of them. He cited and read Vattel again, page 100, section 231, and Blackstone's Commentaries, vol. 1, page 259, to show that by the law of nations, it is left in the power of all states to take such measures about the admission of strangers as they think convenient : that so long as their nation continued at peace with that in which they resided, and they behaved themselves peaceably, they were under the protection of the government of that nation, though liable to be sent or ordered away, whenever that government saw occasion, or its safety required it. If there were nothing then, he said, in the Constitution of the United States, respecting the migration of persons, the doctrine of the law of nations which he had read, was sound, and the general government might by that lawfully restrain or regulate the entry of aliens, and order them away if necessary. But the Constitution had a clause in it upon that subject, being the first clause of the ninth section of the first article, which he read, in these words : "The migration or importation of such persons as any of the states now existing shall think proper to admit, shall not be prohibited by the Congress prior to the year 1808 ; but a tax or duty may be imposed on such importation, not exceeding ten dollars for each person." This clause then, he said contained a recognition of the right of Congress to prohibit migration or importation after the year 1808. In his opinion too, the prohibition of the right of Congress by that clause, extended only to such states as were *existing* at the time of framing the Constitution ; which showed that Congress of course might regulate the migration of persons to such states as were established after that time ; and that was exemplified by the prohibition by Congress of the admission of slaves into the new states. The clause read, then, took away from Congress the right of prohibiting migration within a limited time. But though the *entry* was prevented, the question then recurred, was their *removal when dangerous* prevented also? The question was of great importance. When these states, he said, declared themselves independent, they entered into articles of confederation. That was a system composed of one body : there was no executive, no judiciary. By that system, that single body could enact nothing binding on the people. It was consequently dependent on the several states for the execution of all its measures. The old Congress wished to establish a duty of five per centum only on goods imported, but it could not be carried into effect by reason of the opposition of the states. To obviate that mischief the Federal Convention was appointed, which assembled ,and framed the present Constitution. That took from the several states all matters, of a general nature ; all matters relating to foreign nations. It established legislative, executive, and judiciary branches, which acted upon the several matters coming within their respective spheres ; and it certainly intended that all matters of general national concern should be confided exclusively to the general government. There was a general consent of the people that such matters should be vested in the general government, and taken from the states. He then read the list of powers vested by the Constitution in the general government. By the general law of nations, he said, the admission of aliens into a country was altogether a matter of grace. They might therefore be removed by the government of the country, whenever it was deemed necessary. If the general government, then, possessed not the power of removal, one great mischief of a general nature, which it was intended to remedy, would remain as before. The union would be dependent upon sixteen sovereign and jealous states, for carrying into effect such a measure. Some of these states, too, might be on the verge of insurrection. An alien banished from one might be admitted into another, which would protect him, and thereby the general welfare in that instance defeated, and Congress laid at the mercy of the particular states. He asked what was the situation of America and France at that time? It was true there was no declaration of war between them, but they were not at peace. He enumerated their various acts of hostility towards us, and then asked if there was no danger to be apprehended from aliens of that country. He himself thought there was. He related also the numerous designs and machinations which they had been contriving against us. He deemed it therefore highly necessary that the general government, established for general benefit and common protection, should possess the power of removing them. But, if the law of Congress were to be construed unconstitutional, the general government could not remove them. He read the observations of Mr. *Jefferson* respecting the necessity of a government having the powers of defence and protection; also Mr. *Madison's* speech in the Convention of Virginia to the same effect; and applied them to the case in question. It was true, he said, that the Constitution prohibited the general government from preventing the migration of foreigners prior to the year 1808: but at the same time, the principles of protection must induce a belief that the Constitution did not intend or enact, that when here, they should not be removed, however dangerous to the general weal. Still, however, it was objected, that by the twelfth amendment to the Constitution it was declared, that the powers not granted to Congress, were retained by the people, or the states respectively. It was clear, he said, that even without that amendment, no power could have been exercised by Congress, which was not expressly given to it, or did not follow by necessary implication. The case, he said, was still the same. In regard to an express grant, there could be no dispute; and the doctrine of necessary implication was proved by the Constitution, when in the last clause of the 8th section, it grants to Congress the power "to make all laws which shall be necessary and proper for carrying into execution the foregoing powers, and all other powers vested by that Constitution in the government of the United States, or in any department or officer thereof." From that clause, then, he said, the power of Congress to pass the law in question, was clearly sanctioned by necessary implication. All cases arising under the Constitution, could not be foreseen and enumerated: therefore, that clause was inserted for the purpose of enabling Congress to carry into effect the powers expressly given it by the Constitution. Whatever then necessarily flowed from these express powers, were within the scope of Congress. He then asked if there were anything in the Constitution, from which the law in question could necessarily and properly proceed? To discover that, he first proceeded to examine the preamble. That, he said, declared the Constitution to be formed in order to form a more perfect union, establish justice, insure domestic *tranquillity*, provide for the common defence, promote the general welfare, and secure the blessings of liberty to ourselves and our posterity. The passage of an alien law then, he said, was justifiable for the purpose of answering the four great ends last mentioned in the preamble, which showed the object and intention of the Constitution. But he said, there was something in it more positive. He called their attention to that clause in the enumeration of the powers of Congress "to define and punish piracies and felonies committed on the high seas, and *against the law of nations;*" and said, that aliens came within it, since for an alien to conspire against the peace of the nation, which permitted him a residence therein, was an offence against the law of nations. He further read the clause declaring that the United States would guarantee to the several states a republican form of government, and *protect each of them against invasion.* He relied much upon the term *protect* used in that clause. Protection, he said, was a preventing, a guarding against. He would compare it to a *shield,* which an individual cast before him to protect himself against the javelin before it reached him; for it would be no protection, if he waited till the wound was inflicted. He observed, that whatever flowed from a grant, followed the grant itself. Congress, therefore, in *protecting* the states, might enact cautionary laws for the purpose. A law sending away dangerous aliens was a cautionary law, tending to *protect* the states. Every society had as much right to prevent the mischief which aliens might do, as to punish them for it after it was done. Aliens might be punished for crimes as well as citizens. So, laws might be passed for preventing the commission of crimes by them, as well as for preventing the commission of them by citizens. But such a law must always be temporary. It could not be permanent. It would continue only so long as danger existed. It would affect only dangerous persons. Aliens could only be dangerous in time of war, or in times verging towards war. In times of safety, such a law would be unnecessary and improper. He agreed, therefore, that a permanent law of that kind including all aliens, passed before 1808, would be unconstitutional; since it might absolutely defeat the 9th section. But that a temporary law passed only for the purpose of ordering away *dangerous aliens,* was a law of *protection* to the states. It was a necessary power for every government to possess. A government would be worth nothing without it, since it could not protect the people. He then proceeded to take the Constitution altogether, recapitulated the several clauses before cited, and said it was a rule of construction of all instruments, that all the parts should be taken and considered together, that they might stand together, and be reconciled with one another if possible. He called their attention to two clauses of the Constitution, the ninth section of the first article reserving to the states the right of permitting migration, &c., and the fourth section of the fourth article, which declares that the United States shall protect each state against invasion. When one part, then, of the Constitution, he said, reserved to the states the right of permitting migration, and another granted to Congress the power and duty of passing all such laws as would protect the states from invasion or violence, would not the same operate as a proviso qualifying the former general expression, and allow Congress from principles of protection, to expel dangerous aliens? He thought at

3

any rate the power in that case contended for, a necessary one, even were it not in the Constitution. And in such a case, the legislature ought to recommend an amendment to the Constitution for the purpose. Since the adoption of the Constitution, he said, Congress had passed laws for erecting forts in different parts of the United States. He asked what part of the Constitution gave them that power? They must derive it from the fourth section of the fourth article only, the same being for the purpose of protection. There was a necessity for exercising this power at that time. We had amongst us a number of dangerous Frenchmen. The chief author however of the plots had sneaked off, as well as his associates. He said he was happy to be clear of them. Since they were gone, that law was no longer necessary: Congress might then properly repeal it. Yes, he said, the incendiaries were gone. He congratulated America upon it. He hoped they never might return. But an objection had been made that the alien law had taken away from the poor alien the trial by jury. He said that aliens were not a party to the compact, but citizens only. The Constitution secured *rights* to citizens, and declared that they should not be deprived of them, but by trial by jury. But, aliens not being a party to the compact, were not bound by it to the performance of any particular *duty*, nor did it confer upon them any *rights*. He referred to Vattel again, to show that by the law of nations, the admission of aliens into a country was not a matter of right, but of favour; and observed that ordering away an alien, was not divesting him of any right, but withdrawing from him a favour; and that it was new doctrine that a favour could not be withdrawn, but by trial by jury. He then observed that the alien law did not touch life, liberty, or property; but only directed the alien to be removed. If he would not remove himself, however, when ordered away, but remained obstinate, he might then be imprisoned. He read, and relied upon the favourableness of that clause of the law which extended to the suspected alien the right of proving to the President that he was harmless. He still asserted that the law of nations gave a power to the government to remove aliens when dangerous; and that, by the law in question, neither life, liberty, or property was touched, except in cases of contumely. He then stated the case authorized by our municipal laws, respecting surety of the peace; and asked, how did the trial by jury stand in that case? The citizen, he said, was deprived of it, and that too in a free country. The case of the alien then, was not harder. The trial by jury was dispensed with in the case of the peace-breaker; therefore, the same might be done in the case of an alien. He said, that the terms upon which aliens were admitted, were, their not intermeddling with the concerns of the nation. Should they do so, and, upon being required to withdraw, continued obstinate, they must be committed in the same manner as citizens who refused to give surety of the peace.

Another objection had been made, that if they were sent out without trial by jury, they might next be deprived of life and property without it. This, he said, could not be done. An alien was entitled to them as *natural rights;* and therefore, as they were rights, could not be deprived of them without a trial by jury. The case was quite different in regard to his removal, as his admission into the country was not matter of right, but was merely a matter of *favour*. It had been also objected, that the three powers of government were all blended in the President by the alien law. He said that they were not. But, if such a power in regard to aliens were necessary, it must be entrusted somewhere. It could not be with a private individual. It could not be with the judiciary. It could not be with the legislature; but might most properly be with the executive. He, by the Constitution, was bound to execute the laws: therefore, it was most properly entrusted with him, being the executive officer, with whom all persons and bodies whatever were accustomed to communicate. It could least of all be entrusted with a court which transacted its business publicly. For these matters must be in confidence. That was often necessary for nipping things in the bud. Secrecy then being absolutely necessary, and a court of law being publicly held, and at stated periods, the proceedings might be divulged, or the explosion take place, before they could obtain information, or try the fact. And all that too, not for the sake of a matter of right, but mere courtesy. It could not be entrusted to the legislature, unless its sittings were permanent: it could, then, only be entrusted with the president. To prove the justice and fairness of this regulation, he again introduced the case of a man brought before a magistrate to give surety of the peace. On the complaint of A., he said, the magistrate might arrest and imprison B., until he gave security to be of good behaviour. In that case, a man was deprived of liberty without a trial by jury; but that was right, because society was bound to *protect* as well as *vindicate* its citizens; and before a trial of the fact could be had, the person apprehending danger might be murdered. He again cited Mr. *Jefferson's* piece to prove, that no cases under the law of nations were ever submitted to a jury to be tried. He cited also part of a speech of Mr. *Madison*, in the Convention of Virginia, nearly to the same effect; and thereupon observed, that the trial by jury was only used in municipal regulations, where citizens and others were concerned under the particular laws of the state, and not in cases between the government and aliens, which arise under the law of nations. That even in matters of right, the right of the individual ought to yield to the good of the community. He then read that clause in the Constitution concerning the suspension of the writ of *habeas corpus*, and said, that the suspension of that writ might take place during the existence of rebellion or invasion. In that case, a citizen might, at the will of the President, be committed and confined until the existing danger was over. And if a citizen, invested with all civil rights, might thus be confined in a time of danger, so ought an alien, who had no positive political right whatever, when the good of the community required it. He said, he might produce many other instances, to prove the propriety of necessary implication. He then mentioned the subject of foreign intercourse, and asked whence was that power derived? He knew no part of the Constitution which particularly authorized it. It could be derived only from that clause of the Constitution, which prohibited to the states, the power of making any treaties, or entering into any agreements. It had been observed by the gentleman from Caroline, that Congress had passed a law to send away alien enemies, and that was a good law. Where was that power to be found? Nowhere, except it were derived from that, protective power, which was to be gathered from the Constitution by means of implication only, or by implication from the power given to declare war. He further asked, at what time those laws were passed, and what was the cause? And then observed, that whatever construction led to an absurdity, was erroneous. He then supposed the case of the states having the power of admitting aliens, and the General Government not having the power of removing them. The Assembly of Virginia might think a whole army of aliens admissible. Suppose, he said, that Bonaparte and his army (if they could ever get out from the Nile again) were to arrive within the state, and they should think them too, admissible; by the construction of the resolutions before them, Congress in such case ought not to remove them. The right of protection, he said, was a natural right, appertaining to each individual, and that a number of individuals had as much right to protect themselves as one individual. Did the Constitution prohibit such a right? He then observed, that both the Constitution of the United States, and of this state, directed that the trial by jury should be held sacred. He said, he would then proceed to examine if that right had never been pretermitted by any law of the state; and requested that the law of Virginia, for removal of aliens, passed in 1792, should be first read. (It was read accordingly by the clerk.) He then observed, that although the Constitution of the state directed that the trial by jury should be held sacred, yet that law " authorized the Governor to apprehend, and secure, and compel to depart out of the commonwealth, all suspicious persons, &c., *from whom the President of the United States should apprehend hostile designs against the said states.*" In that instance, then, a previous legislature had acknowledged as a matter indisputable, what this legislature disputed, that a suspicious alien might be sent away at the instance of the President. Their law even authorized the sending away the alien without a trial, and in the mean time his being imprisoned. Yet that legislature, in passing that law, did not suppose it had violated the Constitution. He then read the act of Congress under consideration. He compared both acts together, and said that he looked upon them to be nearly the same. If there were any difference between them, he said it was, that the law of the state was more severe than the law of Congress, inasmuch as the former subjected the alien to imprisonment at all events: the latter only in case of his refusal to remove himself. It was remarkable, too, he said, that the same law of the state, although passed in 1792, was re-enacted from one passed in 1785, thirteen years ago, and so many years nearer than the present time to the Revolution, when it is to be supposed the principles of that Revolution were much purer than they were at the present time. He then contended that there was the same reservation to the people of all powers not granted to the state government, as was to the states of all powers not granted to the General Government. Consequently, the trial by jury being declared sacred by the bill of rights, the legislature of the state could have no more power by the Constitution to pass such a law, than Congress had by the Constitution of the United States. Yet no complaint against such a law had ever been heard until the law of Congress was passed. All the clamour had been reserved for that alone. He again observed, that no other state legislature had passed any such resolution as the one before them. They must be presumed to be equally watchful: they must be presumed to have wisdom too, and that it was not exclusively confined to this legislature. They should hesitate, therefore, in making such a declaration as was then contemplated. He then called for the reading of the law of the state, which authorized the delivering up a citizen committing a crime in a foreign country, at the instance he said of the United States, without trial by jury, on mere suspicion and on demand. (The clerk read the law.) Mr. *Taylor* then called the attention of the committee to the last clause of the law, from which it appeared that the offender might be tried by a jury for the offence in this state, but was deprived of such a trial by the fourth section, where he was delivered up to a foreign nation on requisition. He ascribed the reason for dispensing with the trial by jury, in the latter case, to be, because it was a case within the law of nations, which admits no trial by jury, and still that law was thought not incompatible with the Constitution. He observed that the gentleman from Caroline had dilated much upon the probable effects of the law of Congress in question. He would indulge himself in the same manner.

What, said he, would be the situation of this country, were it once known that Congress had no such power as that of removing aliens? He begged them to recollect what horrid scenes of devastation and carnage had been exhibited by Frenchmen in their own island of Saint Domingo. If France would abandon her people there, and desolate the fairest colony in the world, could it be supposed, that they would love us more than themselves: that they would spare their foes. He begged them to recollect too, the doubtful state of affairs between our country and France. It was true that the two nations were not at war, since no declaration of war had been on either side, but they were not at peace, since each party was seizing the vessels of the other. War then might ensue, and at the time the alien law was passed, it was a thing extremely probable. Every nation, before it struck, prepared as deadly a blow as possible. He then asked if the French could wound us in any respect so vitally, as by arming the slave against his master. Attempts, he said, had been already made, by French emigrants, to excite our slaves to insurrection. Suppose then, they were to attempt the thing again, and an insurrection should accordingly take place, what would be the consequence? In that common calamity, he said, the ranks of society would be confounded; the ties of nature would be cut asunder; the inexorable and blood-thirsty negro would be careless of the father's groans, the tears of the mother, and the lamentations of the children. The loudest in their wailings would be their wives and daughters torn from their arms, with naked bosoms, outstretched hands, and dishevelled hair, to gratify the brutal passion of a ruthless negro, who would the next moment murder the object of his lust. He then asked how all that was to be prevented? By vesting the general government with that power to remove such aliens, which it had already so generously exercised for the purpose, in the law then under consideration: a law particularly calculated for the protection of the southern states. He then mentioned what success the French had had, in other countries into which their emigrants had been admitted. What intrigues they had carried on in Venice, Switzerland, Holland, &c., all which countries had been expunged from the list of republics, and added to the already over-grown dominions of France. These events, he said, had been brought about chiefly by stirring up the people to discontent, by alien incendiaries. It was necessary then, that the United States should adopt proper measures to prevent such mischiefs. To that end, said he, let us cherish the law passed for the purpose. He then proceeded to relate the late conduct of the French towards us, and what description of persons had migrated from that country to the United States,—the most noted characters of whom were Volney and Talleyrand. He made several remarks upon the con-duct of both of them while in this country, but gave a particular account of the peregrination of the latter from Europe to America, thence back again to Europe: how he was denounced and proscribed by his country-men, restored to favour again, and in the end preferred to the ministerial office which he then held. It behoved the people of this country, there-fore, to be on their guard against him and all the rest. He wished, he said, to conclude; for he was conscious that he had fatigued himself, and he supposed the committee also. He should be glad, however, to be permitted at some other time to deliver his sentiments in regard to the sedition law. He thought indeed, that the best way thereafter would be to discuss one law at a time. He further observed, that the members of that Congress which had passed those laws, had been, as far as he could understand, since generally re-elected: therefore, he thought the people of the United States had decided in favour of their constitutionality, and that such an attempt as they were then making to induce Congress to repeal the laws, would be utterly nugatory.

MR. RUFFIN arose next, and said that he was convinced his abilities would not enable him to place the subject in such a light as it would be placed before it was finished. However, as it was a matter of much importance, he was induced to assign his reasons for the vote which he was about to give. He should confine himself, he said, to two points: the constitu-tionality of the laws, and the consequences. The alien law, he said, was unconstitutional in two points: and, after observing that, although an alien did not enjoy all the rights of a citizen, yet he enjoyed some, he proceeded to show in what points that law was unconstitutional. He thought it so for two reasons: 1st. Because it blended several powers in one person; and 2dly. Because it contained powers not granted to Congress by the Constitution. He then proceeded to state how the alien was to be deprived of the trial by jury, and to be banished for particular acts, at the time of their commission, innocent, but which might, by a retrospective operation of the said act, (the President being thereby armed with legislative and judicial, as well as executive power,) be made criminal. The gentleman from Prince George, he said, had admitted that if Congress were to pass a law to exclude all aliens for ever, prior to the year 1808, it would be unconstitutional. Mr. Ruffin then begged leave to inquire as to the diffe-rence of the effect which such a law would have from the present alien act of Congress, should Congress annually think proper to re-enact the law as it now stood, until 1808. The principle and effect, he said, were the same. The only rational conclusion, then, to be drawn from the concession of the gentleman was, that if Congress be incompetent to the passage of a permanent law, (except, indeed, where the Constitution interposes,) they must be incompetent to the passage of a temporary one. But the gentleman, he said, had attempted to prove the constitutionality of that act, by saying that Congress had passed, or might pass, laws respecting alien enemies. The cases, however, Mr. *Ruffin* said, were extremely different. Congress alone could determine upon war or peace : consequently, alien enemies were proper subjects for congressional legislation : but that alien friends were exclusively subject to the sovereignty of the several individual states ; as the twelfth article of the amendments to the Federal Constitution expressly declares, that " the powers not delegated to the United States, by the Constitution, nor prohibited by it to the states, are reserved to the states respectively, or to the people." And as at the same time, he said, the only power given by that compact to the general government, over alien friends, was in the ninth section of the first article, it must follow that this was one of the rights reserved to the states. The gentleman last up, he said, had contended however, that this power was rightfully exercised by Congress, and had taken the broad ground of construction and implication, upon which to erect his fabric. Construction and implication, Mr. *Ruffin* said, was a doctrine which he had hoped was banished from the councils of America. It was a doctrine which the people of America had unanimously and uniformly protested against. It was the exercise of this kind of right by the British parliament which involved us in a war with that government. It was to guard against the exercise of such a power, that the state constitutions were formed : and it was that abhorrence in America to constructive and implied rights, that induced the specific delineation of congressional powers. Let them admit, he said, the position of the worthy member, and then mark the extent to which it would carry them. In the preamble to the Constitution, the ends designed to be produced by that compact, are enumerated. Amongst them the following : " to provide for the common defence, promote the general welfare :" and in the eighteenth clause of the eighth section of the first article, " to make all laws which shall be necessary and proper for carrying into execution the foregoing powers, &c.," were the parts of the Constitution, by which it was contended, that those constructive and implied rights are given : Suppose, said Mr. *Ruffin*, the general government should be of opinion that those objects would be produced in a higher degree by continuing the present members in office for ten years, or for life? Was there any person who then heard him, who would think such an exercise of power legitimate ? Certainly not. Yet he contended that such a power was as impliedly given by the Constitution, as that which Congress had taken upon itself to exercise over alien friends. Mr. *Ruffin* then concluded by observing, that as it was then late, and the committee appeared to be fatigued, he should reserve the rest of his observations for another opportunity.

The committee then rose, reported progress, asked and had leave to sit again.

IN THE HOUSE OF DELEGATES,

Saturday, December 15, 1798.

The House resolved itself into a committee of the whole House, on the state of the commonwealth, Mr. *Brackenridge* in the chair, when Mr. *John Taylor's* resolutions being still under consideration,

MR. MERCER arose and said, that he felt great difficulty in prevailing upon himself to take a part in the very interesting discussion which had arisen, and would probably be continued, upon the resolutions submitted to the committee. This difficulty was produced, not by any want of confidence in the rectitude of the opinion which he entertained, or in the purity of the motives that would ultimately direct his vote. On the one hand, he was deeply impressed with the importance of the subject; on the other, he felt and acknowledged his own inability to do justice to its merits; but, in proportion to the magnitude of the question, was his solicitude to explain the principles upon which his opinion was formed. The manner in which the laws complained of had been defended here, and elsewhere, was to his mind more alarming than the laws themselves. It showed that gentlemen were ready to defend, not only existing violations of the federal Constitution, but any infractions which might hereafter be committed upon it. For, if the opinions which the gentleman from Prince George submitted to the committee yesterday, be correct, the nature of that Constitution was changed. It was not what the people and states understood it to be at the time of its ratification. Its powers were enlarged to a dangerous extent. It could no longer be considered as producing a confederation, but certainly established a consolidated government.

Every question, Mr. *Mercer* said, which related to the respective powers of the state and general government, was, in itself, of magnitude sufficient to engage the whole attention of gentlemen who were desirous of preserving to each its proper powers, and to maintain that entire independence which belongs to each, and which each had a right to enjoy. He was, therefore, surprised, when he heard the member from Prince George, yesterday, calling the attention of the committee to subjects, which, however interesting in themselves, could not be supposed to have the most remote connexion with the resolutions upon the table. Those, said Mr. *Mercer*, embrace several constitutional questions, which ought to be considered by themselves; they point out a plan by which the friends of the paper believe a repeal of the supposed unconstitutional acts would be most readily obtained. It was a solemn appeal to the understanding of the committee; yet, the injuries of France to America, her excesses in Europe, always magnified and misrepresented by the enemies of freedom in every quarter of the world, and the misfortunes of St. Domingo, had been pressed with considerable force by that same gentleman. This effort, Mr. *Mercer* said, had been practised with great effect in the community. It was scarcely possible to consider the measures of our own government, and candidly to examine their influence upon the public happiness, without being subject to the imputation of an undue attachment to a foreign power. He rejoiced in knowing, that as long as the charge had existed, and as often as it had been repeated, not a single instance had been produced throughout America, by which it could be supported. It was used as the apology for a system of measures which could not have been adopted, without receiving the universal disapprobation of all who have a knowledge of the principles of the federal Constitution, and of the clear limitation of power contained in that instrument. For his part, he did not see how a view of the insults offered to America by France, could decide the merit of the resolutions. He hoped the committee were ready to repel the former, as well as to consider the latter. To preserve the Constitution, was to preserve the union; and to maintain that, upon the principles upon which it was originally formed, was to bid defiance to every foreign power, whose conduct might be hostile to the independence and rights of our country.

The gentleman from Prince George had told the committee that the resolutions introduced by the gentleman from Caroline were calculated to rouse the people to resistance, to excite the people of Virginia against the could result from their adoption. They contained nothing more than the federal government. Mr. *Mercer* did not see how such consequences sentiments which the people in many parts of the state had expressed, and which had been conveyed to the legislature in their memorials and resolutions then lying upon the table. He would venture to say, that an attention to the resolutions before the committee would prove that the qualities attempted to be attached to them by the gentleman could not be found. He begged leave to read the first and second clause, in which it is declared, "that the General Assembly doth unequivocally express a firm resolution to maintain and defend the Constitution of the United States, and the constitution of this state ; and that they will support the government of the United-States in all measures warranted by the former," and to maintain the union, "it pledges all its powers." Language less calculated to rouse resentment could not be used : nor were the resolutions addressed to the people, and if they were, Mr. *Mercer* said they would not have been objected to by him on that ground. If the people were not to be confided in, we were wretched indeed. In whom were we to confide, if not in the people? In their virtue and patriotism were all his hopes placed. The history of government had been the history of crime and usurpation. In the purity of administration he could not solely confide. The people were the best, and the only defenders of their liberties; when they became ignorant of the proceedings of their own governments ; when public virtue should cease to be their ruling principle, their liberties would experience the same fate, which those of other nations had undergone : power would stand in the place of the Constitution. He hoped no arguments derived from the probable consequences upon the people of adopting the resolutions, would prevent the judgment of the committee from being calmly exercised upon them.

The right of the state government to interfere in the manner proposed by the resolutions, Mr. *Mercer* contended, was clear to his mind. He asked, what were the rights belonging to the state governments prior

to the existence of the federal Constitution? They were those which belong to all sovereign and independent states. They were perfect and complete. The federal Constitution derived its powers from the people and
the states, and could give none but what had been previously in the possession of the states or the people, and by them delegated to the general
government. It would not be said, that all power was delegated to the
general government; though it had indeed been improperly said, as he
should attempt to show before he took his seat, that the powers of the
federal government were general. He should attempt to show they were
special, and that none but what were specially delegated could be exercised. It appeared to him, that, from the operation of the two separate
governments in the same community, there resulted three species of rights
to be exercised. There were rights which the "federal government
could exclusively exercise, without any interference on the part of the
state government; there were rights which could be exercised by each
government at the same time, and there were rights which belonged exclusively to the state government. The latter embraced all which had not
been delegated in the federal Constitution to the general government, or
prohibited to the states by that instrument. That portion of power which
had been delegated to the federal government, did not affect the sovereignty
of the states" over the reserved rights; that sovereignty continued entire;
and remained as to the reserved rights, what it had been with respect to
all the rights, before the federal Constitution. If the remaining rights are
sovereign, the states whose sovereignty is invaded by any act of the general government have it as fully in their power to defend and protect these,
as they would have had to defend any of their rights if attacked by a foreign power, before the general government had a being. The state believed some of its rights had been invaded by the late acts of the general
government, and proposed a remedy whereby to obtain a repeal of them.
The plan contained in the resolutions appeared to Mr. *Mercer* the most
advisable. Force was not thought of by any one. The preservation of
the federal Constitution, the cement of the Union with its original powers,
was the object of the resolutions. The states were equally concerned, as
their rights had been equally invaded; and nothing seemed more likely to
produce a temper in Congress for a repeal, than a declaration similar to
the one before the committee, made by a majority of states, or by several
of them. The states had the power of communicating together in producing amendments to the federal Constitution. A proposition for this
purpose had been presented to the legislature, during the present session,
from the state of Massachusetts, and would be acted upon before their
adjournment. It appeared strange that the states might communicate together to amend the Constitution, and were not permitted to do so, in
order to protect the same when amended; that they might communicate
together when they chose to give away their rights, but could not do it
when their reserved rights were invaded. The reverse of this Mr. *Mercer*
was happy in believing was true. The opinion contained in the resolutions was coeval with the Constitution itself, and had been maintained by
the most enlightened commentary which had been produced in America
upon that instrument (he alluded to a collection of papers written under

the signature of Publius, in the state of New York), when the Constitution
was under consideration, and generally known by the name of the Federalist. The union of talents exercised in the production of this work had
justly entitled it to the attention of every American who is anxious to know
the true meaning of the federal Constitution, and the real intent of its
powers; and though some of its opinions may be erroneous, it was still
the best authority that could be produced. The time of its being written
was extremely favourable to the impartiality of its sentiments, as that vindictive party spirit which had now so unhappily extended its baneful influence to almost every individual in the community, could not have affected its supposed authors, one of whose merits had so justly been resounded
a few days ago from every side of this house. This authority, when
speaking of the checks which the state governments would always have
upon the general government, and of the little probability of the latter en-
grossing powers unobserved, uses the following strong and decided language: "If the majority (in the general government) should be really
disposed to exceed the proper limits, the community will be warned of the
danger, and will have an opportunity of taking measures to guard against
it. Independent of parties in the national legislature itself, as often as the
period of discussion arrived, *the state legislatures,* who will always be not
only vigilant, but suspicious and jealous guardians of the rights of the citizens *against encroachments from the federal government,* will constantly
have their attention awake to the conduct of the national rulers, and will
be ready enough, if anything improper appears, to sound the alarm to the
people, and not only to be the *voice,* but, if necessary, the *arm* of their
discontent:" vol. 1st, page 166. Their sentiments embraced the plan proposed in the resolutions. They spoke a language much stronger than
any which these would be found to contain. We do not wish, said Mr.
Mercer, to be the *arm* of the people's discontent, but to use their *voice.*
The same authority has maintained the right of the states to interfere in
the manner expressed in the resolutions submitted to the committee, in
terms still more applicable. " *It may safely be received as an axiom in
our political system, that the state governments will, in all possible contingencies, afford complete security* against invasion of the public liberty
by the national authority. Projects of usurpation cannot be masked under
pretences so likely to escape the penetration of select bodies of men, as of
the people at large. The legislatures will have better means of information. They can discover the danger at a distance; and possessing all
the organs of civil power, and confidence of the people, they can at once
adopt a regular plan of opposition, in which they can combine all the resources of the community. *They can readily communicate with* each
other in the different states; and unite their common forces for the protection of their common liberty:" vol. 1st, page 176. Here, said Mr. *Mercer,*
we see the opinion of the resolutions so clearly admitted, as to be considered a " *political axiom in our system.*" The right of two different
states " *to communicate with each other,*" is here supported by the best
defence which the federal Constitution ever received; not only this right
is defended, but were the states to " adopt a regular plan of opposition, in
which they should combine all their resources," this authority, addressed

to the people at the time the Constitution was under consideration, would justify the measure. But no such wish was entertained by the friends of the resolutions. Their object in addressing the states is to obtain a similar declaration of opinion with respect to several late acts of the general government, which seem to violate some of the most invaluable rights secured by the charter of their own existence; and thereby to obtain a repeal of measures unconstitutional in their nature, and hateful in their tendency; measures so justly obnoxious to the people, that they would have found few advocates, but for the vain pretence of their being necessary to defend us against the attempts of France; measures that have divided the community at a moment when union of sentiment is ardently to be wished for by every friend to the interest of his country.

The gentleman from Prince George had introduced the opinions of a learned writer upon the law of nations, to prove which were the rights of aliens. Though, Mr. *Mercer* did not believe this class of men stood, in a foreign country, upon the narrow ground in which it was attempted to place them, yet, he deemed it entirely unnecessary to inquire what was the nature and extent of their rights; he should contend that the federal government possessed no power over aliens in time of peace; and, therefore, whatever power a sovereign state could exercise with respect to them, under the general law of nations, that power belonged to the state, and not to the general government; the rights of sovereignty did not attach to the federal government in all their extent: it was sovereign only with respect to the rights which it could exercise *exclusively*: it was limited in its operation, and the boundaries of its authority clearly ascertained; unless, therefore, this power over aliens should be found vested in the general government by the terms of the Constitution, he could not admit it to be derived from implication, or from any general clause in that instrument. Implication would lead us into an endless discussion. The plain sense and meaning of the Constitution should be our guide. In some part of the gentleman's argument he admitted the limited powers of the Constitution; in others he certainly advanced opinions destructive of that limitation. To show that the powers under the Constitution were limited and special, Mr. *Mercer*, begged leave to refer to the Constitution itself. In the eighth section and first article, there was found a special enumeration of powers; most of the great powers of Congress were here particularly defined. Those which they had a right to exercise, and which were not in this section, were as clearly ascertained in other parts of the instrument: why was this cautious enumeration of powers necessary, except to keep Congress within the strict and literal meaning of the Constitution, and to prevent the assumption of power under any general clause? It was intended to prevent them from exercising any power, but what was given. If opinions cotemporaneous with the original discussion of the Constitution in Virginia, can serve us in ascertaining its true meaning, (and they certainly ought,) he would refer gentlemen to the debates in the Convention of this state. The opponents of the Constitution were apprehensive, that by implication, or some general phrases, Congress might assume powers not intended to be conveyed. The advocates of that paper declared, in every day's debate, that these apprehensions were without foundation: that the language was so clear, and its powers so well defined, that none could be exercised under it by implication, or that was not found upon its face. Though the evidence of every member who wished the Constitution ratified, might be produced upon this subject, he would mention the opinions of only two gentlemen belonging to that body. "Mr. *John Marshall* asked if gentlemen were serious when they asserted that if the state governments had power to interfere with the militia, it was by implication. If they were, he asked the committee whether the least attention would not show they were mistaken: *each government was to act according to the powers given it.* Would any gentleman deny this? He demanded if powers not given were retained by implication? Could any man say so? Could any man say, that this power *was not retained by the states, as they had not given it away?* For, does not a power remain till it is given away? The state legislatures had power to command and govern their militia before, and have it still, *undeniably, unless there be something in this Constitution that takes it away.*" Though the limited powers of the Constitution were in this opinion insisted on, there was still higher authority. It was the instrument of ratification adopted in the Convention of Virginia, which had been mentioned by the gentleman from Caroline. It contained the opinion of the Convention, and declares, " that *every* power not granted, remains with the people and at their will: *that, therefore, no right of any denomination,* can be *cancelled, abridged, restrained,* or *modified,* by the Congress, by the Senate, or House of Representatives, acting in any capacity, by the President or any department or officer of the United States, except in those instances in which power is given by the Constitution for those purposes; and that, among other essential rights, the liberty of conscience and of the press, cannot be cancelled, abridged, restrained or modified, by any authority of the United States." We see what was the opinion of the State of Virginia, with respect to the powers of the Constitution, when she was called upon to ratify or reject it. But, to remove all doubts, immediately upon its going into operation, certain amendments were made, among which is the following: "The powers not delegated to the United States by the Constitution, nor prohibited by it to the states, are reserved to the states, respectively, or to the people." This amendment, now a part of the Constitution, ought to fix the real extent of the powers of Congress. But, the gentleman was not satisfied with it, because the word *expressly,* was not to be found there. Mr. *Mercer* hoped the committee would not believe this single term essential to ascertain the limitation of power under which Congress were bound to act. The words of the amendment were general, and conveyed a certain meaning. It was that which the face of the Constitution, in its original form, would warrant, which cotemporaneous opinions had maintained, and which the Convention of Virginia had declared to be true. It was impossible for language to be so explicit as to produce a clause that might not be subject to similar objections; for, if this term had been used in the amendment, gentlemen might have thought it still defective, as others equally strong might have been left out. He therefore supposed, as these evidences ascertained the power of the Federal Constitution to be special, and as no power over aliens, such as has been exercised by Congress, in the law so generally obnoxious, had been, or in his opinion, could be shown to exist in that body, the law itself must be considered repugnant to the Constitution, and as invading the rights of the states.

Many of the remarks of the gentleman from Prince George, were in-tended to show the expediency of the law, and the inconveniences that might arise from the want of the power in Congress to pass it. Mr. *Mercer* considered these remarks entirely foreign from the inquiry before the committee. The only question ought to be, whether it was constitu-tional or not : if it was not, in his opinion, a violation of the Constitution, which ought to be held sacred, he declared that he would not at this time thus publicly deny its expediency. But there would be no period so criti-cal, as to justify silence upon a departure from the Constitution. It might be believed, that temporary advantages would result ; but permanent evil would be the certain consequence : for, if there was a maxim in American politics, it must be, that no law could be expedient, which was unconstitu-tional. If it was found inconvenient that Congress had not this power, the remedy was plain : perhaps it was the best feature in the instrument that pointed out the manner in which itself could be amended. It did not consider the present provisions in it as the unalterable effort of the best reason, but left them to the operation of time and experience, by which their defects might be unfolded : when these appeared, the remedy was in amending the Constitution, and not in usurping powers by constructions, so highly forced, as to leave its meaning entirely uncertain ; and to lay the foundation for administering the government upon principles unac-knowledged by the Constitution, and unknown to the states and the people at the time of its adoption. But the gentleman had supposed, that under the aid of necessary implication, Congress possessed the power of passing the alien friend law ; and made his appeal to the last clause in the eighth section, which said, that Congress should have the power " to make all laws which shall be necessary and proper to carry into execution *the fore-going powers*, and all other powers *vested by this Constitution* in the go-vernment of the United States, or in any department or officer thereof." Mr. *Mercer* said, this clause had been called in the Convention of Virginia, by the opponents of the Constitution, the *sweeping* clause. But it was evident, it referred only to the powers expressly " *vested*" in Congress by the Constitution. It could give no new power. It would be absurd to suppose, that after a special enumeration of powers, limited by the terms of the grant, that *any* general expressions could so operate, as to produce an increase of authority. It had not been shown to his satisfaction how the law complained of, was " to carry into execution" any power vested by the Constitution " in the government of the United States, or in any de-partment or officer thereof." Under the construction that had been given to it, it involved new powers, nowhere to be found delegated in that instru-ment : for the true exposition of this clause, he would now refer to the opinion of the other gentleman in the Convention, to whom he had alluded. Mr. *Madison*, speaking of this clause, said, " It is only superfluity. If that latitude of construction, which he (Mr. *Henry*) contends for, were to take place, with respect to the sweeping clause, there would be room for those horrors. *But it gives no supplementary power.* It enables them to execute the *delegated powers.* It is at most explanatory; for when any power is given, its delegation necessarily *involves authority to make laws to execute it.*"

"With respect to the *supposed* operation of what was denominated the sweeping clause, the gentleman, he said, was mistaken; for, *it only extended to the enumerated powers.* Should Congress attempt to extend it *to any power not enumerated,* it would not be warranted by the clause." This opinion must be considered as the just one. It had been maintained by the writer which he had cited, the Federalist. The Constitution itself warranted the truth of it; but, there ought to be no doubt after reading the amendment, which had already been stated. If the power exercised in the law, was not enumerated, neither this, nor any other general clause, could give it to Congress.

. The gentleman had called upon the committee, to show in what part of the Constitution the powers of Congress, with respect to foreign nations, were stated. Mr. *Mercer* hoped he did not mistake his remark, for it was a very important one. If it was true that these great powers, certainly exercised by Congress, were not vested in that body by express terms, but were derived to them by construction or implication, the deduction that would naturally flow from such a truth, would be fatal to the Constitution. It was, if powers so great could be used, without being specially delegated, it showed the extent of implication; and under its operation other powers equally important, and among them, that which Congress had exercised over aliens, might be assumed, but such a position is destructive to the Constitution. Mr. *Mercer* rejoiced in believing it could not be supported by any argument drawn from the powers of Congress over foreign relations; for none were more expressly delegated than these; he begged leave again to refer to that instrument, which should be our constant guide. In the 10th section of first article, it is declared that "no state shall enter into any treaty, alliance, or confederation." And that "no state shall, without the consent of Congress, enter into any agreement or compact with another state, or with a foreign power, or engage in war, &c." This proved that all power with respect to foreign connexions was taken from the states. It was not among their reserved rights; nor could they exercise it conjointly with Congress, because they were deprived of it by negative words in the Constitution. It belonged *exclusively* to the general government. To show this, he read the following clauses in the Constitution : "The Congress shall have power to regulate commerce with foreign nations." "To establish an uniform rule of naturalization." "To declare war and grant letters of marque and reprisal." When speaking of the powers of the President, it says, "He shall have power, by and with the advice and consent of the Senate, to make treaties," &c. "And shall nominate, and by and with the advice and consent of the Senate, shall appoint ambassadors, other public ministers and consuls." "He shall receive ambassadors and other public ministers." These clauses embrace all the great objects of a foreign intercourse; they make it clear, that the powers of the general government upon this subject, are expressly delegated, and depend not upon nice constructions or implication.

In these remarks, Mr. *Mercer* said, he had attempted to show that the federal Constitution was a limited grant of power: that the power which Congress had exercised in the case of the alien law, had been nowhere delegated to them by that instrument, and ought not to be considered within their reach, from implication. That if Congress did not constitutionally possess the power over aliens, which they had exercised, the exercising it was an invasion of the sovereignty of the states; and whenever this took place, the states had a right to communicate with each other, in the manner contemplated by the resolutions now before the committee. But if he had been convinced that this power was vested in Congress, the manner in which they had used it, was equally repugnant to the Constitution, and subversive of some of the most valuable provisions contained in it. It was as necessary they should preserve the distribution of powers actually delegated, according to the mode prescribed in the Constitution, as it was for them not to assume powers which had never been delegated. It was as necessary that one department of the government should not be permitted to use authority, to the constitutional exercise of which only the three branches were competent, as that the whole should assume powers which neither had a right to exercise. The objections to this act had been so often urged, and the public attention so much excited, that it would be useless to dwell upon them at this time: he would briefly mention the objections which he felt to the act, even if Congress had the power over aliens which they had exercised. His first was, that it placed in the hands of the President an union of authority, which by the principles of free government, should always be kept separate and distinct. It gave him the right to exercise legislative, judicial, and executive powers, which were intended to be kept apart by the Constitution, and never could be united in the same individual, or in the same department of government, without producing a real despotism. To prove that legislative power was vested in the President by this law, he asked what was the distinguishing characteristic of that power, or the highest act that could be performed by it? It was to prescribe a rule of conduct, commanding what was right, and prohibiting what was wrong. What was the rule of conduct prescribed to the alien by this law? What was he commanded to do, and what to avoid? There was no rule of conduct laid down in the law. There was no crime defined. Even the President was not required to say what the alien's duty should be. Everything was confined within his own breast. The class of men intended to be involved under this law, could not know they had sinned, until the punishment was upon them. If he then prescribed the rule of conduct for aliens, he also had the right under the law to *judge* when that rule was violated: he was the executive department of the government constitutionally, and the duties of legislating and judging were annexed to his new office by this law. The second objection was, that it destroyed the trial by jury, which he considered was extended to all persons by the Constitution. The terms were as general, and as comprehensive, as language could make them. He begged leave to refer to them. "The trial of *all crimes*, except in cases of impeachment, shall be by jury." "*No person* shall be held to answer for a capital or otherwise infamous crime, unless on a presentment or indictment by a grand jury, &c."

" Nor be deprived of *life, liberty,* or *property*, without due process of law."
" In *all criminal* prosecutions, the accused shall enjoy the right to a speedy
and public trial, by an impartial jury, &c.," " be *informed of the nature
and cause of the accusation:* to be confronted with the witnesses against
him : to have compulsory process for obtaining witnesses in his favour ;
and to have the assistance of counsel for his defence." These just, humane,
and most invaluable of all privileges, were taken from the alien: his
" *liberty*" was to be suspended without any "*crime*" being defined, which
he ought to avoid ; without any " trial by jury," of which " no person" is
to be deprived under the Constitution ; there was no " information of the
nature and cause of the accusation" to be communicated to him ; he was
" to be confronted with no witnesses ; counsel could not be heard in his
favour ;" his liberty depended upon the mercy and justice of an individual.
The third objection was, that it virtually destroyed the right of the states,
under the ninth section of the first article of the Constitution ; for though
the states might admit the " migration or importation" of such persons as
they might think proper prior to a certain period, it was to little purpose,
if the President, influenced by his own suspicions, could send them away.
The argument of the gentleman from Prince George, seemed to relinquish
the point. He observed, that the law would have been unconstitutional,
if it had been a permanent one, passed prior to the year 1808, since it
would then defeat this section. Mr. *Mercer* said, he could not see how its
being temporary, would prevent the same effect from being produced : for,
if the power of Congress could pass such a law for two years, it might extend to the year 1808. If they possessed the right to originate the law,
and keep it in force for any term, however short, they could certainly
defeat the ninth section altogether ; because, as often as the period arrived
when this temporary law was to expire, they had only to pass it again for
a limited time ; and by thus keeping it temporary, bring about the year
1808; after which the gentleman supposed the right would be in Congress.
The law being only a temporary one, therefore, could not possibly prove
it to be constitutional.

Much had been said, by the member from Prince George, respecting the
conduct of aliens, and the dangers that were to be apprehended from them.
Mr. *Mercer* did not suppose that the friends of the resolutions felt it their
duty to defend, or to blame that conduct, whatever it might have been,
without having ever understood any acts to have been performed by that
class of men by which American rights had suffered. The statement of
the gentleman might be true, and still it did not affect the question before
the committee. The object of the resolutions was not to defend aliens,
but to protect the Constitution, which had been violated in the case of
these men. If, under the intention of removing dangerous aliens, the
principles of that instrument would be openly violated, and some of its
wisest provisions set aside, the same might take place with respect to native citizens. If it was infringed upon in one instance, the same might
happen in any other.

With respect to the sedition law, as it was generally called, Mr. *Mercer*
said he would not take up the time of the committee in making any observations upon it. He was willing to let the proof of its unconstitutional

quality rest upon the argument of the gentleman from Caroline. He would only say, it was odious in his sight. It was certainly unnecessary, unless the general government had reason to doubt the virtue and patriotism of the people. If that government would pursue measures compatible with the Constitution, and calculated to preserve the country in a state of peace, and not hasten that unhappy crisis with which we were threatened, when war should be found unavoidable, every citizen would be ready to defend his country's rights against the attempts of any nation upon earth. Mr. *Mercer* believed, if it had not been for the unfortunate difference between America and France, there would have been few voices ready to approve of several of the late acts of the general government. That difference had been made the pretext for exercising power in a manner which, two years past, would have been universally condemned. He hoped the committee would distinguish between the aggressions of France, and the operations of our own government. The alarm of foreign invasion, created by government, was not a modern thing. When power wished to encroach, the same had been excited in every age and country. At this time, two instances occurred to him. When Charles the Seventh of France wished to establish a standing army in that country, he told the people it was necessary to be ready against invasions from England. But when all danger was removed, the army was kept up, and afflicted the nation for centuries. Charles was the first king of France who levied a tax without the consent of the states-general. When Cardinal Ximenes introduced a standing army into Spain, the people were informed it was necessary to protect them against the invasion of the Moors from Africa; but when these were expelled the country and their power destroyed, the army was continued. History afforded many similar instances. It proved, that the moment for power to enlarge its privileges was that of public agitation and alarm; he would make no inferences with a view of applying them to the general government. Every gentleman in the committee might make his own deductions. Mr. *Mercer* concluded by observing, that he should vote for the resolutions, unless arguments could be offered to prove to his satisfaction, that the acts complained of were constitutional.

Mr. POPE arose next, and made several general observations in answer to those which had fallen from Mr. *George K. Taylor*, respecting the necessity of deliberation before decision in favour of the alien law, and concerning Volney and Talleyrand. He then proceeded to observe, that as to Talleyrand, the gentleman from Prince George was not correct as to what he had related of him; but besides, that he had not related the whole story. He had represented him to be a great rascal indeed, and a very great rascal he himself would acknowledge he was. But that he would still give them a further account of that Mr. Talleyrand, as true as that which the gentleman from Prince George had related. He then proceeded to mention that, in the course of Talleyrand's stay in America, he had been for some time much countenanced by some of the conspicuous characters in New York, of whom he particularly mentioned the gentleman who never broke a command, who never disturbed the quiet or repose of any family; that gentleman who inviolably kept the sacred vow he made

to his bride on the day of marriage.   But as soon as these gentlemen discovered his political opinions to be different from what they supposed
them to be when they admitted him into their society, they instantly broke
off all communication with him, and ever afterwards reviled and persecuted him.   He made some observations respecting Volney ; and then asked
how the gentleman from Prince George had found out the story which he
had related of Volney, when Porcupine or Goodloe Harper never could ?
Perhaps he had learnt it from Billy Wilcox ; and who was he ?   A mere
automaton.   He could say this—he could say that—anything or nothing.
He was directed altogether by the breaker of the matrimonial vow.   The
gentleman from Prince George had spoken of Frenchmen *sneaking* away.
But sneaking as they were, he said, he believed all Europe sneaked before
them.   However, he said, he was no champion for the French, any more
than for the British.   He thought we had no business with either of them.
He then spoke of British aggressions upon our commerce.   But these, he
said, were not felt by the executive of the United States, as well as many
of its citizens.   He then complimented Mr. *George K. Taylor* upon his
talent in moving the passions.   He had exercised that talent so effectually
a session or two before, as to draw tears from the members of that house,
(alluding to the speech delivered in favour of the new criminal law,) and
he himself must confess, indeed, that the gentleman had, on the subject
then before them, dealt more in pathos than in argument.   He then asked
why the gentleman, when reviling Genet, did not say something of Liston
too ?   He believed that he (Liston) had done us as much harm as ever
Genet did.   As a proof, he instanced the Spanish transaction.   But when
that was stated to that great man, Mr. Pickering, he said that we were to
pay no kind of credit to it, for he was satisfied that our good allies, the
British, did not intend to injure us.   The gentleman from Prince George,
he said, had introduced a damsel, and that was the damsel of liberty.
When he had done so, he, (Mr. *Pope*,) cold as his blood was, confessed
that he was seized with an ecstacy.   But when, at the same time, the
gentleman would not permit that damsel to remain within these walls, he
acknowledged that his feelings were very much wounded indeed.   For he
(Mr. *Pope*), was fond of all damsels, but particularly so of the damsel of
liberty.   And if he were so, cold as his blood was, what might they not
expect from that young, athletic gentleman, whose warmth of blood was
so plainly visible.   The same gentleman, he said, had also dwelt upon
the Saint Domingo horrors.   The alien law, he (Mr. *Pope*) said, had
not removed them.   He believed all the emigrants from that place were
aristocrats : but they had not been removed.   The gentleman had also
mentioned the determinations of the other states.   As well as he could
recollect, he said, he conceived that such determinations extended only to
an approbation of the measures of the Executive in regard to the negotiation with France.   But, be they what they would, we were not bound
to follow their example.   Kentucky had differed from them.   He asked
who had knocked at the doors of the aristocratic Senate of the United
States but Virginia ?   She had been the chief means of opening them.   In
that instance, then, she had weight.   He wished, therefore, that on this
occasion they should do what they thought right.   That, too, might pro-

bably have weight. If it should not, they would at least discharge their duty. . At any rate, he thought the determination, according to the resolutions which they were about to make, would not lead to war, as was apprehended; and therefore they might safely agree to pass them. However, he said, he did not feel himself so rigidly attached to the resolutions, but that he would be willing to. agree to any modification of them to accommodate gentlemen, provided the substance of them should be so retained as to go to declare the laws of Congress under their consideration, unconstitutional.

Mr. JOHN ALLEN arose next, and said he was not accustomed to make apologies for anything he wished to say in this house, nor should he do so in the present case; the subject was of too much importance to require any. And, notwithstanding his' ill state of health, he rose to give his feeble aid in favour of the wounded daughter of liberty. In deciding on a constitutional question, he did not expect that the understanding was to be banished, and the passions only left to be their guide. But, he found that the gentleman from Prince George, through the whole of his lengthy harangue, relied solely on the force and effect of the latter. That gentleman informed them that he should confine his observations to the alien law, and attempt to prove it constitutional. How did he do this? By describing, in the most terrific colours, the conduct of the French towards us, and other nations; and then asserting, that the alien law was made to protect us from the French. But, before the gentleman indulged himself in his description of the cruelties and aggressions committed by the French, he should have proved that this law related *only* to that nation. But it clearly was not so. It extends to all nations alike, and without discrimination. The law need only be read to prove the truth of this assertion.

Unless, then, it appeared that we were threatened with, or had danger to apprehend from, all the nations on earth, that law could not be justified, even by the gentleman's own arguments. The gentlemen had further observed, that if this law had been permanent, it would be unconstitutional; but, if temporary, it would not. Mr. *Allen* said, in his opinion, there was no difference between the cases. He could not discover how a clause in a law declaring that it should expire at a particular period, could make the law constitutional. But, the gentleman did not appear to rely much on that argument; only that it gave him an opportunity of returning again to his favourite theme, a description of French cruelties. But, said the gentleman, the admission of aliens in a country was a matter of favour, and not of right. But, Mr. *Allen* averred, that the admission of alien friends into a country was not a matter of favour; and even if it were, when they were in a country they were entitled to certain rights, which he enumerated, and which, he said, were derived to them from the laws of nature, nations, and humanity. The gentleman admitted that an alien could not be deprived of life or property without a trial, and that by jury. If so, surely they should not be deprived of their liberty without trial, and that too by jury. But, perhaps, in these modern days, life and property only are to be held sacred, while liberty is to be exposed to the whim or caprice of a single man. If, indeed, this be the case, and liberty is considered of less value than property, then the argument of the gentleman should have some weight. But, we are taught by the Constitution to rank liberty next to life. If, therefore, an alien cannot be deprived of his property without trial by jury, he certainly should not be deprived of his liberty without the same kind of trial. On that account, then, he said, the law was apparently unconstitutional. But suppose, he said, it was absolutely necessary to provide by law for sending aliens out of this country, who had the power to do so? Congress, or the states? He declared that the states had. He read the first clause of the ninth section respecting the migration of persons prior to the year 1808, as proof of the assertion. But, even if Congress had such a power, they had no right to vest it in the President, for reasons that had already been given, and that were too apparent not to be understood. He then proceeded to point out the danger of placing too much power in the hands of the Executive. He stated instances of the unhappy effects proceeding from it in Britain; and was afraid we had much danger to apprehend from a desire in Congress to increase executive power. This law, vesting in the President such enormous powers, the gentleman from Prince George observed, was made for the purpose of getting rid of two individuals, and as they had sneaked out of the country, there was no farther necessity for the law. To what extremity, said Mr. *Allen*, must the United States have been reduced. How must they be degraded, when we are informed that it was necessary to make the President absolute tyrant over perhaps a million of people, to get rid of two men.

But it was urged as an objection to the adoption of the resolutions under consideration, that the people were the proper tribunal to decide upon the constitutionality of the laws, and that they would shortly decide the question at the next election. Mr. *Allen* contended, that was not a proper mode for the decision of such a question, for that the people often voted from personal or local attachments; and that they were not always apprised of the opinions of the different candidates; and he instanced his own district as proof of the latter assertion. But, he said, if this was a proper mode of deciding this question, he believed there was no doubt how the people would determine. And this house, by the re-election of a senator of the United States the other day, had already decided the question. Mr. Allen then concluded by making some general observations on the dangerous consequences of deriving powers from implication; and said, that he at that moment experienced too much bodily pain to be able to proceed further.

On motion of Mr. *Magill*, the committee then rose, the chairman reported progress, asked, and had leave to sit again.

IN THE HOUSE OF DELEGATES,
Monday, December 17, 1798.

The House resolved itself into a committee of the whole house, on the state of the commonwealth, Mr. *Brackenridge* in the chair, when Mr. *John Taylor's* resolutions being still under consideration,

Mr. Barbour arose, and observed, that being a young man, he did not intend to have troubled the committee with any remarks upon the subject under discussion, but the solicitude he experienced had impelled him forward. He observed, that the moment on which he arose, might be called the first of his political existence, and yet in that moment he was called upon to decide a question, in which, not only his own fate as a politician, but the welfare of his country was materially involved. Mr. *Barbour* asked, what must be the sensations of a young man the first instant he stepped on the theatre of public life, to be called on to act a part, in which such important consequences are implicated? He observed, he experienced those sensations to an eminent degree. But having formed · a rule, by which he meant to be governed in his political career, which was, to pursue the line of conduct his judgment dictated as the most proper, he would announce to the committee, and through the committee to the world, the motives which actuated him to give the vote he was about to pronounce, which would be in favour of the adoption of the resolutions. He observed, it had been remarked by every gentleman, whether *pro* or *con*, that the event of the present discussion was important. He begged leave to add his testimony likewise to the importance of the subject. And he believed he should not use language too strong, was he to assert, that in the proceedings of this Legislature might be read the destinies of America: for issue was joined between monarchical principles on the one hand, and republican on the other ; and they were the grand inquest who were to determine the controversy. For should so important a state as Virginia sanction the measures complained of in the resolutions, (which she would do if the resolutions should be rejected,) it would become a step-stone to ·. farther usurpation, until those great rights, which are guaranteed by nature and the Constitution, will be destroyed one by one, and a monarchy erected upon the ruins thereof. But on the contrary, if she discountenanced those measures, (as she would do by the adoption of the resolutions,) and could obtain the co-operation of the sister states, it might overawe tyranny, for tyranny in embryo was timid. He asked, could it be necessary, to conjure the members of the committee to be tremulously alive to the importance of the subject, and viewing it free from prepossessions, should give that opinion, which would redound most to their own fame and eventuate in the welfare of their country. He then read the resolutions, and observed, the gentleman from Prince George had remarked, that those resolutions invited the people to insurrection and to arms. But Mr. *Barbour* said, if he could conceive that the consequence foretold would grow out of the measure, he would become its bitterest enemy, for he deprecated intestine commotion, civil war, and bloodshed, as the most direful evils which could befall a country, except slavery. A resort to arms was the last appeal of an oppressed and injured nation, and was never made but when public servants converted themselves, by usurpation, into masters, and destroyed rights once participated ; and then, it was justifiable. But he observed, the idea of that same gentleman was in concert, as would appear by reference to a leading feature in the resolutions, which was, their being addressed not to the people, but to the sister states ; praying, in a pacific way, their co-operation in arresting the tendency and effect of unconstitutional laws. He observed, it had been said by some gentlemen that they admitted the unconstitutionality of the laws, and yet they would vote against the resolutions, for that the subject exclusively belonged to the people, and if their servants had violated their trust, they ought to substitute others. In answer to this, Mr. *Barbour* observed, that doctrine like this was pregnant with every mischief. For once admit, said he, that the states have no check, no constitutional barrier against the encroachment of the general government, we should thereby lessen that weight to which the state governments are entitled in the political machine, which, in America, is a complex one. We should thereby destroy those checks and balances, which are the *sine qua non* of their mutual existence and welfare. And the consequence then would be, that instead of harmony and symmetry which has hitherto prevailed, chaos, confusion, and all the evils incident to that situation, would be the inevitable result. In theory this doctrine is alarming, but fortunately for the liberties of America, when it comes to be tried by the rules of reason and sound argument, it is found monstrous and absurd, and therefore its advocates must be few. He observed, that he would undertake to demonstrate that, although the people possessed the right of excluding those who advocated the obnoxious measures, and he hoped would exercise the right, yet the state legislatures not only had a concurrent right, but were equally bound to exercise that right. He asked, who were the parties that formed the compact? Were they not the people and the states? If it had been formed exclusively by the people, he supposed a majority of the people would have been sufficient to have confirmed the compact. But what was the fact? Did not the Constitution require, that the consent of nine of the states shall be an indispensable preliminary to its adoption? Again, did it not permit three-fourths of the legislatures to alter the Constitution, without the intervention of the people? And cannot the states admit new parties to the compact, to wit, by the erection of new states? Again, are not the state legislatures to the Senate, what the people are to the Representatives? And if the latter possess the power of censure and discharge (which as yet no gentleman would deny), must it not follow by a parity of reasoning, that the former possess the same power relative to the body elected by themselves? Again, the President is elected by electors, who represent the states as well as the people; for the number of electors is not in proportion to the number of the people alone, but the states as well as the people: for example, the state of Delaware has three electors, when it is entitled to but one representative; whereas Virginia has only twenty-one electors when she is entitled to nineteen representatives. It must follow, then, as an incontrovertible deduction, that the states are parties to the compact, and being parties, if the compact was violated (as it was violated) the states have the right, and ought to exercise it, to declare that those proceedings, which are an infringement upon the Constitution, are not binding. The state legislatures being the immediate representatives of the people, and consequently the immediate guardians of their rights, should sound the tocsin of alarm at the approach of danger, and should be the arm of the people to repel every invasion. If, said he, the alien and sedition laws are unconstitutional, they are not law, and of course of no force. For what are the necessary ingredients to the Constitution and the force of a law? It was not only essential they should receive the sanction of the constituted authorities, but the act itself must be in unison with the Constitution; for, if an agent should transcend his limited authorities, he would be guilty of usurpation; and all usurpation being founded in wrong, whatever has that only for its support, must be void. This being the case, the legislature would be guilty of misprision of treason against the liberties of their constituents if they did not denounce the violations offered to the Constitution through the medium of the alien and sedition laws. He observed, it remained for him to show, that the laws alluded to, were unconstitutional.

The worthy gentleman from Caroline having proven, in a clear and perspicuous manner, the unconstitutionality of the sedition law, and delineated, in masterly and eloquent language, the consequences of that act, which is entitled to the infamous pre-eminence in the scale of guilt, and as no gentleman had undertaken its defence, Mr. *Barbour* said, that his remarks would be confined to the alien law alone. And, in order to ascertain whether this law was constitutional or not, reference must be had to the nature of the Constitution. The government must be either limited or unlimited. If the latter, it was omnipotent, like the Parliament of Great Britain, and was adequate to the purpose of passing any law, however impolitic, absurd or dangerous it might be to the liberties of the people. But, if it were limited, (which was a principle he supposed so clear, that to consume the time of the committee in proving it, would be a supererogation,) it would remain then to be inquired, whether in the limited power granted, a power be given to pass a law like the one now under discussion, or not. He observed, that to comprehend the nature of the Constitution of the general government, it might not be unimportant to recur to the political situation of America, prior to the adoption of the federal government. In 1776, the thirteen United States, then the colonies of America, after having been lacerated to the midriff, by the vulture fangs of British persecution, threw off their colonial subjugation, and took a stand among the nations of the earth. At this time, there were thirteen independent sovereignties tied together by the feeble bands of the articles of confederation. So long as the pressure of external danger was felt, so long the bond of union was found sufficiently strong. So long as all jealousies and rivalships were sacrificed on the altar of public good, the defects of that system were, in some measure, concealed. But, so soon as the pressure of foreign invasion was removed, so soon it was discovered that the system of union created by the confederation, was inadequate to the sublime purposes for which it was intended. The people of America saw and deplored the situation with which they were menaced; and the Virginia Legislature, sensible of the jeopardy to which their well earned liberties were exposed, were the first to recommend a reformation in the compact by which the states were connected, notwithstanding the senseless yell and malicious calumnies with which certain hireling papers to the east teem, of a disposition in this state to shake off the union. Influenced by this spirit, the convention met in the year 1786, in Annapolis, but broke up without doing any thing effectual. In the year 1787, the convention which met in Philadelphia, gave birth to the Federal Constitution. The object of the general government *ex vi termini*, must be for general purposes; and the powers necessary to carry those purposes into effect, were expressly defined; and it was the sense of the American people, cotemporaneous with the adoption of the general government, when the attributes and qualities of that government were best understood, that all powers not granted were retained. As an evidence of which, let reference be had, he said, to the twelfth amendment of the Federal Constitution; which expressly declares, that all powers not granted to the general government, were retained to the states, or the people, respectively. It was then urged, (with propriety too, as the sequel has evinced,) that the Federal Constitution was defective, in consequence of its wanting a bill of rights. It was answered by the advocates of the Constitution, (amongst whom was Mr. *Lee* of Westmoreland, who now displayed great zeal in support of administration, and consequently, amongst the friends of administration, should have some weight,) that the Constitution was better without, than with a bill of rights; for, if there had been, (Mr. *Lee* observed,) an enumeration of particular rights, with the friends to forced construction there would have been a claim, as residuary legatee, to all rights not expressly retained; but in the present government, there were only particular powers granted, and consequently, all powers not granted, are retained to the states, or the people, respectively: a doctrine which he (Mr. *Barbour*,) observed before, had been recognised in the twelfth amendment to the Constitution. Mr. *Barbour* then observed, that he having shown that the government could exercise no power but what was specifically enumerated, it behooved the authors or supporters of the law to show that the power of making a law like the one which was now the subject of discussion, was designated in the list of specific powers. If they could not show it, it must follow, it was an usurpation of power not warranted by the Constitution. To ascertain the truth upon this subject, which in argument was desirable, let reference be had, he said, to the section which enumerates the powers that Congress can legally exercise, (being the eighth section of the first article.) Any power which Congress should exercise, not warranted by that charter, would be an usurpation upon the rights of the states, or the people; and in proportion to the extent of the usurpation, should be the execration of every friend to republican government and the liberties of the people. It would be discovered, when reference was had to the section of the Constitution alluded to above, that no power to make an *alien* law is granted. When gentlemen are called upon to justify the assumption of power, they desert the ground of the law being justifiable agreeable to the letter of the Constitution, and take refuge behind the sanctuary of implication. Mr. *Barbour* then described the danger of implied power, in a warm and animated manner. He begged the committee to be alive to the mischief with which this doctrine was teeming. If, said he, we once abandon the high road which the wisdom of our ancestors has established, and in which the constituted authorities were directed to walk; if we once abandon that palladium of civil liberty, our rights will be immediately gone. No, said he, let us, if our servants turn either to the right or to the left, smite them as of old was Balaam's ass, so that they turn not away from the path to which, if we mean to keep our liberties, they should adhere with unde-

viating regularity. Promulge it once, said hĕ, to the world, or rather to
Congress, that they have a right to exercise powers by implication, and it
requires not the aid of prophecy to foretell, if we may judge of the future
by the past, that those great and inestimable rights which flow from nature,·
and are the gift of nature's God, will be assassinated by the rude ·and
unfeeling hand of ferocious despotism. That body will not only pass
alien and *sedition* laws, which they have had the audacity to pass in the
tenth year of the Constitution, but will go on to increase the already black
catalogue of crimes, new fangled, and existing only in the brain of suspicion
and political villany, till some of the best patriots are sacrificed, and the
purest blood of which America boasts, streams. The friends of liberty will
be sacrificed, as so many obstacles to their ambitious designs, and despotism, covered with the gore of patriots, will stalk with impunity amongst
us. But, Mr. *Barbour* said, he had determined to pursue the gentleman
from Prince George through all the meanders and twistings of his argument, and expose its fallacy and danger; that there should be no ground
upon which the supporters of this law should find rest: like the dove of
old, they should be compelled to take refuge in the ark, which, by the
resolutions, was prepared for their reception. For this reason, for the sake
of argument, but for that only, (God forbid it should be for anything else,)
he would admit the principle that Congress might legislate by implication,
yet it could have no power of the kind which appears to have been exercised in making the alien law. But before he went into that subject, it
was necessary he should take notice of some miscellaneous remarks which
had fallen from the gentleman from Prince George. That gentleman had
observed that Congress had passed the law, and that we should hesitate
before we declared it unconstitutional; for if it was unconstitutional, the
people ought to resort to arms. In answer to this, Mr. *Barbour* observed,
that the circumstance of Congress having passed it, if it was intrinsically
unconstitutional, did not render the law less so; and although he had a
high respect for some of the members of Congress in both houses, on
account of their talents and integrity, yet some of the warmest advocates
of this law and executive measures, were suspicious characters from their
situation in life, which was so desperate as not to be endangered, but on
the contrary they might try to be bettered by revolution and convulsion.
Political profligacy in a republican government sooner or later will meet
its fate, the execration of an injured people; but by a change, the Judases
of American liberty will aspire to the acme of opulence in the sunshine·of
monarchy, the most genial climate for the growth of everything which is
abhorrent to republican simplicity and virtue. But, he said, if he had the
highest estimation both for their virtue and wisdom, he should exercise his
own judgment, with 'which he had been blessed by the God of nature, and
if· that condemned it, he should not hesitate to declare in strong terms his
disapprobation. He trusted, he said, that the American people were not
prepared for unconditional submission and non-resistance. A doctrine like
this would have disgraced the last century, and was fit only for the miserable regions of the East, where ignorance, superstition and despotism their
sad dominion keep. He trusted that the American people did not intend
to attach to servants the attribute of infallibility : if not, the adoption of the

law under discussion, by Congress, would have no weight upon the mind of the committee. The gentleman urged that we should hesitate, before a declaration was made that the law was unconstitutional. Mr. *Barbour* asked, what had been the conduct of the committee? Had they rushed precipitately into a determination? On the contrary, had not the subject been discussed for several days; and would it not continue to be discussed for several days more? Had not every gentleman an opportunity of delivering his ideas upon the subject? And had not a depth of judgment and a brilliancy of talent been displayed in the discussion, which would do honour to any deliberative body? In short, had not the subject been treated in a manner suited to its importance? · What more, then, could be asked? The gentleman from Prince George was for the people's rising *en masse*, if the law was unconstitutional. For his part, Mr. *Barbour* said, he was for using no violence. It was the peculiar blessing of the American people to have redress within their reach, by constitutional and peaceful means. He was for giving Congress an opportunity of repealing those obnoxious laws complained of in the resolutions ; and thereby effacing from the Amercan character a stain, which, if not soon wiped off, would become indelible. The gentleman from Prince George had further said, that all the other states in the union had met and adjourned, and tacitly acquiesced in the measures which had been pursued by the general government. The gentleman was incorrect in point of fact.

The state of Kentucky had, in language as bold as could be used, expressed their execration of some of the leading measures·of the general government adopted at their last session ; but upon none more particularly than upon the laws complained of in the resolutions. The state of Tennessee was in such a situation, as to require or authorize the Governor to convene an extra session. About what could it be, if it was not the uneasiness experienced by the people of that state at the usurpation of the general government? In respect to the other states being not adverse, he would not contradict the gentlemen. But what weight would this remark have upon the committee? Was the conduct of the other states to be the criterion whereby to govern this state? He trusted not. He hoped, that so long as this state kept its independence, it would think and act for itself. Virginia had been always forward in repelling usurpation of every kind ; and he trusted she never would forfeit the reputation she had acquired ; but always would be the champion of the rights and liberties of America. But, he said, having answered the desultory remarks of the gentleman from Prince George, he would return to the doctrine of implication. That gentleman read the preamble to the Federal Constitution, to prove that, as the liberty and general welfare of the whole were the object of the Constitution, Congress had a right to do anything which might be necessary, in their opinion, to effect that purpose. The inference, Mr. *Barbour* observed, which had been deduced, was by no means tenable. To assert that the preamble to the Constitution should alter or subvert the Constitution, or that the preamble gave powers not given in the Constitution, was in theory such a monstrous solecism, and so much opposed to every principle of construction, that he did suppose it would be subscribed to but by few. The preamble, to be sure, explains the end of the Constitution. It was to secure the liberties and welfare of the American people, but upon what terms? Why, upon the terms designated in the Constitution. The people of America and the states, knew that the powers conceded to the general government by the Federal Constitution, were adequate to the ends contemplated. Then to pretend to assert that, although those powers, which the states and people designated as those only, which should be exercised, were not the only powers that were granted, was a calumny against the framers of the Constitution; for they must have intended to ensnare the people. For what mind could hesitate to pronounce, that the object of enumerating the powers must have been to fix barriers against the exercise of other powers? And Mr. *Barbour* demanded to know, what was the use of a specific enumeration of powers, if it was intended to invest the general government with sweeping powers? For what could be more awkward or ridiculous, than to see the wisdom of America defining the particular powers, which its government might legally and constitutionally act upon, and in the conclusion, investing it with general powers, which from the expression, must have included all those specific powers, which had been previously granted. Mr. *Barbour* then referred to Publius, 2d vol., pages 46, 7, 8, as an author, who had treated this subject very fully and ably. The gentleman from Prince George had said, that the last clause of the 8th section of the 1st article, commonly called the sweeping clause, the substance of which is, " That Congress shall have power to pass all laws which shall be necessary to the carrying into effect the foregoing powers," would justify Congress in making the laws complained of. Mr. *Barbour* asked, what was the object of that clause? It was not to create new powers, but to complete the other powers before granted. This clause was indispensable; without it, the Constitution would have been a dead letter. For if Congress possessed not the power of making laws to carry into effect the powers specifically enumerated, the powers granted would have been useless; since to possess rights which cannot be carried into effect, was just the same as if there were no rights. But no other construction could attach; for that clause speaks only of those powers which before had been granted. And if no power relative to aliens had been granted, this clause could have no possible effect, which he hoped he had sufficiently demonstrated. Mr. *Barbour* said that the gentleman from Prince George had relied upon the fourth section of the fourth article of the Constitution, by which Congress guarantees to each state a republican form of government, and binds itself to protect each state from invasion, &c., as one out of which the implied power of making alien-laws grew. For he asked how could the general government protect from invasion, without the power of passing a law like the alien; and that it was indispensable the general government should possess the power of expelling aliens; for, if they had not the power, the state of Virginia might admit Bonaparte's army, with him at their head, (if he should ever escape from the Nile.) If, said Mr. Barbour, no other reason could be assigned in favour of the alien law, than an idea so wild as the danger of admitting Bonaparte and his army, its supporters must be in pitiful distress. To anticipate danger of this kind, was to attach to this, state not only criminality, and that too of the blackest kind, but stupidity bordering on idiocy, and to set at defiance the uniform experience of man-kind. For was it ever yet known that a nation participating the blessings of liberty and peace, invited into its bosom a powerful foe, by which those invaluable blessings might be rifled. An idea of this kind was the child of a mind labouring to but little purpose to find some justification for the opinions it advances. But who could have supposed that the section alluded to, which had for its object only imposing an obligation, should by some be converted into a source of power? What, Mr. *Barbour* asked, was the object of that section? It was to impose on Congress the duty of defending each state from invasion. Congress, in the eighth section, had the power of declaring war; yet, without this section, Congress was not bound to exercise this power; and but for this section, Congress might have seen a state invaded, and yet by the letter of the Constitution, would not have been bound to have defended it from invasion, but might have left her to her own resources. To guard against this inconvenience was this section inserted; yet out of this, the committee were, told new powers are derived to the general government. Mr. *Barbour* observed, it appeared to him a bold and unjustifiable assertion to say that the expul-sion of alien friends was necessary to prevent invasion. For his part, his small intellectual faculties could not perceive the connexion. He could readily perceive the necessity of expelling alien enemies; a right which Congress possessed, and upon which they had acted; but that the expul-sion of a friend was necessary to the prevention of invasion, created in his mind a confusion of ideas. It was asked by the gentleman from Prince George, by what authority did Congress exercise control over foreign intercourse, if it was not by implication? Mr. *Barbour* answered, that the power was granted, he thought, by the third clause of the eighth section of the first article, the second clause of the second section, and the third section of the second article of the Federal Constitution. By the first, Congress has power to regulate commerce with foreign nations. By the second, the President, by and with the advice and consent of the Senate, may make treaties, and shall likewise appoint ambassadors and other public ministers and consuls. And by the last, the President is vested with the power of receiving ambassadors and other public minis-ters; from which it is apparent, that without the aid of implication, the general government possesses the power of regulating foreign intercourse.

It was asked, too, by the same gentleman, by what power did Congress erect forts, if it was not by implication? Mr. *Barbour* answered, by the last clause but one of the eighth section of the first article there was this language: " Congress shall have the power to exercise exclusive legisla-tion in all cases whatsoever over such district, &c.:" "And to exercise like authority over all places purchased, by the consent of the legislature of the state in which the same shall be, for the erection of forts, maga-zines, &c." Mr. *Barbour* concluded upon this point, by observing that surely the gentleman had not read the Constitution, for if he had he would not have propounded the question, when he must have known the answer would recoil upon him. It was asked, too, by the gentleman from Prince George, if Congress possessed not the power to make the law now under discussion, by what authority did they make a law relative to alien enemies. Mr. *Barbour* answered he was happy he was able to instruct the gentleman upon the subject of the Constitution, which he (Mr. *Taylor*) had not read, or if he had, it was in a cursory and inattentive manner. He referred the gentleman from Prince George to the eleventh clause of the eighth section of article the first. By that, Congress had the power of declaring war. So soon, then, as war shall be declared, by the law of nations, alien enemies become prisoners of war; and being prisoners of war, and Congress having the sole power of declaring war, Congress had a right to say what should be done with the prisoners, whose destiny Congress alone could decide. Again, the power of declaring war was the *genus.* The prisoners, which shall have been made under that declaration, might be called a *species.* Now, as the *genus* has been granted, the *species*, which is subordinate to the *genus*, has been granted likewise; it being an axiom in reason, that the less is always included in the greater. To deny the truth of this position, would be as absurd as to say, when A. has transferred to B. a parcel of land, that the house or the wood upon the land are not granted likewise. Or, when a transfer in fee simple is made, that the life estate is not given also. But it had been said, that Virginia had passed a similar law, and, therefore, Congress must have the right. Doctrine like this should be a warning to the Virginia Legislature not to deviate from the principles of liberty, or the spirit of its Constitution, lest it should become a pretext to justify the worst of purposes in the hands of the general government. He observed, that he would not say whether Virginia had done right or wrong, in passing the law alluded to, because it was unimportant in the present discussion. He observed, the doctrine contended for by the gentleman from Prince George, namely, that Congress had a right to pass the law, because Virginia had done so, deserved the most serious attention and unreserved disapprobation of the committee. For, if it be true, the government of the United States would become an absolute consolidated government; and the sovereignty of the States annihilated; from which situation, said Mr. *Barbour*, good Lord deliver us! But fortunately for us, he said, the position existed only in the mind of its author. The state legislature had a right to regulate the mode of descents. Agreeably to the doctrine of the gentleman from Prince George, Congress would have a right to pass a similar law. Congress would possess the power of reviving the old feudal monarchical principle of primogeniture; and he had no doubt that it would be done, because it would be in unison with the other acts of the general government. Yet, no sober man, at this time, would say that Congress has a right to to say anything relative to the rules which shall be observed in the descent of estates. It must be clear and obvious to every man, not infatuated with political fallacy, that there is a line of demarcation drawn between the powers of the state and general governments; and to assert that Congress can do whatever the state can do, is as absurd as to say, the state can do whatever Congress can do; a position he did suppose the advocates of congressional omnipotence would be unwilling to admit. Mr. *Barbour* asked, in what cases Congress had a right to call in the aid of implication,—admitting, for argument's sake, that, on particular occasions, they might resort to that alternative? For allow the supporters of the principle the utmost latitude for which they contended, it could only be resorted to when the Constitution had given a power that cannot be consummated without implication. Wherever the Constitution was explicit, implication must be excluded. He said he would illustrate his idea by assimilating this case to the doctrine which would prevail in the instance of presumptive and positive evidence. Where positive evidence, from the nature of the case, cannot be procured, presumptive evidence is admissible, but where positive evidence can be procured, presumptive evidence is inadmissible. The Constitution, too, in the ninth section of the first article, is expressly in point. It is to this effect: " The migration or importation of such persons as any of the states, now existing, shall think proper to admit, shall not be prohibited by the Congress prior to the year 1808." This then, explicitly declaring that Congress shall not inhibit the migration of aliens, if the state should think proper to admit them, must unquestionably exclude the idea of implication, and, consequently, the deductions drawn from that source, (the source itself being corrupt), must be fallacious. But it might be answered by a quibbler, that the alien-law did not prevent the landing of aliens here. But where, Mr. *Barbour* asked, was the difference between their being prevented from landing, and the very moment they landed being sent off? He begged leave to state a similar instance, which would prove this was a distinction without a difference; namely, if a man should suffer another to come into his house, and the moment he stepped in, should kick him out, would this not be as bad, nay worse than if he had prevented him from coming in at all? The liberal mind looked down with pity and disdain upon such subterfuges; and hesitated not to declare that the alien-law did, beyond question, violate the Constitution of the United States in this part thereof. This part of the Constitution being violated should excite universal alarm; because to it was attached particular inviolability by the fifth article which declares that in this particular the Constitution should not be amended prior to the year 1808. Mr. *Barbour* said, the gentleman from Prince George having exhausted the doctrine of implication, had resorted to that of expediency, and contended that although Congress had neither express nor implied power to pass the law, yet it being expedient, it was correct. He said if that doctrine be true, the Constitution, instead of being the main pillar of American liberties, was but an institution calculated to ensnare. By the provisions in the Constitution, which the American people supposed as so many guarantees to their liberties, they had been trepanned into a fatal apathy, whilst they indulged themselves in what they supposed a well-grounded reflection, that the checks in the Federal Government were inviolate. They were now, as it were, awakened from the fatal repose into which they had been carried by misplaced confidence; and as the people of Caroline well expressed it, this boasted Constitution of their own choice, and the rights which it secured, are to *evaporate in the crucible of legislative expedience.* He said he felt himself unusually agitated at the bare mentioning of such monstrous doctrine. Go, said Mr. *Barbour*, and read the historic page: it would there be found that 'expediency has been' the invariable pretext of tyranny: it has been with that engine that the liberties of a free people were eternally assailed. If, said he, the time should ever come (which

God forbid) when that doctrine should prevail, we might date it as the era of the downfall of American freedom. From that moment, let the votaries of liberty be shrouded in sackcloth, and with ashes upon their heads, deplore the departure of their protecting genius. And, if from America the genius of liberty should ever take her flight, like the vital spirit, it would return no more to re-animate the body from which it had flown. The gentleman too, to support the necessity or expediency of the law, resorted to the situation of this country as it related to France. This he said was the favourite theme: this was a ground he had anticipated; it was not new; it had been successfully adopted by the higher orders of government. The conduct of France towards this country had been echoed by the friends of administration from every part of America, and under the momentary delusion created by the dispatches of the American envoys, it was hoped that principles of usurpation might be pushed. The jealous friends of the Constitution and the liberties of the people, if they had fortitude to oppose the impulse of the moment, and declare that the general government was bent upon the subversion of republican princi- ples, were branded with the opprobrious epithets of being disorganizers, French partizans, and enemies to all order; and the President of the United States, confident of success from the supposed wisdom of his operations, has condescended to become the head of the party, and has used language which, from its billingsgate style, as a man he treated with supercilious contempt; but as an American, he would feign shed an obliterating tear, which should efface it for ever. As coming from the chief magistrate of the Union, it would inflict an indelible stigma upon the American name.

Mr. *Barbour* said, he would not pretend to justify the conduct of France to this country. It was such as met with his disapprobation. It was an event, he said, that would be long deplored, and the consequences thereof were incalculable; for it had become the pretext of those measures, of which he complained. But, he said he felt indignant at the idea, that domestic usurpation was to be justified upon the ground of the maltreat- ment of a foreign nation; and that the President of the United States should dare brand the guardians of the rights of the people with the offensive name of a faction; and, to use his own language, that this faction should be ground into dust and ashes. Whom did Mr. Adams mean to call a faction? A majority of the yeomanry of America. For it was a fact not susceptible of any doubt, that a large majority of real native Americans were opposed to his election, and his political opinions; which Mr. *Barbour* said he would denounce as being hostile to republi- canism. For, although Mr. Adams was elected by a majority of three votes, yet it was well known that the majority was produced by artifice and coalition of federal officers, persons deeply concerned in funding and banking systems, refugees, foreigners, (whose whole life had been but a life of warfare against the principles of free government,) bankrupt speculators, and, to complete the group, all those who could profit by change and convulsion. Mr. *Barbour* said he would not be understood to pass an indiscriminate censure against all the friends of Mr. Adams; be- cause he believed there were as virtuous and as enlightened characters friends to his election, as were opposed to it. Neither should he have made any remarks upon the nature of parties, had not the gauntlet been thrown: from that circumstance, he thought himself justifiable in taking it up, and causing it to recoil upon the head of its author. He said he supposed he was one of that party, whose fate had been anticipated; but he felt an elevating pride when he was classed with the names of *Jefferson* and *Madison;* names which to the latest time, so long as worth and real patriotism should be respected, would cast a shade upon the author of such sentiments. Mr. *Barbour* said, for his part he could not perceive the connexion between the conduct of France, and the conduct of our own government; and although the friends of administration had been able by their dexterity in the arts of delusion, to gain a momentary advantage; although the passions of the people were excited for the instant, by which, reason, the noblest inhabitant of the human mind had been dethroned, yet they (for the people think generally right), at last, under the influence of truth, when generally disseminated, would regain their reason unclouded by passion, and at that moment they would spurn from them, with inexpressible detestation, the authors of their delusion. He hoped, then, that no more would be said of the conduct of France, in justification of alien and sedition laws. But the gentleman from Prince George had attempted to alarm the committee into his opinions, by delineating the fate of the island of St. Domingo. He told us that the fertile plains of that island had been deluged with seas of blood, and strewed with mangled carcases and mutilated limbs; and that if the alien-law had not passed, by which all dangerous aliens were excluded, the same fate might have befallen the Southern States. The committee were almost taught to tremble at the idea of their houses being wrapt in flames; their property a prey to rapine; their lives to massacre; their wives, their daughters, and their sisters falling victims to the brutal and indiscriminate lust of the negro; and in short everything to misery and ruin. But, Mr. *Barbour* said, he respected too highly the good sense and judgment of the committee, to suppose for a moment that attempts of that kind would succeed: he knew they would be deemed the meagre, unimportant chink of the moment, that would scarcely survive the instant that gave them birth. That gentleman's sensibility was aroused only by imaginary evils; it was not at leisure to deplore the situation to which the unfortunate aliens, by this law, will be reduced. Instead of this class of people moving in the elevated sphere of freemen, which they occupied before the adoption of this law, they will be sunk into the despicable grade of slaves, whose destiny was suspended upon the arbitrary nod of one man. Mr. *Barbour* said, the committee were told, too, of a conspiracy, which had for its object a schism in the empire, by which we were to lose the western country. Where was the evidence of that? Before he was willing to legislate, he said, he must have evidence of the fact, of a fact apparently so incredible, and so derogatory to the character of his country. He believed the western country, particularly *Kentucky*, was inhabited by as virtuous and as patriotic characters as the world ever produced: men who possessed that genuine and fervent regard for the cause of liberty that goes to elevate human nature a grade in the scale of animated nature, from which they look down with ineffable disdain upon such calumnious charges as those.

Conspiracies, plots, and wild chimeras were always resorted to in justification of tyrannic measures. The popular pretext of public good was the
auxiliary called in to palliate measures pregnant with public evil. And
too frequently under the mask of a zeal for the welfare of the commonwealth, were concealed designs which would eventuate in the destruction of the liberties of the people. But they had been told by the gentleman from Prince George, that the law was made for two characters,
to wit, Talleyrand and Volney; and that those characters had, in consequence of the same, sneaked off. Independent of the absurdity of the
principle, namely, the making a general law to suit a particular case, the
gentleman was most egregiously mistaken in point of fact; for Talleyrand
was minister for foreign affairs for France, and in France at the time the
law passed. How then the law could pass to operate on Talleyrand, was
to him astonishing. For the character of Talleyrand, Mr. *Barbour* referred
to the statement which had been made by the gentleman from Prince
William. It was sufficient to say, that so long as he was supposed to be
a martyr to the cause of monarchy, so long he was bosomed by Mr.
Hamilton and his party. As to Mr. Volney, he said, the cause of truth
and virtue required he should speak more at large. He had the pleasure
of seeing that meritorious character whilst in America, but he knew him
better by history than from personal acquaintance. He from maturity
had been influenced by the benevolent desire of ameliorating the condition
of mankind by illuminating the mind, and dispelling superstition. It was
for this sublime purpose we saw him traversing Asia, and sitting, in medi-
tative silence, amidst the ruins of Palmyra, drawing wisdom from experience, and developing the causes which contribute to the dissolution of the
elements of society, and the overthrow of empires, and his capacious
mind filled with materials of knowledge of the best kind. We saw him
returning thence to his native country, to publish to the world his acquire-
ments, as so many beacons by which those who sit at the head of affairs
might guide the vessel of state free from those shoals upon which they
have so frequently shipwrecked. Unfortunately for this philosopher,
for France, and for the world; Robespierre was at this time at the acme
of power. Robespierre, the most infamous of mankind, always the
enemy to rational and genuine liberty, wherever it was found, confined
this friend to the species in the instrument of despotism, a gloomy jail.
By the working of events, a revolution takes place in France, by which
this sanguinary tyrant met the fate which all usurpers merit. Liberty
reared its head, and emancipated one of its votaries, the enlightened
Volney. No sooner was he free from incarceration, than he left, once
more, his native country in pursuit of wisdom, and steered to Columbia,
once happy land. He explored this extensive continent, and returned
once more to Europe to analyze his knowledge, and to benefit mankind
by disseminating the useful information which he had acquired. This,
then, was the character against whom such unfounded calumnies have
been uttered. But unless some evidence was exhibited, he should take
the liberty to say that they were the offspring of the gentleman's own
imagination, begotten by the phantom of delusion.

The gentleman from Prince George observed, that the power of making a law like the one under discussion should belong to Congress; other-wise, Congress would be dependent upon sixteen states. This doctrine would perhaps do, if the gentleman was in Convention, and was ascer-taining the powers which should be exercised by the Congress; but, the committee were not inquiring what these powers should be, but what they were. This reasoning, he made no doubt, was urged in Convention; but, the representatives of the large states, which were but thinly inhabited, were opposed to the power being conceded to the General Government; and he had shown, in a former part of his argument, that the power of restraining the migration of such persons as the states should think pro-per to admit, was expressly inhibited by the Constitution. The same gentleman descanted at large upon the conduct of France towards the European powers. Subterfuges of this kind evidently demonstrated the distress to which the supporters of this law were reduced. For what had the conduct of France to do with an abstract inquiry upon the constitu-tionality of the law under discussion? Arguments of this kind were cal-culated only to inflame the passions at the expense of reason. But, since the Committee had been driven into this subject unavoidably, Mr. *Barbour* said he. would examine what had been the conduct of France to the European powers. Why, she had done to those powers what those powers intended to do to her. She had subdued them, and out of the rotten governments, under which those countries groaned, had established four republican governments. The gentleman said, that the French in-trigues succeeded only in republics, whilst in monarchies they had no effect. This was a calumny against republican government, *en masse*, and required serious attention and refutation.

Mr. *Barbour* asked, where was the republican government, the over-throw of which that gentleman so much deplored? Was there a republi-can government in Europe? No; there were some which had impudently assumed the name; but it was a fact not to be controverted, that in those countries the governments were completely aristocratic; than which, no government could be worse. But perhaps that gentleman had become a disciple of the new philosophy which had sprung up under the influence of the present administration, the head of which had declared, that aris-tocracy is the dictate of nature, is indispensable to the order of society, and the happiness of mankind, (alluding to Mr. Adams's answer to the address of the people of Harrison County.) If this principle were admit-ted as orthodox, the world should lament the ruin of aristocracies; but, if it were false, (which he believed the greater part of America would not deny,) so far from mourning their downfall, it should diffuse general joy. Mr. *Barbour* said he had now pursued the gentleman through all the argu-ments which he had given into on the score of expediency, and trusted he had demonstrated their fallacy. He would now call the attention of the committee to a contrast he was about to draw between the law and the Constitution. Let it then, for argument's sake, be admitted that Congress had a power to make a law relative to aliens; yet might not Congress violate that right? As for example, Congress have the power of laying a direct tax, yet Congress might violate that right in laying a tax without reference to the inhabitants of the state upon which the tax was to be laid.

The alien-law, Mr. *Barbour* said, violated the sixth amendment of the Constitution, (the substance of, which was, " that no warrant shall issue, but upon probable cause, and that, too, supported by oath or affirmation,") in this, that the President, without probable cause, without an oath, and barely upon suspicion, had a right to apprehend the alien, against whom some mercenary informer may have lodged a complaint. It likewise violated the seventh amendment, in this; that by the alien-law the President was invested with the power of consigning to banishment, without the formality of trial, this unfortunate class of people, of which he supposed we had myriads amongst us, when by that amendment it is declared, " that no person shall be held to answer for a capital or otherwise infamous crime, unless on a presentment, or indictment of a grand jury."

By the eighth amendment it is declared, too, that in all criminal prosecutions the accused shall enjoy a speedy and public trial by an impartial jury of his vicinage, and be informed of the nature and cause of the accusation; be confronted with the witnesses against him; have compulsory process for obtaining witnesses in, his favour; and have the assistance of counsel for his defence. It was only necessary to read the alien-law, to show the palpable violations of the Constitution. ·No oath or affirmation was requisite; no presentment or indictment by a grand jury necessary; no trial by jury; his accusation, conviction and punishment, were all to be announced by the Presidential officer in one breath. It was true, there might be a kind of mock trial before a tribunal filled with characters selected by the President: a tribunal not under the solemnity of oath, not under the least responsibility to public opinion, but from the nature of their institution, are taught to kiss the hand from whom they receive their authority: a tribunal unknown to our Constitution; and in fact, as far as it went, was an epitome of the star chamber and high commission courts. But, Mr. *Barbour* said, he had been told that the aliens were not parties to the compact, and therefore were not entitled to the benefit of the compact. He contended that by the law of nations, but what weighed still more strongly upon his mind, upon principles of reason and humanity, they were entitled to the benefit of the rights secured under the Constitution. The Law of Nations, Vattel, page 171, section 135, declares that the sovereign authority of a state has no right to prevent the migration of persons into its country without a good reason. As for example, China has a right to refuse the admission of aliens, because its country is completely populated, and because the admission of aliens would operate an insuperable injury to its citizens. But what good reason could America assign for refusing admittance to strangers, with a country extensive, fertile beyond, exception, and uninhabited. Had not the persecuted alien, then, a claim upon us not to be frittered away by the ingenuity of sophistry? Mr. *Barbour* said, having shown that strangers had a claim upon us, and that, by the laws of nations, they have a right to come amongst us, he would proceed to prove that when they were in this country, they were entitled to the benefit of the law. For this purpose, he would refer to Vattel's Law of Nations, page 160–1. It is there said, that the law of the land is not only applicable to the particular subjects, or citizens of the sovereign authority, but applies to all orders of people of every description. It appeared to him a doctrine of the most cruel kind, and which he trusted he should never again hear re-echoed from these walls, to attempt to narrow the operation of an instrument for the purposes of despotism. A benign philosophy would dictate, that the Constitution should receive a liberal construction, when the welfare of thousands required it. But Mr. *Barbour* said, that aliens were parties to the compact, so far at least as relates to security against oppression. For, by coming to this country, they tacitly agree to be bound by the Constitution and laws thereof. If an alien committed an offence, how in ordinary cases was he tried? As citizens. How was he punished? As citizens. Surely, then, as he was to be punished by the laws, he should be entitled to their protection. And Vattel further mentions, that an injury done a stranger should be punished by the sovereign authority, in as exemplary a manner as if done to a citizen.

But it had been said, that the sending off of aliens was no punishment: it was a kind of preventive justice. Language like this, was the offspring of a cold heart and muddy understanding. What! Was it no punishment to banish a fellow-man from a country where he has invested his all? Where he has formed the strongest imaginable ties? And in which he expected to find an asylum from the fangs of despotism? And perhaps to consign him back to the country, from the persecuting tyranny of which he might have fled? Let those who advocate this doctrine, bring the case home to themselves, and inquire if they would not conceive it a punishment to be banished from a country which contained their all. Mr. *Barbour* observed, that the alien-law had violated the Constitution in a very obvious manner, by destroying the main pillar upon which all free governments stand, namely, a separation in the three great elements of government. By it, the President was invested with legislative, executive, and judicial powers, which Montesquieu defines to be the essence of despotism. He first gave his assent to the law as President. He then legislated in establishing a rule by which the alien is to be tried, and every rule was a law. The law itself has established no rule; has pointed out nothing which the alien shall avoid; nor yet prescribed anything which he shall do. The President, in the gloomy, dark and inaccessible recesses of his mind, was then to prescribe the rule, and make it known only when he intended to punish under the rule ; there, then, he legislated. He then was to judge whether the alien had violated his own rule, and if he should conceive or suspect that he had, he was then to carry his own sentence into effect. If he had been called on to delineate a picture of frightful despotism, Mr. *Barbour* said, he should think he had discharged the task by copying the alien-law. The President of the United States was invested with the pleasing and humane power of pardoning. What kind of a figure would the President exhibit, when he had accused and condemned the poor unfortunate alien, to be applied to for a pardon? Was it ever yet known in a country which had participated freedom, and had progressed in jurisprudence, that the same man or set of men had the power of condemning and pardoning at the same time? The enlightened Montesquieu has observed that it would create a confusion of ideas, and the world would be at a loss to know whether the culprit had been acquitted, or condemned and pardoned. In consequence of the measures which had been pursued, the executive branch of the government had acquired an undue preponderance of power, which had derogated from the other branches; the result of which was, that instead of their moving in the dignified sphere of planets, they had dwindled into the pitiful character of satellites, which played around the executive with servile complaisance. And the liberties of the American people, which revolve around the Constitution as the centre of their system, should that be destroyed, would be precipitated into ruin likewise. America was destined, he said, to increase the already extended catalogue of despotic nations, and we should be compelled to admit the melancholy truth, that man is not susceptible of self-government, but is doomed to be governed (he trembled whilst he related it) by arbitrary, accursed arbitrary sway. But notwithstanding all this, we were told, Hail Columbia, happy land! That the people of America were the happiest in the world! What then, were the people to wait till the pressure of the evil principle was felt? No. As an elegant author expressed it, they augur misgovernment at a distance, and snuff the approach of tyranny in every tainted breeze. The political horizon of America, which some years ago shone with undiminished lustre, and which attracted the admiration of all the world, was now darkened with clouds of domestic usurpation, which waited but for some incentive, to burst in dreadful violence upon our heads. What an august melancholy scene was here! That at the conclusion of the eighteenth century, a time which twenty years ago, by the sanguine admirers of the rights of mankind, would have been anticipated as the birthday of a general jubilee of emancipation, when distant nations would have heard and have quickened into public life by the sound, the Virginia Legislature was brought to decide whether, even in America itself, the birthplace and cradle of liberty, liberty shall be preserved, or whether, bound hand and foot as it was, it shall be offered up as a sacrifice upon the altar of vice and ambition. Mr. *Barbour* then expressed himself in the following strong and animated manner: Legislators of Virginia! The voice of the people speaks to you; the eyes of the friends of liberty throughout the continent, are upon you; and the friends of mankind throughout the world are waiting in anxious solicitude the result of your deliberation. The road to immortal honour is open before you; the temple of fame is within your reach, and the welfare of your country calls eminently upon you. By the adoption of the resolutions you raise a rampart against the inroads of usurpation, and your names will be wafted down on the stream of time, crowned with laurels, and as they pass, will be hailed by a grateful posterity with plausive acclamations. But if you reject, you give additional weight to the already overgrown power of the general government, by which the liberties of the people will be subverted; and in some after time, when our country shall consider us, the people pointing you out shall say, there go the authors of our misfortunes.

He then concluded by thanking the committee for the attention they had given him.

On motion, the committee then rose, the chairman reported progress, asked and obtained leave for the committee to sit again.

IN THE HOUSE OF DELEGATES,

Tuesday, December 18, 1798.

The House resolved itself into a committee of the whole House, on the state of the commonwealth, Mr. *Breckenridge* in the chair, when Mr. *John Taylor's* resolutions being still still under consideration,

Mr. MAGILL said, that he arose with sensations never before experienced by him; that he conceived the peace of the United States to be involved in the decision which the committee were about to make; for the question appeared to him to be whether the states should remain united under the federal Constitution, or that instrument which they were bound to support, be declared of no force or effect; that in delivering his sentiments to the committee, he would address himself to the reason of the members, and avoid an appeal to their passions; for if the opinion he advocated could not be supported upon this ground, he would not resort to any other. That he had attended to the arguments of the gentleman from Orange, and those of the gentlemen who preceded him on the same side: with their eloquence he was pleased, and their talents he admired, but the judgment he had formed upon the laws, after the most serious reflection, so far from being shaken, had received additional force by the manner in which the debate had been conducted. When gentlemen of first-rate talents amuse the fancy with eloquent harangues, instead of attempting to inform the understanding, to him it was evident that they thought their positions untenable. He said we are to decide upon the constitutionality of the "alien and sedition laws," as they are generally called, and in so doing are we not erecting ourselves into a court of justice, particularly so as the resolutions declare those laws null and void; for where is the department of the government, except the judiciary, that can exercise this power? He said that the present Assembly was chosen by the people for the ordinary purposes of legislation, and he begged to know the source from whence their judicial powers, even over a law passed by themselves, in a case where their jurisdiction was complete, could be derived. If, said he, it be admitted that we cannot judicially act upon a law passed by this or any other Assembly of this commonwealth, and that our courts alone can do so, where is that law, point out that feature in the federal Constitution, that gives to this body the power now about to be exercised? He said that the public papers had teemed with invectives against Congress for passing these laws. Could gentlemen say this was a criterion to judge them by? He said, that in all the publications he had seen, and the arguments he had heard used, the authors had taken for granted what remained to be proved. Admit the premises, and the conclusion may fairly be drawn. The gentleman from Orange, Mr. *Magill* said, had observed that the President of the United States was a friend to monarchy, or in favour of a monarchical government. Admitting this, for argument's sake, to be correct, what relation, said he, can it have to the subject now under consideration? Will it enlighten the mind of a man when he is called upon to form an opinion upon an important point, to have his judgment drawn from that object, by suggesting one foreign and entirely unconnected with it? He said, that for his own part, Mr. Adams possessed his highest confidence; that he viewed him as the tried and true friend of his country; that the happiness of his fellow-citizens was his first object; that he looked up to the virtues and talents of Mr. Adams with veneration, and would only add, that his administration had in his opinion been pure and uncorrupt. These sentiments, though unpopular here, I ever have and will avow, said Mr. *Magill* so long as the measures heretofore pursued, be continued. He then contended, that the statement of the gentleman from Prince George, respecting the rights of aliens, was correct, and the contrary one of the gentleman from Orange not so, and gave his reasons for this opinion. He observed, that he meant to be concise in his replies to the arguments against the alien-law, as the gentleman from Prince George had opened that part of the debate, and would, in concluding it, notice all such as he should omit. He said that he adopted this mode, supposing that the opening of the sedition act, which had been assigned to him, would take up as much time as the House could on that day allow him. He then defined as necessary to a perfect knowledge of the subject, the powers of the general and state governments. He observed, that the only true and natural foundations of society are the wants of individuals. He said this rule applied to the states, considered as such, at the time this Constitution of the United States was formed. The insufficiency of the old confederation, said he, evinced their wants, and to prevent again experiencing these wants, this Constitution was formed. He observed, that to him the Constitution of the United States should be thus explained, as giving to the Federal government a control over the national affairs; to the state governments, the care of state or local concerns. Upon this definition, and the Constitution taken together, he proceeded to inquire if the alien-law had violated the Constitution in any respect; and he agreed with the gentleman from Prince George in his statement respecting aliens, that Vattel's doctrine was solid, and to be relied upon. He insisted, that the safety of a nation could not be secured, without such a power as this law gave being deposited somewhere. He agreed with the gentleman from Spottsylvania, that the dispute with France, if it could be avoided, ought not to be introduced; but how, said he, can this be done? The unjust, and infamous conduct of France, should make our government careful how its citizens introduce themselves amongst us, with their diplomatic skill; and to guard against attempts of that nation and its citizens, this law perhaps was passed. He then adverted to Volney and Talleyrand, of whom the gentleman from Prince George had spoken, and said, that that gentleman had not been correctly understood by the gentleman from Prince William, and others, when they alluded to his remarks upon Talleyrand and Volney. The gentleman from Spottsylvania had mentioned the independence of the state governments at the time of the adoption of the Constitution. He admitted that to be true, but said the argument was of no weight, unless it could be proved that they were independent now, as their situation at that period was the subject. He then made some remarks in answer to the gentleman from Brunswick, upon the first clause of the ninth section of the Constitution, restraining Congress from prohibiting migration; and he

said, the gentleman from Caroline had not relied upon that clause, but the
gentleman from Orange had. He said, that he thought the clause last
mentioned, related only to slaves, and his reason for thinking so, was
founded upon the language used in the latter part of the clause, and the
whole Constitution taken together. He then quoted the opinion of Mr.
George Nicholas, delivered at the time of the adoption of the Constitution,
in effect the same as his own. He here read the opinion delivered by Mr.
George Mason, in the debates of the convention in Virginia, in regard to
the clause referred to, respecting migration and importation extending to
slaves only. He took this to be the opinion of Mr. *Mason*, inasmuch as
his observations, as well as those of others, were confined to that description of persons alone. He then mentioned the alien-law of Virginia, not,
he said, with a wish that if it were erroneous, it should be a precedent,
but to show what was the opinion of the legislature of this state at that
time. They had been told, that the Legislature of Virginia had a right to
pass such a law, and that Congress had not. He contended on the contrary, from the Constitution, that the state had a power to pass such a law,
only until Congress should interfere, by passing one upon the subject. He
assimilated this to the case of citizenship, upon which laws had been passed
by the state, that were set aside when Congress passed a general law, by
the force of that law. He then said, that the clauses in the Constitution
of the United States, and in the bill of rights of Virginia, securing the trial
by jury, were couched in general terms, and neither were ever supposed to
be infringed until the passage of the alien-law by Congress. The people
of this state had passed such a law for the same reason, as had induced
Congress to pass one, to wit, to insure domestic tranquillity. Let me ask,
said he, if here we ought not to pause, and not hastily condemn a former
legislature of our own state. He then proceeded to show, that by the
suspension of the writ of *habeas corpus*, (which the Constitution warranted
in a particular case,) the trial by jury was taken away even from a
citizen. Would not then, he said, the true meaning and spirit of the same
instrument allow it to be taken away from an alien, a person entitled to
no absolute rights, and who was no party to the compact, in a similar case.
He then stated at large, the proceedings which took place in the case of
the suspension of the writ of *habeas corpus;* and observed, that a person
then charged, must remain in prison without a hearing, until the emergency
had ceased. That case then, he said, was in principle the same as the
alien-law. The cause for the suspension of the writ of *habeas corpus*
was temporary, and when the cause had no longer an existence, the effect
would also cease. He then contended, that when the alien-law had passed,
there was good cause to apprehend danger from without, and from aliens
within our territory: to guard against their attempts was proper. He
said, the gentleman from James City had urged the necessity of aliens
being informed of the rule of conduct which should govern them upon
their arrival in America. In reply to this, he, Mr. *Magill*, would observe,
that aliens must know that rule from the law of nations, which is a part
of the law of every country, and is simply this, "interfere not in the
governmental affairs of a foreign country, and confine your attention to
your individual concerns whilst in that country." He thought this power

given by the law, of removing aliens, properly vested in the President. He stated his responsibility, and the eminent services rendered by the present President, together with his known attachment to his country, as a pledge that he would not act cruelly or unjustly.

The gentleman from Caroline had argued upon the condition upon which the Constitution was adopted in Virginia, and upon that point he had understood him to say, that the condition being broken, we were no longer bound by the ratification. This, Mr. *Magill* said, was an alarming doctrine. He then recapitulated his several arguments, in order, he said, to impress upon them what he attempted to prove, and said, that he would then consider the sedition-law : and here he requested the attention of the committee, this law being in its nature particularly important, citizens being affected by it. The freedom of the press, correctly understood, and as it was considered by the framers of the Constitution, he contended was not abridged by the law. He then read the sedition-act, and said the passage of this law was opposed in Congress by those gentlemen who had opposed the defensive measures adopted against a foreign nation, and in Virginia it was reprobated on the ground of its being unwarranted by the Constitution. He asked, is there by this law an addition to our penal code, and said, that in his judgment no new offence was created by it, everything it forbids being before an offence at. common law. He said, here it will be proper to inquire, whether the doctrines of the common law apply, or form the basis of our laws : that they do so, he took to be clear and evident ; such was the opinion entertained in the Virginia Convention. He said, that what the doctrines of the common law were prior to, and at the establishment of the Constitution of the United States, must then be the rule, and the term liberty of the press, as then understood, an important consideration. He then read the history of the liberty of the press, as laid down by Blackstone, in the fourth volume of his Commentaries, and said, this then is the history of the term freedom of the press. It was an exemption from all power over publications, unless previously approved by licensers. To show that it did not extend to an exemption from legal punishment, according to the principles of the common law, he said, let us again return to the same author : " Libels are malicious defamations of any person, and especially a magistrate, made public, by either printing, writing, signs or pictures, in order to provoke him to wrath." He proceeded to read Blackstone's definition, with the mode of proceeding against persons charged with libellous publications. The liberty of the press, as he had stated it, he said was essential to a free state, and drew the distinction between the liberty and licentiousness of the press. He said, with this definition of the freedom of the press, as it was before them, with Blackstone's rational observations in their view, can we for a moment suppose that Congress, when they concurred in recommending the third article of the amendments, and the assemblies of the different states, when they ratified and approved that article, intended to procure an exemption for writings false, scandalous, and malicious, from punishment, according to the principles of the common law. Doth not the judicial power of the United States expressly extend to controversies, to which the United States shall be a party? Can there be a case, in which the United States shall be called a party, if not to those which are offences against the United States, their people and government? Was it intended that the government should be destitute of the means of defending itself or its members? Have not Congress power, " to make all laws necessary and proper for carrying into execution the powers vested by the Constitution in any department of the government of the United States?" He said, let us now see what construction hath been put upon the twelfth clause of the bill of rights in Virginia, by the Assembly of that state, for a law by that body is an express declaration of the opinion it entertains. The twelfth clause is, " That the freedom of the press is one of the great bulwarks of liberty, and can never be restrained but by despotic governments." The Constitution of the United States says, in the third article of the amendments, " Congress shall make no law respecting an establishment of religion or prohibiting the free exercise thereof, or abridging the freedom of speech, or of the press, &c." In substance the language is the same. Amongst the laws passed in 1792, is one to be seen in page 219 of the Revised Code, entitled, " An act against divulgers of false news;" which law enacts, " That whereas," &c. He then read the law. The legislature was then of opinion, that divulgers of false news, whether printers or others, were not protected by this clause in the bill of rights. Are we, he asked, wiser than a former Assembly? This law in our code, upon being compared with the law of Congress, will be found much more severe than the latter. By the law of Congress, the accused may give in evidence in his defence, the truth of the matter contained in the publication charged against him, &c. But, said he, is it known to the people that in a prosecution for a libel in Virginia, under the state laws, you can neither plead nor give in evidence the truth of the matter contained in the libel. He said, in a civil action, the truth could be pleaded in bar of the suit, and upon proving the plea, a verdict would be found for the defendant. He here pointed out the mode of proceeding by indictment against a person accused and tried under the state law for a libel ; and said here is a material distinction between the two laws. He contended, that the freedom of the press was not abridged, no new offence being created. He asked, how can the officers of government carry the laws of the union into effect, without possessing the confidence of the people? He said, what is this law designed to prevent, is it the circulation of false and malicious slanders? And if so, can any man wish to exercise such a right, even admitting him to possess it, the bare use of which would cover him with infamy? He said a law passed by us is right, but a similar law passed by Congress, having equal power upon the subject-matter, is wrong. He repeated his several arguments in order, and said that the committee had been so indulgent, that he would now pass on to the resolutions offered : And here, he said, it appeared to him that the wisdom of man could not devise a more certain mode of preventing a repeal of the laws complained of, than that which the resolutions pointed out. Are gentlemen serious, he said, in wishing a repeal? He said, the moment that the paper under consideration was adopted, he should consider as giving birth to a serious and alarming contest. He said, are we sincere in our professions of friendship to the government of the United States? If so, why snatch with avidity an opportunity of resorting to a measure violent in its nature, before we have made an attempt, moderate and temperate. Would this conduct, he said, be pursued by an individual wishing to be reconciled to his friend? He said the resolutions are certainly incorrect. The states alone are parties! What, are the people entirely excluded? He contended, that there is not a state in the Union that hath so unequal a representation in the state legislature as Virginia. Are the people of Virginia represented according to numbers? No! It is the name of a county. Two hundred freeholders have the same voice in this Assembly, as one thousand. This statement, he said, the committee knew was accurate, and the two counties could be named. He then referred to the third amendment to the Constitution of the United States, which secures the right of petitioning for a redress of grievances. The states, he said, could never be injured whilst that power existed; and could he be convinced that the people were aggrieved, he would join in a constitutional, moderate way to obtain a redress. He said, the Kentucky resolutions, as did ours, declared these laws null and void. If they are so, let the proper courts say so. He then proceeded to show that the states could not form a coalition; for by the Constitution they are prohibited from entering into any confederacy, or making any agreement with each other. In substance, he said, this was forming a confederacy. He then read an extract from the Federalist, in the writing of which the gentleman from Spottsylvania had said Mr. *Madison* was concerned.

He said he thought the laws constitutional, and then enumerated the consequences of adopting the resolutions before the committee. He enlarged upon this subject, and again entreated the committee to pause and seriously to reflect upon the awful question before them, for such he really considered it.

Mr. Foushee arose next, and asked if it would be necessary for him to tell the committee that the subject was *important*, after what the gentleman last up had said: " that *peace* or *war* was to be the consequence." And being so important, he (Mr. *Foushee*) thought that they should most seriously consider the matter previous to a decision on the resolutions before the committee. He then made some remarks upon the quotations from the law of nations, used by Mr. *George K. Taylor* and Mr. *Magill*, to show that sovereignty must reside in every independent nation, and the power consequently attached to sovereignty. This doctrine he did not deny, but said, if the states individually were sovereign before and at the time of the adoption of the Constitution, which he contended they then were, and still are, he asked could any one lay his finger on that part of the Constitution of the United States which had taken away their sovereignty in those cases embraced by the alien and sedition laws? That the Constitution was a limited compact, and contained no powers but those granted. But the common law and implication had been resorted to by gentlemen, in support of a contrary doctrine. By admitting the common law and this construction to have force, he said, Congress might, under these, and the terms *general welfare*, pass any act whatever; thereby setting the Constitution at naught, and making it a dead letter; and nothing would be reserved to the states, or to the people. He was alarmed, he said, at the method which the gentleman from Prince George had adopted, in selecting the alien from the sedition law, in his arguments, and confining himself to the former. In doing so, he (Mr. *Foushee*) feared, he discovered an intention, under the guise of attacking aliens only, who were certainly the most unpopular inhabitants amongst us, to lay a foundation for inflicting similar injuries, in future, on such of our citizens, as might give offence, and that he thought the selection of this law might keep the danger he apprehended out of general view. Mr. *Foushee* made several observations in answer to Mr. *G. K. Taylor*, respecting the rights of aliens; and observed, that, by the alien law, they were deprived unconstitutionally of liberty, which he (Mr. *Foushee*) contended was one of their rights, as well as life and property, to which it was acknowledged they were entitled; for the loss of their liberty, however, he said, the gentleman from Prince George expressed no pity nor offered any excuse, except one, which might be the plea of any tyrant. Mr. *Foushee* then said, he thought and feared, that the alien law was but a step to something else, to wit, a *precedent* under which citizens might in future be attacked. Danger too, he said, had been assigned as the cause of passing those laws. That cause, he observed, might be raised up at any time by an artful President, who could perhaps previously get such a treaty made as to suit his purpose; and, under the idea of danger, to produce a state of preparation, by which his power might be increased, and which might become injurious by the extension of influence arising from patronage; for instance, &c. What direful acts and effects of usurpation, said he, may not ensue under the pretence alone of danger? The unconstitutionality of these laws, he observed, had been so fully proved, that it would be unnecessary then for him to say anything further on that head; and that, if there was an act at which the human mind could revolt, it would be, in his judgment, the denial of such unconstitutionality. He then said, that if the doctrine of some gentlemen on the floor of Congress, and that contended for by a certain modest pamphleteer, as lately published, and which some days past had been so copiously detailed by the member from Prince George, and which he (Mr. *Foushee*) had since seen, could be established, he admitted the resolutions must be wrong; but, as he was well satisfied such doctrine could not be supported, he thought the resolutions ought to receive the sanction of the committee. He mentioned the subject of implication again, and dwelt on its direful consequences, many of which he particularly enumerated. He then proceeded to answer quotations made by gentlemen from certain laws of Virginia, particularly the alien-bill, endeavouring, as he supposed, to deduce from thence, power to the general government over aliens. He urged, that the latter particularly was a proof that the state, and state only, had a right to pass such a law; and consequently, that Congress had not the right.

But, he said, the gentleman from Prince George had urged, that if Congress had not the power of passing such a law, Virginia might admit under the description of aliens, an army of soldiers, for instance, Bonaparte and his whole army (if they could get out of Egypt). Mr. *Foushee* asked, what idea must that gentlemen have of the virtue and patriotism of his fellow-citizens, in urging such an argument? He said, it might justly be called, in the gentleman's own words, a *monstrous idea.* He then asked, where would those doctrines contended for by gentlemen in opposition to the resolutions, leave us? Would it not be in a mass of *consolidation?* Could not freemen, he said, assert their rights, without being charged with an intention or wish of dissolving the government of the United States? He then stated the observations of several gentlemen, in regard to the consequences of opposition, as they termed it. That he differed, however, from them in regard to the consequences they apprehended, to wit, an invitation of foreign invasion, &c.; and he contended strongly for the right of free communication and consultation. He observed, that the gentleman from Prince George had said, that these acts of Congress having been passed by a majority of that body, the members of which had taken an oath to support the Constitution of the United States, could we suppose they were unmindful of it? The members of this Assembly, Mr. *Foushee* said, had taken the same oath, in addition to other obligations. That they must therefore pursue their duty, in discharge of their solemn obligations to this state and the United States, without regard to the conduct of other people, although they may have acted also under oath. He then recapitulated various arguments of those who approved the resolutions, and observed, it had been said by the member from Prince George, that this law (meaning the alien-law), although passed, would affect very few comparatively, indeed it would be almost as one man only. In this light, he (Mr. *Foushee*) considered it so much the more to be dreaded, as an exertion for its repeal might not be sufficiently made, and thus a *precedent* be established. Small beginnings, he said, often produced great ends, and required, therefore, to be more narrowly watched. He then made a comparison between the structure of the *Constitution* and the *universe.* The latter he represented to be a system composed of atoms. If, said he, it were once to be ascertained that we had a power to destroy or annihilate one atom, it would soon be seen that we had a power to destroy more atoms; and thereby we should establish a principle, which might go to the total destruction of the universe. The same consequences as to the right of power over the Constitution, he said, might ensue, for the power over each was limited. Danger too, he said, had been repeatedly assigned as a cause for those laws. He again asked, what would be the consequence of subscribing implicitly to that doctrine? The principles of such a measure, he repeated, would be to establish in a designing man, or set of men, at the head of the government, *all power,* which might be continued, even when the danger spoken of no longer existed. Precedent, he again said, would be thus founded and resorted to; and be urged upon us on every occasion, by saying, *the same thing has been done before.* But if danger alone, added he, had been the cause of passing those laws, and they could be justified, even on that score, that danger, he said, was now nearly over, or greatly lessened. He then referred to historical facts to prove the force of his remarks. These, he said, were worthy of being attended to. He again declared himself in favour of the resolutions, especially the first. After which he observed, that he had confined his observations generally to the alien-law, as he

had understood the gentleman from Prince George to say, early in the debate, that the arguments on the sedition-law would not be gone into, until
those on the alien-law had been urged and decided on. However, he said,
he considered the sedition-law of much the greater consequence of the
two, as the evils were by that law, in his judgment, much aggravated;
and that all the arguments urged against the alien-law applied with accu-
mulated force against the sedition-law; and that he could as yet only
account for the selection of the alien-law in argument, as being the most
distant from, and least to be felt by, the citizens at large. He then proceeded to state the purport of the sedition-law, the construction which had
been given to it, and the consequences resulting from its operation. And
although he admitted, that speaking might not be expressly enumerated,
yet he said the free communication of opinion was prevented, and particularly in the mode of writing, printing, &c. He then stated the beneficial
effects resulting from a free communication of sentiment, and the greater
benefits still, flowing particularly from the freedom of the press; by means
of which, knowledge was most extensively diffused. He made several
observations in favour of the manly language of the resolutions, particularly the first, as holding out our express determination to resist usurpation by every constitutional mode, as well as invasion; and which he
thought would be the most effectual means of curing the present evil, as
well as preventing similar attempts in future. He then made a short re-
capitulation of the unconstitutionality and inexpediency of those laws, and
observed, that injustice and deception were particularly evident, in his
judgment, on the face of the sedition-law, to wit: four specified acts,
" writing, printing, uttering, and publishing," independent of other prohibitions, were made punishable. That it had been urged, those various
acts might be justified, if they contained the truth. He urged in reply,
that the justificatory clause only enumerated two items, " writing and
publishing." That printing and uttering were not in that clause; and
therefore, justification could not be pleaded in excuse for a prosecution
founded on either of these.

Mr. BROORE arose next, and said that he never could consent to sanction
the passage of resolutions having so alarming and dangerous a tendency
as those which had been presented to them by the gentleman from Caroline; and before he gave his vote upon the subject, he would beg leave to
state to the committee, without adverting to the particular merits of the
laws that were the subject of those resolutions, the reasons that would
govern him in his vote upon that occasion.

Resolutions such as these, said Mr. *Brooke*, declaring laws which had
been made by the government of the United States to be unconstitutional,
null, and void, were in his opinion, in the highest extreme dangerous and
improper, inasmuch as they had not only a tendency to inflame the public
mind; they had not only a tendency to lessen that confidence that ought
to subsist between the representatives of the people in the general government and their constituents, but they had a tendency to sap the very foundation of the government, by producing resistance to its laws, and were in
the eyes of all foreign nations evidence, fatal evidence, of internal discord

in this country, and of imbecility in our government to protect itself against domestic violence and usurpation. For these reasons, he said, he was opposed to these resolutions, and did not hesitate to declare himself equally opposed to any modification whatsoever of such resolutions, that might be intended as an expression of the. general sentiment upon this subject, because he conceived it to be an improper mode by which to express the wishes of the people of this state upon the subject. By what mode then, said he, were this Assembly to understand and to express the will of the people of Virginia upon the laws that had been called in question? By an act of the Virginia Legislature, declaring these laws to be unconstitutional, null, and void? No! But by the laws of the general government, to whom the power properly belonged of making these laws; and by which their will had been already expressed. The government of the United States, he said, was one organ of the will of the people; the Legislature of Virginia was another organ of the public will. Those two organs, then, of the public will were at variance. One of these organs made laws for the government of the United States: another of these organs, the inferior one, declared these laws to be unconstitutional, null, and void; and the question then was, which of these organs were they to obey? The government of the United States, he said, most indubitably; because in the government of the United States, the representation of the people of this state is more pure and more equal than it is or could possibly be in the state government, under the existing state Constitution. In the general government, said he, every thirty thousand persons are represented; but in the state government, from the great inequality in the representation, under the existing state Constitution, it was utterly impossible, under existing circumstances, by this mode to express the sentiments and wishes of the people of Virginia upon the laws that had been called in question. In some counties in the state, said he, fifteen hundred or two thousand freeholders constitute the number of electors, who are entitled to but two representatives: in other smaller counties, one hundred and fifty or two hundred freeholders constitute the number of electors, who are entitled to the same number of representatives: so that, from this apparent inequality in the representation, circumstanced as he was, and a number of other gentlemen in the House, how could they form any sort of estimate of the general will of the people upon the subject of the laws in question. In the county of Prince William, he knew not what the people thought of the laws. The representation from Loudoun, Berkeley, Frederic, and many other large counties, were in the same situation. To what standard then were they to resort in order to ascertain the general will upon the subject? To the laws themselves, he said, he would again reply, which have been passed by the general government, where we are equally represented, and to whom the authority properly belongs by the Constitution. Since the representatives of the people in the general government, then, had made these laws, as a good citizen he would obey; as a good citizen he valued the Constitution of the United States, which he had sworn to support, and which he conceived to be invaded by the resolutions before them; and when the people of that part of the country which he had the honour to represent, became so exceedingly degenerate, so lost to all regard for the great advantages and benefits resulting from a connexion between the states under the federal Constitution, as to give.him instructions to vote for the adoption of resolutions having so alarming and dangerous a tendency as those which had been offered by the gentleman from Caroline, he should go in mourning for them; he should bid adieu to legislation, and seek an asylum in some other region of the globe, among a race of men who had more respect for peace and order, and who set a higher value upon the blessings of good government. But sensible as he was that his constituents would have discernment and patriotism enough to think with him that the resolutions offered for our adoption by the worthy member from Caroline, teem with principles hostile to the very existence of the general government; that they would think with him that any attempt in the state legislature to control the operations of the general government by the adoption of resolutions inviting the sister states to a cooperation in resisting its laws, was equally dangerous and improper as it is unnecessary, he should give a negative to these resolutions, and before he sat down, beg leave to offer a resolution as a substitute for those which had been presented by the member from Caroline. He offered it, he said, at this stage of the business, because the tocsin of rebellion had been that day sounded in the House by the resolutions accompanying the Governor's letter from the state of Kentucky. The sooner then, he said, our determination not to co-operate in resisting the laws of the general government should be announced to that state, the sooner our determination to support the American government should be announced to the nations of the earth, the better. And for this purpose he would offer the resolution which he had before referred to. He then read his resolution, in the following words: " *Resolved*, That as it is established by the Constitution of the United States, that the people thereof have a right to assemble peaceably, and to petition the government for a redress of grievances, it therefore appears properly to belong to the people.themselves to petition when they consider their rights to be invaded by any acts of the general government; and it should of right be left to them if they conceive the laws lately passed by the Congress of the United States, commonly called the ' alien and sedition bills,' to be unconstitutional, or an invasion of their rights, to petition for a repeal of the said laws." After reading the said resolution, Mr. *Brooke* handed it in to the clerk's table, where the same being again read, was laid upon the table.

.,On motion of Mr. *Johnson*, the committee then rose, the chairman reported progress, asked, and had leave for the committee to sit again.

IN THE HOUSE OF DELEGATES,

Wednesday, December 19, 1798.

The House resolved itself into a committee of the whole House, on the state of the commonwealth, Mr. *Breckenridge* in the chair, when Mr. *John Taylor's* resolutions being still under consideration,

Mr. Pope arose and said, that he was not accustomed to make apologies; but that he looked upon it as necessary, after what he had said
before on the subject. He could assure the committee, that what he had
said at first, was not intended as a speech; and he had no doubt but that
it was so understood by others. The observations were of a ludicrous
turn, and intended only as an answer, of that kind, to the gentleman from
Prince George's introducing the French into the debate. This he thought
not proper; and the object of his former remarks therefore, was to treat
it in a ludicrous manner. But on the present occasion, he said, he considered himself as called upon by his colleague. He would speak, therefore, while the thing was fresh. And in order that he might not be mistaken in it, he had noted the substance. He meant not, he said, to go
into the subject before them. There had been enough, he thought, in the
harvest-field already. He himself would only glean a little. His colleague had said, that he was not instructed: but that if his constituents were
so degenerate, or *debased*, he (Mr. *Pope*) was not positive which of these
terms he had used, but it was no matter which, it was the same thing, as
to instruct him to vote for such resolutions as those which had been offered
to them by the gentleman from Caroline, he would go into mourning;
that in case the resolutions were *adopted*, it would be, in his opinion, nothing more than the tocsin of rebellion; and in such a case, he would go
to some other country to seek an asylum. Mr. *Pope* then observed, that
he would pause to give an opportunity for correction, if he had misstated
anything. But as he was not corrected, he said he would proceed to
reason from those observations of his colleague. He considered them as
applying to himself, being one of those in favour of the resolutions; but
still he did not believe the gentleman had intended them as such. He
knew him better. However, he said, both that gentleman and the gentleman from Frederic, whose coolness and moderation must be admitted,
had sounded the alarm: they had called the resolutions the tocsin of rebellion: they would be drawing the sword as it were, and that we might
date the destruction of the liberty of the people from the day on which
they passed. He then proceeded to read the resolutions offered by the other
side (meaning those offered by Mr. *George K. Taylor*), and to comment
on the language of them. The gentlemen who were in favour of these,
he said, displayed boldness. Could they be afraid, then, of the resolutions
offered by the gentleman from Caroline. There was something in that
he did not understand. He said he must make a deduction from it. The
gentlemen surely must be hypochondriac. He compared their case to the
conceit of Don Quixotte about the windmills; otherwise they could not be
alarmed about our having an army of Frenchmen at our doors. His
colleague, he said, had observed that we were more equally represented
in Congress than in this Assembly. In answer to which, he asked, if the
people of New-Hampshire could more equally represent us than the
Legislature of this State. He then stated what was the usual language of
the eastern people in Congress respecting the Virginians. They were
called by them disorganizers, jacobins, &c. He then proceeded to show
which of our members in Congress had voted in favour of those laws, and
concluded that Mr. *Evans* was the only one, General *Morgan* and Mr.

Machir, as well as he could recollect, at the time of the passage of the laws, being either at home, or on their way home. So much then, he said, in answer to the observations of his colleague. He then proceeded to answer the observations of the gentleman from Frederic, in regard to the gentleman from Prince George's introducing the French into the debate. The gentleman from Frederic, he said, seemed to disapprove it. He (Mr. *Pope*) did so too. He could not imagine how the gentleman from Prince George, himself, could think it proper. And how happened it, that this gentleman could not, in the course of his reflections think of Ireland too. But British enormities, he supposed, would not suit his purpose. He then proceeded to enumerate them; and afterwards adverted to the quotations made from Publius, by the gentleman from Frederic, respecting a resort to be made to the people in such a case as the present one. He (Mr. *Pope*) thought that the Legislatures ought to take up the matter first; and the people only in the last resort. He stated the nature of the bargain made, at the time of adopting the Constitution, which was, that of the people giving up certain rights, and reserving the rest to themselves. This, he said, was proved by the twelfth amendment, which he read. He then observed that the greater part of the Constitution extended to the prohibiting of powers to the States. This amendatory clause, therefore, reserved to them what was not prohibited. He then read the resolution offered by Mr. *Brooke*, and observed, that the gentleman from Frederic had also acknowledged the people's right to assemble. But how did that right stand? The article securing it, he said, was invaded. He stated an instance of his receiving a wound in his left breast; in such case he would be less able to protect himself from receiving a wound in the right breast, or elsewhere. This he compared to the case of the clause above referred to, and declared that our most important rights, secured by that clause, were destroyed. Of what account then would be the right of petitioning? If they were to lose the resolutions offered by the gentleman from Caroline, he said, he would pronounce our liberty to be gone. But whenever that was mentioned, he observed, that many of the members on the other side would frown and spurn at it. He then made several contemplative observations upon the consequences of our rights being destroyed, and afterwards observed, that he would recur to that part of the speech of the gentleman from Prince George, in which he had introduced the goddess of liberty; upon which Mr. *Pope* concluded his observations in the following words: "Methinks I heard that gentleman say to this fair goddess, by your name we aroused the American people to oppose the tyranny of Great Britain! By your name we brought into the field large armies! By your name we drove from our country the mercenary troops of George III. and established our independence! We have now no further use for you: we only meant to change men, not measures."

Mr. DANIEL said, that he stood up to express that opinion, which his feelings and his judgment compelled him to render on this occasion. He said, he did not flatter himself, that he should be able to afford any considerable aid to the discussion, or to give very material information to the committee. But the importance of the question, and the solemnity of the appeal, which had been made by the people to the Assembly, in his opinion, required a liberal discussion to be had; that the subject, being contemplated in various points of view, might be the better understood. He should therefore beg the indulgence of the committee, while he took a short view of the subject. In doing this, he said he should follow the track which had been led by the gentlemen opposed to the resolutions before the committee, beginning with the "alien-act" so called; and first, with an examination of the arguments of the gentlemen from Prince George and Frederic. He said, it must have been observed, that in the progress of their observations, these gentlemen had assumed three principles, which could not be yielded to them, to wit: that the government of the United States was a consolidated government,—that the doctrine of implication supplied it with all necessary powers, and that the necessity and expediency of any measure authorized its adoption. These principles, he said, were assumed in aid and maintenance of their arguments, although they were not stated in express terms. But it would be easy to show, that the government was not a consolidated government in principle, however it might be in practice; that the doctrine of implication could not extend the powers of government beyond the specific grant of the Constitution; and that no necessity or expediency ought to authorize a violation of the Constitution.

The Constitution of the United States, he said, was a deputation of power from the several States, for the purposes of a Federal Government; wherein the several states were sovereign and independent as to powers not granted, and the Federal Government sovereign and independent as to those powers which were granted. The doctrine of implication could not increase the powers of the Federal Government, but could only go, as it was expressed by the Constitution, to authorize it to make such laws as might be necessary to carry the powers *granted* into effect. Having premised these things, he proceeded to examine the arguments which had been urged in favour of the "alien-act."

The gentleman from Prince George, he said, prefaced his observations on this subject, by saying that this was an act of the Congress of the United States, in which were combined the wisdom and deliberation of all America; that the determination of this combined wisdom and deliberation, was the strongest evidence of the constitutionality of the act, and that it was therefore dangerous for us to interfere on this subject. Mr. *Daniel* hoped this mode of reasoning would make no impression on the committee. He said, it was an argument that would equally apply to every possible measure of the Federal Government; and by this rule, any act of the government, however palpably violating the Constitution, and prostrating the rights and liberties of the people, might be maintained. It might be said of every act, that the *combined wisdom and deliberation of Congress* had sanctioned it.

The objections which that gentleman made to the mode of remonstrance adopted by the resolutions, he said, had already been so handsomely and conclusively answered by a worthy member, (Mr. *Mercer*,) who preceded him in this discussion, that there was no necessity for him to give them any attention.

The same gentleman, he said, in maintaining the constitutionality of the "alien-act," had observed, that aliens had those rights only in the United States, which they have in other countries by the law of nations ; and produced Vattel to show, that the sovereign of any nation had a right to prohibit the entrance of strangers into its territory; to prescribe the condition upon which they may enter; to command their departure when necessary ; in short, that it was matter of grace, and not of right, that strangers were suffered to enter the territories of any nation.

If this doctrine, said Mr. *Daniel*, be admitted true in the extent in which the worthy member quoted it, it was easily seen and could not be overlooked, that the authority applied to a consolidated government, where there was but one sovereign of the nation ; but it could not apply to the United States, where there exist the several sovereignties of the state governments, and the sovereignty of the Federal Government: of the state governments, as to powers not granted : of the Federal Government, as to powers which are granted in the Federal Constitution.

But, said Mr. *Daniel*, this power over strangers, resulting from the right of domain to every nation, and which every independent nation will exercise, does rest somewhere among the American people. It remained, then, to be inquired, where this power was lodged in the distribution of powers, among the several sovereignties which existed in the United States, in the manner which he had before stated ? The Constitution, he said, gave the answer. By section ninth, article first, it was declared, that " the migration or importation of such persons as any of the states now existing, shall think proper to admit, shall not be prohibited by the Congress, prior to the year 1808." Thus the power of admitting aliens into its territory, was left to the several states, respectively. It followed then, that each state had the right to prescribe the terms and conditions upon which aliens should be admitted, and was the judge when those terms and conditions were violated. Aliens, said he, are admitted into the territory of a nation or state, upon certain conditions. They could not therefore, be sent off, or commanded to depart, without injustice, so long as they observed the conditions upon which they were admitted. *That power*, which was the sovereign judge of the propriety of admitting aliens into its territory, must be the sovereign judge of the *necessity and justice* of sending them away. This *necessity and justice* could not exist, so long as the conditions, upon which they were admitted, remained unbroken. Each state had this power over its respective territory, by the clause of the Constitution which he had just recited. Each state, said he, was therefore, the sovereign judge of the propriety and justice of commanding aliens and strangers to depart from the limits of its respective territory.

But, said he, the gentlemen contend, that this article of the Constitution cannot apply ; and here they differ in their construction ; the gentleman from Frederic maintaining, that this clause related only to the importation of slaves; the gentleman from Prince George insisting, that this clause does only secure to the states the right of *admitting* aliens, but does not declare that Congress shall not have power to send them away. He said he would examine the objections as they stood in order. With respect to the opinion of the member from Frederic, (Mr. *Magill*,) the words

of the clause, " migration or importation," were, from their very terms, a
sufficient refutation : and he believed, if they were to seek the reason why
this clause was inserted in the Constitution, they should find, that the
Southern States insisted upon it, not only to secure their right of continuing
the abominable slave-trade, but that they might also have it in their power
to encourage and effect the settlement of their back lands. The gentleman,
he said, had urged no reason of his own, in support of the opinion which
he gave, but read to the committee parts of the speeches of Mr. *Mason*
and Mr. *Madison*, delivered in the Virginia convention, when the Constitution was under discussion. But, said Mr. *Daniel*, when this document
was examined, it would be found that those gentlemen, in the parts of
their speeches to which the worthy member referred, did simply state,
that the right of continuing the slave-trade was secured by this clause to
the Southern States, and that they did not advance any sentiment or idea,
which could, in the remotest degree, maintain the opinion, that this clause
related to the "*importation* of slaves only, and did *not* relate to the *migration*" of aliens into the several states.

With respect to the objection of the member from Prince George, (Mr.
G. K. Taylor,) that although this clause secured the right of admitting
aliens to the several states, yet it did not deny the right of Congress to
send them away, it might be observed, that the objection itself admits the
sovereign power of the states to permit strangers to enter their respective
territories. He said he had before endeavoured to prove that *this power*
involved, necessarily, the rights of prescribing the conditions upon which
aliens might enter, and of controlling them after they had entered the territory of any particular state. But to meet the objection more pointedly,
he would take a view of the powers of any particular state, unconnected
with and separated from the other states. Virginia, for instance, independent of her federation and union with the other states, would be completely
sovereign, and have all possible power and right on this subject to admit
aliens into her territory, and to control and send them away at pleasure,
regarding only the rules prescribed by the law of nations. He would now
ask what power and right Virginia had given up on this subject, in her
connexion with the other states, by the Federal Constitution? It was
yielded by the gentleman that she had power and right to admit aliens
into her territory. He again demanded, had she granted the power and
right of sending them away, to the general government? But, said he, it
is declared by the twelfth amendment to the Constitution, that " the
powers not delegated to the states by the Constitution, nor prohibited by it
to the United States, are reserved to the states respectively, or to the people ;" therefore, he insisted, this power of sending away aliens from the
territories of the particular states, not being delegated to the United States
by the Constitution, remained with Virginia, as it respected the limits of
her own particular territory. But, said the gentleman from Prince
George, Mr. *Daniel* continued, this article of the amendments must be
understood that whatever is not *expressly* reserved to the states is given
up to the Federal Government, *if necessary*. Besides the perversion of
the plain meaning of this article, by this construction, said Mr. *Daniel*,
the gentleman should have remembered that he stated in his argument

that a construction which leads to *absurdity* was not true. This construction would make this article of the amendments answer no purpose; it was,
therefore, he joined with the gentleman, *absurd and untrue.*

The powers of the federal government being *expressly* defined, "it was
true as a general principle," that powers not granted were retained by the
states, said Mr. *Daniel*; but so jealous were they of their rights, and so
fearful of the greedy doctrine of implication, that this amendment was
recommended and annexed to the Constitution, for the purposes of security
and safety.

The gentlemen, he said, finding it impossible to maintain their ground
by the aid of any clause of the Constitution, wherein power was *expressly*
delegated, had sought the assistance of several general phrases and expressions, such as, "to provide for the general welfare," "to repel invasions," "to make laws necessary to carry the foregoing powers into
effect," by which they endeavoured to maintain that the general government has other powers than those expressly given by, and enumerated in
the Constitution, and unlimited power as to all subjects of a general
nature. If this be true, said he, if these general expressions and clauses
give general and unlimited power, the special enumeration of power in
the Constitution was absurd and useless. Those sage and patriotic poli-
ticians who formed the federal plan of government, puzzled themselves to
no purpose in defining, enumerating, and limiting power: they had nothing
to do but to organize the government; say there should be an executive,
judicial, and legislative body; prescribe the mode in which the members
of the several departments should be brought into office; and declare that
"*they should have power to provide for the general welfare.*" This
would be precisely such a Constitution as gentlemen contended was our
Federal Constitution, in which the powers of the several branches of the
government were so specially enumerated, limited, and defined. And it
was, Mr. *Daniel* said, a wilful and studied design that misapplied these
general terms and clauses of the Constitution, for they are necessarily explained by the special grants of power: they must be understood, that
"Congress shall provide for the general welfare," according to the Constitution of the United States, and the powers therein granted. "Congress
may repel invasions," according to the Constitution, and the powers therein
granted. "Congress shall have power to make all laws which shall be
necessary and proper for carrying into execution the foregoing enumerated
powers:" not to increase and extend their authority, but to carry into
effect those powers which are enumerated in the Constitution.

He said, he presumed enough had been said in answer to the gentleman's arguments in favour of the *rightful* power of Congress to legislate
on this subject: he would now proceed to examine the arguments which
had been urged with an intent to maintain the opinion that the "trial by
jury" was not violated by the "alien-act." The gentleman from Prince
George had said, that aliens were not entitled to a trial by jury, because
they were not parties to the Constitution, were under no obligations to the
government, and that no duties could be demanded of them. That citizens
alone had a right to a trial by jury, because they were parties to the Con-

stitution, which secured that right, and on account of their obligations and duties to the government.

Mr. *Daniel* said, if the worthy member had been as attentive to the authority of Vattel on this point, as he was when he hoped to draw something from it to support him, he would have found the reverse of almost everything he stated relative to aliens, to be true; he would have found that they had rights to be protected, and duties and obligations to discharge; that they were bound to obey the general laws of the land, and that they a right to be tried according to the general laws of the land. He would have found that, " in countries where a stranger may freely enter, (as in this,) the sovereign is supposed to allow him access only upon this condition, that he be subject to the laws, I mean the *general* laws made to maintain good order, and which have no relation to the title of *citizen* or subject of the state. The public safety, the rights of the nation, and of the prince, necessarily require this condition; and the stranger tacitly submits to it as soon as he enters the country, as he cannot presume upon having access upon any other footing. The empire has the right of command in the whole country, and the laws are not confined to regulating the *citizens among themselves,* but they determine what ought to be observed by *all orders of people* throughout the whole extent of the state. In virtue of this submission, the strangers who commit a *fault,* ought to be punished according to the laws of the country." Vattel, book 2d, chap. viii. p. 267, sect. 101 and 102. And again, page 268, section 104, he would have found that, " the sovereign ought not to grant an entrance into his state to make strangers fall into a snare: as soon as he receives them he engages to protect them as his own subjects, and to make them enjoy, as much as depends on him, an entire security," according to the general laws of the land. He trusted that the committee were sufficiently satisfied that aliens have rights which are under the protection of the laws of that state wherein they reside; that they have duties and obligations to discharge to that state, and that if they commit a *fault,* they have a right to be tried and punished according to the general laws of that state. The worthy member from Prince George, as if he foresaw his defeat on this ground, took refuge under that clause of the " alien-act," which provides that " an alien may prove the falsity of the charge." Mere mockery of justice, said he, to prove the falsity of suspicion ! Prove the falsity of being suspected of what he did not know, of what he was not informed ! There was no rule established, by observing which he could avoid suspicion : there was no rule directing what shall be done, and what shall be avoided by the alien : he could only know that it was dangerous for him to become suspected by the President of what he did not know, and that he might, if he could, prove the falsity of a suspicion to which some conduct of his, but what particular conduct he could not tell, may have given birth. He then observed, that the same gentleman, quitting all constitutional principles, appealed to the doctrine of *necessity,* and insisted that it was absolutely necessary to compel dangerous aliens to depart from our country, and that the President of the United States ought to be authorized to enforce their departure. But, Mr. *Daniel* said, he would insist that some rule should be established, instead of the *bare suspicion*, to decide who were, and who were not, dangerous aliens.

He should require proof, that the Constitution authorized Congress to invest the President with such a power; this had not been shown, it could not be shown. He contended, therefore, that this power was lodged in the several states respectively, and wisely lodged. For, in case of emergency, each state had it in its power to act immediately, before the President could be informed of the danger. The authority of each state was always at hand; could be immediately applied to, and would be readily inclined to take efficient measures for the safety of its citizens. The member from Prince George, he said, had observed, that such a provision as the one marked by the alien-act was necessary to guard against the French and their intrigues. If so, he said, the states were competent to make the provision. He believed they were as much disposed as any other body would be, to adopt all necessary and constitutional measures. He hoped, that Virginia had virtue and patriotism sufficient to view with indignation, and to suppress with vigour, any intrigues of a dangerous nature, whether meditated by France or any other nation. But, in adopting such a measure, he wished to observe the laws of nations. He could not consent, under the pretence of guarding against aliens, who were citizens of France, to violate the rights of other aliens among us, who might be citizens of any other nation. He contended, that the alien-act was general, and equally applied to all aliens, whether citizens of France, or subjects of another power. He stated a case from the law of nations, to prove that such a regulation, if made at all, should be particularly directed against the citizens or subjects of that nation from whom danger is apprehended.

The member from Prince George, he said, had read a clause from the Virginia laws, which he assimilated to the alien-act passed by Congress, and from which he argued the right of Congress to pass the law in question. He requested that the law might again be read. (It was accordingly read by the clerk in the following words: " It shall and may be lawful for the Governor, with the advice of the Council of State, to apprehend and secure, or cause to be apprehended and secured, or compelled to depart this commonwealth, all suspicious persons, being the subjects of any foreign power or state, who shall have made a declaration of war against the said states, or from whom the President of the United States shall apprehend hostile designs against the said states, provided information thereof shall have been previously received by the executive from him.") Mr. *Daniel* then said, that the law which had been read, pursued the law of nations; and clearly recognised the distinction which he had before laid down, that it did not authorize the Governor to apprehend and send away all aliens whom he might suspect; but such suspicious aliens only whose nation was at war with these states, or from whose nation, hostilities were apprehended. That this law was not general, but particularly directed against those aliens, whose nation was at war with this country, or from whose nation there were reasons to expect war. That this law, instead of furnishing an argument in favour of the right of Congress to pass the law in question, was a strong proof that the legislature of Virginia, at the time of its passage, entertained the opinion, that the power to regulate this subject belonged to the state. He said, it was remarkable that the gentleman from Prince George, on this occasion, following the example of the present administration, had indulged himself in declamation against the intrigues of the French nation ; had inveighed with the utmost bitterness, against their policy and injustice; had threatened us with the horrors of another St. Domingo; that our slaves would be let loose upon us; that our wives, our daughters, our sisters, would be forced into the rude embraces of the ruthless negro, who would butcher them before our eyes, immediately after having satisfied his lustful appetite. Mr. *Daniel* said, this language was addressed to the feelings and passions, and not to the understanding of the committee. For his part, he should consider the subject upon principle. To the intrigues of France he opposed the virtue and patriotism of our citizens in general; the vigilance and activity of our officers and magistrates ; and the wisdom of the state legislature to observe all necessary measures, an evidence of which was seen in the law which had been read. That invectives against France could not prove the constitutionality of the law in question. That if they were intended to excite the indignation of the committee against that republic, the gentleman had spent his time in vain ; for that the injustice and rapacity of that nation, without the aid of the gentleman's elocution, had already inflamed the mind of every member into bitterness and resentment. But, amid this universal glow of indignant feelings, he wished to see our glorious Constitutions saved inviolate. Secure me in this point, said Mr. *Daniel;* save the Constitutions of my country from innovation and violence, and I will join hands with the gentleman, and swear eternal enmity to France, and all other nations of the earth, who shall be hostile to the liberty and independence of the United States. But, said he, it would seem as if the injustice of France to other nations ; her base attack upon our neutral rights, and undefended, unoffending commerce, had so affrighted gentlemen, that they were ready to abandon those principles which were once so dear to all America. Inglorious sons, however, were they, who for distant and feeble alarms would forsake those principles and those rights which our forefathers sought at every hazard, and maintained amidst the threatening ruin of war and bloodshed. In vain, said he, are we told that the French government is a military despotism, which proscribes the liberty of the press, and carries its measures by force of the bayonet! It cannot reconcile us to like measures in the United States. It cannot reconcile us to a sedition-law and to a standing army, which will probably produce the same miserable effects here, as they have done in France. It cannot prove to us the constitutionality of the acts in question.

. He said, before he took leave of this part of the subject, he would take notice of a charge which had been made by the gentleman from Frederic, against those who advocated the resolutions, that they addressed arguments to the humanity of the committee. He would reply, that the opposers of the resolutions addressed arguments to the fears of the committee ; that admitting the charge to be true, (which was by no means the case,) it was much more honourable, both for those who make the address, and those who are addressed, that application be made to the feelings of humanity, rather than to those which are excited by fear and alarm. That the gentleman, himself, had threatened us with confusion and darkness, and foreboded the hasty setting of the sun of American glory, if we adopted the resolutions; and his coadjutor from Prince George had invaded our country with a French army, and slaughtered our best and dearest friends before our eyes. This mode of argument, however unfair, was by no means novel. When our gallant forefathers conceived the mighty design of declaring the American world independent and free, the same doctrine of terror and alarm, of dangers from abroad, and mischiefs and ruin incalculable within, was pressed and repeated. But, resting firm on principle, they steadily pursued truth, and achieved the glorious deed of American independence. As then, so now, he hoped, this doctrine of terrorism would make no impression; but that the committee would consider the subject upon principle, and determine upon its merits.

Mr. *Daniel* observed, that in the course of the observations which he had made, to obviate exceptions which gentlemen had taken to the resolutions proposed, it was to be discovered, that his principal objections to the "alien-act" were, that it violated the sovereignty of the state governments; that it blended legislative, executive, and judicial powers; that it violated the right of trial by jury, contrary to the Constitution.

With respect to the first objection, he had shown by the foregoing arguments, that the state governments were sovereign as to those powers not granted to Congress, and this subject, not only not being granted, but prohibited Congress by the ninth section, first article of the Constitution, it followed, that as to this subject, the states were severally sovereign; and that any attempt by Congress to legislate on this subject, within the limits of any particular state, was an attack upon the sovereignty thereof.

As to the second objection, that the alien-act blended legislative, judicial, and executive powers, it might be observed, that legislative power is the authority to prescribe a rule of conduct: this rule is the act of the legislative power, declaring what shall be done, and what shall be avoided. The "alien-act," said Mr. *Daniel*, does not declare what the alien shall do, and what he shall avoid: it does not declare a rule of conduct, which he can know and observe: the President has the power to prescribe this rule of conduct for the alien, by bringing him to the bar of suspicion, if he does not observe a line of conduct, which, not being designated by the "alien-act," is only known and subject to the President's will. But to declare this rule of conduct is a legislative act; the President, by this law, has effectually the right to prescribe this rule: therefore, he contended, that the President was invested with effectual legislative power. He certainly had the power to judge when the alien came within the rule prescribed by his suspicion: and in this, as in all other cases, he was invested with executive power. Thus in one person, contrary to the Constitution, was to be seen the lawgiver, judge, and executioner.

With regard to the third objection, that the "alien-act" infringed the right of trial by jury, he referred the committee to the seventh article of the amendments to the Constitution, where it is found, that "*no person* shall be deprived of his life, liberty, or property, without due process of law." He contended, that an alien was a person, who had rights of life, liberty, and property, and was therefore within the provision of this part of the Constitution. He had before shown, that by the law of nations, an alien had the right of being tried according to the *general* laws of the land. It was here evident, that an alien was a person who could not be deprived of his "liberty" without due process of law. It remained then to be inquired what was this "due process of law?" This "due process of law," he said, was to be found in the seventh and eighth articles of the amendments to the Constitution, that "*no person* shall be held to answer an accusation, unless on a presentment or indictment by a grand jury;" that "the accused shall enjoy the right to a speedy and public trial by an impartial jury, of the state and district wherein the crime shall have been committed; to be informed of the nature and cause of the accusation; to be confronted with the witnesses against him; to have compulsory process for obtaining witnesses in his favour; and to have the assistance of counsel for his defence." This mode of trial pointed out by the Constitution, this "due process of law," was disregarded, and entirely abolished by the "alien-act." Having taken this short view of the alien-act, he said he would proceed to consider the "sedition-law," as it was commonly termed. He could have wished that gentlemen had given their opinions freely on this subject. The gentleman from Prince George, he said, had given some apology why he declined the discussion: he had committed himself a day or two past, by declaring that the sedition-law was already *sufficiently odious.* It was, therefore, Mr. *Daniel* said, he supposed the gentlemen thought it best not to meddle with it. He would receive the gentleman's apology, and proceed to examine the law, according to his own ideas on the subject, in which he would occasionally take notice of what the gentleman from Frederic had urged.

He stated that the acts enumerated in the first section of the sedition-law, as offences to be punished with heavy fines and long imprisonment, were "to combine or conspire together with intent to oppose any measure, or to impede the operation of any law of the United States," or to intimidate any officer under the government of the same, from undertaking, performing, or executing his trust or duty; or to counsel, advise, or attempt to procure any insurrection, riot, unlawful assembly, or combination, whether such counsel or advice had effect or not. The offences enumerated in the second section of said law, he said, were, "to write, print, utter, or publish, or to cause the same to be done, or to aid in writing, printing, uttering, or publishing, any false writings against the government, the President, or either house of the Congress of the United States, with intent to defame the government, either house of Congress, or the President, or to bring them, or either of them, into *disrepute;* or to excite against them, or either of them, the hatred of the people; or to excite any unlawful combination, for opposing any law, or act of the President of the United States, or to *defeat any such law or act.*" These were the provisions of the act. The provisions of the Constitution were, "Congress shall make no law respecting an establishment of religion, or prohibiting the free exercise thereof; or *abridging* the freedom of speech, *or of the press;* or of the right of the people peaceably to assemble, and to petition the government for a redress of grievances." Third article of amendments to the Constitution. He requested gentlemen to read the one and the other; to compare them, and to reconcile them if possible. He was one of those who believed, that the first clause of the law would, in its operation, effectually destroy the liberty of speech; and the second clause did most completely annihilate the freedom of the press. "To *combine, conspire, counsel, and advise together*," was a natural right of *self-defence*, belonging to the people; it could only be exercised by the use of speech; it was a right of self-defence against the tyranny and oppression of government; it ought to be exercised with great caution; and never, but upon occasions of extreme necessity. Of this necessity, the people are the only judges. For if government could control this right; if government were the judge, when the necessity of exercising this right has arrived, the right never will be used; for government never will judge that the people ought to oppose its measures, however unjust, however tyrannical and despotically oppressive. This right, although subject to abuse, like many other invaluable rights, was nevertheless essential to, and inseparable from the liberties of the people. The warmest friend of any government would not contend that it was infallible. The best of governments may possibly change into tyranny and despotism. Measures may be adopted violating the Constitution, and prostrating the rights and principles of the people. He hoped never to see the time; but, if it should so happen, no man would deny but that such measures ought to be opposed. But, he would ask, how they could be effectually opposed, without the people should "combine, conspire, counsel, and advise" together? One man could do nothing. This right of adopting the only efficient plan of opposition to unconstitutional, oppressive, and tyrannical measures, whenever they should occur, he hoped never would be given up. This right had been well exercised on a former occasion against England; and it would probably be well used again, if our liberties were sufficiently endangered, to call forth its exertion. But for the spirited and energetic exercise of this right; but for the "combining, conspiring, counselling, and advising" together of the American people, these United States, now independent and free, would have remained under the tyrannical and despotic domination of the British king. It had been said, that this doctrine leads to anarchy and confusion; but, said Mr. *Daaiel*, this doctrine gave birth and success to our revolution; secured our present liberty, and the privileges consequent thereupon. The contrary doctrine, said Mr. *Daniel*, leads to passive obedience and non-resistance, to tyranny and oppression, more certain and more dangerous. If a measure was unpopular, and should give discontent, it would be discussed: if it should thereupon be found to be tolerable, it would be acquiesced in. If, on the contrary, measures should be adopted of such dangerous and destructive tendency, that they ought to be opposed, he would ask, how this could be done but by the means which are forbidden in the first section of the law in question? These were the only means by which liberty, once trampled down by tyrants and despots, could be reinstated: and if the general government continued its rapid progress of violating the Constitution, and infringing the liberties of the people, the time he feared was hastening on, when the people would find it necessary again, to exercise this natural right of defence.

Mr. *Daniel* said he would now turn his attention to that part of the law which affects the freedom of the press, in which the Constitution was most palpably, and most dangerously infringed. On this subject, he said, the gentleman from Frederic had contended, that the Constitution was not violated; that the common law was a part of the Constitution; and that the offences enumerated in the act, were always punishable at common law. If this be the fact, said Mr. *Daniel,* the law in question is nugatory; and the clause of the Constitution on this subject, which had been read, was of no effect. By the gentleman's common law, which he had read, offences against the king and his government, were precisely such as were enumerated as offences in this law, against the President and government of the United States; substituting the word "President," in the latter case, for the word "king," in the former. These offences might be "by speak-ing, or writing against them; or wishing him (the king in England, and the President in America,) ill, giving out scandalous stories concerning them (the King and his government in England, and the President and his government in America,) or doing anything that may tend to lessen him (the King, or President, as the case may be) in the esteem of his subjects; weaken the government, or raise jealousies among the people." (4 *Black-stone's Commentaries, page* 123.) When our "sedition law" was so like the law of England, he did not wonder that the gentleman had supposed that the law of England was in force here; one being the copy of the other, with the necessary change of names, and some other trivial cir-cumstances; nor did he wonder that the gentleman should say, in confor-mity to that authority, that "the liberty of the press, properly understood, is by no means infringed or violated" by such regulations, "but consists in laying no *previous restraints* upon publications;" and is otherwise "li-centiousness," (4 *Blackstone, p.* 151;) that a printer may publish what he pleases, but must answer the consequence, if a certain set of men shall adjudge his writings to contain "dangerous and licentious sentiments." If this be true, he said, he would be glad to be informed for what purpose was it declared by the Constitution, that "the freedom of the press should not be restrained;" and how we were more free in the United States, than the people of any other nation whatsoever? The most oppressed of Eu-rope; the slaves and subjects of the most despotic power on the earth, he said; had the right to speak, write, and print whatever they pleased, but were liable to be punished afterwards, if they spoke, wrote, or printed any-thing that was offensive to the government: that there was very little dif-ference as to the liberty of the press, whether the *restraints* imposed were "*previous*" or subsequent to publications. If the press was subjected to a *political licenser*, the discretion of the printer would be taken away, and with it his responsibility; and nothing would be printed but what was agreeable to the political opinions of a certain set of men; whereas *subse-quent restraints* have the same operation, by saying, if you do "write, print, utter, or publish," anything contrary to the *political opinions,* re-putation or principles of certain men, you shall be fined and imprisoned. In vain, he said, were we told that the accused may prove the truth of his writings or printing, and that we are only forbidden to write or print false facts. The truth was that it was not the facts, but the deductions and conclusions drawn from certain facts, which would constitute the offence. If a man was to write and publish that the Congress of the United States had passed the "alien and sedition acts," that the provisions of the said acts were in these words, reciting the laws as they are; that the Constitution was in these words, reciting the provisions of the Constitution truly; and conclude that the said acts violated the Constitution; that the Congress and the President, in enacting the same, had assumed powers not granted to them, and had encroached upon the liberties of the people, who ought to take measues "to defeat" these laws, and this "act of the President." Here the facts stated, that the laws had been passed, and that the Constitution was in terms stated, could be proved, and would not constitute the offence, but the inference from these facts, that the Congress, in enacting the said laws, had violated the Constitution, assumed powers not delegated to them, and usurped the rights and liberties of the people, in which usurpation the President had joined, would certainly have a tendency "to defame the government, the Congress, and the President, and to bring them into *disrepute* and hatred among the people," and would therefore constitute the offence. The inference or conclusion from certain facts might be true or not, and was mere matter of opinion. It was opinion then, *political opinion*, which was the real object of punishment. The deduction made from the facts just stated, he said, was in his opinion true; the consequence of which was, that the Congress and President of the United States had not his confidence; with him they were in "disrepute." But he could not prove that the opinion was true, as a fact; he could offer those reasons which convinced his mind of its truth, but they might not be satisfactory to a jury summoned with a *special regard* to their political opinions, or to a judge of the United States, most of whom had already pronounced their opinion on the subject, either in pamphlets, or political instead of legal charges to the grand juries of the several circuits of the United States; thus prejudging a constitutional question, which they knew would be made, if ever the law was attempted to be carried into effect.

He said he would state one more case to exemplify his opinion. If at the time of British oppressions, when the parliament of England boldly implied the right to make laws for, and to tax the American people, without representation, any man had by writing maintained that representation and taxation were inseparable, and that it was an usurpation and assumption of power by parliament to impose taxes on the American colonies, who were not represented in parliament, the fact here stated would not offend, because true; but the conclusion, the charge of usurpation, made upon the British government, would certainly have a tendency to bring it into "disrepute and hatred" among the people, as it did most effectually in America, and would have constituted the offence. This opinion, though now clearly admitted to be true, was then new, and could not be proven true to an English judge and jury, for they were so impressed with its falsity, that the nation undertook and carried on a bloody and expensive war, to correct its error. He concluded that the provisions of this act abridged and infringed the liberty of the press, which at the time of the

adoption of the Constitution had no other restraint than the responsibility
of the author to the individual who might be injured by his writing or
printing; that they destroyed all inquiry into political motives, silenced
scrutiny, weakened the responsibility of public servants, and established
political and executive infallibility ; that the solicitude discovered by the
government to defend itself against the attacks of its own citizens, was an
evidence that its acts would not deserve their confidence and esteem ; that
the solicitude thus expressed by threats of fine and imprisonment, to keep
the President for the time being, from coming " into disrepute," was evidence
of a fear that a comparison of *motives and views* would prove favourable
to his competitor, and was calculated to keep the real merits of competition
out of view, inasmuch as the merits of one of the proposed candidates could
not be insisted on to advantage, without exposing the demerits of the other,
which would tend to bring him " into disrepute." And if the one to whom
the want of merit should be ascribed, should be President for the time
being, thus to bring him into " disrepute," would be to bring the person
discussing the subject into the pains of fine and imprisonment.

It had been contended, said Mr. *Daniel,* by the gentleman from Frederic,
that the adoption of the resolutions would be an infringement of the right
of the people to petition. He, Mr. *Daniel,* would state, that this right
might be exercised by an individual, by an assemblage of individuals, or
by the representatives of the people ; which last mode was preferable,
when the sovereignty of the state, as well as the appropriate rights of the
people were attacked, as in the present case. He conceived, however,
that the law in question had very much abridged the right of the people
to petition and remonstrate. The necessity and propriety of petitions and
remonstrances could not be seen but by discussion : the right itself could
not be effectually used, without " *counselling and advising together.*"
Three or more persons would constitute an " unlawful assembly ;" for it
would be easily said, that they were unlawfully assembled, when they
intended, by discussing certain *acts* of the President, or laws of the government, " *to defeat*" the same, by inducing the people to petition and remonstrate ; or if the same were not defeated, by virtue of such petition and
remonstrance, to bring the government and President into " disrepute,"
for continuing such acts and laws in operation, against which the people
had petitioned and remonstrated. But those things being offences, and so
enumerated in one clause of the law, an assembly of three or more persons, contemplating the objects just described, would be " unlawful,"
within the purview of the act, and subject to fine and imprisonment. Again,
he said, the dangerous and ruinous tendency of certain measures, might
not be observed by the people of any particular district. A few, however,
might wish a petition to be made, to remove the grievance of the measures;
in order to which, they would individually address the district by writing,
in which they would expose and censure the evil tendency of the said
measures, to excite the people to petition and remonstrate, " to *defeat*" the
same, or necessarily to bring the friends of the continuance thereof into
" disrepute." This would be an offence within the purview of the second
clause of the law. Thus, said he, by one act we have seen, that that
clause of the Constitution, which secures the right of speech, of the press,

of petition, of the free exercise of religious opinion to the people, is pros-
trated in every respect, except as it relates to religion. And this last and
most invaluable right, he had no doubt would soon be invaded, inasmuch
as he had been informed, that the friends of the present measures had
already begun to insinuate, that an " *established church* was one of the
strongest props to government;" and inasmuch, that the same reasons
might be urged in its favour, as in favour of the abridgment of the liberty
of the press. But it was said, that the press was still left *free* to print
truth : "its licentiousness and abuse" are only forbid. So it might be
said of religion : true religion only ought to be tolerated : the *abuse* of
religion ought to be forbidden : the " licentiousness" of particular sectaries
ought to be restrained.

He said, he was fearful that he had already trespassed upon the patience
of the committee, and he would hasten to a conclusion, with a few remarks
on the particular shape and address of the resolutions. It had been ob:
jected by gentlemen, that it was going too far to declare the acts in question, to be " no law, null, void, and of no effect :" that it was sufficient to
say they were unconstitutional. He said, if they were unconstitutional, it followed necessarily that they were " not law, but null, void, and of no effect."
But, if those particular words were offensive to gentlemen he had no objection
to any modification, so the principle were retained. As to the objection, that
they were improperly addressed to the other states, Mr. *Daniel* said, he supposed that this mode was extremely eligible. If the other states think with
this, that the laws are unconstitutional, the laws will be repealed, and the
constitutional question will be settled by this declaration of a majority of the
states : thereby destroying the force of this precedent, and precluding from
any future Congress, who might be disposed to carry the principle to a more
pernicious and ruinous extent, the force of any argument which might be
derived from these laws. If, on the contrary, a sufficient majority of the
states should declare their opinion, that the Constitution gave Congress
authority to pass these laws, the constitutional question would still be
settled ; but an attempt might be made so to amend the Constitution, as to
take from Congress this authority, which in our opinion was so pernicious
and dangerous.

He then concluded by saying, that something must be done : the people
were not satisfied : they expected that this Legislature would adopt some
measure on this subject : that the Constitution of the United States was
the basis of public tranquillity ; the pledge of the sovereignty of the states,
and of the liberties of the people. But, said he, this basis of public tranquillity, this pledge of liberty and security is but a name, a mere phantom,
unless it be strictly observed. It became our duty to watch attentively,
to see that it was not violated ; to see that it was equally observed by
those who govern, and by those who are destined to obey. To attack the
Constitution was an offence against society ; and if those guilty of it were
invested with authority, they added to the offence a perfidious abuse of the
power with which they were intrusted. It was our duty, said he, to suppress this abuse with our utmost vigour and vigilance. It was strange to
see a free Constitution openly and boldly attacked by those who were put
in power under it. It was generally by silent and slow attacks, that free
7

governments had progressively changed, till very little of their original tex-
ture and principles remained : that the doctrine of implication had introduced innovations, under the influence and operation of which, the freest
governments had been enslaved. It was our duty to guard against innovations. The people of Virginia had been attentive to this subject. The
petitions and remonstrances, which had been read to the committee, proved
that the people were seriously alarmed at the innovations of the Federal
Government. He said they proved more : they proved that the people
thought that their servants, in the administration of the Federal Government, were not even modest enough to wait the increase of their power
by progressive change. That their ambition exceeded the resources of
the doctrine of implication : that their thirst of power could not be satiated,
but by a direct attack upon the Constitution, and a prostration of the great
rights of the people. He said, this apprehension of the people, which he
thought just, *would* be ' satisfied. He thought the mode proposed _by the
resolutions was most likely to effect this purpose, as well as other important purposes. He said, if they who were the representatives of the people,
would not act for them when called upon, the people will speak for themselves ; and as the voice of God, they would be heard. He hoped this
final and dreadful appeal would never be necessary. He preferred the
resolutions, and hoped they would be adopted by the committee.

Mr. CURETON arose next, and said, that he wished to make some few
observations. He confessed, that he had before had some doubt about the
alien-law; but that the gentleman last up had convinced him of the propriety of it, and was proceeding to show how, but observed, that as the
committee appeared to be impatient, he would not trouble them any longer,
and therefore moved that the committee should rise, but upon General
Lee's rising to speak, he withdrew his motion.

General LEE then proceeded to observe, that as the subject required the
fullest deliberation, he hoped that all the papers respecting it would be read
that evening, to prevent any interruption in the debate the next day. By
this arrangement time would be saved, and perspicuity in argument pro-
moted. It was too late in the evening then, to enter at large upon the
subject. This he would defer till the next day, when he should with
frankness and candour deliver his sentiments, with a view of showing the
pernicious tendency of the resolutions on the table.

He begged to know how many counties in the state had presented petitions to the Assembly on this subject ; any one of which petitions, with the
alien-law, he must trouble the clerk, he said, to read, as he believed this
law particularly, to be much misunderstood. He himself considered it as
going only to enable the chief magistrate to remove dangerous aliens,
thereby preventing the commission of crime, and not punishing crimes
committed.

The sedition-law, he said, so far as he recollected it, was free from the
charges contained in the resolutions. If then, on examination, it was
found that these laws were constitutional, the resolutions proposed must
be rejected. If they were found unconstitutional, it was proper to interfere

and restore the Constitution to its original purity. In this salutary wish
he would cheerfully join, but he must take steps becoming a portion of the
same people to take, full of friendship, full of mutual respect, and tending
to perpetuate union and brotherly love, not disunion and hatred.

Mr. NICHOLAS arose next, and said that the gentleman last up wished
to save time, by having all the papers read that evening, but he wished to
know how that would save time? The gentleman had said too that the alien
law extended to *prevent* only, and not to punish crimes. Mr. *Nicholas*
asked, if banishment was no punishment? He had always understood,
he said, that it was; and then observed, that he should have been glad
that the gentleman had been present from the commencement of the discussion, that he might perfectly have understood the nature of it.

Mr. *John Taylor's* resolutions were then read, together with those laid
upon the table by other gentlemen, and the memorial from the people of
Caroline County.

Mr. BROOKE then arose, and observed, that labouring under all the
diffidence that a person unaccustomed to public speaking would naturally
feel, in delivering his sentiments upon so momentous an occasion as the
present, he was sensible of the disadvantage he must have laboured under,
in delivering his sentiments upon the subject the day before; and on this
account, he felt more sensibly the attack made upon him by his colleague,
and the attempt made by him to distort the observations, which, in the
midst of his confusion and embarrassment, Mr. *Brooke* said, had fallen
from him. These observations that gentleman had undertaken to carica-
ture. A more proper person for a task of this kind could not have undertaken it. He would do justice to every subject he ever did undertake.
Mr. *Brooke* then said, that he would proceed to repeat to the committee
his observations just as they were expressed, which, notwithstanding the
diffidence he felt on the occasion, he perfectly recollected; and he believed
that other gentlemen, not disposed to distort his meaning, would agree with
him in his statement. He had observed, he said, that he was opposed to
the resolutions offered by the gentleman from Caroline, however modified;
that he was under no instructions; and that if the people of his county
should be so *degenerate* (to the best of his recollection was the term; but if
the term *debased*, which his colleague had stated as a stronger expression,
would suit his purpose better, it might be so) as to instruct him to vote for
resolutions having so dangerous and alarming a tendency as those referred
to, he should go into mourning; he should bid adieu to legislation, and
seek an asylum in some other region of the globe, amongst a race of
mortals who had more respect for peace and order, and who set a higher
value upon the blessings of good government. Mr. *Brooke* then concluded
by observing, that he had thus recapitulated the observations used by him,
no less to gratify his colleague who had called upon him, than that the
people of his county might know that these were his sentiments.

Mr. BOOKER then moved that the committee should rise.

Mr. JOHN TAYLOR hoped that the committee would not rise, but that they would proceed. Several days, he said, had already been spent in the discussion of the business before them ; and much more time might be spent, unless they should adopt a different mode. They had, until then, been in the habit of receiving only one speech a day; and the only way to dispatch the business he thought, would be to meet early and sit late.

Mr. GEORGE K. TAYLOR said, that he intended to say something further upon the subject, but wished not to hurry the committee.

Mr. COWAN also observed, that he intended to deliver his sentiments to the committee, tending to show that the alien law was constitutional, but wished not to press the matter then.

Mr. NICHOLAS hoped that the committee would not rise. They had as yet proceeded but slowly. He hoped, therefore, that the gentleman last up would proceed : he should be glad to hear him.

The same being also requested by others at the same time,

Mr. COWAN proceeded, by observing that much had been said upon the subject already. It was a question of great importance, and the great attention which had been given by the committee, was a proof of the talents of the speakers. He confessed that he had no such claim, but came forward on another ground. He felt it a duty to his constituents and the whole community, to engage in the discussion. He had noticed, he said, that the observations of the gentleman from Prince George had been objected to on one particular ground, that of their mingling the affairs of France with the subject of the laws under consideration. But he (Mr. Cowan) thought that could not be avoided. The present question, he said, had its root in French transactions. The rights of citizens and aliens, he thought, had been confounded ; and in order to have a clear apprehension of them, a standard ought to be fixed upon to try them. That standard he pronounced to be, as to citizens, the Constitution; as to aliens, the law of nations. Every sovereign nation, he said, was possessed of certain rights. Amongst them the right to govern aliens was a perfect right. It vested a power to restrain them. That right, he said, contained two things ; the first was that of obliging aliens to depart, the second was to allow them to remain.

An alien, said Mr. Cowan, entering into a country, as the condition of such entrance, doth agree to submit to the laws of its sovereignty. Submitting to them did imply, that when required, he was bound to retire. Where did the exercise of this power rest? By the Constitution, the power to exclude remains in the states for a limited time. It was true that the powers not particularly granted are reserved. It had been said that the states were sovereign. It was so, but not in the latitude contended for. For, if it were so, the clause in the Constitution respecting the migration and importation of persons, was an argument to the contrary. How did the states derive this right? If they had it before the adoption of the Constitution, the Constitution gave it to no purpose. It was a supererogation. By the adoption of the Constitution, Mr. Cowan conceived, the states excepted that right. Where was it then? It was with the people, who, in order to the distribution of powers therein specified, and for that purpose, had resumed their full, their native rights. That, indeed, was a matter of moment. For, could they once ascertain where the right then was vested, they might then find the key to unlock the Constitution, so as to find the power to pass an alien-law. If Congress had not the right, the states must have a paramount right to protect aliens. If Congress had it not, the states could suffer aliens to remain within them, in despite of Congress. Could the states then confer a perfect right on aliens? If they could not, they had no power to keep them here. For, if they could keep them here one hour, they might keep them here until 1808. But, Mr. *Cowan* said, he would attempt to show that the states had no such right. He hoped gentlemen would answer him on that point. A state could confer a perfect right only in two ways: First, by naturalization; but this subject was conveyed to Congress. Secondly, by treaty with the state from which the alien comes; but this power, too, was vested in Congress, and prohibited to the states. Could an act of Assembly confer a perfect right? No; because, "a perfect right is that to which is joined the right of constraining those who refuse to fulfil the obligation resulting from it." An alien could not oblige a compliance with the terms of it. It had been said that the alien-law violated that part of the Constitution which gives the state a right to exclude aliens, if it thinks proper. But, if the state could not give the right to them to remain, it must be with Congress, and therefore no violation. By the Constitution, a power was given to Congress to repel and to protect against invasion, and to make any law to carry its measures into effect. What could be the meaning, then, of those clauses? The terms to *repel* invasion, and *protect* against invasion, gave different powers. Could it be thought proper, that the general government should have no power to defeat a plan before it was matured? It must be inferred, then, from such words, that Congress had the power to take such measures as would secure the people. There was no necessity, then, of resorting to the last clause of the eighth section of the first article, for the power in question. The general powers of Congress would be sufficient to give it. When bound to accomplish an end, are not, said he, the means included? Or are they withheld? But, if the state had no such power, it was in Congress. For, if it was not there, where was it? Thus much, Mr. *Cowan* said, for the constitutionality of the alien-law. He proceeded next to discuss its nature. It had been said, that it blended different powers. But, Mr. *Cowan* said, that the Constitution of the United States, in his opinion, was not such an one as that the powers of government were necessarily kept separate and distinct. It was true, they were so in the state Constitution; but that they are not so in the former, was proved by the instance of the President's ratifying a treaty. For, as the treaty when made, becomes a law, his ratification has the effect of a legislative act. He must often act with a union of powers. By approving laws, particularly, he legislates; and in cases where no person is pointed out by a law to enforce its execution, the President perhaps is the proper person to do it. This is proved by that clause in the Constitution which directs, that the President shall take care that the laws be faithfully executed. Therefore, even if the President had not been named to carry the alien-law into effect, by the Constitution, he must have done it so far as was executive. Two powers, then, are united by the Constitution in him.

Mr. *Cowan* then observed, that if the committee could be convinced that the law was constitutional, they certainly must conceive the wisdom of Congress adequate to the policy of such a law. The alien-enemy laws passed by the Legislature of this state, and also by the Congress of the United States, had been admitted by the gentleman from Caroline to be necessary. He (Mr. *Cowan*) considered that law of Congress as being very analogous to the law now the subject of debate. For, if such enemy-alien law be necessary in a state of war, the law of Congress now under the consideration of the committee, under defensive operations, was necessary in proportion. It had been urged too, that aliens, by the law of nations, had the same rights *as* citizens. But that the alien was *so* entitled, he said, was necessary to be shown. There certainly was a distinction between the alien and citizen. An alien is not subject to all the laws of a country, but such only as regulated the affairs of private life. Mr. *Cowan* then read the seventh amendment to the Constitution, containing the principles and regulations which were to govern in criminal cases. Gentlemen had derived rights to aliens under this clause, and seemed to rely much upon the word *persons* used in this clause. But he (Mr. *Cowan*) asserted that aliens were entitled to their privileges from a principle of the law of nations, and not under the Constitution, as a party thereto. For the alien could not be made a soldier, he owing allegiance elsewhere. The expressions, too, used in the seventh amendment, "except in cases arising in the land or naval forces, or in the militia when in actual service, in time of war or public danger," prove that aliens were not the persons contemplated by that clause, but citizens, they only being subject to those kinds of service. Indeed, an Indian or a negro might, by such doctrines as gentlemen held, be as well entitled as an alien. But none of these were parties to the Constitution. Gentlemen who argued thus, would prove too much for an alien. They would place him in a better situation than our own citizens. It had been said banishment is a punishment. But banishment of a citizen, said Mr. *Cowan*, exists not under the Constitution. He said, also, that an alien on coming into, admitted the right of sovereignty of the country over him. This was the condition of his admission into every country: to illustrate which, he repeated the observations which he had before made upon that point. He also recapitulated his preceding arguments about perfect right, and then observed that it had been said that this Assembly ought to adopt the resolutions before them, and not use force; but by means of them, produce an effect on the general government. And it was further said that the compact was between states. But, Mr. Cowan said, he could not agree with gentlemen in these points. What effect could the resolutions have? It ought to be supposed that Congress had wisdom: that, if they thought they were right they would not recede. If they thought they were wrong, he believed they would endeavour to do what was right. He thought, too, that the compact contained an union both of the states and people. What, said he, would be the effect of declaring the laws null and void? The principle would extend to all laws of Congress whatever. What then would be the result? It would shake the foundations of tranquillity. It would shake the faith of the people in their government, as well as the faith of foreign nations in it. It would be setting up powers paramount to the government. Because a few of the people had directed them to act upon the subject, could they think they had the power? Had the people empowered them to declare the laws null and void? On the contrary, if the people on their return, should hold a different language, how could the members of this House justify themselves to the people? Would it be by telling them that they, their representatives, had all powers? He again stated the consequence of exercising such a power. And if the compact were to be dissolved, he asked, what would be the consequences? The resolutions would give a pause to the acts under consideration. For they recommended to the people to obey or not obey. And if without power from the people, this Assembly should attempt to exercise their rights to control the general government, he asked what would be the consequences? He enumerated them much at large, and concluded with an earnest request that they would not adopt the mode proposed by the resolutions.

On motion, the committee then rose, the chairman reported progress, asked, and had leave for the committee to sit again.

IN THE HOUSE OF DELEGATES,

Thursday, December 20, 1798.

The House resolved itself into a committee of the whole House, on the state of the commonwealth, Mr. *Breckenridge* in the chair, when Mr. *John Taylor's* resolutions being still under consideration,

General LEE arose, and said that he was sorry he had been prevented from attending his duty in the House earlier in the session. He had thereby lost the opportunity of combating the pernicious system in operation at its commencement, as well as that of obtaining the information which previous discussion must have afforded. Disadvantageously, however, as he felt himself situated, he could not refrain from presenting to the committee those reasons which influenced him in opposing the resolutions. There were, he believed, three propositions on the table: the resolutions proffered by the worthy member from Caroline: counter resolutions proposed by his worthy friend from Prince George, and a resolution proposed by a worthy member from Prince William. To the counter-resolutions he gave his cordial assent: to the last proposition he also assented, as it breathed a spirit congenial to true American policy, and afforded an innocent way of disposing of the resolutions from Caroline. But inasmuch as the rejection of the first resolutions would necessarily involve the approbation of those proposed in opposition, he should apply his observations to effect that object only.

General *Lee* then contended, that the ruling principle in the resolutions was erroneous. They asserted as a fundamental position, that the existing Constitution was a compact of states. He denied this position: declaring the Constitution to be a compact among the people. The ancient confederation was a compact among the states; it was so in style, manner, and power. But the government under which we now live, was precisely the reverse. What is its style? " We the people." What is its manner? Executed by functionaries appointed mediately or immediately by the people. What is its power? That of the people; derived from them, and based upon them. How then could it be asserted that the present Constitution is a compact of states? And would the committee sanction by their approbation, a declaration palpably wrong? It was true, there was to be drawn from the Constitution some faint support for this erroneous construction. The Senate, one branch of the Federal Government, was elected by the states, as states. This deviation from the general system could not be relied on to destroy the system itself. It was the result of our peculiar situation. The smaller states could not be induced to renounce their existing equality entirely. It was necessary to compromise, in order to obtain the happy Constitution we possess.

To this compromise was attributed the federal feature just mentioned. But this partial departure from the general principles of the system, could not be regarded as covering the broad ground taken in the resolutions. All the branches of government ought to be elected by the states, as states, to maintain the position assumed.

This was not the case, and consequently the resolutions were radically erroneous.

General *Lee* then proceeded to the examination of the alien and sedition laws. He began with the alien law, which he contended was not a breach of the Constitution. If the law was unconstitutional, he admitted the right of interposition on the part of the General Assembly; nay, it was their duty, and every good citizen was bound to uphold them, in fair and friendly exertions, to correct an injury so serious and pernicious. He would himself cordially contribute his humble mite; but even in that case, he should adopt a very different manner from that contained in the resolutions. Friendship should be the ground, friendship the dress, and friendship the end of his measures. The resolutions inspired hostility, and squinted at disunion.

The objections made to the alien-law were: 1st, It transcends the power of Congress. 2d, It violates that article of the Constitution which leaves to the states the right of admission of emigrants. 3d, It deprives an alien-friend of trial by jury. 4th, It unites legislative, executive, and judicial powers. To the two last, he said, he should particularly attend, as gentlemen preceding him had, he understood, fully noticed the two first. General *Lee* read some passages from the law, tending to show that the prevention of commission of crime, and not the punishment of a crime committed, was its only object.

He then proceeded to show that trial by jury could only apply on charge of crime committed. It was ludicrous to attempt to apply it in the alien-law; and it was consequently absurd to stigmatize that law, and those who framed it, with violation of the Constitution, by denial of trial by jury, where trial by jury could not possibly apply. The law was in its nature preventive, and sprung from the right of duty of government to protect the states from invasion. The exercise of this right belonged to Congress, and they were the sole judges of the expediency. In their decision, all ought to acquiesce. In case of error or vice, the revolving elections presented a proper corrective, which could be applied to without commotion or disturbance; and which, fairly and judiciously applied, could not fail to cleanse the body politic.

During the debate, it had been well observed by the worthy member from Lunenburg, that the injustice of France might be considered as the *root* of these measures, and that it was not easy to discuss the latter, without reference to the former. This remark was certainly true, and must have been felt by every gentleman engaged in the discussion. In case of an invasion, a measure dependent only on its practicability, of which practicability our venomous and insatiable foe was the sole judge, what keen and operative aid might not be afforded by the numerous aliens, long fostered by American hospitality, and anxious for an opportunity to display their ingratitude, if we might be permitted to form an opinion of their future conduct by the zeal with which they laboured to expel from the breasts of our citizens all respect for religion and government; preparing, as far as was in their power, the American people for the reaction of the French and Saint Domingo tragedies.

Ought not then Congress to have taken measures to rid their country of such eventual misery? It was their first duty so to do; and supineness on their parts would have been criminal.

But it seems that aliens have rights under our Constitution. It was wonderfully kind, he said, in our fathers to devote their time and money to the care of the Turk, Gaul, and Indian, when the proper object was that of their children. This spurious doctrine, however confidently asserted, was not credited by the gentlemen themselves. They might impose on others, but the discernment of their own minds forbade success in imposing on themselves. An alien would claim no right in this country, unless he could show a treaty for it; excepting his participation in the usual rights of citizens, which he held upon courtesy, and which courtesy could be withdrawn at the pleasure of the sovereign power. Be done then, he said, with all these pretences. They were groundless, and seized only to excite more and more the begun ferment.

The sedition-law, General *Lee* said, was also declared to be a violation of the Constitution. Let us, said he, examine it. Let us refer to the clause in the Constitution securing the freedom of the press, which we are told by the above law is abridged. By the law you must conspire to oppose a measure of government; or utter, write, or publish, with the intention of opposing, or exciting opposition to government. The publication must also be false, malicious, and scandalous.

General *Lee* then asked, if government was worth preserving? If not, let it be annulled. If it was, deny not to it, he said, the means of preserving itself. The Constitution must be very defective, if it held not the power of self-preservation. It was not defective; and a fair construction of it would warrant the sedition-law. Government with us depended for its existence upon the affections of the people. In its preservation the people were interested. Any attempt, by the publication of falsehood to discredit government, and thereby to impair the public confidence in it, was an offence against the people; it was wrong in morality, and ought to be punished. What honest man would complain of a law, which forbids the propagation of malice, slander, and falsehood? What good citizen would not delight in a law, which, while it punishes the above vices, tends to perpetuate the government of his choice? And yet a law of that sort, he said, afforded a fertile topic of abuse and misrepresentation.

General *Lee* then observed that, " thou shalt not lie," was one of the ten commandments : it was one of the injunctions of the sedition-law. Whoever considered the freedom of speech abridged by the divine law? No man unless lunatic ; nor could the freedom of the press be so deemed, without a misconstruction of the Constitution, or of the sedition-law.

This state, he said, had from the Revolution enacted laws of the same sort. In 1776, a committee was appointed for the revision of our laws. Messrs. *Pendleton, Wythe, Jefferson, Mason* and *Lee,* composed the committee ; able, honourable, and eminent citizens. Among their proposed bills, was to be found one on the subject of libels. A reference to this bill would show its minute resemblance to the sedition-law. Authority such as that just quoted, General *Lee* said, could not fail in guarding the committee from accrediting the intemperate censures issued against Congress. He would proceed, he said, to another authority in point of time and subject, though one of the respectable gentlemen just named, and the very one of all others to whom gentlemen on the other side attached most weight. Mr. *Jefferson,* in his correspondence with Mr. *Madison,* respecting the new Constitution, maintains, said General *Lee,* the doctrine we contend for. He (Mr. *Jefferson*) expressly says, that in preventing the abridgment of the freedom of the press, punishment for uttering falsehoods ought not to be inhibited. (3 Jeff. Mem. 25.) The same doctrine is expressed by the same gentleman, in his Notes on Virginia. (Notes on Va., Appendix No. II., p. 233.)

However, General *Lee* said, he would refer to an authority still higher, the General Assembly of this state in 1776. That august body, the champions of American rights, the patriots who composed our state Constitution, passed a law on this subject in the following words : " That, if any person residing, or being within this commonwealth shall, from and after the publication hereof, by any word, open deed, or act, advisedly and willingly, maintain and defend the authority, jurisdiction, or power of the king, or parliament of Great Britain, the person so offending, being legally convicted thereof, shall be punished with fine and imprisonment, to be ascertained by a jury, so that the fine exceed not the sum of twenty thousand pounds, nor the imprisonment the term of five years :" " and that any person who shall maliciously and advisedly endeavour to excite the people to resist the government of this commonwealth as by law established, or persuade them to return to a dependence upon the crown of Great Britain, or who shall maliciously, or advisedly terrify and discourage the people from enlisting into the service of the commonwealth, or dispose them to favour the enemy, every person so offending, and being thereof legally convicted, shall be punished with fine and imprisonment as aforesaid."

These men, General *Lee* said, formed our Constitution, and these men passed the law of which the quotation is an extract. They must have understood their own work; they could not mean to violate the Constitution. The law then was not unconstitutional in their opinions, and yet it must be so, if the doctrine now advanced be accurate.

The Constitutions of the state and of the United States, provide in terms equally strong for the security of the freedom of the press. The law above quoted, passed by the state, and the sedition-law, passed by Congress, were of the same sort in word, spirit, and object. If the first be no violation of the state Constitution, the second could not be deemed a violation of the United States Constitution. Other laws passed by the state, all tending to justify the opinions which he and those who thought with him held, General *Lee* said, might be referred to; especially the law against the divulgers of false news and the law against treason. It had been fully observed by the worthy member from Prince George, that the word " freedom" of the press had a definite meaning; and he had proved incontestably what this technical meaning was, to wit, a freedom from every restraint in printing, but not a freedom from punishment, if the printing was in its tendency injurious to an individual or to the community.

It appeared plainly to his mind then, that the resolutions asserted an untruth, when they charged the two laws with violation of the Constitution. But it seems, he said, that the laws are inexpedient and unwise. Of their expediency and wisdom the people have made Congress the sole judge. They have the best information; their object must be the public good, and it was presumable that the measure was wise and necessary, or their adoption would not have taken place. He would not, he said, examine the question of expediency of the laws, but would examine the expediency of the resolutions. Admitting for a moment, that the laws were unconstitutional, he contended that the course pursued by the resolutions was inadmissible. Prudence frowned on the indecorum and hostility which their face showed, nor was it to be presumed that contumely to the sovereignty of the Union was the likeliest way to obtain a repeal of the laws. The very reverse must happen. Why, then, recur to such an expedient, if the object of repeal be the real object? He hoped that he should be pardoned, he said, when he suspected that repeal of the laws was not the leading point in view. Promotion of disunion and separation of the states, struck him as objects which the resolutions covered. What evils so great could befall the American people? Every measure squinting at such disasters ought to be spurned with zeal. Let us, then, said he, put our veto on the resolutions. Was an individual, he observed, to apply to his friend for redress of some supposed injury, the application would be conveyed in terms polite and friendly. So ought it to be when a state applied to the United States. But why not wait for the operation of the constitutional checks? The united system was made by the whole people, for the management of all affairs national. The same people instituted state governments, for the management of all state affairs. These systems held concurring jurisdiction over some subjects, and of course might occasionally interfere. Who, then, was the proper arbiter between them? Not the state government: the people had given them no such power. The people themselves, the creators of both systems, were the proper judges. Their decision was obtainable under the rules of the Constitution in the revolving elections. The judiciary also was a source of correction of legislative evil; a source fixed by the Constitution, and adequate to cure violations of the same like those now alleged. The state legislatures might also act, but it must be by proposing amendments to the Constitution in either way therein delineated.

If then the laws were deemed unconstitutional, let the question, he said, be left to the people, to the judges: or let the legislature come forward with a proposition for amending the doubtful parts of the Constitution; or with a respectful and friendly memorial, urging Congress to repeal the laws. Thus would our union be strengthened, our friendship perpetuated.

The state judges, he said, had on many occasions interposed when this legislature had passed laws unconstitutional. The remedy had cured the disorder, and tranquillity remained undisturbed. So would the federal judges. They were as respectable, as trustworthy as were the state judges; in them as much confidence ought to be reposed. For his part, he said, he felt as much confidence; nor could he admit the force of those distinctions which gentlemen laboured to establish, tending to discriminate in favour of state judges and state officers. They were all citizens alike, bound to do their duty; clothed with the authority of the people, and directed by the will of the people. Whether called state or federal judges, sheriff or marshal, was a light and unimportant circumstance.

The resolutions, General *Lee* said, struck him as recommending resistance. They declared the laws null and void. Our citizens thus thinking, would disobey the laws. This disobedience would be patronised by the state, and could not be submitted to by the United States. Insurrection would be the consequence. We have had one insurrection lately, and that without the patronage of the legislature. How much more likely might an insurrection happen, which seemed to be advised by the Assembly? The scene in Pennsylvania turned out to be a comedy: the same attempt here, he feared, would issue in tragedy. ·Let us, said he, avoid these numerous ills. All the states are interested in our decision, both as to their reputation and tranquillity. He requested gentlemen then to be temperate, to reject the proffered paper, and adopt some other course.

Division among ourselves at this time, he said, encouraged invasion. He could not bring himself to believe that gentlemen meant to invite the enemy to our country. He could not attribute to gentlemen such motives. But what signified the goodness of their intentions, if their measures produced the effect?

General *Lee* then concluded by entreating gentlemen to pause. Take this one rash step, said he, and you will be carried step by step till you land in misery, or submit quietly with derision settled upon your heads. Should my efforts, Mr. Chairman, be unavailing, I shall lament my country's fate, and acquiesce in my country's will; and amidst the surrounding calamities, derive some consolation from recollecting my humble exertions to stop the mad career.

Mr. CURETON said, that there had been silence in the committee for some time; and if no other gentleman was disposed to speak, he hoped the question would then be put. The debate had engaged their attention for several days past, and he expected that every member of the committee had made up his mind upon the question.

Mr. *John Taylor's* resolutions were read by the clerk.

Mr. PETER JOHNSTON then arose, and acknowledged his incompetency to throw any light upon the subject, but hoped to be indulged with a few observations in answer to the gentleman from Westmoreland. He had contended that the states were not parties to the compact, but the people. Mr. *Johnston* denied the position, and said that every fact in the history of the government would contradict it. If the confederation was formed by states, the states alone possessed the power of dissolving it. And when it was found incompetent, the *states*, and not the people, directed a convention to frame the Constitution. When that was framed, their power was at an end. The members of it, it was true, were the representatives of the mass of the people of America. But, when the system was framed, it was submitted to the conventions of the people of the several states. If those conventions then assembled under the auspices of the legislatures of the different states, the states were parties. Should the words, " we the people," then change the nature of the compact, contrary to the historical facts of the day? He thought not.

Mr. *Johnston* then cited the fourth section of the fourth article of the Constitution, which declares, " that the United States shall guarantee to every state in this Union a republican form of government, &c." Also the fifth article, which declares, that " the Congress, whenever two-thirds of both houses shall deem it necessary, shall propose amendments to this Constitution, or on the application of the *legislatures* of two-thirds of the several states, shall call a convention for proposing amendments, which in either case shall be valid to all intents and purposes, as part of this Constitution, when ratified by the legislatures of three-fourths of the several states, or by conventions of three-fourths thereof, as the one or the other mode of ratification may be proposed by the Congress, &c." From these clauses, he conceived, an irrefragable argument was deducible in favour of his idea. It had been said, however, that from the expression *conventions* in this article, the states were not parties. Mr. *Johnston* contended that they were, as the other expressions in this article were as strongly in favour of the states being parties, as the word *conventions* could be in favour of the people being parties. The truth was, that both the states and the people were parties.

He then made several observations in answer to General *Lee's* argument upon the matter of compromise between the states. This gentleman, too, he said, had asserted that the alien-law extended to prevent offences, and not to punish them. This Mr. *Johnston* denied, and proceeded to point out the real case of the alien under the law of Congress. He understood the law was designed for alien-friends. There was also an alien-enemy law; and if the former related to alien-enemies, it would have had reference to the latter. But it was general; it related therefore to both. He mentioned the argument of General *Lee* respecting the entry of aliens into a country, but observed that this point had been before spoken to.

Mr. *Johnston* also referred to the remarks of Mr. *George K. Taylor* upon the rights of aliens, and contended that an alien was entitled to justice. If so, he was entitled to the means of obtaining justice, to which a fair trial was indispensable, but was deprived of it by this law. It was in vain to say that the President would not abuse the power. If it was not warrantable by the Constitution, it was still objectionable. It had been said, too, that citizens might live in peace notwithstanding the law. That neither, was any argument if the law was unconstitutional. The gentleman from Westmoreland had placed a particular construction on the word *persons*. In doing that, the gentleman should have recollected the case of a certain description of persons excluded by the laws of this state from entering the same. The same gentleman had read extracts too from the sedition-law, to show that there must be *intent* and *purpose*, in order to bring men within the law. Mr. *Johnston* asked how intent and purpose were to be made out but by words? To illustrate which he mentioned Lyon's case; and then asked how an intent could be proved, but by deductions from words? Was that any security? An evil intent might be deduced from words, by which none was ever designed. He mentioned as an instance, the story lately circulated amongst them respecting Mr. Tazewell, our senator. It would be, moreover, in the power of the tools of government to place a construction on words which might destroy the person speaking them. The gentleman from Westmoreland had also read extracts from the law of the state respecting aliens, and insisted that Congress had the same right as the state to pass such a law. This Mr. *Johnston* denied, and contended that the states in that respect had sovereign power, and that Congress had no such power, but a defined and limited power only. To prove which he read the first clause of the ninth section of the first article, in the following words: "The migration or importation of such persons as any of the states now existing, shall think proper to admit, shall not be prohibited prior to the year 1808, &c.;" and then asked, if any law having that effect, had been passed before the adoption of the Constitution? There had not; therefore such clause was inserted. Mr. *Jefferson's* letter too, had been produced, but was that to be quoted to govern the committee on the occasion? The Constitution should be their guide. And even Mr. *Jefferson's* letter, as it was stated, did not extend to the business in question; it related only to private regulations.

Mr. *Johnston* then proceeded to consider the consequences of the sedition-law; and among others, conceived that the public opinion, heretofore found so useful, would be repressed, would be punished by it. Was that the liberty which was guaranteed by the Constitution? No; it was a shameful attack upon both. All the gentlemen who had spoken upon this question, (except the gentleman from Caroline,) instead of arguing the constitutional point, had addressed themselves to the passions. He then asked what would be the consequence if responsibility was taken from public servants? The style of the resolutions too had been complained of. But whether the laws were said by the committee to be null and void, or not, was a matter, he thought, of little consequence. For if they were unconstitutional, they, of course, were null and void. He justified the mode of communication which the resolutions proposed. The people might petition if they thought proper. But the state, when addressing its own servants, ought to act as the resolutions proposed. It had a right to instruct its senators, and the people their representatives. However, Mr. *Johnston* said, as the subject was exhausted, he would be satisfied with the remarks he had made.

Mr. CURETON arose next, and proceeded to deliver his opinion in respect to the powers of the general government and the state governments. How were their powers derived? From the people. The convention that framed the Constitution was called by the states. The Constitution when framed was submitted to the people, who, by convention, ratified it. He asked what would be the consequence of an opinion that the states had the balance of power alone? What was it? One-sixteenth part only. He considered that the people had powers; and contended that they had the only right to act upon the sedition law. And if Congress had usurped a power, which should appear to be an innovation on their rights, they would have the power in March next to make an example of those who had trampled on those rights; and this mode of proceeding was consistent with the Constitution. He then asked why did the resolutions embrace both laws? He also made several observations respecting the power of passing such a law as the alien-law. He agreed with the gentleman from Lunenburg, that the power properly belonged to Congress; and asked how could aliens dangerous to the country be sent out of it, if the power was not vested in the President.

Mr. *Cureton* then proceeded to answer the objections of gentlemen in respect to the corruption of the officers of the general government; and hoped that they should be confined to the constitutionality of the laws: but he still contended that the people had the only right to act upon the sedition-law. The states never had the power alone; therefore it could not be reserved. It belonged to Congress, who were under the correction of the people only. As far as the resolutions related to the alien-law, he had no objection, he said, to do what was proper: for instance, if it should appear that the law was an infringement on the state government, to recommend it to our senators in Congress to endeavour to have the same repealed; for that was sanctioned by precedent. But the plan of the resolutions, Mr. *Cureton* said, was a new one. He looked upon it as an innovation on the rights of the people, and stabbing fundamental principles. He concluded by hoping, therefore, that the resolutions would not be agreed to.

Mr. JOHN TAYLOR arose next, and observed that though it was late, and the debates had been protracted to great length, he hoped the importance of the subject would be considered as a justification for his replying to the extraordinary and dangerous arguments which had been urged in opposition to the resolutions he had introduced.

A member of Lunenberg had even asserted them to be an act of perfidiousness to the people; because, by undertaking to declare one law of
Congress unconstitutional, the legislature would assume a power of declaring all their laws unconstitutional. Let the proposition then be reversed, to discover if there be perfidiousness in the case, the side to which
it attached. Would it be said, that the Legislature could not declare this
law of Congress unconstitutional, because it could declare no law of Congress unconstitutional? · Admitting such a position, did not these consequences evidently follow, that the check meditated against Congress in the
existence of the state governments, was demolished; that Congress
might at its pleasure violate the constitutional rights of these governments;
that they must instantly become dependent, and be finally annihilated.
Could it be perfidious to preserve the freedom of religion, of speech, of the
press, and even the right of petitioning for a redress of grievances? Gentlemen, in defining the laws of Congress, had taken their stand upon this
broad principle, namely, "That every government inherently possesses
the powers necessary for its own preservation." Apply this principle to
the state governments: for, if it be a sound one, they are equally entitled
to the benefit of it, with the general government. Under this principle
then, to which his adversary had resorted, and which he therefore could
not deny, it followed that the state governments have a right to withstand
such unconstitutional laws of Congress, as may tend to their destruction,
because such "a power is necessary for their preservation." To illustrate
this, suppose Congress should be of opinion, that an arrangement of men
into different ranks would tend to the order of society, and should, as pre-
paratory to this end, intermeddle with inheritances, and re-establish primogeniture. It could be only urged against such a law, that it was unconstitutional; but if the state could not declare any law of Congress
unconstitutional and void, even such an one as this must be submitted to,
and of course all powers whatsoever would gradually be absorbed by, and
consolidated in, the general government.

He observed, that the right of the state to contest the constitutionality
of a law of Congress could, however, be defended upon better ground, than
by the reaction of the doctrines of gentlemen on themselves. That a
principle literally constitutional, theoretically sound, and practically useful,
could be advanced, on which to rest it. It was this: the people and the
states could only have intended to invest Congress with a power to legislate constitutionally, and the Constitution expressly retains to the people
and the states, every power not surrendered. If therefore Congress
should, as was certainly possible, legislate unconstitutionally, it was evident that in theory they have done wrong, and it only remained to consider whether the Constitution is so defective as to have established limitations and reservations, without the means of enforcing them, in a mode, by
which they could be made practically useful. Suppose a clashing of
opinion should exist between Congress and the states, respecting the true
limits of their constitutional territories, it was easy to see, that if the right
of decision had been vested in either party, that party, deciding in the
spirit and interest of party, would inevitably have swallowed up the other.
The Constitution must not only have foreseen the possibility of such a

clashing, but also the consequence of a preference on either side as to its construction. And out of this foresight must have arisen the fifth article, by which two-thirds of Congress may call upon the states for an explanation of any such controversy as the present, by way of amendment to the Constitution; and thus correct an erroneous construction of its own acts, by a minority of the states; whilst two-thirds of the states are also allowed to compel Congress to call a Convention, in case so many should think an amendment necessary for the purpose of checking the unconstitutional acts of that body. Thus, so far as Congress may have the power, it might exert it to check the usurpations of a state, and so far as the states may possess it, an union of two-thirds in one opinion might effectually check the usurpations of Congress. And, under this article of the Constitution, the incontrovertible principle before stated, might become practically useful; otherwise no remedy did exist for the only case which could possibly destroy the Constitution, namely, an encroachment by Congress, or the states, upon the rights of the other. The case was even strongest in favour of a check in the hands of the states upon Congress: for although Congress could never alter or amend the Constitution, without the concurrence of three-fourths of the states; yet such a concurrence would be able so to alter or amend it, as to check the encroachments of Congress, although the whole of that body should disagree thereto. The reason for this will exhibit the unconstitutionality of the argument, which supposes, that the states hold their constitutional rights by the courtesy of Congress. It was this: Congress is the creature of the states and of the people; but neither the states nor the people are the creatures of Congress. It would be evidently absurd, that the creature should exclusively construe the instrument of its own existence; and therefore this construction was reserved indiscriminately to one or the other of those powers, of which Congress was the joint work; namely, to the people, whenever a convention was resorted to, or to the states, whenever the operation should be carried on by three-fourths.

Mr. *Taylor* then proceeded to apply these observations to the threats of war, and the apprehension of civil commotion, towards which the resolutions were said to have a tendency. Are the republicans, said he, possessed of fleets and armies? If not, to what could they appeal for defence and support? To nothing, except public opinion. If that should be against them, they must yield; if for them, did gentlemen mean to say, that public will should be assailed by force? If so, should a minority, by the help of the powers of government, resort to force for its defence against public opinion; and against a state which was pursuing the only possible and ordinary mode of ascertaining the opinion of two-thirds of the states, by declaring its own, and asking theirs? How could the fifth article of the Constitution be brought into practical use, even upon the most flagrant usurpations? War or insurrection, therefore, could not happen, except Congress should attempt to control public opinion by force; and this it could not be supposed they would ever do, not only because the will of the people is the sovereign in all republics; but also, because both that will and the will of the states, were made the constitutional referee in the case under consideration. Hence a movement towards this referee could

8

never be admitted as leading to war or commotion, except in those countries where an armed and corrupt minority· had usurped the government,
and would of course behold with abhorrence an arbitrament of a majority.
Such, however, he hoped would be the respect to public opinion, that he
doubted not but that the two reprobated laws would be sacrificed, to quiet
the apprehensions even of a single state, without the necessity of a convention, or a mandate from three-fourths of the states, whenever it shall be
admitted, that the quiet and happiness of the people is the true end and
design of government.

With respect, he said, to the remedy proposed in the talents and integrity
of the continental judges, without regarding the prejudices which might
probably exist in favour of the government, from which an appointment
should flow, it might be remarked, that the judges by the Constitution are
not made its exclusive guardians. That if continental judges were the
proper referees as to the constitutionality of continental laws, state judges
were the proper referees as to the constitutionality of state laws; that
neither possessed a power over the other, whence a clashing of adjudica-
tion might ensue; and that if either had been *superior*, the same consequences would result as would flow from a superiority of Congress, or of
the states over the other, with this additional aggravation; that the people
could not by their elections influence a constitutional question, to be decided
by the judges, as they could to a certain extent, when it was to be decided
by a general or state legislature: an influence, however, insufficient; because it would require six years to change the Senate of the United
States, and four that of Virginia, during which an unconstitutional law
would have done its mischief, which was yet greatly preferable to no
influence at all.

He observed, that the resolutions had been objected to as being couched
in language too strong and offensive, whilst it had also been said on the
same side, that if the laws were unconstitutional, the people ought to fly to
arms, and resist them. To this he replied that he was not surprised to
hear the enemies of the resolutions recommending measures which were
either feeble or rash. Timidity, it was known, only served to invite a
repetition of injury, whilst an unconstitutional resort to arms would not
only justly exasperate all good men, but invite those who differed from
the friends to the resolutions to the same appeal, and produce a civil war.
Hence those who wished to preserve the peace, as well as the Constitution,
had rejected both alternatives, and chosen the middle way. They had
uttered what they conceived to be truth, in firm yet decent language; and
they had pursued a system which was only an appeal to public opinion,
because that appeal was warranted by the Constitution, and by principle;
and because it gave an opportunity to the general government to discover
whether they would be faithful to the same principle, and thereby establish
a precedent, which would both now and hereafter have a strong tendency
against civil war. That this firmness, which was both exhibited and felt,
was really necessary as an act of friendship to the general government, if it
was true, as some thought, and as the commotion in the public mind
plainly indicated, that a farther progress in their system was full of danger
to itself, and misery to the people. If, said he, we beheld our *friend*

already advanced to the brink of a precipice without having discovered it, ought we in friendship slightly to admonish him that the very next step might precipitate him into an abyss below, or strenuously to warn him of his danger? Again: If a country was to be defended, into which the foe could only enter at a single pass, which was fortified and garrisoned, ought the resistance of this garrison to be feeble and cowardly, and ought they traitorously to surrender this key into their country, from a confidence in the enemy? Liberty was that country—our Constitution the fortress —and ourselves the garrison. Shall we, he said, desert our post without even a parley with the assailants? If we did, the inevitable consequence must be a consolidation of these states into one great sovereignty, which will, from its vast extent, as inevitably settle with rapidity into a monarchy, and like all other great empires it must resort to those oppressions to support itself, which make the cup of life bitter to man. That such a degree of timidity would be as dishonourable as the violent measures which gentlemen on the other side recommended in cases of constitutional infractions, would be immoral and unconstitutional.

That firmness as well as moderation could only produce a desirable coincidence between the states, an example of which having been already set by Kentucky, it behooved us so to act as to avoid a difference of opinion as to the mode, when we united in the end ; because divisions respecting either would undoubtedly destroy every hope of a successful issue. In opposition to the propriety of soliciting this coincidence, the Constitution, prohibiting the states from entering into a confederation among themselves, had been quoted. In reply to which he would ask, if an application from one state to another to learn its sentiments upon a point relative to the Constitution, was to be considered as unconstitutional, as amounting to a confederation? In what way could two-thirds of the states consult or unite, so as to exercise their right of calling a convention under the fifth article, or in what way could three-fourths ever amend the Constitution? This observation evinced the incorrectness of such a construction, as had also the practice of the states, in submitting each other's resolutions to mutual consideration, in a variety of instances.

Mr. *Taylor* then said that the constitutionality of the laws had been defended by the common law. It had been said that the common law attaches the rights arising from the law of nations to a sovereignty wherever it resides: that therefore a power over aliens devolved under the common law upon Congress, and that sedition being also a common law offence, they had a right to punish it. If the common law bestowed powers upon Congress, it was unnecessary to controvert these laws, because there was hardly any species of oppression which it would not justify. Heresy and witchcraft were common law offences ; the former was a complete engine for tyranny. But the Constitution of the Union did nowhere adopt the common law, or refer to it as a rule of construction. That as the state constitutions or laws had done so under different forms, it evinced that the states must have considered an adoption necessary to give it force, and thinking so, it was impossible that the state conventions which assented to the Constitution, could ever have supposed that they were establishing a government which could at pleasure dip their hands into the inexhaustible treasuries of the common law and law of nations, and thence extract as much power as they pleased. On the contrary, the Constitution of the Union does in its face plainly erect a government of powers expressed and limited, and not left to be new-modelled at random, or by ambition, by a reference to obsolete or little known codes of law, which had never been taken into contemplation during its discussion in any state convention.

Having now gotten rid of objections rather collateral, Mr. *Taylor* said that he would come to those which more immediately referred to the objectionable laws. It had been said that aliens had no rights: that if they had, such rights were only held by the law of nations, which allows them to be removed whenever their residence is thought dangerous by the sovereignty; and assuming it as granted that the sovereignty of America is in Congress, it was therefore concluded that the law was constitutional.

In reply to this argument, he observed, that Congress only possessed a special and limited sovereignty, to be exercised in a special and limited manner, so as not to conflict with that portion of sovereignty retained to the several states, and so as not to violate those constitutional principles prescribed for the preservation of liberty. That aliens, under the law of nations, were entitled and subjected to the sanctions of municipal law; and however their rights as foreigners may be unimportant to us as natives, yet it was of vast importance that the fundamental principles of our municipal law should not be destroyed, because an alien only was the present victim, since it established precedents, and produced consequences, which would wound citizens through the sides of aliens. To apply this general remark, he said, the Constitution was a sacred portion of municipal law. It had empowered Congress "to define and punish offences against the law of nations," and it had declared, "that the judicial power shall extend to all cases in law and equity arising under this Constitution, or the laws of the United States; and that the trial of all crimes shall be by jury." The law of nations was therefore in contemplation whilst defining the judiciary power. If an alien has done wrong, must it not be a *case in law or equity, or a crime?* At any rate, must it not be a *case arising under the Constitution, or the laws of the Union?* If so, his punishment, supposing the act criminal, is to be inflicted by a jury: if not criminal, it is yet referred to the judiciary, by the comprehensive terms "all cases." Might not precedents then, violating these essential principles of our municipal law, be dangerous to citizens, when it was recollected that no difference is contemplated by the law of nations, or that municipal law, between aliens and citizens touching these rights, during the residence of the former. Again: were not the checks contemplated by the Constitution weakened by making a President in fact a king of the aliens? Our towns will abound with men whose every interest depends upon executive pleasure. Might they not be used to influence elections? And what would prohibit their being forced into the volunteer corps, then to be armed and officered by the executive? Here then, except for the virtues of a temporary chief magistrate, was a mode struck out, by which a large force might be embodied and armed, possessing no rights, and completely dependent on the will of one man. Was this to adjust the balances? Or did it comport with the principles of republicanism? If not, in this mode also might citizens be wounded through the sides of aliens.

A gentleman from Prince George, he said, had urged, that except for this law, the state of Virginia might admit a French army with Bonaparte at their head. Of this, he said, there would certainly be as little danger, as that under it a President should admit an English army. Because, although it was obvious no nation would call in a foreign force to destroy itself, yet history was not deficient in cases wherein individuals have resorted to a foreign force to enslave the nation. That he meant not to insinuate anything to the injury of the present President; but by retorting the argument, to show its weakness, by exhibiting the difference between suffering the residence of foreigners to depend upon the national legislatures, and surrendering it as a great prerogative, to one man.

It had been argued too, that the power given to Congress to protect each state against invasion, comprised a power of expelling dangerous incendiary aliens; for that Congress ought to be enabled to nip dangerous designs in the bud.

If power could be gotten by inferences as loose as these, all attempts to limit it might be relinquished. Dangerous designs ought to be nipt in the bud. Was it the danger to which the power attached, and not the alienage? If so, dangerous incendiary citizens might also be nipt in the bud without trial, and exported at executive will. The protection of a state against invasion, is imposed upon Congress as a duty, secondary only to the guarantee of a republican form of government, and not bestowed upon them as an enlargement of power; and the reason of it is, that the states are prohibited from keeping troops or ships of war in time of peace, which prohibition does not extend to the Union. Greatly as this argument had been relied on, the propriety of this construction was evinced by two observations; one, that the states might as far as they could protect themselves against invasion, and even raise troops in time of war, proving that this was a duty imposed upon Congress, and not an executive power. The other, that it is also made the duty of Congress to protect the states against domestic violence, *but only on application of the state legislature or executive.* The jealousy evidently exhibited here against the interposition of Congress, even in cases of actual domestic violence, by no means warrants the supposition, that they might interpose where apprehensions of danger only existed. Further, if Congress obtained the power constructively from that of repelling invasions, there was nothing to limit its exercise to aliens. Again, and again, the committee were told of the common law and the sovereignty of Congress. An attempt to excite an insurrection had been called an offence at common law; and a power to regulate all cases arising under the law of nations, it was said, follows sovereignty. Thus every power was bestowed arising from these copious sources. He asked, by what part of the Constitution Congress were empowered to punish all common law offences, and whether that barbarous, feudal, gothic and bloody criminal code was to be let loose upon us by inference and implication? Domestic violence, said he, is insurrection. Why was Congress specially directed how to act in this common law offence, if they had an unlimited power to punish all common law offences? As to these rights of sovereignty, it was fair reasoning to urge, that a particular donation of a part excluded the idea of a donation'of the whole by way of inference. If this splendid thing called sovereignty had invested Congress with all the powers arising from the law of nations, why was it necessary particularly to invest Congress with the power of punishing offences against the law of nations? And if Congress, under this sovereignty, derived to themselves an unlimited power over aliens, how could it have been necessary to bestow upon Congress the special power of naturalizing these very aliens? This doctrine of the rights of sovereignty was as dangerous as false. Dangerous, because its extent could be never foreseen : false, as violating the idea of limiting a government by constitutional rules. From this unlimited source, the British Parliament derives its claim of unlimited power. King, lords and commons, because sovereign, may do everything. If it was. admitted here, being in fact a common law doctrine, it not only would absorb the common law powers, and those arising from the laws of nations, but also the royal prerogatives, and whatever else it bestows upon the British Parliament. Such a sovereignty would speedily swallow up the state governments, consolidate the Union, and terminate in monarchy.

Mr. *Taylor* said, that the laws objected to had been largely defended within and without doors, upon the ground of laws with similar provisions having been passed in this state.

Without stopping, he said, to point out the strong distinguishing features between the state laws and those of Congress, it would suffice to show the inefficacy of the argument upon other grounds. The powers surrendered to Congress and reserved to the states, are by the Constitution evidently designed to be defined, and whether successfully or not, it was yet impossible to deny the intention of that instrument to concede certain powers to the one, and to reserve certain other.powers to the other. If then it was a sound argument to assert, that Congress may legislate upon a subject because a state has already done so ; that is, that the exercise of the reservation by a state shall enlarge the concession in favour of Congress, it followed that the reservation so soon as it was used was lost, and that even the limitations upon congressional power ought to be understood as only designed to extend it. Further, perhaps no state constitution in America exhibits that clear and explicit restraint upon a legislative interposition respecting the freedom of religion, the press, and petitioning, which was to be found among the amendments of the general Constitution. Was it defensible then to assert that Congress, though opposed by this positive constitutional barrier, were yet empowered to legislate co-extensively upon these subjects with a particular state having no such obstruction to surmount.

He said that this extravagant and unjustifiable mode of construing the Constitution had even been carried so far as to quote Blackstone, and a private letter of Mr. *Jefferson* ; so that if this instrument was to be expounded, not by itself, but by the law of nations, the common law of England, the laws of the several states, the opinions of English judges, and the private letters of individuals, it had only launched us upon the ocean of uncertainty, instead of having conducted us into a safe and quiet

harbour.   That Blackstone's definition of the liberty of the press, considered as accurate by the gentleman on the other side, amounted to this:
" the right of publishing anything not prohibited by law without the necessity of obtaining a *previous license.*"   He wholly quibbles away the liberty
of the press, in the whim of considering the necessity of a license as the
only mode of destroying it, whilst he also admits that government may
prohibit it from printing whatever it pleases.   Was it not obvious that the
end meditated by the liberty of the press, can as effectually be defeated in
one mode as the other, and that if a government can by law garble, suppress and advance political opinion, public information, this great end,
upon which public liberty depends, will be completely destroyed.   According to this construction, the Constitution of America has only declared
that Congress shall not intercept writings by a previous examination, and
allowance or rejection; but that they may make whatever writings they
please illegal and penal in any extent.   Read, said he, the Constitution,
and consider if this was all it meant to secure.

   Mr. *Jefferson's* letter, he said, was written before the amendment to the
Constitution which it recommended: but upon which it could not of course
be a comment; and therefore this letter, if it had lent any aid to the gentlemen on the other side, would be more than balanced by that sublime
and just construction of the Constitution itself, as to the liberty of the
press, to be found in the negotiations of the late envoys to France.   But
this letter, as well as plain legal principles, had been egregiously misunderstood, and both upon examination, would be found to support the argument against the laws.   The letter, whilst recommending those securities,
for which the amendment to the Constitution was afterwards designed,
urges as an argument, that all were legally answerable for *false facts published injuring others.*   This is the letter, and this the legal principle upon
which a common action of slander was grounded: and laws reaching this
evil, existed before the sedition-act, in every part of the Union.   By a
small but important deviation both from the letter and the law, a great
and dangerous delusion was resorted to by the gentlemen on the other
side.   Falsehood, said they, is punishable by law, and Mr. *Jefferson* admits that it ought to be so; and the sedition-law punishing falsehood only,
both the laws and Mr. *Jefferson* have united in its approbation previous to
its existence.   The great error in this doctrine arose from dropping the
word " fact," and taking that of " falsehood," which includes " opinion,"
as well as fact.   Fact was capable of proof, opinion was not.   To say
that such laws as the alien and sedition existed, would be to assert a fact,
and if he (Mr. *Taylor*) was prosecuted for it, it might be proved.   But to
assert that these laws were unconstitutional and oppressive, and productive of monarchy, would be an opinion, constituting a degree of criminality
under the sedition-law, subjecting a man to punishment, and yet it was
not a fact capable of being proved.   Hence, therefore, the laws of the
land, and Mr. *Jefferson's* letter, unite in confining punishment to the publication of false facts, and hence opinions were only made punishable in
tyrannical governments; because there was no standard to determine the
truth or falsehood of opinion.

   But he said, it had been violently objected that, supposing these laws are unconstitutional, the state legislature could have nothing to do with the subject; because the people alone are parties to the compact, called the Constitution of the United States.

To this objection he answered, that although the framers of the Constitution chose to use the style, "we, the people," yet it was notorious, that in every step, from its commencement to its termination, the sense of the people respecting it, appeared through the medium of some representative State Assembly, either legislative or constituent. That the Constitution itself, in many parts, recognises the states as parties to the contract, particularly in the great articles of its amendment, and that of admitting new states into the Union without a reference to the people; and that even the government of the Union was kept in motion as to one House of the legislature, by the act of the state sovereignties. That added to these incontestable arguments to show that the states are parties to the compact, the reservation of powers not given, was to the states as well as to the people, recognising the states as a contracting party, to whom rights were expressly reserved. From all which it followed, though it be not denied that the people are to be considered as parties to the contract, that the states are parties also, and as parties, were justifiable in preserving their rights under the compact against violation; otherwise their existence was at an end; for, if their legislative proceedings could be regulated by congressional sedition-laws, their independency, and of course their existence, were gone. And although it had been within and without doors often asserted, that the sedition-act does not extend to words spoken, yet if any gentleman would read the first section, and consider the terms " counsel or advise," he would find that *words* are clearly within its letter, and that this part of the law seems particularly adapted for a deliberative assembly. He said he could not but observe, that this doctrine, that the people are to be considered as the only parties to the compact, was incomplete. The idea of a person's contracting with himself was absurd. Where was the other party? He feared, though it was not avowed, that the gentlemen were glancing towards the old doctrine of a compact between government and people; a doctrine which effectually destroyed the supremacy of the people and the independence of government, no less than the monstrous doctrine of allegiance and protection, which falsely supposes, that the people are indebted to the government for safety, whereas it is they who erect, support, and protect the government. That it was also curious to observe, that gentlemen allow the state governments to have been proper organs of the will of the people, whilst binding them by the measures leading to the Constitution, and that they still allow these organs to be capable of expressing their will in the election of senators, and doing any other acts for the execution of the Constitution, whilst they deny that they are any organs of public will, for the sake of opposing an infringement of the same Constitution. Thus, in framing it, and in executing it, in a great variety of ways, the will of the people was allowed to express itself through this medium; but in saving it from violation, it shall be closed up against them; so that there shall be as few obstacles as possible against this violation. The people may petition Congress, said gentlemen, against the violation, and this was the only proper remedy. Let us, said Mr. *Taylor*, apply this remedy to another case. Suppose a state should, by law, violate the Constitution. Would there be no other remedy, but for the people to petition that state, or for the judges of that state to decide upon the constitionality of the law? Why would there be another remedy? Because the Constitution, having bestowed rights upon the general government, a violation of the Constitution which should infringe those rights, would justify that government to take measures for its own preservation; because the Constitution does not leave the remedy to depend upon a petition of the people to the aggressor. Reverse the case, said he. If Congress should unconstitutionally infringe rights reserved to the state governments, should they depend upon a petition of the people to the aggressor for their defence? They were then conducted, he said, to this clear position, that as Congress holds the rights bestowed by the Constitution under that, and independent of the states; so the states hold the rights reserved by the Constitution under that, and independent of Congress; and of course that each power possesses the further right of defending those constitutional rights against the aggressions of the other; for otherwise it would follow, that the power having constitutional rights, to maintain which was however unconstitutional, must presently disappear.

He said, that the last argument in favour of the sedition-act had been drawn from the law of Virginia respecting treason, which had been read. With respect to this law, he replied, that the same arguments applied, which he had before used, to show the impropriety of quoting state laws, to justify congressional. It would be as just to say, that a state could pass laws for raising fleets and armies, because Congress had done so, as that Congress could infringe the liberty of speech, because the states had done so. The states are expressly forbid to do the one, and Congress the other. But this reference to the treason law of Virginia furnished a strong argument to prove the unconstitutionality of the sedition-act. The law evidently considers sedition as being one species constituting that genus called treason, which was made up of many parts. It therefore accurately expresses the idea of Virginia of the word "*treason*," and shows how she understood it, as used in the Constitution. By that, treason is limited to two items, with the punishment of which only, the general government is entrusted. Hence it was evident, that Virginia could not have conceived that Congress could proceed constitutionally to that species of treason called sedition; and if this was not the true construction, what security was derived from the restriction in the Constitution relative to treason? Congress might designate the acts there specified by that term, and they might apply other terms to all other acts, from correcting which, that clause of the Constitution intended to prohibit them; by doing which, as in the case of sedition, they might go on to erect a code of laws to punish acts heretofore called treasonable, under other names, by fine, confiscation, banishment or imprisonment, until social intercourse shall be hunted by informers out of our country; and yet all might be said to be constitutionally done, if principles could be evaded by words.

Mr. *Taylor* concluded with observing that the will of the people was better expressed through organized bodies dependent on that will, than by tumultuous meetings; that thus the preservation of peace and good order

would be more secure; that the states, however, were clearly parties to
the Constitution, as political bodies; that rights were reserved to them,
which reservation included a power of preservation; that the legislature
of the state was under a double obligation to oppose infractions of the
Constitution, as servants of the people, and also as the guardian of those
rights of sovereignty, and that qualified independence reserved to the state
governments by the Constitution; and to act up to this duty was the only
possible mode of sustaining the fabric of American policy, according to
the principles prescribed by the American Constitution.

Mr. BAYLEY arose next to reply, he said, to the very extraordinary
arguments which had fallen from the gentleman from Caroline, and was
proceeding to do so; but finding that such a noise prevailed, from the im-
patience of the committee to rise, that he could not be distinctly heard, he
declined, and sat down.

On motion, the committee then rose, the chairman reported progress,
asked, and had leave for the committee to sit again.

IN THE HOUSE OF DELEGATES,

Friday, December 21, 1798.

The House resolved itself into a committee of the whole House, on the
state of the commonwealth, Mr. *Breckenridge* in the chair, when Mr.
John Taylor's resolutions being still under consideration,

Mr. GEORGE K. TAYLOR arose, and said that when these resolutions
were first submitted to the committee, they had been disapproved by him;
and that the time which had since elapsed, with the most mature reflection,
had quickened his disapprobation into complete aversion and entire disgust.
The resolutions contained doctrines and principles the most extravagant
and pernicious; declarations unsubstantiated by fact; and an invitation to
other states to concur in a breach of that Constitution which they professed
to support. To substantiate this charge, he would beg the pardon and
patience of the committee, while he examined and criticised certain parts
of the resolutions, and while, agreeably to a promise given on a former
occasion, he should offer some few remarks on the constitutionality of what
is called the sedition-law.

The third clause of the resolutions begins in the following terms:
"That this Assembly doth explicitly and peremptorily declare that it
views the powers of the Federal Government as resulting from the compact to which the states *alone* are parties." This-declaration, however
explicitly and peremptorily made, was unfounded and false: the *states* are
not the *only* parties to the federal compact. Considered as particular
sovereignties of detached parts of the Union, they did not give it birth
or organization: the state legislatures were not consulted respecting its

adoption. It was the creature of the *people* of United America; their voice spoke it into birth; their will upholds and supports it. To demonstrate this it would be necessary to recur to the history of the present Constitution, and to examine some of its features.

When the British colonies in America, now the United States, dissolved their connexion with the parent country and declared themselves independent, they entered into certain articles of confederation and union. This was an act of the *states*. It was begun by the state representatives in Congress. The articles of confederation, when digested, were sent to the *legislatures* of every state for consideration. They were ratified by the *legislature* of each state in the Union. They profess themselves to be articles of confederation and perpetual union between the *states*: they relate; in every article, not to the *people*, but to the *states*: they were submitted to, and adopted by, not the people, but the states; and of them it may truly be said that they were "a compact to which the states alone were parties."

As these articles of confederation acted exclusively on the states, and as they prescribed no method of compelling delinquent states to obey the requisitions of Congress, their weakness and inefficacy became shortly visible. The most pressing demands were disregarded, or partially obeyed; and the evils and expenses of war were thus protracted and increased. Still, however, the American spirit and love of freedom rose superior to every difficulty, and obtained, after an arduous struggle, peace and independence. No sooner was the danger removed which had hitherto compelled some respect to the recommendations of Congress, than the impotence of that body became conspicuous, and the futility of that plan of government which possesses no sanction to enforce obedience to its laws was demonstrated. In defence of our liberties a considerable debt had been incurred. Justice and policy called on the United States to pay the interest of this debt, if they could not discharge the principal; but they called in vain. Congress indeed recommended that a duty of five per cent. ad valorem, should for this purpose be laid on all goods imported into the United States; but their recommendation was disregarded. The certificate given to the soldier for his toil and blood in the day of battle, depreciated and became worthless; every public contract was uncomplied with; a total disregard prevailed as to national sentiment and honour; symptoms of distrust, jealousy, and rivalship among the several states appeared. The Union seemed fast crumbling into annihilation, and the national character at home and abroad was sunk and degraded. The people of America began to be sensible of their situation. Delegates were at first sent from a few of the states to Annapolis, for the purpose of devising and recommending commercial arrangements. These delegates recommended that a convention from the several states should be appointed for the purpose of revising and amending the articles of confederation. Their idea was adopted. Each state appointed delegates to this convention, and it assembled at Philadelphia, for the purpose of *proposing amendments to the articles of confederation.*

The deliberation of a few days convinced the convention that an amendment of that instrument was impracticable, and that no government could

be efficient or permanent which operated not on the individuals of the community, but altogether on the state, sovereignties, and which could not
compel obedience to its laws by the punishment of the disobedient and refractory.   They adopted, therefore, a plan at once bold and judicious. It
was to recommend a new form of government for, general purposes, by
taking from the states the control of all matters relating to the general
welfare, and vesting these in the government of the Union : by dividing
this government into legislative, executive, and judiciary departments,
which should at once prescribe and enforce the rules of general conduct,
without the aid or intervention of the state legislatures, and which should
have power to punish the disobedient and refractory.

Here it was to be observed, he said, that the convention acted without
the express authority of the state legislatures.   They were deputed to
amend the *old articles of confederation :* they were not authorized to propose new forms of government.   Their love of country, indeed, induced
them to attempt a scheme or project of government to be submitted to
their fellow-citizens, and their wisdom enabled them to accomplish its
structure.   But the *state governments* were no parties to this project, since
they deputed the authors of it for different purposes, and were ignorant of
the change about to be recommended.

That the convention itself did not consider that the states were, or would
be the only parties to this compact, was evident from the language used
in the commencement of the new Constitution : " We the *people* of the
United States, in order to form a more perfect union, &c. ;" not " we the
states of New Hampshire, &c. ;" yet they had the old articles of confederation before them, where the states were constantly mentioned, and the
people not once named.   Why was the word " states" purposely discarded,
and the word " people" purposely introduced, if, as these resolutions declare, the states alone are parties to the compact ?

The convention, after having finished the Constitution, came to the following resolutions :

" *Resolved,* That the preceding Constitution be laid before the United
States in Congress assembled, and that it is the opinion of this convention
that it should afterwards be submitted to a convention of delegates chosen
in each state by the people thereof, under the recommendation of its legislature, for their assent and ratification ; and that each convention assenting
to and ratifying the same, should give notice thereof to the United States
in Congress assembled.

" *Resolved,* That it is the opinion of this convention, that as soon as
the conventions of nine states shall have ratified this Constitution, the United States in Congress assembled, should fix a day on which electors
should be appointed," &c.

The former articles of confederation being in truth a compact *of the
states,* were submitted to the state legislatures.   The Constitution of the
United States was " submitted to a convention of delegates chosen in each
state *by the people* thereof."   The articles of confederation were assented
to and ratified by the *state legislatures.*   The Constitution of the United
States was assented to and ratified by conventions chosen in each state *by
the people* thereof.   If the *states* in their political corporate capacity, be as

the resolutions declare, the only parties to the latter compact, why was its consideration submitted not to the *state legislatures*, but to the *people* of the United States, in their several conventions?

Again : so soon as the conventions of nine states should have ratified the Constitution, the convention recommended that a day should be fixed for the appointment of electors, &c., in order that the government should be put into operation. Why should the commencement of the operations of the government be postponed until the conventions of nine states should have ratified the Constitution? Because the states were extremely unequal in size and population, and consequently a majority of *conventions* might have ratified the Constitution, when in truth a majority of the *whole people* had rejected it: but this could not be the case when the conventions of nine states had ratified it; because any nine states formed a majority of the *people* contained in the thirteen. Did not this circumstance then prove, that the present is a government proceeding from the *people*, and that they are material, if not the exclusive original parties to it? If so, how could it be said that the states alone are parties to the compact?

Further : the fifth article to the Constitution declares that " the Congress, whenever two-thirds of both Houses shall deem it necessary, shall propose amendments to this Constitution, or on the applications of the legislatures of two-thirds of the several states, shall call a convention for proposing amendments." In each of these modes of obtaining amendments, the *people* are evidently recognised as parties to the compact :—" Congress, whenever two-thirds of both Houses shall deem it necessary, shall propose amendments :" but one House of Congress, the House of Representatives, is the immediate representative of the *people*, the other House, the Senate, is the immediate representative of the *states ;* whenever then, two-thirds of the representatives of the *people* and two-thirds of the representatives of the *states* shall concur in deeming it necessary, they may propose amendments. Was not this a recognition that the people generally, as well as the particular state sovereignties, are interested in the operations of the government? How then could the *states alone* be said to be the parties to it? "Or, on the applications of the legislatures of two-thirds of the several states, shall call a convention for proposing amendments." Here the idea was still supported, that the representatives of a majority of the *whole people* must combine in the application, which majority it is supposable, will be two-thirds of the *states.* The article proceeds " which (amendments) in either case shall be valid to all intents and purposes, as part of this Constitution, when ratified by the *legislatures* of three-fourths of the several *states*, or by *conventions* in three-fourths thereof, as the one or the other mode of ratification may be proposed by the Congress." Thus Congress might if they should think proper, divest the *states* in their political corporate character, of all agency in ratifying amendments by submitting them not to the *legislatures of the states*, but to *conventions of the people.* Did this prove that the states alone are parties to this compact?

At the time of our separation from the government of Great Britain, the people of each state in the Union, represented in convention, established for that *state*, a constitution or form of government. This having been established by the immediate representatives of the people, deputed

for that particular and especial purpose, is not amendable or alterable except by the same people or their representatives, deputed for that special
purpose; yet the second clause of the sixth article of the Federal Constitution, is in the following words: "This Constitution and the laws of the
United States, which shall be made in pursuance thereof, and all treaties
made, or which shall be made under the authority of the United States,
shall be the supreme law of the land, and the judges in every state shall
be bound thereby, *anything in the constitution* or laws of any state to
the contrary notwithstanding." By this clause, the Constitution, laws
and treaties of the United States, are declared to be paramount and
superior to the *constitution* and laws of every particular state; and
where they may come into collision, the latter must yield to the former.
Who could have deprived the state constitutions of their former supremacy,
and made them subservient not only to the Constitution, but to constitutional laws and treaties of the United States, except the *sovereign people*,
the source and fountain of all power? And after this should we be told
that the *states alone* are parties to the compact, when so plain and palpable a proof was exhibited to the contrary?*

Let those, said Mr. *Taylor*, who charge us with anti-republican sentiments, and with political blindness or heresy, examine this part of their
own creed, and declare whether it savours of republicanism or orthodoxy?
We have long and fondly cherished the idea, that all government in
America was the work and creature of the *people;* we have regarded
them with reverence and bowed down before their supremacy. But it was
reserved for this period and for this Legislature to convince us of our
error, and to prove that in America, as in Turkey and in France, the
people are nothing, and that the *state legislatures* are everything.

The fourth clause of the resolutions is in the following words: "That
the General Assembly doth express its deep regret, that a spirit has in
sundry instances been manifested by the Federal Government to *enlarge*
its powers by *forced constructions* of the constitutional charter which defines them; and that indications have appeared of a *design* to expound
certain general phrases, (which having been copied from the very limited
grant of powers in the former articles of confederation, were the less
liable to be misconstrued,) so as to *destroy* the meaning and effect of the
particular enumeration, which necessarily explains and limits the general
phrases, and so as to *consolidate the states* by degrees, into one sovereignty,
the obvious tendency and inevitable result of which would be to transform
the present republican system of the United States into an *absolute*, or at
best, *a mixed monarchy*."

The charge against the Federal Government, contained in this clause,
Mr. *Taylor* said, was of the most serious nature, and merited mature deliberation before it should be adopted. If it be true, that government was
criminal, indeed, and merited, not reprehension only, but the severest
chastisement; if it be true, the present administrators of that government
should be hurled from their seats with universal execration, and submitted
to the vengeance of a justly enraged people. If it be true, it was our duty

---

* The answer to this ingenious train of reasoning is given in the *Report, post*, p. 191.

to advise, and it was the duty of our constituents to practise opposition and resistance ; to draw the sword from the " sleep of its scabbard," and to cut out this foul cancer before its roots shall have taken too fatal a spread. But, was it true? If it be, in what instance was it so? The resolutions declared, that " a spirit to *enlarge* its powers, and to CONSOLI- DATE THE STATES, so as to introduce MONARCHY, has been manifested by the general government in sundry instances." What were those instances? Would it not have been kind and proper to enumerate them, when it was to enlighten the blindness of those less keen-sighted than our legislative illuminati? For we, said he, who approve not these resolutions, discern not in the government these " forced constructions of the constitutional charter ;" those " designs to consolidate the states by degrees into one sovereignty ;" those unconstitutional efforts " to enlarge its powers so as to transform the present republican system into an absolute, or at best, a mixed monarchy." On the contrary, said he, we suppose that we see the best form of government ever devised by human sagacity, wisely adminis- tered, so as to promote and increase the general prosperity and happiness of the people. We ask, where is there seen so much real happiness, prosperity, and liberty as in these United States? We demand, whether the sun, from his rising in the morning, until his setting beams are quenched in the west, beholds so fortunate a people? Why, then, should we interrupt their repose, disturb their harmony, and poison their tran- quillity, by unfounded suggestions, that their government means to rivet monarchy upon them? The " sundry instances" of this intention, men- tioned during this debate, were a fleet, an army, taxes, the alien and sedi- tion-laws. What causes have given birth to these measures? A precon- certed plan of the government to introduce monarchy? No! They derive their origin from a more noble source; from a determination to reject, with disdain, the insolent demand of tribute to a foreign nation ; from a proper care to protect our commerce from the piratical depredations of that nation, and from a fixed resolve to vindicate our soil from hostile in- vasion. Let us, I pray you, said he, recollect the history of late events. Has not our government sent repeated embassies to France, and have not those embassies been repeatedly and contumeliously rejected? Was not General Pinckney threatened with imprisonment? Were not the three envoys insulted with a demand that their country should become tributary to France? and was not that country threatened with the fate of Venice if the demands should be refused? Was there a man among us who could bear the idea of paying tribute to any foreign country? And when the consequence of the refusal, has been aggravated depredations on our trade, and the threat of erasing us from the list of nations, was there one so base who would not prepare for defence? What was the situation of things when our small navy was first equipped? Numbers of French picaroons at the mouths of all our principal rivers, lay in wait for our ships, and few of them escaped. What, said he, has been the consequence since that navy has been equipped? These pirates have been chased to their homes ; our coasts are no longer insulted ; the price of the produc- tions of our soil has increased, and our flag floats on the ocean, respecta- ble and respected. Was not this measure more wise, more patriotic, and more economical than to have permitted our trade still to be the prey of French cruisers, and to have suffered a vital wound to be inflicted on the industry and happiness of our citizens, from the diminished value of their commodities, which would have been the unavoidable result? Will not, said he, this navy enable us, in case of invasion, to transport men and the munitions of war immediately and expeditiously from one port to another of the Union? Will it not be able to gall and distress an invading enemy? Why, then, shall so wise and so necessary a measure be construed into an effort to crush republicanism and establish monarchy on its ruins?

But the regular army which is to be raised will be the death of our liberty. Standing armies in all countries have been the engines of despotism, and they will become so in this.

Fortunately there are two clauses in the Constitution of the United States, which prove that so long as the representatives of the people remain uncorrupt, no great danger can be apprehended from standing armies. The first clause of the seventh section of the first article declares, that " all bills for raising revenue shall originate in the House of Representatives." The twelfth clause of the eighth section of the same article gives Congress power to " raise and support armies," but declares, " that no appropriation of money for that use shall be for a longer term than two years." It is Congress, and not the President, who are to " raise and support armies." Armies cannot be raised and supported without revenue. The bills for raising this revenue must originate in the House of Representatives. Appropriations of money to raise and support an army, shall not be for a longer term than two years. The House of Representatives itself is elected for two years only. After a first, or at most a second appropriation for this purpose, a new election of representatives must take place. If the new House of Representatives deem the army useless or dangerous, they will refuse to appropriate for its support, and it must be disbanded. Thus the danger to be apprehended from an army raised *for an indefinite period* appears not to be great. But the present army, from the terms of its enlistment, was to continue in service only during the existing differences with France. After they shall cease it will be disbanded, and while they continue it must be necessary. For let it be remembered that our foe possesses a lust of dominion insatiable ; armies numerous and well-disciplined, inured to conquest and flushed with victory, officers alert and skilful, commanders distinguished and renowned. Let it be remembered that she is as destitute of friends as of principle, and that as she has sent one army under Bonaparte to pillage the East, as a compensation for their services she may send another for the same purposes to rifle the West. Against this host of invaders, hungry as death and insatiable as the grave, shall we oppose only militia? In such a conflict what would be our chance? A band of militia ill-armed and completely undisciplined, to measure weapons with men inured to blood, and with whom murder is a science! How long would our militia be able to remain in the field? Each man among them would at first be hurried from his plough, and from the embraces of his wife and children, with scarcely a moment's warning. That wife and those children would soon require his return, or the farm would remain uncultivated, and distress and misery would be their portion. The first detachment of militia must then within three or four months be relieved by another. At the moment when they have formed an idea of the first rudiments of war, they would be succeeded by others completely new and undisciplined. Was an army thus composed, likely to prove effectual in resisting the invasion of veterans inured to combat and accustomed to victory? Did the experience of the late war with Great Britain demonstrate the superlative efficacy of militia? Why were the Southern States plundered, ravaged, and for a time subdued by Cornwallis? Because he was opposed principally by militia, whose want of skill could not resist the British bayonet. Was the patriotism of the men of 1776 to be now disputed? It could not be ; yet they had recourse to regular soldiers, by whom the great and important victories of America were obtained, and who, when peace was re-established, although unpaid and distressed, returned peaceably to their homes and their firesides. Of whom was that army composed? Of our fathers and our brethren. Of whom will the present army be composed? Of our brethren and our sons. Who led that army to battle and to conquest? Washington. Who will conduct this? The same great and good Washington. Will he whose virtue and honour have been proved in the most trying seasons; whose fame has never been surpassed in the annals of mankind, and who is the constant theme of applause and admiration throughout the globe, in his latter days prove so degenerate as to become the tool of ambition and the destroyer of liberty? Of that liberty which his exertions established, and of that Constitution which he contributed to frame, to organize, and to administer? The idea was too absurd to be seriously entertained, and therefore this part of the subject, he said, he would dismiss with the following observation :—A regular army was principally composed of men who, having from choice embraced the military profession, did not by their absence materially impede the labour of the society, or occasion domestic difficulties and distress : of militia, a great proportion were fathers of families, whose absence from their homes was extremely inconvenient and ruinous. The death of the regular soldier was of little comparative importance—the death of the militiaman, who leaves behind him a wife and family of young children, was a serious evil. The regular army was prompt, skilful, and effectual ; the militia army must always be languid in its operations, undisciplined, and ineffectual. Instead, then, of aiming at monarchy, our government labours, by the establishment of this army, to secure success to our efforts for freedom, and to spare a lavish and ruinous waste of the blood of our citizens.

Taxes, he said, are the necessary result of warlike preparations. These we have been compelled to adopt, by the insolence, the machinations, and the hostilities of France. They are the present price of our independence : and where the stake is so precious, no real American could begrudge them.

In the fifth clause of the resolutions, " the General Assembly doth particularly protest against the palpable and alarming infractions of the Constitution, in the two late cases of the alien and sedition-acts passed at the last session of Congress."

On the subject of the alien-law, Mr. *Taylor* observed, that he had before given his ideas at large, and should at present only repeat that from the authorities adduced by him on a former occasion, and from the reason of the thing, it appeared that the entry of an alien into any country was matter of favour in the sovereign power of that country, and not matter of right on the part of the alien. During his stay, the country to which he has migrated affords him hospitality and protection: during the same period, he owes respect and obedience to its laws. But the country exacts from him no allegiance: he is not bound to fight the battles of that country: he is exempt from serving in the militia: he is not subject to the taxes that have only a relation to the citizens: he retains all his original privileges in the country which gave him birth: the state in which he resides has no right over his person, except when he is guilty of crime: he is not obliged like the citizens, to submit to all the commands of the sovereign: but, if such things are required from him as he is not willing to perform, he may at will quit the country. The government has no right to detain him except for a time, and for very particular reasons. The writers on the law of nations therefore universally agree that the nation has a right to send him away whenever his stay becomes inconvenient or dangerous to its repose.

The Constitution of the United States, from its preamble, and from every article and section of the instrument, demonstrates that it was the intention and design of its framers to vest every power relating to the general welfare and tranquillity of the Union in the General Government. Each particular case could not be foreseen; and therefore the powers are given in general terms, and conclude with the particular power "to make all laws which shall be necessary and proper for carrying into execution the foregoing powers, and all other powers vested by the Constitution in the Government of the United States, or in any department or officer thereof." With this palpable intention of its framers in our view, we ought to give to the instrument a liberal as well as candid interpretation. If the General Government possesses not the power of removing dangerous aliens, but that power is vested exclusively in the particular states, one of the principal views of the old confederation would remain in all its vigour. While through the instrumentality of these characters insurrection and treason are maturing into birth, the Government will of itself be unable to avert the mischief, and must humbly supplicate sixteen independent and jealous sovereignties to carry its designs for the public safety into effect. It must disclose to each state the most important and delicate secrets, as that state will require testimony before it begins to act. It may in repeated instances be subjected to the mortification and danger of a refusal, and the alien might frequently depart from one state willing to exclude him, and take refuge in another determined to protect him. Thus the peace and safety of the Union might at all times be endangered; and the same government which can declare war against the foreign nation, shall not before that event takes place, be able to exclude from its soil the most dangerous and abandoned subject of that nation, although his residence may be the bane of public tranquillity.

Congress has power "to provide for calling forth the militia, to execute the laws of the Union, suppress insurrections, and repel invasions." When the insurrection or invasion *has taken place,* Congress may by the militia suppress the one, and repel the other. But the Constitution declares further, that "the United States shall guarantee to every state in this Union a republican form of government, and shall *protect* each of them against invasion; and on application of the legislature, or of the executive, (when the legislature cannot be convened,) against domestic violence." The power before recited had given Congress power to call forth the militia to *suppress* insurrections, and *repel* invasions. The section last mentioned directs them to *protect* each state against invasion and domestic violence. Are these two clauses of precisely the same meaning and import? Then the framers of the Constitution were guilty of tautology. But they are not of the same import. The first gives the power of suppressing insurrections, and repelling invasions, when insurrections or invasions *should exist :* the latter directs Congress to *protect* each state against invasions or domestic violence, which might *threaten and impend.* Protection necessarily implies and includes the *prevention* of mischief and danger. In protecting the states then against invasion, Congress must use the means of *preventing* the evil; and the clause before recited gives them in express terms the power to make all laws necessary and proper for carrying into execution any power vested in them by the Constitution. Congress then foresaw, from the dispute existing between the United States and France, that war might be the probable result, and that invasion might be the consequence of war. To protect the states against this invasion, a proper measure appeared to be the exclusion of dangerous aliens. They were vested by the Constitution with power to pass all laws necessary and proper to *protect* the states against invasion, and they therefore constitutionally passed the alien-law.

But against this construction of the Constitution, Mr. *Taylor* said, a gentleman from Orange had given the committee an extract from Publius, of which it could only be said, that the doctrine contained therein, although unquestionably sound and incontrovertible, did not apply to the present question. To prove this, let the extract itself, he said, be read again. It is in the following words : " It has been urged and echoed that the power to lay and collect taxes, duties, imposts and excises, to pay the debts, and provide for the common defence and general welfare of the United States, amounts to an unlimited commission to exercise every power which may be alleged to be necessary for the common defence or general welfare." No stronger proof could have been given of the distress under which these writers labour for objections, than their stooping to such a misconstruction.

Had no other enumeration or definition of the powers of the Congress been found in the Constitution, than the general expressions just cited, the authors of the objection might have had some colour for it; though it would have been difficult to find a reason for so awkward a form of describing an authority to legislate in all possible cases. A power to destroy the freedom of the press, the trial by jury, or even to regulate the course of descents, or the forms of conveyances, must be very singularly expressed by the terms " to raise money for the general welfare." Publius afterwards proceeds to state other arguments exposing the fallacy of the opinion urged by the opposers of the Constitution against this article. But let it be remembered that the subject which Publius was discussing was this, whether the power given Congress " to lay and collect taxes, duties, imposts, and excises, to pay the debts, and provide for the common defence and general welfare," gave to Congress a right of legislating on every subject whatsoever. Now, who among us, said Mr. *Taylor*, has cited this clause in favour of the alien-law? Has any one of us, continued he, contended that Congress possesses the right of legislating on every subject? And because this clause does not give them such a power, did it follow that the power to protect the states from invasion does not authorize them, on the prospect of war, to exclude dangerous aliens? Some authority more applicable must be produced before we shall be proved to be in the wrong. In defence of the alien-law, Mr. *Taylor* observed, that he would make no further observations, but would call the attention of the committee for a few minutes, to what is called the sedition-law. In his remarks on this, from the wide range he had taken, he should be compelled to be much more concise than he had intended to be.

He presumed that it would be conceded by all who heard him, that each individual possessed from nature certain rights of great value and importance. Among these was the right to liberty and to life; and, what was of no smaller importance than the other two, the right to his good name and reputation. For even in a state of nature, where the will of each individual was his law, and his power the measure of that law, and where consequently eternal strife and confusion must prevail, a good name would be of no small importance to its possessor. He, who when chance or misfortune had thrown his brother savage into his power, did not rob or abuse him, but bound up his wounds and dismissed him in peace, would be respected by the man he had benefited, and by all others who should hear of the circumstance, and would in consequence be in some degree secure against insult and attack. But in a state of society the possession of reputation must for obvious causes be of infinite importance. This state was the result of a compact formed by the component individuals for the enjoyment of their natural rights to greater advantage and with greater certainty. Each owes to the regulations of the society implicit obedience; and the society is equally bound to guarantee and to vindicate to each, his natural and social rights. Invasions therefore, against property, liberty, or life, have been punished in every society and under every form of government; but the natural right to reputation is as dear and invaluable to its possessor as any other whatsoever; it is essential to his comfort and happiness; he could never be supposed to have consented to its surrender; and invasions of it ought, therefore, to be punished by the society as well as invasions of property, liberty, or life. For no possession whatsoever is of such real value as an honest fame: in comparison with it, the possession of property is of little consequence. Property, in reality, adds nothing to the respectability of its possessor. When lost it may be regained; or if for ever lost, its former owner may still be respectable. But the loss of reputation is a much more serious mischief. It is irretrievable. Who could bear to be regarded by his fellow-citizens as destitute of principle and honour, and to be viewed by the world with contempt and detestation ? Who would be unaffected at being deprived by the stroke of calumny of the friend he loved ? Whose feelings would remain untortured, when the mistress he adored, whose smiles were those of affection, and whose eyes proclaimed the dominion of love, should be everlastingly estranged from him ? When that bosom which before glowed with genial and sympathetic fires, should, touched by the breath of calumny, become cold and icy as the everlasting snows that envelope the pole ? Such were the mischiefs accruing from the loss of reputation to the individual in his private capa. city. But suppose him possessed of those virtues which dignify human exis- tence, and of those talents which adorn it, and wishing to exert those virtues and those talents in a public capacity for the benefit of his fellow-citizens ; if his reputation be blasted, or his character tainted, he would be spurned by those citizens from their presence : his talents would render him an ob- ject of greater odium : he would remain hated and despised through life, and execrated even after his death. Was the loss of property then to be compared with this injury ? Nay, was not the loss of character equal or superior in mischief to the loss of existence ? The murdered man dies an object of universal sympathy and regret,—the recollection of his virtues is cherished, and his foibles and vices are excused or forgotten. But the man whose reputation is tainted, lives an object of universal contempt and disgust, and dies the theme of infamy and execration. Accordingly in every society, and throughout all time, a remedy has been afforded to the injured individual for calumnious attacks upon his reputation. And what would be the consequence of impunity to such an offence ? The injured man, having no redress from the laws of his country, would arrogate to himself the right of revenge, and a mournful scene of assault, bloodshed and death, would be the unavoidable and melancholy result. These things could not be tolerated in a state of society ; and accordingly slander and libels are punished with us by the common law. By the common law is understood the unwritten law of nature and reason, applying to the com- mon sense of every individual, and adopted by long and universal consent. This common law attaches itself to every government which the people may establish. It existed in Great Britain when our ancestors migrated from that country, and it followed them to this. It prevailed in every state throughout the Union, before their separation from the British empire, and it regulates the whole American people now. A government, then, established by that people for the general safety and general happiness, will of necessity be guided in cases of general interest and concern, by the principles and regulations of the same common law. By that common law, unfounded calumny of magistrates generally, was matter of punish- ment, of a more severe punishment than in cases affecting the reputation of private individuals, because in the former instance the *function* rather than the *man* was the object of attack. And whenever magistrates of a new description are appointed, the old principles of the common law im- mediately apply to them, and calumnies against them are of course punish- able. Thus when these states became independent of Great Britain, a number of officers of government were created unknown to the former co- lonial establishments ; but no one had ever thought it necessary to declare by statute, that slanders of them shall be punishable. When the Constitution of the United States was formed, a new description of officers, before unknown, was created: the common law pervaded and regulated every portion of the people which formed that Constitution; and consequently the rules of the common law immediately attached themselves to those officers. Consequently slanders of the President of the United States, of members of Congress, and of other officers of the general government, are punishable by the common law; because slanders of those characters are injuries not so much to the man, as to the community. Ours is a government which must rest for its support on the public sentiment. While the people approve it, it will flourish; when they withdraw their affections, it must expire. Unfounded calumnies against the officers of government, who administer and conduct it, tend to weaken the confidence and affection of the people for the government itself. The Constitution of the United States, it is acknowledged by all, authorizes the government to punish acts of resistance to its measures. Would it not be strange, if, when it authorizes them to punish acts of resistance, it should prevent them from punishing acts tending to introduce resistance? That the government must look on tame and passive while the mischief is preparing, and be incapable of action until that mischief has ripened into effect, when its actions and operations may perhaps be unavailing. That it shall be fully able to suppress and punish actual insurrection, but shall be incapable of preventing it. This would surely be absurd. And as the Constitution of the United States is the work of the whole American people; as every man of that people is regulated by the common law; as that common law attaches itself to the state governments, established by that people, and punished unfounded calumnies of state magistrates, why shall it be said not to attach itself to the government of the whole American people? And why shall it not punish unfounded calumnies of the magistrates of the general government? Why is the state magistrate protected by the common law? Because he is a public functionary, and calumnies of him injure the public. Was not a magistrate of the general government also a public functionary? Would not calumnies against him also injure the public? And if the functionary *of the part* be protected by law, how shall it be said that the functionary *of the whole* is left unprotected? Surely reason proclaims, that in proportion to the magnitude of the trust reposed in the functionary, would be the mischief arising from false, scandalous, and malicious representations of his conduct. The most unfounded calumnies against the governor of a particular state could only rouse the discontent, or excite the opposition of that state. But unfounded calumnies against the President of the United States, may paralyse, convulse, and destroy the Union. The reason of the common law applies, therefore, more powerfully to the magistrate of the general government than to the magistrate of the state government. But this is the general feature of that law, and of reason, that the person being a magistrate of whatever grade or description, and being vested with the authority of the laws, ought to be protected.

That the principles of the common law apply to the general government, is obvious from the second section of the third article of the Constitution, which declares, that " the judicial powers shall extend to all cases in law and equity, arising under this Constitution, the laws of the United States, and treaties made, or which shall be made under their authority," and "to controversies to which the United States shall be party." The judiciary, in cases arising under the laws of the United States, will be regulated by those laws : and in cases arising under treaties, by those treaties and the law of nations ; but what cases can arise under the Constitution, as distinguished from cases arising under the laws of the United States and under treaties, except cases to be decided by the rules and principles of the common law? And these in "controversies to which the United States shall be party," will, unless altered or modified by law, operate in their full extent.

This is not the only instance in which the common law is recognised in the Constitution ; for the ninth amendment is in these words: "in suits at *common law*, where the value in controversy shall exceed twenty dollars, the right of trial by jury shall be preserved; and no fact tried by a jury shall be otherwise re-examined in any court of the United States, than according to the rules of the *common law*." When in the re-examination of facts tried by a jury, the courts of the United States are expressly prohibited from observing any other than the rules of the common law, the Constitution itself declares, that the common law applies to those courts ; and if it applies in one instance, it must apply in all others coming within their sphere, unless where it is altered by act of Congress.

The common law has been thus shown to apply to the government of the United States as well as to the governments of the particular states and to particular individuals. One rule of the common law is, "that he who writes, utters or publishes a false, scandalous, and malicious libel against a magistrate or the government, shall be punished by fine and imprisonment." The writer, utterer or publisher, therefore, of a false, scandalous and malicious libel against the government of the United States, or any magistrate thereof, is at common law, punishable by fine and imprisonment.

The objection to the punishment of libels, that truth is the sufficient antagonist of error, and needs no assistance, Mr. *Taylor* said, was not correct: that falsehood was light and volatile; she flew on the wings of the wind, she spread her mischiefs with inconceivable velocity : that truth was the child of experience, and the companion of time; she scarcely ever outstripped, and rarely kept pace with her companion. What mischief in all ages and in all countries have been occasioned to individuals, and to the public, by malignant falsehoods, before truth could arrive to detect and protect them. How would these mischiefs be aggravated, if they should remain unpunished by the laws? The fairest reputation, when frequently assailed, must be diminished in the public esteem. Each scandalous report finds some believers; and at length the most charitable will be disposed to think that such repeated charges could not be made without some foundation. They will increase in proportion to the talents and the station of the injured individual, and unless they be punished by the laws, the most splendid abilities, and unsullied virtues, must cease to be useful, and sink into disgrace.

Mr. *Taylor* said, from what had been said, it would appear that the right to punish libels against governments, or their officers, is founded in the principles of nature, of reason, and of common law. The act of Congress on this subject, said he, punishes nothing before unpunishable: it creates no new crime: it inflicts no new punishment: but on the contrary, it mollifies and alleviates the rigours of the common law; for at common law, the amount of the fine, and the time of imprisonment, are unlimited, and regulated only by the discretion of the court trying the offence: by the act in question, the fine is limited at the utmost to two thousand dollars, and the imprisonment to two years.

But the opposers of this law assert, that however the principles of the common law may apply to the government of the United States, in ordinary cases, and whatever might have been their original power to punish libels, this power is now taken away by the third amendment to the Constitution.

This amendment is in the following words: " Congress shall make no law respecting an establishment of religion, or prohibiting the free exercise thereof, or abridging the freedom of speech, or of the press."

The difference of the terms used in this amendment, Mr. *Taylor* said, was remarkable. " Congress shall make no law *respecting* an establishment of religion, or prohibiting the free exercise thereof."   Consequently, they dare not touch the subject of religion at all.   But further, they " shall make no law *abridging* the freedom of speech, or of the press;" not " *respecting* the freedom of speech, or of the press." When religion is concerned, Congress shall make no law *respecting* the subject: when the freedom of the press is concerned, Congress shall make no law *abridging* its freedom ; but they may make any laws on the subject which do not abridge its freedom.   And in fact, the eighth section of the first article of the Constitution authorizes them in express terms " to promote the progress of science and useful arts, by securing for limited times, to authors and inventors, the exclusive right to their respective writings and discoveries."   Now if Congress could not make any laws *respecting* the freedom of the press, they could not secure for limited times to authors their respective writings, by prohibiting those writings from being published and vended, except by those whom the authors should expressly permit. They may consequently make laws respecting the press, provided they do not *abridge* its freedom.   To *abridge* the freedom of the press, Mr. *Taylor* said, was to impose upon it restraints or prohibitions which it did not experience before; or to increase the penalties attached to former offences accruing from its licentiousness. If then the sedition-law does impose upon the press restraints or prohibitions which it did not experience before that act was passed, or if it increases the penalties attached to former offences arising from its licentiousness, it was conceded to be unconstitutional.

But it had been demonstrated, he said, that the common law embraces and attaches itself to the constitution and government of the United States; and that it punishes with indefinite fine and imprisonment the writing, uttering, or printing false, scandalous, and malicious libels. When the act in question, then, only punishes the same false, scandalous, and malicious writing by fine and imprisonment to a *definite* amount, and for a *definite* period, it does not impose upon the press restraints or prohibitions which it did not experience before, nor does it increase former penalties; it therefore does not *abridge* its freedom, and is consequently constitutional. To suppose that because Congress are prohibited from making laws abridging the freedom of the press, they cannot punish the vile slanders and infamous calumnies which from time to time issue from it, against the government, Mr. *Taylor* said, was to suppose that the people of America had given a solemn and constitutional sanction to vice and immorality; that they had completely privileged the infamous offence of lying; and that every individual had consented, in case of his being employed by the United States, to release the society from the protection and vindication of his natural right to reputation.

The persons who framed the amendments to the Constitution of the United States, were certainly men of distinguished abilities and information. Among them was a great proportion of lawyers, whose peculiar study had been the common law. Perhaps every one of them had read and maturely considered Blackstone's Commentaries; these would inform him, that in England, the terms "freedom of the press," had an appropriate signification, to wit: exemption from previous restraint on all publications whatever, with liability, however, on the part of the publisher, to individuals or the public, for slanders affecting private reputation or the public peace. Certainly every one of them was acquainted with the laws of his own state, where the terms "freedom of the press," had precisely the same meaning as in England. When, then, in the amendments to the Constitution they speak of "the freedom of the press," must it not be presumed they intended to convey that appropriate idea, annexed to the term both in England and in their native states? And a reference to Blackstone will clearly point out, both the emancipation of the press in that country from its former shackles, and the true import and meaning there and here, of the term "freedom of the press." "The art of printing," says that valuable writer, "soon after its introduction, was looked upon (as well in England as in other countries) as merely a matter of state, and subject to the coercion of the crown. It was, therefore, regulated with us by the king's proclamations, prohibitions, charters of privilege and of license, and finally, by the decrees of the Court of Star Chamber, which limited the number of printers, and of presses which each should employ, and prohibited new publications, unless previously approved by proper licensers. On the demolition of this odious jurisdiction, in 1641, the long parliament of Charles I. after their rupture with that prince, assumed the same powers as the Star Chamber exercised with respect to the licensing of books, and in 1643, 1647, 1649 and 1652, issued their ordinances for that purpose, founded principally on the Star Chamber decree of 1637. In 1662, was passed the statute 13 and 14 Car. II. c. 33, which (with some few alterations) was copied from the parliamentary ordinances. This act expired 1679, but was revived by statute 1 Jas. II. c. 17, and continued till 1692. It was then continued for two years longer, by statute 4 W. & M. c. 24; but though frequent attempts were made by the government to revive it in the subsequent part of that reign, yet the parliament resisted it so strongly, that it finally expired, *and the press became properly free* in 1694. and has ever since so continued." The same writer thus elegantly defines the *liberty of the press.* "The liberty of the press is, indeed, essential to the nature of a free state; but this consists in laying no *previous* restraints upon publications, and not in freedom from censure for criminal matter, when published. Every freeman has an undoubted right to lay what sentiments he pleases before the public: to forbid this, is to destroy the *freedom of the press;* but, if he publishes what is improper, mischievous or illegal, he must take the consequence of his own temerity. To subject the press to the restrictive power of a licenser, as was formerly done, both before and since the revolution, is to subject all freedom of sentiment to the prejudices of one man, and make him the arbitrary and infallible judge, of all controverted points in learning, religion, and government. But, to punish (as the law does at present) any dangerous or offensive writings, which, when published, shall, on a fair and impartial trial, be adjudged of a pernicious tendency, is necessary for the preservation of peace and good order, of government and religion, the only solid foundations of civil liberty. Thus the will of individuals is still left free; the abuse only of that free will, is the object of legal punishment. Neither is any restraint hereby laid upon freedom of thought or inquiry; liberty of private sentiment is still left; the disseminating or making public of bad sentiments, destructive of the ends of society, is the crime which society corrects." "A man (says a fine writer on this subject) may be allowed to keep poisons in his closet, but not publicly to vend them as cordials. And to this we may add, that the only plausible argument heretofore used for the restraining the just freedom of the press, 'that it was necessary to prevent the daily abuse of it,' will entirely lose its force, when it is shown (by a seasonable exertion of the laws) that the press cannot be abused to any bad purpose, without incurring a suitable punishment; whereas it never can be used to any good one, when under the control of an inspector. So true will it be found, that to censure the *licentiousness,* is to maintain the *liberty* of the press."

In England, said Mr. *Taylor,* the laying no *previous* restraints upon publications, is *freedom of the press.* In every one of the United States the laying no *previous* restraints upon publications hath always been, and still is deemed the *freedom of the press.* In England, notwithstanding the freedom of the press, the publication of false, scandalous, and malicious writings is punishable by fine and imprisonment. In every one of the United States, notwithstanding the freedom of the press, the publication of false, scandalous, and malicious writings is punishable in the same manner. If the freedom of the press be not therefore abridged in the government of any particular state, by the punishment of false, scandalous, and malicious writings, how could it be said to be abridged when the same punishment is inflicted on the same offence by the government of the whole people?

If it should be thought that this point required further elucidation, let us, said Mr. *Taylor,* look for it in the Constitution of the state of Virginia. It had been said that the general government, being constituted for particular purposes, possesses only such powers as are granted: and this was conceded to be true. It had been also said that the state governments, being constituted for the general regulation of the people in each state, possess all powers which the people have not expressly retained to themselves; and this, for the sake of argument, shall also be granted. Yet it would not be disputed that the powers retained by the people to themselves in their state Constitution, are as sacred and inviolable as those retained by the people to themselves in the Constitution of the United States. Now the people of Virginia, in their state constitution, appear to have been as jealous of this freedom of the press, as were the people of the United States in the formation of the Federal Constitution. For if the Constitution of the United States declares, that Congress shall " make no law abridging the freedom of speech or of the press," the Constitution of Virginia, in the twelfth article of the bill of rights, declares, " that the freedom of the press is one of the great bulwarks of liberty, and can never be restrained but by despotic governments." The legislature of Virginia therefore, Mr. *Taylor* said, could no more pass a law *restraining* the freedom of the press, than Congress could pass a law *abridging* the freedom of the press. The liberty of the press could not be *restrained* without being *abridged.* Yet it had never been doubted that false, scandalous, and malicious writings are punishable in Virginia. In the year 1792 the legislature of this state passed a law " against divulgers of false news," and no one suggested that the liberty of the press was thereby *restrained.* In the same session another act was passed, declaring " that any person who shall, by *writing* or advised speaking, endeavour to instigate the people of this commonwealth to erect or establish any government separate from, or independent of, the government of Virginia, within the limits thereof, without the assent of the legislature of this commonwealth for that purpose first obtained, shall be adjudged guilty of a high crime and misdemeanour, and on conviction, shall be subject to such pains and penalties, not extending to life or member, as the Court before whom the conviction shall be, shall adjudge." Neither was this law deemed unconstitutional. Now if the legislature of Virginia could pass laws punishing divulgers of false news, and writers advising the people to particular detrimental acts, without *restraining* the freedom of the press, could not the legislature of the Union punish false, scandalous, and malicious writings tending to destroy the government, or to bring it into hatred and contempt, without *abridging* the freedom of the press? To say that they could not, was to declare that punishing the *licentiousness*, is abridging the *freedom*, of the press; and that licentiousness and freedom are synonymous terms.

Every man, continued Mr. *Taylor*, has a right to freedom of action; but no one supposed that this bestowed upon him the right to assault another on the highway. Every one has a right to the freedom of the press; but should he use it so as to assault the happiness of an individual or the repose of society, without being liable to punishment for the mischief he had occasioned?

It had been said that false, scandalous, and malicious libels against the government of the United States, or any officer thereof, are punishable in the courts of each state respectively; but this was believed to be incorrect. Libels against state magistrates, or such officers of the general government as reside in Virginia, are punishable in our state courts, because the injured persons reside within the limits of the state, contribute to its support, and are entitled to protection from it : but libels against the magistrates of a foreign nation, or of a sister state, or of the general government, residing out of this state, are not punishable in our courts, because the injured individuals in these cases are not bound by our state laws, do not sustain the burdens, or contribute to the support of the commonwealth; and are consequently not entitled to its protection. But it would not be denied, that an infamous slander of the President of the United States, tending to produce insurrection, was equally mischievous, if published by a citizen of Virginia, as if published by a citizen of Pennsylvania. The courts of the United States, therefore, must take cognizance of the case, or the offence would remain unpunished. Every public incendiary would, by palpable misrepresentations and abominable falsehoods, continually agitate and convulse the minds of the people. That affection towards the government which alone supports it, would shortly be withdrawn, and would speedily fall, to rise no more.

On the sedition-law, Mr. *Taylor* said, he would make no further remarks, but would proceed to other parts of the resolutions.

The seventh resolution is in the words following : " That the good people of this commonwealth having ever felt and continuing to feel the most sincere affection to their brethren of the other states, the truest anxiety for establishing and perpetuating the union of all, and the most scrupulous fidelity to that Constitution which is the pledge of mutual friendship and the instrument of mutual happiness, the General Assembly doth solemnly appeal to the like dispositions of the other states, in confidence that they will concur with this commonwealth in declaring, as it does hereby declare, that the acts aforesaid are *unconstitutional and not law, but utterly null, void, and of no effect,* and that the necessary and proper measures will be taken by each for *co-operating* with this state, in maintaining unimpaired the authorities, rights, and liberties reserved to the states respectively, or to the people."

On this resolution, Mr. *Taylor* said, two remarks would be submitted. The legislature of one state in the Union declares two acts passed by a majority of the representatives of the whole American people, to be *unconstitutional and not law, but utterly null, void, and of no effect.* They declare this, not as an *opinion,* but as a certain and incontrovertible fact; in consequence of which the people of the state owe no submission to the laws. Have, continued he, the representatives of a *part,* a power thus to control and to defeat the acts of the *whole ?* In the Congress of the United States, the people of each state are fairly and equally represented in proportion to the population of that state. If, after a majority in that Congress have decided that certain laws are constitutional and expedient, the legislature of Virginia hath a right to annul those laws by declaring them to be unconstitutional, the old republican maxim that the majority must govern was exploded, and the Union would be dissolved. If the state of Virginia could repeal and annul the alien and sedition-laws, she could repeal and annul any other acts of Congress; and if *she* hath the right, every other state must possess it likewise.

If any act passed by Congress be unconstitutional, the judges of the federal court, who are unbiassed by party, and unwarped by prejudice, and who are selected for their superior talents and integrity, afforded a constitutional check upon the legislature. The people themselves are another most powerful check ; for they will know the vote of their representatives, and if they deem the law for which they voted to be unconstitutional, they will order them to depart at the ensuing election, and replace them with others more wise and more virtuous. Here were two peaceable and happy modes of correcting the mischief: whereas, for one or more jealous state legislatures to endeavour to repel or control the acts of Congress by their sovereign power, was at once to introduce disunion and civil war. The government of the Union, which might have yielded to fair reason and argument, will never give way to the threats or force of these rival sovereignties. If they do, the powers and energies of the Federal Government would be from that moment destroyed. They will determine to try the experiment whether the Union shall govern a few states, or a few states shall rule the Union. The certain consequence will be a resort to arms, civil war, and carnage, and a probable dismemberment of the Union.

Of such consequences, in such an event, the framers of the Constitution were aware. They, therefore, wisely in the tenth section of the first article declared that " no state shall, without the consent of the Congress, enter into any *agreement* or *compact* with another state or with a foreign power." The resolution last cited, however, invited the other states to " take the necessary and proper measures for *co-operating* with this state in maintaining unimpaired the authorities, rights, and liberties reserved to the states respectively, or to the people." Could other states *co-operate* with this for these purposes, unless by virtue of some previous *agreement* or *compact?* To *co-operate*, was to *act in concert*. Must not some agreement or compact among the states precede their acting in concert? It must in the nature of things. Does not the Constitution forbid this agreement or compact in positive and express terms? Were we not, then, inviting our sister states to a deliberate and palpable breach of the Constitution; and this at the moment when we were so liberally reviling Congress for an imputed breach of the same instrument? Did their example authorize us to violate what we had solemnly sworn to support and preserve? Or did an act which was not to be tolerated in the *wicked* Congress, become venial or laudable when committed by the *saints* composing this Assembly?

These resolutions, continued Mr. *Taylor*, must have some ultimate object ; and it had been demanded what that object was? The gentleman from Caroline had answered, that it was ultimately to induce the states to call another general convention for the amendment of the Constitution. How unfortunate and ruinous such an experiment would be, the reflection of a few moments must convince us.

When the circumstances and the time when the convention assembled which formed our present Constitution, and the importance and difficulty of the task which they undertook and executed, were considered, we had ample cause to return our fervent thanks to the Almighty for the issue of their labours. At that time the weakness and inefficacy of the articles of confederation was perceived and acknowledged by us all ; our contracts were undischarged ; our credit was destroyed ; and our character as a nation was contemptible both at home and abroad. All America united in the sentiment that change was essential: all America deputed members to the convention which introduced that change. Foreign nations despised us too much to interfere in the deliberations of that body, or of the state conventions which afterwards adopted the instrument. Even under these circumstances, the harmony with which the plan was recommended, and the unanimity with which it was adopted, were subjects of amazement and wonder.

But what would be the consequence and effect of a convention summoned to amend the Constitution at the present moment? Now, said he, party-spirit unfortunately flames and rages. Some think the Constitution as perfect as it could be made, while others consider it as the harbinger of monarchy, and others again, supposed that the powers of government require an increase of energy and power. A spirit of mutual concession could no longer be expected. The delegates from the northern and southern parts of the Union would behold each other with jealousy and suspicion. They would never unite in the same project. They might agree indeed, in pulling down the present building, but they would never agree in erecting another.

This too, is a period when the whole European world is convulsed and in arms; our rising importance attracts their attention and excites their fears. Even in the present state of things, their ministers and agents were continually intriguing among our citizens. Would they remain idle and unemployed while the convention was deliberating? Would they not afford fuel to the flame of party, and prepare the public mind to reject every scheme which might be proposed? Was it not reasonable to be expected that the consequence of their exertions, and our own ferments, would be confusion, anarchy, civil war, and disunion? Enjoying, then, as we do, every happiness to which reason can aspire, shall we, said he, wantonly attempt a change by which little could be obtained, and everything might be sacrificed.

In Virginia, Mr. *Taylor* said, the general sentiment was that the government of the United States verges towards, and will ultimately settle in, a monarchy. But the measures of that government are supported by a majority of the House of Representatives, and by a still greater majority of the Senate. From this obvious proof of the prevailing sentiment throughout the Union, was it to be expected that another government would be framed vesting smaller or fewer powers in the executive, than he at present exercises? Would not our object, on the contrary, be defeated, since the general convention would probably enlarge instead of diminish the powers of the national government? No other consequence, therefore, could at the present time, and under existing circumstances, follow such an experiment, but increase of dissatisfaction and disgust, and a more ardent disposition to dissever the bonds of union which now connect all America.

In such a convention, in vain should we reckon on the superior importance, power, and influence of Virginia. A majority of states would never agree to summon another convention unless it should be previously agreed and declared that the votes shall be taken as in the former convention, by *states*. In such a convention, where the influence of Delaware or Rhode Island would be as great, and their respective votes would weigh as much as those of Virginia and Pennsylvania, what would be our chance of carrying our particular objects into effect. The smaller states already behold us with jealousy and apprehension. Each representative would come prepared to watch, to oppose and circumvent every other. Northern and southern, eastern and western parties and interests would immediately appear; and the convention, after a restless and turbulent session, which would increase instead of diminish the rage of faction among their constituents, would rise in confusion. The sound of peace would be no longer heard; the sentiment of union would no longer continue, but the sword would be drawn, the union for ever dismembered, and the bloody history of Europe would be retraced in the melancholy annals of divided and hostile America.

How sad and gloomy a contrast would such a state of things afford to the present flattering and happy aspect of our affairs. At this day, said Mr. *Taylor*, America, united under one government, experiences an increase of wealth and population unknown to any other country. Mild and equal laws, industrious and enterprising citizens, peace among ourselves and respect from foreign nations, render us the envy of every other part of the globe. Mr. *Taylor* then concluded with the following observation: May HE who rules the hearts of men, still dispose us to yield obedience to the constitutional acts of the majority; may He avert the mischiefs which these resolutions are calculated to produce; may He increase the love of union among our citizens; may no precipitate acts of the Legislature of Virginia convulse or destroy it; and to sum up all in one word, may it be perpetual!

Mr. GILES arose next, and said, as he had but lately appeared before the committee, he would not have obtruded any observations upon it, had not some remarks which had fallen from gentlemen made some impression upon him. Therefore, though unprepared, he would make a few observations. He then observed, that for several years past he had had an opportunity of considering the systems pursued by both the state government and General Government. Of those he considered the system of Virginia the best and mildest. For after twenty years' operation, little mischief could be proved to have proceeded from it; but, on the contrary, much good had been done by the administration of it in that time. There had been no complaint that he had heard respecting the injury of person or property; and there had been at the same time less energy in it than in any other government whatever. The injunctions of law had been duly obeyed, and of the laws of the United States particularly, of as much so here as in any other state. What had been the cause of this? Not the rigour, but the mildness of the laws. And were such principle always to be attended to, the necessity of energy in the executive branch would never exist. Mr. *Giles* then asked what was that energy? It was despotism. Whence had sprung the distinction of parties? Not while Virginia was left to herself. He then proceeded to pass a high eulogium on her system, which had been felt by him in private life; for he confessed that he had never acted

in a public character in this body before? Whence then did party-spirit
arise? It had been since that new doctrine had taken place of strength-
ening the hands of the executive of the United States, to give it an energy.
And he proceeded to show of what kind that was.

Since that period, he said, efforts to resist had originated. Mr. *Giles*
then requested the committee to examine the powers of the General
Government, and observe what was the opinion formed of them at its commencement. He then mentioned certain systems which had been established in the course of its operation, such as the funding-system, bank,
&c. These systems being established, it would be thought necessary from
time to time, to give them energy. He said, there was a kind of sophistry
used by the General Government in assigning that for the means which
was in fact the end; and stated for example the case of invasion and
insurrection. The sedition-law had been called the means for preventing
them; but he (Mr. *Giles*) declared the contrary to be the fact. The sedition-law was truly the end, and an invasion was made use of as the means
to introduce it. He would examine the Constitution, he said; and there
he found the language as plain as the English language could be. Still,
however, that language, plain as it was, was avoided by calling an end a
means. The sedition-law, then, was an end to suppress a certain party
in the United States. But it had been predicted by gentlemen, that many
mischievous consequences would attend the adoption of the plan proposed
by the resolutions before the committee. Mr. *Giles* contended, however, that
if such consequences did take place, they would not proceed from any act
of this Assembly, but from these acts of Congress already passed. As for
himself, he wished as much as others to preserve happiness. His efforts
were tending to that end. An oath, too, had been spoken of. What was it?
" To support the Constitution of the United States." It became then the
duty of the members of this Assembly, who had taken such an oath, to
support the Constitution. But it had been said, that on this occasion a
resort must be made to the judiciary and to the people. Why so? said
Mr. *Giles*. The members of this Assembly have taken the same oath to
support the Constitution as the judiciary and the people. It became then
as much their duty to support it, as it was that of the others. He then
asked, how was the Constitution to be supported; and said, that it was
by resisting *all* attacks upon it, not any particular acts only. But the
right of the members of this Assembly to speak their opinions upon the
subject was questioned. It was said, that they must inform the people so:
that they must do it, that the judges must do it, and that they their representatives wished not to do it themselves. Mr. *Giles* then said, that
the measures of our present government tended to the establishment of
monarchy, limited or absolute. It had been said, too, that the people only
were parties to the compact. But Mr. *Giles* asked what was an association of people? A federal? No; it was a social compact. How then
would they support it as a federal compact, if it were only a social compact? The state government was truly of the latter kind. The General
Government was partly of each kind. The objection to the word *only*
then was correct, and before he concluded, he should move to strike it
out. But he acknowledged that they were then acting as a state. The

gentleman from Westmoreland had delivered his opinion respecting the formation of the government. In this opinion, Mr. *Giles* said, the gentleman was partly correct, and partly incorrect. The United States would perhaps have been in a different situation, if what the gentleman had asserted had been established. He then proceeded to show in what manner several states in the Union appointed their electors to choose a President, which was by their legislatures. The federal idea, then, of the other side was not correct. And if, on the other hand, the government were a social compact, he pronounced monarchy to be near at hand, the symptoms and causes of which he particularly pointed out: and concluded that the state legislatures alone, at this time prevented monarchy. He then said, that in proportion as the powers of the government were extended, new excuses for more energy would arise. And what was energy? A coercing of the public will. He then observed how little energy was exerted in Virginia. The energy of the laws was sufficient. He hoped, then, that the right of the committee to proceed to examine the subject would not be denied. The gentleman from Prince George had dwelt upon the present happiness of the people, to disprove which Mr. *Giles* called to mind the rigorous proceedings of the government, and particularly cited the case of *Matthew Lyon*, whom, notwithstanding the reports propagated to his prejudice, he said he would aver to be a man of much worth. The effects of these laws of Congress were not yet sufficiently known. The medium of information had heretofore been contracted and imperfect. This House was then undertaking to make them more known. The critical situation of the United States, too, had been mentioned: that France and England both had a view towards us; and that therefore great caution should be used.

He then proceeded to take notice of the measures adopted by the last Congress. The cause for them held out, was the danger to be apprehended from a certain foreign power. This cause had produced the laws respecting the navy, the army, aliens, and the sedition-law, which last operated upon citizens, and not foreigners. Those gentlemen, he said, who never had been about the seat of government, could form no conception of the exertions of persons who were continually infusing into men's minds, the notions of energy. Mr. *Giles* then read an answer of the President of the United States, to show what he had in view in respect to that foreign power, so much feared. It was his answer to the address of the people of Bath. He read it, and proceeded to comment on the latter part of it respecting a party in Virginia to be crushed into dust and ashes. He asked what was that party? They were said to be French partisans. But by whom were they so called? He asked, too, who were the favourers of the resolutions? Not Frenchmen, but good citizens. This was the party then to be crushed, before the schemes of the President could be effected. He said that he could produce more answers of the President, avowing the same principles and design, as that already cited, but he would not tire the committee with them. He declared himself, however, to be as good a citizen as the President. Why then was he to be crushed into dust and ashes? He then expressed his disapprobation of the measures adopted by the government respecting the army and

10

navy. He asked, of what characters would they be composed? Of the idle and dissipated part of the community? On the contrary, who were the patriots who would protect their country? This very party mentioned by the President would repel any invasion. It was true they had no arms, but they would find arms. Mr. *Giles* then said that he approved of the argument used by the gentleman from Caroline, respecting the volunteers, but wished it to be somewhat more extended. He thought it a much more serious matter than any other. The gentleman from Caroline had used it in regard to the President's enlisting aliens merely. But Mr. *Giles* said he would ask, further, of whom those companies were to be composed? Not of farmers or farmers' sons, but chiefly of aliens. He himself believed that the operation of the last-mentioned law was intended to unite both. But it was said the people would protect the Constitution; that the judges would protect it. He then observed, that opposition to foreign power was always the pretence to usurpation. To prove that, he instanced the case of Rome. There, he said, whenever the people found themselves oppressed, and solicited redress, they were told by their rulers that was not the time; that the commonwealth was in danger; that the Volsci were at their gates. Mr. *Giles* then said, that by the measures adopted by the last Congress, nothing had been left undone to carry us into monarchy. But union was now said to be necessary. What was that union for? To abridge the freedom of the press. Was that desirable? He compared this to the case of robbers forming an union for the purpose of robbing. And said, that *good* was the object of the union of the states, and not *mischief.* He then adverted to the distinction between opinion and fact. He said Mr. *Jefferson's* was a good distinction. And that the assertion of false fact was punishable before the sedition-law was passed; but the assertion of false opinion was not. There was no standard to ascertain that; there was, however, in respect to false fact. This sedition-law, then, deprived men of the freedom of speech. It prescribed the punishment of a new thing. Opinion heretofore, had ranged at large, had always prevailed. Mr. *Giles* then asked, how was the restriction of opinion introduced in France. It was brought about in Robespierre's reign of terrorism. He then asked how this party mentioned by the President was to be crushed? Incarceration would not be sufficient. In regard to the restriction of opinion, he compared our situation to that of France, in the reign of Robespierre. As for himself, he feared not the system, but thought the most effectual mode was now pursued to introduce the same despotism here as had prevailed in France. He approved the mode adopted by the resolutions, in making a declaration to conflict with other opinions. He then referred to our situation, and said that he felt himself as much interested as any one to ward off war, but he thought the worst of all things was ultimately submission; and that a constitutional violation was more degrading than anything. But the resolutions had been charged with containing invective. He said if there were any, it must arise from simple language, expressing simple truths. However, if better could be used he would be willing to agree to it. But he doubted whether should even the Lord's Prayer be introduced before them, and undergo a criticism, they could be brought to agree to it. It had been said, that if this Assembly critically examined the measures of the general government, they should use more pleasant terms. But Mr. *Giles* said they were not terms, but truths that were unpleasant. He proceeded next to consider the alien-law, and to answer the observations of gentlemen in respect to aliens having no rights. In advocating the rights of aliens, he said, he did not consider what was popular, but what was justice. A stranger coming into a country had a *right* to protection. It was not a matter of *favour* only. A great number of persons already admitted into this country, he said, were not citizens. They would be affected by this law. He insisted that aliens were not only entitled to a trial by jury, but to that particular benefit of a jury *de medieta telinguæ*, by the law in force both in England and here. It had been said, however, that this was not a trial of guilt, but to prevent it. That, he said, made no difference. A trial was still necessary. He conceived that there was no foreign, but a domestic reason for this law. It was said that the French were ambitious. But was this a ground for the laws to affect our domestic operations? If they were repealed the government would be as firm as it was now. The administration, he said, was not the government. The government could subsist without it. For instance, it was once thought in Switzerland that it was necessary to keep a bear amongst them, for their prosperity and safety. After awhile the bear broke his chain and run away. For some time after, the people continued to lament his escape, and expected that some dreadful calamity would befall them. But, after waiting some time, and finding that no such calamity arrived, they began to bring themselves by degrees to believe, that the bear was of no use, and that they could do as well without him, as with him. Mr. *Giles* then said that he was as much in favour of government as any man, and would contribute as liberally to its support, but was not an advocate for improper measures. He then proceeded to consider the sedition-law. He observed, that the gentleman from Prince George had mentioned the God of Heaven. But he had nothing to do with the Constitution. If he had, it was omnipotent. On the contrary, Mr. *Giles* said, that the powers of government were derived from the Constitution, and not from the reason and nature of things. Implication, he said, was a dangerous doctrine. There was an express prohibition of all powers not granted by the Constitution. The Constitution and this law convey to the mind different impressions. The derivation of power, he again insisted, could not be proved otherwise than from the Constitution. The powers not given by that were retained to the states, or to the people. What, then, was given to each? The general government, he said, should not be entrusted to decide upon character, or in case of murder. That power was reserved to the states. That was the proper authority for regulating and deciding upon these matters. Mr. *Giles* made some further observations on the last clause of the law last mentioned, and then said, that declaring these acts of Congress unconstitutional, satisfied the oaths of the members of this Assembly. He would agree to stop after that, if they thought proper, and to strike out everything beyond it. If gentlemen thought the laws were unconstitutional, they were bound to say so, otherwise it would be a dereliction of the oath which they had taken. For his part, he said, he should vote for something which would express his opinion upon the subject. He would, however, at any rate, move to strike out of the resolutions before the committee, the word *alone*.

Mr. NICHOLAS seconded Mr. *Giles's* motion for striking out of the resolutions the word *alone;* and further observed, that either the gentleman from Prince George or himself, misunderstood the gentleman from Caroline, in respect to calling a convention. He hoped, therefore, that the gentleman from Caroline would explain himself upon that point. Mr. *Nicholas* then stated what he understood that gentleman to say, which he himself approved ; but on the contrary, did not approve the calling a convention.

Mr. BOLLING said, that he understood the gentleman from Caroline in the same manner that the gentleman who was last up did, in respect to calling a convention. Mr. *Bolling* also made several observations to show that the gentleman from Prince George had misunderstood Mr. *Jefferson's* letter which had been quoted by him.

Mr. JOHN TAYLOR said he would explain in a few words what he had before said. That the plan proposed by the resolutions would not eventuate in war, but might in a convention. He did not admit, or contemplate, that a convention would be called. He only said, that if Congress, upon being addressed to have those laws repealed, should persist, they might, by a concurrence of three-fourths of the states, be compelled to call a convention. Mr. *Taylor* further said, that while up he would himself move to strike out certain words of the resolutions, if the same were in order ; which being agreed to without a question taken, Mr. *Taylor* proceeded to do so.

The original resolutions offered by him to the House, and referred to the committee of the whole House on the state of the commonwealth, were in the following words :

Resolved, As the opinion of this committee, that the General Assembly of Virginia doth unequivocally express a firm resolution to maintain and defend the Constitution of the United States, and the Constitution of this state, against every aggression, either foreign or domestic, and that it will support the government of the United States in all measures warranted by the former.

That this Assembly most solemnly declares a warm attachment to the union of the states, to maintain which, it pledges all its powers ; and that for this end it is its duty to watch over and oppose every infraction of those principles, which constitute the only basis of that union, because a faithful observance of them can alone secure its existence, and the public happiness.

That this Assembly doth explicitly and peremptorily declare that it views the powers of the federal government as resulting from the compact, to which the states *alone* are parties, as limited by the plain sense and intention of the instrument constituting that compact ; as no further valid than they are authorized by the grants enumerated in that compact ; and that in case of a deliberate, palpable, and dangerous exercise of other powers not granted by the said compact, the states, who are parties thereto, have the right, and are in duty bound, to interpose for arresting the progress of the evil, and for maintaining within their respective limits, the authorities, rights, and liberties appertaining to them.

That the General Assembly doth also express its deep regret that a spirit has, in sundry instances, been manifested by the federal government, to enlarge its powers by forced constructions of the constitutional charter which defines them; and that indications have appeared of a design to expound certain general phrases (which having been copied from the very limited grant of powers in the former articles of confederation, were the less liable to be misconstrued), so as to destroy the meaning and effect of the particular enumeration, which necessarily explains and limits the general phrases, and so as to consolidate the states by degrees into one sovereignty, the obvious tendency and inevitable result of which would be to transform the present republican system of the United States into an absolute, or at best, a mixed monarchy.

That the General Assembly doth particularly protest against the palpable and alarming infractions of the Constitution, in the two late cases of the "alien and sedition-acts," passed at the last session of Congress, the first of which exercises a power nowhere delegated to the federal government; and which by uniting legislative and judicial powers to those of executive, subverts the general principles of free government, as well as the particular organization, and positive provisions of the Federal Constitution; and the other of which acts exercises in like manner a power not delegated by the Constitution, but on the contrary expressly and positively forbidden by one of the amendments thereto; 'a power which more than any other ought to produce universal alarm, because it is levelled against that right of freely examining public characters and measures, and of free communication among the people thereon, which has ever been justly deemed the only effectual guardian of every other right.

That this state having by its convention which ratified the Federal Constitution, expressly declared, "that among other essential rights, the liberty of conscience and of the press cannot be cancelled, abridged, restrained, or modified by any authority of the United States," and from its extreme anxiety to guard these rights from every possible attack of sophistry or ambition, having, with other states, recommended an amendment for that purpose, which amendment was in due time annexed to the Constitution, it would mark a reproachful inconsistency and criminal degeneracy, if an indifference were now shown to the most palpable violation of one of the rights thus declared and secured, and to the establishment of a precedent which may be fatal to the other.

That the good people of this commonwealth having ever felt, and continuing to feel the most sincere affection to their brethren of the other states, the truest anxiety for establishing and perpetuating the union of all, and the most scrupulous fidelity to that Constitution which is the pledge of mutual friendship, and the instrument of mutual happiness, the General Assembly doth solemnly appeal to the like dispositions of the other states, in confidence that they will concur with this commonwealth in declaring, as it does hereby declare, that the acts aforesaid are unconstitutional, and

not law, but utterly null, void, and of no force or effect, and that the necessary and proper measures will be taken by each, for co-operating with
this state in maintaining unimpaired the authorities, rights, and liberties
reserved to the states respectively, or to the people.

That the Governor be desired to transmit a copy of the foregoing resolutions to the executive authority of each of the other states, with a request
that the same may be communicated to the legislature thereof.

And that a copy be furnished to each of the senators and representatives, representing this state in the Congress of the United States.

The word, "*alone*" in the third clause, and the words "*and not law,
but utterly null, void, and of no force or effect,*" in the seventh clause, were
stricken out of the foregoing resolutions.

Mr. *John Taylor's* resolutions thus amended, being then read by the
chairman, Mr. *Brooke* moved, to amend the same, by substituting in lieu
thereof the resolution which he had offered to the committee on Tuesday,
the 18th instant, and which was then laid upon the table. The question
was put thereupon, and the amendment disagreed to by the committee.
The main question was then put on Mr. *John Taylor's* resolutions as
amended by himself, and agreed to.

The committee then rose, and Mr. *Breckenridge* reported, that the committee of the whole House on the state of the commonwealth had had the
same under their consideration, and had come to certain resolutions
thereupon, which he handed in to the clerk's table, (being Mr. *John
Taylor's* resolutions, as above stated, amended and agreed to by the committee.)

General LEE then arose and observed, that although desirous of ending
the debate, yet wishing, with the gentleman from Amelia, to *meliorate* the
paper before them, by striking out some other part of the resolutions, he
would move an amendment to that effect. He then read the fourth clause
of the resolutions, and objected to the same as containing assertions which
he could not believe, and at the same time also a high charge against the
general government. He therefore moved to strike out that clause.

Mr. BOLLING said, that in order to convince the gentleman from Westmoreland of the futility of his proposition, he hoped that no other gentleman would disgrace himself, and the wisdom of the House, by gratifying
the gentleman with a reply on the occasion. He (Mr. *Bolling*) had arisen,
therefore, to second the gentleman's motion, and to give him complete
satisfaction by bringing the question to an end.

Mr. GILES made some remarks in favour of the clause proposed to
be stricken out. He stated several reasons to show why it should be
retained; and concluded by expressing his objection to its being stricken
out.

Mr. NICHOLAS hoped the motion made by the gentleman from Westmoreland, for expunging the clause in question, would not prevail. Without that clause, it was true, he would vote for the resolutions, but his

anxiety about them would be very much lessened, if it was expunged; for then it would appear, that none of the measures of the Federal Government were objected to but the alien and sedition-bills. This was not the fact; and it must also be in the recollection of many gentlemen in that House, that some of those members who were now most loud in support of the measures of which he and his friends complained, and who denied with most confidence the right of the Assembly to interfere, had themselves upon other occasions acted very differently, and justified that interference. One of the gentlemen distinguished himself in a particular instance, for which he had his most hearty approbation, as he considered it a subject highly interesting to the happiness of his country. How gentlemen could reconcile their opinions at past periods, with those they supported at this day, it was incumbent upon them to show. Mr. *Nicholas* said, it was with the deepest regret that he reviewed the principal measures of the Federal Government, as they appeared to him to tend directly to a consolidation of the state governments, which he believed would eventuate in monarchy. Upon all questions about the division of power, everything had been given to the executive from Congress, everything to Congress from the states. The general phrases in the Constitution, which were only intended to explain and limit the powers of the general government, have been considered as giving powers, thereby destroying the effect of the particular enumeration of powers, and of the security derived from the twelfth amendment to the Constitution. He would state the particular acts which he thought most obnoxious. The first in point of time were the bank and assumption laws, for which he could find no authority in the Constitution of the United States, and by which the commercial and monied interests of this country had been devoted to certain individuals and their theories, and concentred a force more powerful and operative than an army of twenty thousand men. The British treaty and its effects were so well known to this House, that it was unnecessary to dilate upon that subject. The doctrine about appropriations of money was so important in its consequences, that it merited the most serious attention of the people of America. The Constitution declares, that " no money shall be drawn from the treasury but in consequence of appropriations made by law ;" notwithstanding which, it is now contended, that the President may by his single act, bind the Congress to make appropriations, whether they deem them proper or not, thereby transferring from the representatives of the people to the executive magistrate, the command of the national purse. The stamp-act subjects the people to an obnoxious and inconvenient tax, and changes already, and may change still more hereafter, the system of evidence which the state laws required in their own courts. The ultimate effect of this may be to shut up the state courts; for it is even contended, that delivery bonds are subject to the tax. If this be true, other process may be taxed so highly as may amount to a denial of justice : the transferring the important power of borrowing money and raising armies, vested by the Constitution in Congress, to the President : the utter neglect of the militia : the attempt to render them useless and unnecessary, by raising standing armies, and by authorizing the President to employ any number of volunteers that he may think proper, when the only reason for a preference of volunteers that occurred to him was, that the President had the appointment of the officers of those corps, whereas the militia officers were appointed by the state governments, greatly' excited his suspicion. He confessed, his objections to these corps had been very much increased since he had seen a letter from the Secretary of War,* from which it appeared to him that the design was to arm one part of the people against the other. He well remembered, that when the Constitution was under discussion, great stress was laid upon this circumstance; and it was believed it would give great security to the state governments, and to the liberties of the people; but so great a revolution had a few years produced, that some gentlemen were willing to abandon principles that have been heretofore deemed the most sacred. The conduct of the executive in bestowing offices, more in the style of rewards for the support of particular measures, than from any regard to the general merits of the citizens called to fill them, and upon the same ground removing from office every man who ventures to hazard an opinion in opposition to any of the measures that have been pursued, necessarily created alarm. He mentioned the removal from office of Mr. *Tenche Coxe* and Mr. *Gardiner*, in support of what he had said, and expressed a fear, that by these means that numerous and influential class of citizens, who ought to consider themselves as the public servants, might be made the creatures of executive power; and if, said Mr. *Nicholas*, the day should ever come that the office of President should devolve upon an ambitious man, public officers might be made the most powerful instruments to promote his views. The influence would operate upon all those who expect, or want public employment.

Mr. *Nicholas* then observed, there was another subject, which he felt the greatest pain at mentioning. Nothing but its importance and connexion with the subject in discussion should induce him to do it. The judiciary department of every government should be most pure; there should not be a suspicion of a previous bias upon the mind of the judge. Every man who goes into a court ought to consider himself as in a sanctuary. The utmost ingenuity of man had been exercised to form a judiciary that should be beyond the reach of influence. Was the conduct of the judiciary what it ought to have been? He had always supposed courts were instituted to dispense justice between man and man, between individuals and the society; but he feared that facts might be stated from which it might be inferred that it was considered by some that there were other objects, such as the propagating of particular opinions; that there was united in the same man, the duties of a missionary and of a judge. He said this point of his argument was so disagreeable to him, that he

* *Extract of a letter from the Secretary of War to an officer of high rank in the militia of Virginia, who had communicated the wish of several volunteer companies to tender their services.*

"It.being deemed important not to accept of companies composed of disaffected persons, who might from improper motives be desirous to intrude themselves into the army under pretence of patriotic association, it will be proper certificates from prominent and known characters, setting forth the principles of the associates, those of the officers elect, —— especially; and that the company have complied with the prerequisite condition of the law, be also presented."

would not dwell upon it, but would dismiss it with a declaration that he felt great pleasure in saying that there were judges to whom he had never heard extra-judicial interference in political matters attributed. Mr. Nicholas observed, that thinking of the measures that he had stated as he did, he could not consent to expunge the clause. Indeed, if he did not give his full assent to what was stated in that clause, he would have been willing to confine the efforts of the House to procure the repeal of the alien and sedition-bills. But considering these as a part of a system that brought into jeopardy the dearest interests of his country, he thought it was their duty to represent to the other states the whole ground of the public uneasiness. As to the alien and sedition-laws, he had intended at an earlier part of the debate to have made some observations, but other gentlemen on the same side with himself, had expressed his opinions better than he could have done. He would therefore only say that he considered them as - unconstitutional, and that if the principle was once established that Congress have a right to make such laws, the tenure by which we hold our liberty would be entirely subverted. Instead of rights independent of human control, we must be content to hold by the courtesy and forbearance of those whom we have heretofore considered as the servants of the people. Mr. Nicholas said he had been a member of the convention that adopted the Constitution; that he had been uniformly a friend to it; that he considered himself as now acting in support of it; that he knew it was the artifice of those on the other side to endeavour to attach a suspicion of hostility to the government to those who differed with them in opinion. For his part, he despised such insinuations, as far as they might be levelled at him. He appealed to his past life, and to his situation for his justification. Upon what gentlemen's claim to exclusive patriotism was founded, he was yet to learn. The friends of the resolutions yielded to none in disinterested attachment to their country, to the Constitution of the United States, to union, and to liberty. The conduct and the motives of all would be judged of by the people of this country, to whom they were all known. Mr. Nicholas had full confidence that the amendment would be rejected, and the resolutions without further alteration, would meet the approbation of a great majority of that House.

General Lee said, that he wished to refute the observations of the gentleman last up, in favour of retaining the clause. (He was proceeding to do so, when he was interrupted by Mr. Nicholas, who observed that the gentleman had misunderstood him, and then declared in substance what he had before actually said.)

After such explanation, General Lee proceeded to justify the measures of the General Government in respect to the removal of persons from office. As to Mr. Coxe, as far as he could recollect the circumstances of his conduct, he thought his removal proper. And as to Mr. Gardiner, he confessed it was a case with which he was quite unacquainted. In respect to the judiciary being forward in delivering their opinions on public measures, he would observe that the state judges had done, and still did the same. He blamed them not for it. For the appointment of men as judges did not deprive them of their rights as citizens. But nothing of this kind, he said, would prove the propriety of the clause proposed to be stricken out.

General *Lee* then observed, that he considered the argument of the·gentleman from Amelia, in respect to the connexion between the alien-law, and the law concerning volunteers, weak. For his army of aliens being soldiers by compulsion, would turn against the President, instead of assisting him. The gentleman, too, had called in question the *ends·* which the government had in view in raising an army and navy. General *Lee* proceeded to answer the objections upon that head, by pointing out those ends. As to the alien and sedition-laws, he contended ₜthat the only *real view* in passing them, was to protect us from foreign invasion. He denied that there was an inclination in the General Government to crush a party. The construction placed by the gentleman from Amelia, upon the President's answer to the address of the people of Bath was erroneous. General *Lee* then read part of that answer, and placed a different construction upon the expressions which it contained. He conceived the President's meaning only to be, that it *depended* upon Virginia to say *whether or not* there was a party in the United States to be crushed, &c.; not positively *asserting* on his part, that there *was* such a party.

General *Lee* then observed, that if the people could govern themselves, how could that be done but by obedience to the laws? Their freedom could not be preserved by any other mode. For if the principle of obeying the will of the majority was once destroyed, it would prostrate all free government. But the gentleman from Amelia had considered himself as one of the party to be crushed, alluded to by the President. He (General *Lee*) was surprised at such an idea. That gentleman had committed no crime. He had for some time before, been honoured with a seat' in Congress. And there, although he had generally been in a minority, yet it was nothing more than the situation in which he (General *Lee*) had often been placed here. In neither was there any criminality. A difference, it was true, did exist between these cases; and he derived consolation from reflecting, that though he himself was in a minority here, he was still in a majority with that body which properly had the determination of national matters. He concluded with hoping that the₋ amendment would prevail.

Mr. TYLER arose next, and said that an able general would fight and struggle to the last. When driven from one stronghold, he would retreat to another; and finding himself no longer able to oppose superior numbers, he would attempt to divide his enemy. Mr. *Tyler* believed the plan on the present occasion, was to divide the republican members, but he hoped the gentleman's plan would not succeed; and that the clause would be retained. He thought it contained solemn truths. He doubted not·but that many of the measures of the General Government had a tendency to monarchy, absolute or limited. These measures had been pointed out by the gentleman from Albemarle. He would however state them over again. Mr. *Tyler* did so. He particularly relied on the growing influence of the executive, and the probability of an alliance with a corrupt monarchy, and an open rupture with a republic, which he said had been openly advocated by gentlemen of high character. He inquired what had been the effects of executive influence in Great Britain? He said, that by the revolution of 1688, and by several statutes of Parliament passed about that time, many of the great rights of the people, and the principles of freedom had been established; but that it might, at this time, be well doubted if the people were more free than they were before the revolution.' This was to be ascribed to the immense influence of the crown, which had three millions at disposal. He demanded what other cause had prevented a reform in Parliament, upwards of three hundred of whose members were chosen by a fewer number of electors. He asked if there was not some similitude between the systems pursued by our administration, and that of Great Britain? He said that the people of Great Britain were clamorous for peace, and Lord Malmesbury was sent to make peace; but he returned, and made no peace. He would not follow the comparison. Our fears, he said, had been assailed. He inquired whom were we to fear? He feared no man, and no measure, but that of offending the people; and he believed that the people were never offended at any effort to maintain their rights, or to protect their liberties. The gentleman from Westmoreland had said, that the gentleman from Amelia could not consider himself as one of the party to be crushed, and had asked what crime that gentleman had committed. Mr. *Tyler* said, that the gentleman from Amelia had committed a crime; the crime of differing in opinion with the administrators of the government. This was the crime that had incarcerated Mr. Lyon. He asked what prospect have we of a change of these measures, which he viewed as the harbingers, the forerunners of monarchy, either limited or absolute. Were we not told that they must have more men, and a little more money; augment our standing army, and increase our navy; and force the construction of the Constitution to warrant alien and sedition-bills? Mr. *Tyler* concluded by hoping that the clause would be retained. He believed it contained the truth, and was very important; and thought that the people of Virginia called for some such measure.

Mr. *John Taylor's* resolutions, as amended, agreed to by the Committee, and reported to the House (*ante*, p. 149–50), being read the second time, a motion was made, and the question being put, to amend the same by expunging from them the fourth clause in the following words:
" That the General Assembly doth also express its deep regret, that a spirit has in sundry instances been manifested by the Federal Government to enlarge its powers by forced constructions of the constitutional charter which defines them; and that indications have appeared of a design to expound certain general phrases (which having been copied from the very limited grant of powers in the former articles of confederation, were the less liable to be misconstrued) so as to destroy the meaning and effect of the particular enumeration, which necessarily explains and limits the general phrases, and so as to consolidate the states, by degrees, into one sovereignty, the obvious tendency and inevitable result of which would be to transform the present republican system of the United States into an absolute, or at best a mixed monarchy."
It passed in the negative, ayes 68—noes 96.
On a motion made by General *Lee*, seconded by Mr. *Bolling*, ordered,

that the names of the ayes and noes on the foregoing question be inserted in the journal.

The names of those who voted in the affirmative, are Messrs. Bailey, Ware, Anderson, Porterfield, Poage, White, Otey, Logwood, Tate, Baker, Breckenridge, M'Guire, Moorman, Spencer, Bedford, Harrison, Herbert, Magill, Bynum, Reives, John Mathews, Cavendish, Royal, Snyder, King, Fisher, Simons, Godwin, Young, Richard Corbin, Thomas Lewis, Turner, Wallace, Pollard, Gregory, Powell, Clapham, Cowan, Evans, Ingles, James Taylor, Watkins, Upshur, Darby, Claughton, Clarke, Divan, Cureton, George K. Taylor, Brooke, Robinson, Ellegood, M'Coy, Coonrod, Wilson, Glasscock, Caruthers, Andrew Alexander, Davis, Charles Lewis, Blow, Booth, Lee, Bradley, Drope, Crockett, Griffin, Andrews—68.

And the names of those who voted in the negative, are Messrs. Cabell, Nicholas, Walker, Giles, Fletcher, Bolling, William Allen, Colwell, Perrow, John Taylor, Buckner, Tyler, Cheatham, Thomas A. Taylor, Daniel, Roberts, Shackelford, Peterson Goodwyn, Pegram, Booker, Daingerfield, Webb, Jennings, Horner, Haden, Payne, Greer, Benjamin Cooke, Hall, Pleasants, Heath I. Miller, Jones, M'Kinzie, Starke, Thompson, Jackson, Prunty, Selden, Price, Martin, Redd, John Allen, Tazewell, Shearman, Joseph Carter, Callis, Meriwether, Chadwell, Francis Eppes, Hudgins, Litchfield, Roebuck, Hill, Nelson, Mark Alexander, Segar, Richard H. Corbin, Scott, Butt, James S. Mathews, Willis Riddick, Josiah Riddick, Semple, Hurst, Freeman Eppes, Dupuy, M'Kinley, Barbour, Wright, Moseley, Woodson, Purnall, Johnston, Pope, Rentfro, William Carter, Hadden, Barnes, Cockrell, Browning, Gatewood, Dulaney, Mercer, Stannard, Nathaniel Fox, John Fox, Faulcon, Seward, Mason, Cary, Burnham, Hungerford, Meek, Shield, Foushee, Newton—96.

A motion was then made, and the question being put, to amend the said resolutions, by striking out from the word "Resolved," to the end of the same, and inserting in lieu thereof the following words:

"That as it is established by the Constitution of the United States, that the people thereof have a right to assemble peaceably, and to petition the government for a redress of grievances, it therefore appears properly to belong to the people themselves to petition, when they consider their rights to be invaded by any acts of the general government; and it should be left to them, if they conceive the laws lately passed by the Congress of the United States, commonly called the 'alien and sedition-laws,' to be unconstitutional, or an invasion of their rights, to petition for a repeal of the said laws."

It also passed in the negative, ayes 60—noes 104.

On a motion made by Mr. *Brooke*, seconded by Mr. *Griffin*, ordered, that the names of the ayes and noes on the foregoing question be inserted in the journal.

The names of those who voted in the affirmative, are Messrs. Bailey, Ware, Anderson, Porterfield, Poage, White, Otey, Logwood, Tate, Baker, Breckenridge, M'Guire, Moorman, Spencer, Herbert, Magill, Bynum, Reives, J. Mathews, Cavendish, Royall, Snyder, King, Fisher, Simons, Nelson, Evans, Ingles, Jas. Taylor, Watkins, Upshur, Darby, Clarke, Divan, Cureton, George K. Taylor, Brooke, Robinson, Ellegood, M'Coy,

Coonrod, Wilson, Davis, Charles Lewis, Blow, Booth, Lee, Bradley, Drope, Crockett, Griffin, Andrews, Godwin, Thomas Lewis, Turner, Wallace, Pollard, Powell, Clapham, Cowan—60.

And the names of those who voted in the negative, are Messrs. Cabell, Nicholas, Walker, Giles, Fletcher, Bolling, William Allen, Colwell, Perrow, John Taylor, Buckner, Bedford, Harrison, Tyler, Cheatham, Thomas A. Taylor, Daniel, Roberts, Shackelford, Peterson Goodwyn, Pegram, Booker, Daingerfield, Webb, Jennings, Horner, Haden, Payne, Greer, Benjamin Cooke, Hall, Pleasants, Heath I. Miller, Jones, M'Kinzie, Starke, Thompson, Jackson, Prunty, Selden, Price, Martin, Redd, John Allen, Tazewell, Young, Richard Corbin, Gregory, Shearman, Joseph Carter, Callis, Meriwether, Chadwell, Francis Eppes, Hudgins, Litchfield, Roebuck, Hill, Marke Alexander, Segar, Richard H. Corbin, Scott, Butt, James S. Mathews, W. Riddick, J. Riddick, Semple, Hurst, Claughton, Freeman Eppes, Dupuy, M'Kinley, Barbour, Wright, Moseley, Woodson, Purnall, Johnston, Pope, Rentfro, William Carter, Hadden, Barnes, Glasscock, Caruthers, Andrew Alexander, Cockrell, Browning, Gatewood, Dulaney, Mercer, Stannard, Nathaniel Fox, John Fox, Faulcon, Seward, Mason, Cary, Burnham, Hungerford, Meek, Shield, Foushee, Newton—104.

And then the main question being put, that the House do agree with the committee of the whole House in the resolutions as reported,

It passed in the affirmative, ayes 100—noes 63.

On a motion made by Mr. John *Taylor,* seconded by Mr. *Nicholas,* ordered, that the names of the ayes and noes on the foregoing question be inserted in the journal.

The names of those who voted in the affirmative, are Messrs. Cabell, Nicholas, Walker, Giles, Fletcher, Bolling, William Allen, Colwell, Perrow, John Taylor, Buckner, Harrison, Tyler, Cheatham; Thomas A. Taylor, Daniel, Roberts, Shackelford, P. Goodwyn, Pegram, Booker, Daingerfield, Webb, Jennings, Horner, Haden, Payne, Greer, Benjamin Cooke, Hall, Pleasants, Heath I. Miller, Jones, M'Kinzie, Starke, Thompson, Jackson, Prunty, Selden, Price, Martin, Redd, John Allen, Tazewell, Young, Richard Corbin, Gregory, Shearman, Joseph Carter, Callis, Meriwether, Chadwell, Francis Eppes, Hudgins, Litchfield, Roebuck, Hill, Mark Alexander, Segar; Richard H. Corbin, Scott, Butt, James S. Mathews, W. Riddick, J. Riddick, Semple, Hurst, Claughton, Freeman Eppes, Dupuy, M'Kinley, Barbour, Wright, Moseley, Woodson, Purnall, Johnston, Pope, Rentfro, William Carter, Hadden, Glasscock, Cockrell, Browning, Gatewood, Dulaney, Mercer, Stannard, Nathaniel Fox, John Fox, Faulcon, Seward, Mason, Cary, Burnham, Hungerford, Meek, Shield, Foushee, Newton—100.

And the names of those who voted in the negative are Messrs. Bailey, Ware, Anderson, Porterfield, Poage, White, Otey, Logwood, Tate, Baker, Breckenridge, M'Guire, Moorman, Spencer, Bedford, Herbert, Magill, Bynum, Reives, John Matthews, Cavendish, Snyder, King, Fisher, Simons, Godwin, Thomas Lewis, Turner, Wallace, Pollard, William Clarke, Royall, Powell, Clapham, Cowan, Nelson, Evans, Ingles, James Taylor, Watkins, Upshur, Darby, Divan, Cureton, George K. Taylor,

Brooke, Robinson, Ellegood, M'Coy, Coonrod, Wilson, Caruthers, Andrew Alexander, Davis, Charles Lewis, Blow, Booth, Lee, Bradley, Drope, Crockett, Griffin, and Andrews—63.

The House then *ordered* that the clerk do carry the said resolutions to the Senate for their concurrence.

IN SENATE,

Monday, December 24, 1798.

The House, according to the order of the day, resolved itself into a committee of the whole House, on the resolutions of the House of Delegates, concerning certain acts of the Congress of the United States, passed at their last session ; and after some time spent therein, Mr. Speaker resumed the chair, and Mr. *Preston* reported that the committee had, according to order, taken the said resolutions under their consideration, and had gone through the same, and had directed him to report the same without any amendment.

A motion was then made to amend the fifth resolution, by striking out the words " *two late cases of the alien and*," and on the question to agree to the same,

It passed in the negative—Ayes 5, Noes 12.

The ayes and noes were required on the above question.

Ayes—Burwell Bassett, Francis Peyton, Benjamin Temple, John Haymond, John Eyre—5.

Noes—Creed Taylor, Richard Kennon, Thomas Royster, Archibald Stewart, French Strother, Hugh Holmes, George Carrington, John Preston, John Hoomes, Thomas Newton, Nicholas Cabell, George Penn —12.

And then the main question being put, that the House do agree to the said resolutions,

It was resolved in the affirmative.   Ayes 14, Noes 3.

Ordered, That the clerk do acquaint the House of Delegates therewith.

On the above question the ayes and noes were required.

Ayes—Creed Taylor, Richard Kennon, Burwell Bassett, Thomas Royster, Archibald Stewart, French Strother, Hugh Holmes, George Carrington, John Preston, John Hoomes, Benjamin Temple, Thomas Newton, Nicholas Cabell, George Penn—14.

Noes—Francis Peyton, John Haymond, John Eyre—3.

The General Assembly, when these resolutions were adopted, consisted of the following persons :—the federalists' names being in *italics*.

HOUSE OF DELEGATES.

ACCOMAC.
John Wise,
Thomas M. Bailey.

AMHERST.
Wm. H. Cabell,
Wm. Ware.

AUGUSTA.
Andrew Anderson,
Robert Porterfield.

ALBEMARLE.
Wilson C. Nicholas,
Succeeded Jan. 28, 1799, by Wm. Woods,
Francis Walker.

AMELIA.
Alex. Jones,
Succeeded 17th Dec. 1799, by
Joshua Chaffin,
Wm. B. Giles.

BATH.
George Poage,
John White.

BEDFORD.
Isaac Otey,
Thos. Logwood.

BERKELEY.
Magnus Tate,
John Baker.

BOTETOURT.
James Breckenridge,
John Miller.

BRUNSWICK.
James Fletcher,
Wm. Ruffin.

BUCKINGHAM.
Powhatan Bolling.
Wm. Allen.

BROOKE.
Francis M'Guire,
Robert Calwell.

CAMPBELL.
Daniel B. Perrow,
Achilles Moorman.

CAROLINE.
John Taylor,
George Buckner.

CHARLOTTE.
Gideon Spencer,
Robert Bedford,

CHARLES CITY.
Collier Harrison,
Samuel Tyler.

CHESTERFIELD.
Matthew Cheatham,
Th. Augustus Taylor.

CUMBERLAND.
John Hatcher,
Wm. Daniel, Jr.

CULPEPER.
John Roberts, ·
John Shackelford, Jr.

DINWIDDIE.
Peterson Goodwin,
John Pegram, Jr.

ELIZABETH CITY.
George Booker,
W. Westwood.

ESSEX.
John Daingerfield,
James Webb.

FAIRFAX.
Roger West,
(did not attend.)
John Carlyle Herbert.

FAUQUIER.
Augustine Jennings,
Gustavus B. Horner.

FLUVANNA.
Joseph Haden,
James Payne.

FREDERICK.
Archd. Magill,
Lewis Wolfe.

FRANKLIN.
Moses Greer,
Benj. Cooke.

GREENSVILLE.
Turner Bynum.
Nathanl. Reives.

GLOUCESTER.
Mordecai Cooke,
Wm. Hall.

GOOCHLAND.
James Pleasants, Jr.
Heath T. Miller.

GREENBRIAR.
John Mathews,
Wm. H. Cavendish.

GRAYSON.
Minitree Jones,
Greenberry G. M'Kinzie.

HALIFAX.
Wm. Royall,
Richard Howson.

HAMPSHIRE.
John Snyder,
Alex. King.

HANOVER.
Thomas Starke.
John Thompson.

HARRISON.
John G. Jackson,
John Prunty.

HARDY.
Jacob Fisher,
Christian Simons.

HENRICO.
Miles Selden,
Wm. Price.

HENRY.
Joseph Martin,
John Redd.

ISLE OF WIGHT.
Josiah Godwin,
Thomas Whitefield,
Succeeded Jan. 2, 1799, by
James Johnston.

JAMES CITY.
John Allen,
Littleton W. Tazewell,

KING AND QUEEN.
Henry Young,
Richard Corbin,

KANAWHA.
Wm. Morris, Jr.,
Thos. Lewis.

KING GEORGE.
Thos. Turner,
Gustavus B. Wallace.

KING WILLIAM.
Robt. Pollard,
Wm. Gregory.

LANCASTER.
Martin Shearman,
Joseph Carter.

LOUDOUN.
Burr Powell,
Saml. Clapham.

LOUISA.
Wm. O. Callis,
Thomas Meriwether.

LEE.
David Chadwell,
Charles Cooke.

LUNENBURG.
Francis Epes,
Wm. Cowan.

MATTHEWS.
Holden Hudgins,
Zadock Litchfield.

MADISON.
Robert Roebuck,
Henry Hill.

MECKLENBURG.
John Nelson,
Mark Alexander.

MIDDLESEX.
Wm. Segar,
Richard H. Corbin.

MONONGALIA.
John Evans,
David Scott.

MONTGOMERY.
John Ingles,
James Taylor.

NANSEMOND.
Willis Riddick,
Josiah Riddick.

NEW KENT.
James Semple,
John D. Watkins.

NORFOLK.
Josiah Butt,
James S. Matthews.

NORTHAMPTON.
John Upshur,
Nathl. Darby.

NORTHUMBERLAND.
Thomas Hurst,
Wm. Claughton.

NOTTOWAY.
Freeman Epes,
James Dupuy.

OHIO.
Archibald Woods,
Wm. M'Kinley.

ORANGE.
James Barbour,
John Wright.

PITTSYLVANIA.
Wm. Clark,
Robt. Devin.

POWHATAN.
William Moseley,
Frederick Woodson.

PRINCE EDWARD.
Peter Johnston,
John Purnall.

PRINCE-GEORGE.
James Cureton,
Geo. Keith Taylor.

PRINCE WILLIAM.
John Pope,
Edmund Brooke.

PRINCESS-ANNE.
James Robinson,
Wm. Elligood.

PENDLETON.
Wm. M'Coy,
Jacob Conrad.

PATRICK.
Joshua Rentfro,
Wm. Carter.

RANDOLPH.
Wm. Wilson,
John Hadden.

RICHMOND.
Richard Barnes,
George Glasscock.

ROCKBRIDGE.
James Caruthers,
Andrew Alexander.

ROCKINGHAM.
Walter Davis,
Charles Lewis.

RUSSELL.
Simon Cockrell,
Francis Browning.

SHENANDOAH.
John Gatewood,
Wm. H. Dulaney.

SOUTHAMPTON.
Robert Goodwyn,
Wm. Blow.

SPOTTSYLVANIA.
John Mercer,
Larkin Stannard.

STAFFORD.
Nathaniel Fox,
John Fox.

SURRY.
Nicholas Faulcon,
Canfield Seward.

SUSSEX.
Robert Boothe,
John R. Mason.

WARWICK.
Richard Cary,
John Burnham.

WESTMORELAND.
John P. Hungerford,
Henry Lee.

WASHINGTON.
James Bradley,
Samuel Meek.

WYTHE.
Wm. Drope,
Saml. Crockett.

YORK.
Samuel Shield,
Thos. Griffin.

RICHMOND CITY.
Wm. Foushee.

WILLIAMSBURG.
Robert Andrews.

NORFOLK BOROUGH.
Thomas Newton.

SENATE.

The names of the Senators, as far as concerns the subject of the resolutions, appear from the vote already stated.

11

III.

RESOLUTIONS OF KENTUCKY LEGISLATURE.

IN THE HOUSE OF REPRESENTATIVES,

November 10th, 1798.

THE House, according to the standing order of the day, resolved itself into a committee of the whole on the state of the commonwealth, Mr. Caldwell in the chair; and after some time spent therein, the Speaker resumed the chair, and Mr. Caldwell reported that the committee had, according to order, had under consideration the Governor's address, and had come to the following resolutions thereupon, which he delivered in at the clerk's table, where they were twice read and agreed to by the House.

1. *Resolved*, That the several states composing the United States of America, are not united on the principle of unlimited submission to their general government; but that by compact, under the style and title of a Constitution for the United States, and of amendments thereto, they constituted a general government for special purposes, delegated to that government certain definite powers, reserving, each state to itself, the residuary mass of right to their own self-government; and that whensoever the general government assumes undelegated powers, its acts are unauthoritative, void, and of no force: That ·to this compact each state acceded as a state, and is an integral party, its co-states forming as to itself, the other party: That the government created by this compact was not made the exclusive or final *judge* of the extent of the powers delegated to itself; since that would have made its discretion, and not the Constitution, the measure of its powers; but that, as in all other cases of compact among parties having no common judge, each party has an equal right to judge for itself, as well of infractions, as of the mode and measure of redress.

2. *Resolved*, That the Constitution of the United States having delegated to Congress a power to punish treason, counterfeiting the securities and current coin of the United States, piracies and felonies committed on the high seas, and offences against the laws of nations, and no other crimes whatever, and it being true as a general principle, and one of the

amendments to the Constitution having also declared, " that the powers not delegated to the United States by the Constitution, nor prohibited by it to the states, are reserved to the states respectively, or to the people;" therefore, also, the same act of Congress, passed on the 14th day of July, 1798, and entitled, " an act in addition to the act entitled, an act for the punishment of certain crimes against the United States;" as also the act passed by them on the 27th day of June, 1798, entitled, " an act to punish frauds committed on the Bank of the United States," (and all other their acts which assume to create, define, or punish crimes other than those enumerated in the Constitution,) are altogether void, and of no force, and that the power to create, define, and punish such other crimes is reserved, and of right appertains, solely and exclusively, to the respective states, each within its own territory.

3. *Resolved*, That it is true as a general principle, and is also expressly declared by one of the amendments to the Constitution, that " the powers not delegated to the United States. by the Constitution, nor prohibited by it to the states, are reserved to the states respectively, or to the people;" and that no power over the freedom of religion, freedom of speech, or freedom of the press, being delegated to the United States by the Consti- tution, nor prohibited by it to the states, all lawful powers respecting the same did of right remain, and were reserved to the states, or to the peo- ple; that thus was manifested their determination to retain to themselves the right of judging how far the licentiousness of speech and of the press may be abridged without lessening their useful freedom, and how far those abuses which cannot be separated from their use, should be tolerated rather than the use be destroyed; and thus also they guarded against all abridgment by the United States of the freedom of religious opinions and exercises, and retained to themselves the right of protecting the same, as this state by a law passed on the general demand of its citizens, had already protected them from all human restraint or interference : and that in addition to this general principle and express declaration, another and more special provision has been made by one of the amendments to the Constitution, which expressly declares, that " Congress shall. make no law respecting an establishment of religion, or prohibiting the free exercise thereof, or abridging the freedom of speech, or of the press," thereby. guarding in the same sentence, and under the same words, the freedom of religion, of speech, and of the 'press, insomuch, that whatever violates either, throws down the sanctuary which covers the others, and that libels, falsehoods, and defamations, equally with heresy and false religion, are withheld from the cognizance of federal tribunals : that therefore the act of the Congress of the United States, passed on the 14th day of July, 1798, entitled, " an act in addition to the act for the punishment of cer- tain crimes against the United States," which does abridge the freedom of the press, is not law, but is altogether void and of no effect.

4. *Resolved*, That alien-friends are under the jurisdiction and protec- tion of the laws of the state wherein they are; that no power over them has been delegated to the United States, nor prohibited to the individual states distinct from their power over citizens; and it being true as a gene- ral principle, and one of the amendments to the Constitution having also

declared, that "the powers not delegated to the United States by the Constitution, nor prohibited by it to the states, are reservēd to the states respectively, or to the people," the act of the Congress of the United States, passed on the 22d day of June, 1798, entitled "an act concerning aliens," which assumes power over alien-friends not delegated by the Constitution, is not law, but is altogether void and of no force.

5. *Resolved*, That in addition to the general principle as well as the express declaration, that powers not delegated are reserved, another and more special provision inserted in the Constitution, from abundant caution, has declared, "that the *migration* or importation of such persons as any of the states now existing shall think proper to admit, shall not be prohibited by the Congress prior to the year 1808 :" that this commonwealth does admit the migration of alien-friends described as the subject of the said act concerning aliens; that a provision against prohibiting their migration, is a provision against all acts equivalent thereto, or it would be nugatory; that to remove them when migrated, is equivalent to a prohibition of their migration, and is therefore contrary to the said provision of the Constitution, and void.

6. *Resolved*, That the imprisonment of a person under the protection of the laws of this commonwealth, on his failure to obey the simple *order* of the President, to depart out of the United States, as is undertaken by the said act, entitled "an act concerning aliens," is contrary to the Constitution, one amendment to which has provided, that "no person shall be deprived of liberty without due process of law," and that another having provided, "that in all criminal prosecutions, the accused shall enjoy the right to a public trial by an impartial jury, to be informed of the nature and cause of the accusation, to be confronted with the witnesses against him, to have compulsory process for obtaining witnesses in his favour, and to have the assistance of counsel for his defence," the same act undertaking to authorize the President to remove a person out of the United States, who is under the protection of the law, on his own suspicion, without accusation, without jury, without public trial, without confrontation of the witnesses against him, without having witnesses in his favour, without defence, without counsel, is contrary to these provisions, also, of the Constitution, is therefore not law, but utterly void and of no force.

That transferring the power of judging any person who is under the protection of the laws, from the courts to the President of the United States, as is undertaken by the same act, concerning aliens, is against the article of the Constitution which provides, that "the judicial power of the United States shall be vested in courts, the judges of which shall hold their offices during good behaviour," and that the said act is void for that reason also; and it is further to be noted, that this transfer of judiciary power is to that magistrate of the General Government, who already possesses all the executive, and a qualified negative in all the legislative powers.

7. *Resolved*, That the construction applied by the General Government, (as is evinced by sundry of their proceedings,) to those parts of the Constitution of the United States which delegates to Congress a power to lay and collect taxes, duties, imposts, and excises; to pay the debts, and pro-

vide for the common defence and general welfare of the United States, and to make all laws which shall be necessary and proper for carrying into execution the powers vested by the Constitution in the Government of the United States, or any department thereof, goes to the destruction of all the limits prescribed to their power by the Constitution: that words meant by that instrument to be subsidiary only to the execution of the limited powers, ought not to be so construed as themselves to give unlimited powers, nor a part so to be taken, as to destroy the whole residue of the instrument: that the *proceedings of the General Government under colour of these articles, will be a fit and necessary subject for revisal and correction at a time of greater tranquillity, while those specified in the preceding resolutions call for immediate redress.

8. *Resolved*, That the preceding resolutions be transmitted to the senators and representatives in Congress from this commonwealth, who are hereby enjoined to present the same to their respective houses, and to use their best endeavours to procure, at the next session of Congress, a repeal of the aforesaid unconstitutional and obnoxious acts.

9. *Resolved, lastly*, That the Governor of this commonwealth be, and is hereby authorized and requested to communicate the preceding resolutions to the legislatures of the several states, to assure them that this commonwealth considers union for specified national purposes, and particularly for those specified in their late federal compact, to be friendly to the peace, happiness, and prosperity of all the states: that, faithful to that compact, according to the plain intent and meaning in which it was understood and acceded to by the several parties, it is sincerely anxious for its preservation: that it does also believe, that to take from the states all the powers of self-government, and transfer them to a general and consolidated government, without regard to the special obligations and reservations solemnly agreed to in that compact, is not for the peace, happiness or prosperity of these states: and that therefore, this commonwealth is determined, as it doubts not its co-states are, tamely to submit to undelegated and consequently unlimited powers in no man or body of men on earth: that if the acts before specified should stand, these conclusions would flow from them; that the general government may place any act they think proper on the list of crimes, and punish it themselves, whether enumerated or not enumerated by the Constitution, as cognizable by them; that they may transfer its cognizance to the President or any other person, who may himself be the accuser, counsel, judge and jury, whose *suspicions* may be the evidence, his order the sentence, his officer the executioner, and his breast the sole record of the transaction; that a very numerous and valuable description of the inhabitants of these states being, by this precedent, reduced as outlaws to the absolute dominion of one man, and the barrier of the Constitution thus swept away from us all, no rampart now remains against the passions and the power of a majority of Congress, to protect from a like exportation or other more grievous punishment the minority of the same body, the legislatures, judges, governors, and counsellors of the states, nor their other peaceable inhabitants who may venture to reclaim the constitutional rights and liberties of the states and people, or who, for other causes, good or bad, may be obnoxious to

the views, or marked by the suspicions of the President, or be thought dangerous to his or their elections, or other interests public or personal: that the friendless alien has indeed been selected as the safest subject of a first experiment; but the citizen will soon follow, or rather has already followed; for, already has a sedition-act marked him as its prey: that these and successive acts of the same character, unless arrested on the threshold, may tend to drive these states into revolution and blood, and will furnish new calumnies against republican governments, and new pretexts for those who wish it to be believed, that man cannot be governed but by a rod of iron: that it would be a dangerous delusion, were a confidence in the men of our choice, to silence our fears for the safety of our rights: that confidence is everywhere the parent of despotism; free government is founded in jealousy, and not in confidence; it is jealousy and not confidence which prescribes limited constitutions to bind down those whom we are obliged to trust with power: that our Constitution has accordingly fixed the limits to which and no further our confidence may go; and let the honest advocate of confidence read the alien and sedition-acts, and say if the Constitution has not been wise in fixing limits to the government it created, and whether we should be wise in destroying those limits? Let him say what the government is if it be not a tyranny, which the men of our choice have conferred on the President, and the President of our choice has assented to and accepted, over the friendly strangers, to whom the mild spirit of our country and its laws had pledged hospitality and protection: that the men of our choice have more respected the bare suspicions of the President, than the solid rights of innocence, the claims of justification, the sacred force of truth, and the forms and substance of law and justice. In questions of power, then, let no more be heard of confidence in man, but bind him down from mischief, by the chains of the Constitution. That this commonwealth does, therefore, call on its co-states for an expression of their sentiments on the acts concerning aliens, and for the punishment of certain crimes herein before specified, plainly declaring whether these acts are or are not authorized by the Federal compact. And it doubts not that their sense will be so announced, as to prove their attachment unaltered to limited government, whether general or particular, and that the rights and liberties of their co-states, will be exposed to no dangers by remaining embarked on a common bottom with their own: That they will concur with this commonwealth in considering the said acts as so palpably against the Constitution, as to amount to an undisguised declaration, that the compact is not meant to be the measure of the powers of the general government, but that it will proceed in the exercise over these states of all powers whatsoever: That they will view this as seizing the rights of the states, and consolidating them in the hands of the general government with a power assumed to bind the states, (not merely in cases made federal,) but in all cases whatsoever, by laws made, not with their consent, but by others against their consent: That this would be to surrender the form of government we have chosen, and to live under one deriving its powers from its own will, and not from our authority; and that the co-states, recurring to their natural right in cases not made federal, will concur in declaring these acts void and of no force, and will each unite with this commonwealth, in requesting their repeal at the next session of Congress.

EDMUND BULLOCK, *S. H. R.*
JOHN CAMPBELL, *S. S. P. T.*

Passed the House of Representatives, Nov. 10th, 1798.
    Attest,

THOMAS TODD, *C. H. R.*

In Senate, November 13th, 1798, unanimously concurred in.
    Attest,

B. THRUSTON, *Clk. Sen.*

Approved November 16th, 1798.

JAMES GARRARD, *G. K.*

By the Governor.

HARRY TOULMIN,
Secretary of State.

IV.

COUNTER-RESOLUTIONS OF OTHER STATES

IN RESPONSE TO THOSE OF VIRGINIA, &c.

STATE OF DELAWARE.

IN THE HOUSE OF REPRESENTATIVES,

February 1, 1799.

Resolved, By the Senate and House of Representatives of the state of Delaware, in General Assembly met, That they consider the resolutions from the state of Virginia, as a very unjustifiable interference with the general government and constituted authorities of the United States, and of dangerous tendency, and therefore not a fit subject for the further consideration of the General Assembly.

ISAAC DAVIS,
Speaker of Senate.

STEPHEN LEWIS,
Speaker of House of Representatives.

Test,

> JOHN FISHER,
> Clerk of Senate.
> JOHN CALDWELL,
> Clerk of House of Representatives.

Resolved, That the above resolutions be signed by the Speaker of the Senate, and by the Speaker of the House of Representatives; and that the Governor of this state be requested to forward the same to the Governor of the state of Virginia.

JOHN FISHER,
Clerk of Senate.

JOHN CALDWELL,·
Clerk of House of Representatives.

STATE OF RHODE ISLAND AND PROVIDENCE PLANTATIONS.

IN GENERAL ASSEMBLY,

February, A. D. 1799.

Certain resolutions of the legislature of Virginia, passed on the twenty-first day of December last, being communicated to this Assembly,

1. *Resolved*, That in the opinion of this legislature, the second section of the third article of the Constitution of the United States, in these words, to wit: *The judicial power shall extend to all cases arising under the laws of the United States*, vests in the federal courts exclusively, and in the Supreme Court of the United States ultimately, the authority of deciding on the constitutionality of any act or law of the Congress of the United States.

2. *Resolved*, That for any state legislature to assume that authority would be,

1st. Blending together legislative and judicial powers.

2d. Hazarding an interruption of the peace of the states by civil discord, in case of a diversity of opinions among the state legislatures; each state having, in that case, no resort for vindicating its own opinion, but to the strength of its own arm.

3d. Submitting most important questions of law, to less competent tribunals; and

4th. An infraction of the Constitution of the United States, expressed in plain terms.

3. *Resolved*, That although, for the above reasons, this legislature, in their public capacity, do not feel themselves authorized to consider and decide on the constitutionality of the sedition and alien-laws (so called), yet they are called upon by the exigency of this occasion, to declare, that in their private opinions, these laws are within the powers delegated to Congress, and promotive of the welfare of the United States.

4. *Resolved*, That the Governor communicate these resolutions to the supreme executive of the state of Virginia, and, at the same time, express to him, that this legislature cannot contemplate, without extreme concern and regret, the many evil and fatal consequences which may flow from the very unwarrantable resolutions aforesaid of the legislature of Virginia, passed on the twenty-first day of December last.

A true copy,

SAMUEL EDDY,
Secretary.

COMMONWEALTH OF MASSACHUSETTS.

IN SENATE,

February 9, 1799.

The Legislature of Massachusetts, having taken into serious considera-the resolutions of the state of Virginia, passed the 21st day of December last, and communicated by his excellency the Governor, relative to certain supposed infractions of the Constitution of the United States, by the go-vernment thereof, and being convinced that the Federal Constitution is calculated to promote the happiness, prosperity and safety of the people of these United States, and to maintain that union of the several states, so essential to the welfare of the whole; and, being bound by solemn oath to support and defend that Constitution, feel it unnecessary to make any professions of their attachment to it, or of their firm determination to sup-port it against every aggression, foreign or domestic.

But they deem it their duty solemnly to declare, that while they hold sacred the principle, that the consent of the people is the only pure source of just and legitimate power, they cannot admit the right of the state legis-latures to denounce the administration of that government to which the people themselves, by a solemn compact, have exclusively committed their national concerns: That, although a liberal and enlightened vigilance among the people is always to be cherished, yet an unreasonable jealousy of the men of their choice, and a recurrence to measures of extremity, upon groundless or trivial pretexts, have a strong tendency to destroy all rational liberty at home, and to deprive the United States of the most essential advantages in their relations abroad: That this Legislature are persuaded, that the decision of all cases in law and equity, arising under the Constitution of the United States, and the construction of all laws made in pursuance thereof, are exclusively vested by the people in the judicial courts of the United States.

That the people in that solemn compact, which is declared to be the supreme law of the land, have not constituted the state legislatures the judges of the acts or measures of the Federal Government, but have con-fided to them the power of proposing such amendments of the Constitution, as shall appear to them necessary to the interests, or conformable to the wishes of the people whom they represent.

That by this construction of the Constitution, an amicable and dispas-sionate remedy is pointed out for any evil which experience may prove to exist, and the peace and prosperity of the United States may be preserved without interruption.

But, should the respectable state of Virginia persist in the assumption of the right to declare the acts of the national government unconstitutional, and should she oppose successfully her force and will to those of the nation, the Constitution would be reduced to a mere cypher, to the form and pageantry of authority, without the energy of power. Every act of the Federal Government which thwarted the views, or checked the ambitious projects of a particular state, or of its leading and influential members, would be the object of opposition and of remonstrance; while the people, convulsed and confused by the conflict between two hostile jurisdictions, enjoying the protection of neither, would be wearied into a submission to some bold leader, who would establish himself on the ruins of both.

The Legislature of Massachusetts, although they do not themselves claim the right, nor admit the authority, of any of the state governments to decide upon the constitutionality of the acts of the Federal Government, still, lest their silence should be construed into disapprobation, or at best into a doubt of the constitutionality of the acts referred to by the state of Virginia; and, as the General Assembly of Virginia has called for an expression of their sentiments, do explicitly declare, that they consider the acts of Congress, commonly called " the alien and sedition-acts," not only constitutional, but expedient and necessary : That the former act respects a description of persons whose rights were not particularly contemplated in the Constitution of the United States, who are entitled only to a temporary protection, while they yield a temporary allegiance : a protection, which ought to be withdrawn whenever they become " dangerous to the public safety," or are found guilty of " treasonable machinations" against the government : That Congress having been especially entrusted by the people with the general defencè of the nation, had not only the right but were bound to protect it against internal, as well as external foes.

That the United States, at the time of passing the *act concerning aliens*, were threatened with actual invasion, had been driven by the unjust and ambitious conduct of the French government into warlike preparations, expensive and burdensome, and had then, within the bosom of the country, thousands of aliens, who, we doubt not, were ready to co-operate in any external attack.

It cannot be seriously believed, that the United States should have waited till the poniard had in fact been plunged. The removal of aliens is the usual preliminary of hostility, and is justified by the invariable usages of nations. Actual hostility had unhappily long been experienced, and a formal declaration of it the government had reason daily to expect. The law, therefore, was just and salutary, and no officer could, with so much propriety be entrusted with the execution of it, as the one in whom the Constitution has reposed the executive power of the United States.

The sedition-act, so called, is, in the opinion of this Legislature, equally defensible. The General Assembly of Virginia, in their resolve under consideration, observe, that when that state, by its convention, ratified the Federal Constitution, it expressly declared, " That, among other essential rights, the liberty of conscience and of the press cannot be cancelled, abridged, restrained or modified by any authority of the United States," and from its extreme anxiety to guard these rights from every possible attack of sophistry or ambition, with other states, recommended an amendment for that purpose; which amendment was, in due time, annexed to the Constitution ; but they did not surely expect that the proceedings of their state convention were to explain the amendment adopted by the union. The words of that amendment, on this subject, are, " Congress shall make no law abridging the freedom of speech, or of the press."

The act complained of is no abridgment of the freedom of either. The genuine liberty of speech and the press, is the liberty to utter and publish the truth; but the constitutional right of the citizen to utter and publish the truth, is not to be confounded with the licentiousness in speaking and writing, that is only employed in propagating falsehood and slander. This freedom of the press has been explicitly secured by most, if not all the state constitutions; and of this provision there has been generally but one construction among enlightened men; that it is a security for the rational use and not the abuse of the press; of which the courts of law, the juries and people will judge: this right is not infringed, but confirmed and established by the late act of Congress.

By the Constitution, the legislative, executive, and judicial departments of government are ordained and established; and general enumerated powers vested in them respectively, including those which are prohibited to the several states. Certain powers are granted in general terms by the people to their General Government, for the purposes of their safety and protection. That government is not only empowered, but it is made their duty, to repel invasions and suppress insurrections; to guarantee to the several states a republican form of government; to protect each state against invasion, and, when applied to, against domestic violence; to hear and decide all cases in law and equity, arising under the Constitution, and under any treaty or law made in pursuance thereof; and all cases of admiralty and maritime jurisdiction, and relating to the law of nations. Whenever, therefore, it becomes necessary to effect any of the objects designated, it is perfectly consonant to all just rules of construction to infer, that the usual means and powers necessary to the attainment of that object, are also granted: but the Constitution has left no occasion to resort to implication for these powers; it has made an express grant of them, in the eighth section of the first article, which ordains, " That Congress shall have power to make all laws which shall be necessary and proper for carrying into execution the foregoing powers, and all other powers vested by the Constitution in the Government of the United States, or in any department or officer thereof."

This Constitution has established a supreme court of the United States, but has made no provision for its protection, even against such improper conduct in its presence, as might disturb its proceedings, unless expressed in the section before recited. But as no statute has been passed on this subject, this protection is, and has been for nine years past, uniformly found in the application of the principles and usages of the common law. The same protection may unquestionably be afforded by a statute passed in virtue of the before-mentioned section, as necessary and proper, for carrying into execution the powers vested in that department. A construction of the different parts of the Constitution, perfectly just and fair, will, on analogous principles, extend protection and security against the offences in question, to the other departments of government, in discharge of their respective trusts.

The President of the United States is bound by his oath "to preserve, protect, and defend the Constitution," and it is expressly made his duty "to take care that the laws be faithfully executed;" but this would be impracticable by any created being, if there could be no legal restraint of those scandalous misrepresentations of his measures and motives, which directly tend to rob him of the public confidence. And equally impotent would be every other public officer, if thus left to the mercy of the seditious.

It is holden to be a truth most clear, that the important trusts before enumerated, cannot be discharged by the government to which they are committed, without the power to restrain or punish seditious practices and unlawful combinations against itself, and to protect the officers thereof from abusive misrepresentations. Had the Constitution withheld this power, it would have made the government responsible for the effects, without any control over the causes which naturally produce them, and would have essentially failed of answering the great ends for which the people of the United States declare, in the first clause of that instrument, that they establish the same, viz: "To form a more perfect union, establish justice, insure domestic tranquillity, provide for the common defence, promote the general welfare, and secure the blessings of liberty to ourselves and posterity."

Seditious practices and unlawful combinations against the federal government, or any officer thereof, in the performance of his duty, as well as licentiousness of speech and of the press, were punishable on the principles of common law in the courts of the United States, before the act in question was passed. This act, then, is an amelioration of that law in favour of the party accused, as it mitigates the punishment which that authorizes, and admits of any investigation of public men and measures which is regulated by truth. It is not intended to protect men in office, only as they are agents of the people. Its object is to afford legal security to public offices and trusts created for the safety and happiness of the people, and therefore the security derived from it is for the benefit of the people, and is their right.

This construction of the Constitution, and of the existing law of the land, as well as the act complained of, the legislature of Massachusetts most deliberately and firmly believe, results from a just and full view of the several parts of that Constitution; and they consider that act to be wise and necessary, as an audacious and unprincipled spirit of falsehood and abuse had been too long unremittingly exerted for the purpose of perverting public opinion, and threatened to undermine and destroy the whole fabric of the government.

The legislature further declare, that in the foregoing sentiments they have expressed the general opinion of their constituents, who have not only acquiesced without complaint in those particular measures of the federal government, but have given their explicit approbation by re-electing those men who voted for the adoption of them : nor is it apprehended, that the citizens of this state will be accused of supineness, or of an indifference to their constitutional rights; for, while on the one hand, they regard with due vigilance, the conduct of the government: on the other, their freedom, safety, and happiness require, that they should defend that government and its constitutional measures against the open or insidious attacks of any foe, whether foreign or domestic.

And lastly, that the Legislature of Massachusetts feel a strong conviction, that the several United States are connected by a common interest, which ought to render their union indissoluble, and that this state will always co-operate with its confederate states, in rendering that union productive of mutual security, freedom and happiness.

          Sent down for concurrence.

                                        SAMUEL PHILIPS, President.

   In the House of Representatives, Feb. 13, 1799.   Read and concurred.
                                        EDWARD ROBBINS, Speaker.
       A true copy.
                         Attest,   JOHN AVERY, Secretary.

STATE OF NEW YORK.

IN SENATE,

March 5, 1799.

Whereas the people of the United States have established for themselves a free and independent national government. And whereas it is essential to the existence of every government, that it have authority to defend and preserve its constitutional powers inviolate, inasmuch as every infringement thereof tends to its subversion. And whereas the judicial power extends expressly to all cases of law and equity arising under the Constitution and the laws of the United States, whereby the interference of the legislatures of the particular states in those cases, is manifestly excluded. And whereas our peace, prosperity, and happiness eminently depend on the preservation of the Union, in order to which, a reasonable confidence in the constituted authorities and chosen representatives of the people is indispensable. And whereas every measure calculated to weaken that confidence, has a tendency to destroy the usefulness of our public functionaries, and to excite jealousies equally hostile to rational liberty and the principles of a good republican government. And whereas the Senate, not perceiving that the rights of the particular states have been violated, nor any unconstitutional powers assumed by the general government, cannot forbear to express the anxiety and regret with which they observe the inflammatory and pernicious sentiments and doctrines which are contained in the resolutions of the legislatures of Virginia and Kentucky; sentiments and doctrines no less repugnant to the Constitution of the United States, and the principles of their union, than destructive to the Federal Government, and unjust to those whom the people have elected to administer it : wherefore,

Resolved, That while the Senate feel themselves constrained to bear unequivocal testimony against such sentiments‘ and doctrines, they deem it a duty no less indispensable, explicitly to declare their incompetency, as a branch of the legislature of this state, to supervise the acts of the general government.

Resolved, That his excellency the Governor be, and he is hereby requested to transmit a copy of the foregoing resolution to the executives of the states of Virginia and Kentucky, to the end that the same may be communicated to the legislatures thereof.

A true copy,   ABM. B. BAUCKER, Clerk.

STATE OF CONNECTICUT.

At a general assembly of the state of Connecticut, holden at Hartford, in the said state, on the second Thursday of May, Anno Domini, 1799, his excellency the Governor having communicated to this Assembly sundry resolutions of the legislature of Virginia, adopted in December 1798, which relate to the measures of the general government, and the said resolutions having been considered, it is

Resolved, That this Assembly views with deep regret, and explicitly disavows, the principles contained in the aforesaid resolutions; and particularly the opposition to the "alien and sedition-acts," acts, which the Constitution authorized; which the exigency of the country rendered necessary; which the constituted authorities have enacted, and which merit the entire approbation of this Assembly. They therefore decidedly refuse to concur with the legislature of Virginia, in promoting any of the objects attempted in the aforesaid resolutions.

And it is further *Resolved*, that his excellency the Governor be requested to transmit a copy of the foregoing resolution to the Governor of Virginia, that it may be communicated to the legislature of that state.

Passed in the House of Representatives unanimously.

Attest,

JOHN C. SMITH, Clerk.

Concurred unanimously, in the upper House.

Teste,

SAMUEL WYLLYS, Secretary.

STATE OF NEW HAMPSHIRE.

IN THE HOUSE OF REPRESENTATIVES,

June 14, 1799.

The committee to take into consideration the resolutions of the General Assembly of Virginia, dated December 21st, 1798; also certain resolutions of the Legislature of Kentucky, of the 10th November, 1798, report as follows:

The Legislature of New Hampshire having taken into consideration certain resolutions of the General Assembly of Virginia, dated December 21, 1798; also certain resolutions of the Legislature of Kentucky, of the 10th of November, 1798:

Resolved, That the Legislature of New Hampshire unequivocally express a firm resolution to maintain and defend the Constitution of the United States, and the Constitution of this state, against every aggression, either foreign or domestic, and that they will support the government of the United States in all measures warranted by the former.

That the state legislatures are not the proper tribunals to determine the constitutionality of the laws of the general government, that the duty of such decision is properly and exclusively confided to the judicial department.

That if the Legislature of New Hampshire, for mere speculative purposes, were to express an opinion on the acts of the general government, commonly called "the alien and sedition-bills," that opinion would unreservedly be, that those acts are constitutional, and in the present critical situation of our country, highly expedient.

That the constitutionality and expediency of the acts aforesaid, have been very ably advocated and clearly demonstrated by many citizens of the United States, more especially by the minority of the General Assembly of Virginia. The Legislature of New Hampshire, therefore, deem it unnecessary, by any train of arguments, to attempt further illustration of the propositions, the truth of which, it is confidently believed, at this day, is very generally seen and acknowledged.

Which report being read and considered, was unanimously received and accepted, one hundred and thirty-seven members being present.

Sent up for concurrence.

JOHN PRENTICE, Speaker.

In Senate, the same day, read and concurred unanimously.

AMOS SHEPARD, President.

Approved, June 15th, 1799.

J. T. GILMAN, Governor.

A true copy.

Attest,

JOSEPH PEARSON, Secretary.

STATE OF VERMONT.

IN THE HOUSE OF REPRESENTATIVES,

October 30th, A. D. 1799.

THE House proceeded to take under their consideration, the resolutions of the General Assembly of Virginia, relative to certain measures of the general government, transmitted to the Legislature of this state, for their consideration : Whereupon,

Resolved, That the General Assembly of the state of Vermont do highly disapprove of the resolutions of the General Assembly of Virginia, as being unconstitutional in their nature, and dangerous in their tendency. It belongs not to state legislatures to decide on the constitutionality of laws made by the general government; this power being exclusively vested in the judiciary courts of the Union : That his excellency the Governor be requested to transmit a copy of this resolution to the executive of Virginia, to be communicated to the General Assembly of that state : And that the same be sent to the Governor and Council for their concurrence.

SAMUEL C. CRAFTS, *Clerk.*

In Council, October 30, 1799.

Read and concurred unanimously.

RICHARD WHITNEY, *Secretary.*

12

V.

VIRGINIA REPORT OF 1799,

AND ANALYSIS THEREOF.

ANALYSIS OF REPORT.

WAIVING objections to the spirit and manner of the counter-resolutions of other states, the Report proceeds to discuss the resolutions of 21st December, 1798, *seriatim.*

1st Resolution. To maintain and defend the Constitution of the United States, &c.
Not liable to objection.

2d Resolution. To oppose every infraction of the Constitution, &c.
Not liable to objection.

3d Resolution. That the powers of the Federal Government result from the *compact*, to which the *states are parties:* That those powers are limited by the plain sense and intention of the instrument of compact: And that it is the duty of the states to interpose to arrest the deliberate, palpable, and dangerous exercise of powers not granted; wherein consider,

I. The truth of the several propositions affirmed: viz., that,

    1. The powers of the Federal Government result from the compact, or Constitution; wherein of,

        1. The contemporary discussions when the Constitution was submitted to the people of the states for their ratification.

        2. The 12th amendment to the Constitution.

    2. The states are parties to the compact, or Constitution: wherein of,

        1. The different senses of the word *states*, and the meaning as here used.

        2. The sense in which the Constitution was submitted to, and ratified by the *states.*

3. The powers are limited by the plain sense and intention of the instrument of compact; wherein consider that,
   1. The powers granted are valid only because granted.
   2. The powers not granted, are not valid.
4. The states, as sovereign parties to the compact, must construe it in the *last resort*, and decide if it be violated; wherein consider that,
   1. There can be no tribunal superior to the states, in the last resort, they being sovereign.
   2. The federal judiciary cannot be the *final* expositor of the Constitution, except in relation to the other departments of the government; because,
      1. Some usurpations, by the forms of the Constitution, cannot be drawn within its control.
      2. The decisions of the other departments, in cases not subject to judicial cognizance, would be equally authoritative and final.
      3. The usurpations sanctioned, or committed, by the judiciary would be irremediable.
5. The cases for interposition by the states;—only where the violation, by the United States, is
   1. Deliberate.
   2. Palpable.
   3. Dangerous.
6. The object of the interposition :
   To arrest the progress of usurpation, and maintain the authorities, rights, and liberties appertaining to the states.
II. The expediency of declaring the truths aforesaid; wherein of
   1. The general importance of recurrence to fundamental principles.
   2. The particular importance in view of the political doctrines of the day.
4th Resolution. That a spirit has been manifested to enlarge the powers of the Federal Government, by forced constructions, especially of certain general phrases; of which the effect will be to consolidate the states into one sovereignty, and the result a monarchy; wherein of the affirmation—
I. That a spirit has been manifested by the Federal Government to enlarge its powers by forced constructions of the Constitution; whereof the instances are (amongst others),
   1. The Bank-law of 1791.
   2. The Carriage-tax law of 1794.
   3. The Alien and Sedition laws.
II. That indications have appeared of a design to expound certain general phrases, [which although substantially contained in the former Articles of Confederation, were never therein so misconstrued,] so as to destroy the effect of the particular enumeration which explains and limits those phrases; wherein of
   1. What general phrases are referred to,—
      Those which relate to a provision " for the common defence and general welfare," &c.—Articles of Confederation, Art. VIII.

    2. The meaning attached to them, in the Articles of Confederation.

III. Instances of a design so to expound those phrases as to destroy the effect of the particular enumeration of powers ; wherein consider,

    1. What the instances are,

        1. Debates in Congress.

        2. Hamilton's Report on Manufactures, 5th December, 1791, wherein he supposes everything in the power of Congress, which concerns the general welfare, and involves the application of money.

        3. Report of Committee of House of Representatives on Agriculture, January, 1797 ; proposing an Agricultural Society under the direction of the Federal Government.

    2. The result of such exposition to destroy the effect of the particular enumeration of powers ; for,

        1. No power of importance, but may involve the application of money.

        2. It is no limitation of the power to confine it to cases affecting the general welfare, because all cases may be said to do so.

        3. The proper construction of the phrases—
        To limit the Federal Government to those modes of promoting the general welfare which are afterwards specified.

    3. The tendency of such exposition of the general phrases in question to consolidate the states into one sovereignty.

    4. The result of such consolidation, a monarchy ; by,

        1. Enlarging the Executive power as a supplement to the deficiency of laws, which would be greater as the objects of legislative attention were multiplied.

        2. Increasing the offices, honours, and emoluments depending on the Executive will, and thereby enabling the chief magistrate to secure his own re-election from time to time, and to regulate the succession.

        3. Rendering the Executive office such an object of ambition as to make elections so tumultuous and corrupt, that the people would themselves demand an hereditary succession.

5th Resolution. Protests particularly, against the Alien and Sedition-Acts, as palpable and alarming infractions of the Constitution, &c. ; wherein consider,

I. THE ALIEN ACT :—Of which it is said that,

    1. It exercises a power not delegated by the Constitution ; wherein of

        1. Some preliminary observations.

            1. The Federal Government possesses only delegated powers; and those not delegated to it are reserved to the states respectively, or to the people. Hence any power exercised, must appear to be granted by the Constitution.

            2. Distinguish between alien *enemies,* over whom the Federal authority, as incident to the power of making war, is complete ; and alien *friends,* to whom it is denied that its power extends.

            3. Even if the "Alien-Act" contemplated *preventive,* only, and

not *penal* justice, and if the former were within the power of Congress, (which is denied,) yet such preventive justice has not been exercised in a constititutional manner.   Because the principles of the only preventive justice known to American jurisprudence, require,

   1. That some probable ground of suspicion be exhibited to some *judicial* authority ; the act refers it to the President.

   2. That it be supported by oath or affirmation ; the act requires none.

   3. That the party may avoid imprisonment by pledges of legal conduct, sufficient in the judgment of some *judicial* authority; the act denies this privilege, or refers it to the discretion of the President.

   4. The party may have a writ of *habeas corpus* if wrongfully confined; the act allows the President to send an alien off before he can obtain such writ, thus unconstitutionally suspending the privilege of the writ.

   5. The party may be discharged from confinement, by order of the proper *judicial* authority, for good cause ; the act confers the power on the President alone.

  4. But the act contemplates *penal* justice ; involving,

    1. Banishment from the country of the alien's choice; and perhaps of his tenderest relations.

    2. Loss of employment and property.

    3. A sea-voyage ; dangerous in itself, and also from the casualties incident to time of war.

    4. Possible vindictiveness of the country whence he emigrated.

2. Answers to arguments to prove the act constitutional.

  1. The admission of aliens being a favour, it is not therefore revocable by the Federal Government; because,

    1. If revocable at all, it does not follow that the Constitution has given to that government the power to revoke it.

    2. Favours are not always revocable, as grants of land, pardon to a malefactor, haturalization, &c.

  2. Aliens not being parties to the Constitution, it does not follow that Congress may invade, as to them, the rights and privileges it secures; because,

    1. Such absolute authority may have been left to the states, or at least may not have been conferred on Congress.

    2. But aliens, though not parties to the Constitution, are entitled, whilst they conform to it, to its protection, as to the protection of the laws, to which also they are not parties.

    3. Upon similar reasoning aliens might not be banished only, but capitally punished by the President, without a trial.

  3. That aliens, by the law and practice of nations may be removed at pleasure for offences against the law of nations, and that Congress is authorized to define and punish such offences, does not justify the indiscriminate expulsion of all aliens ; because,

1. Alien-*enemies* alone, are thus subject to the law of nations, alien-*friends* (except public ministers), being subject to the municipal law.
2. The act being admitted to be *penal*, must be justified by some offence deserving punishment.
3. Offences for which aliens within the jurisdiction of a country, are punishable, are,
    1. Those committed by their states;.which is the case of alien-enemies, admitted to be subject to the laws of nations, and so within the control of Congress.
    2. Those committed by aliens personally; which is the case of alien-friends, who, like citizens, are subject to the municipal law, and so not amenable to Congress.
4. The laws of nations distinguish between *alien-friends*, and *alien-enemies*, allowing the removal of the latter at discretion, but holding the former to be under a temporary allegiance, and entitled to a corresponding protection.
4. That Congress may grant letters of marque and reprisal, and that reprisals may be made on persons as well as property, does not justify the act; because,
    1. Reprisals are a mode of obtaining justice by seizure of persons or property for injuries done by a state, or its members, to another state, or its members, when the aggressor refuses redress.
    2. No injury is alleged or implied from any particular nation, for which this proceeding may afford reparation. It is directed against aliens of *all* nations.
5. That Congress has power to make war does not justify the act, which is applicable to alien-*friends*.
6. That Congress may protect each state against invasion, and provide for repelling invasion, does not justify it; because,
    1. These powers do not add to the general power of war.
    2. Invasion is only one operation of war; and what is not incident to the power of war generally, cannot be so to any of its operations.
    3. A power to act when a case occurs, does not include a power over all means which *tend* to prevent the occurrence; which would frustrate every practicable definition of limited powers. Thus it would involve,
        1. A power over religion, lest a bigoted and tyrannical state should invade us on account of our belief.
        2. A power over popular instruction, and over the provision for the poor, as *tending* to prevent insurrections, &c.
7. That the Constitution has *given to the states* no power to remove aliens, and that there would be, else, no power in the country to send away such as are dangerous, does not justify the Alien-act; because,
    1. Several powers are withheld from both the federal and state governments,—as to tax exports; so that the non-possession of

a power by the state governments, does not imply its possession by the federal government.

2. The powers of the state governments are not the *gift* of the
Federal Constitution, but the residuum remaining in the states,
after the delegation of certain specific powers to the Union.

8. The Alien-Act is not vindicated by the example of the Virginia law of 1785, re-enacted in 1792, which referred to alien-
enemies.

2. The Alien-Act unites legislative, executive, and judicial power in the
hands of the President.

1. Legislative: Because details, especially as to crimes, are essential
to the idea of a law; and here every circumstance of *danger, suspicion,* and *secret machination* is to be defined by the will of the
President.

2. Judicial: Because the President is to judge whether the circumstances exist, which he, as a legislator, has resolved shall be suspicious, &c.

3. Executive: Because he is to execute his own decrees, by removal
of the party suspected.

3. This union of powers subverts the general principles of free government, which require the three great functions to be kept in distinct
hands.

4. It also subverts the particular organization of the Federal Constitution, which provides for the separation of those powers.

II. THE SEDITION-ACT:—*Of which it is said that,*

1. It exercises a power not delegated by the Constitution, wherein of

1. The argument that the common law is part of the law of the
United States in their national capacity: therein consider;

1. That before the Revolution, the common law, however it may
have existed, with more or less modification in all the colonies,
did not pervade the whole as one society; because,

1. It was not the same in any two colonies: the modifications
being materially different in many.

2. There was no common legislature to enact, nor common
magistracy to enforce it.

2. That the Revolution did not imply, nor introduce it as a law of
the Union; because,

1. The fundamental principle of the Revolution was, that the
colonies were united by a common executive, but not by a
common legislative sovereign.

2. Parliamentary regulation of trade [mere practice without
right], was acquiesced in without inquiry, but the assumption
of a power to legislate *in all cases,* resulted in the conclusion
that Parliament could not legislate *in any case.*

3. The interval between the beginning of the Revolution and the
final ratification of the Articles of Confederation, did not introduce it; the nature and extent of the Union being, in that interval, determined by the crisis only.

4. The Articles of Confederation did not adopt it; because,.

    1. Nothing in the instrument countenances such an idea.

    2. Every power, jurisdiction, and right, not *expressly* delegated, is retained.

5. The present Constitution did not introduce it; wherein consider,

    1. That particular parts of the common law may have a sanction from the Constitution; being,

        1. So much as is comprehended in the technical phrases thereof.

        2. Such other parts as Congress may adopt as means necessary and proper to carry into effect the powers delegated.

    2. The clause supposed to justify the conclusion that the common law, generally, is the law of the Union, viz. :

That which extends the judicial power to all *cases in law and equity*, arising under the *Constitution*, laws, &c., of the United States; wherein consider,

        1. That cases may arise under the *Constitution*, distinct from such as arise out of laws and treaties, without supposing the common law part of the Constitution, viz. :

            1. Cases involving restrictions on states; as to emit bills of credit, &c.

            2. Cases between citizens of different states, &c.

        2. That the phrase, " cases in law and equity," refers only to *civil* cases : whereas the common law includes criminal cases also; because,

            1. *Criminal cases in law and equity*, would be a language unknown to the law.

            2. Appellate jurisdiction, in such cases of "law and equity," is given (with one or two exceptions) to the Supreme Court, both as to *law and fact*, which excludes criminal cases.

            3. The judicial power is not (by Amendment XI. of Constitution) to be construed to extend to any suit in *law or equity*, of an individual against a state; which also excludes the idea of criminal cases.

        3. That the phrase, " cases in law and equity," referring at any rate only to *civil* cases, could not justify the Sedition-Act, which is a *criminal* statute.

        4. That the clause in question, though it involved the common law, both in *civil and criminal* cases, defines the extent of the *judicial*, and not of the *legislative* power.

    3. That the descriptions in the Constitution of the law of the United States, do not embrace the common law, viz. :

        1. That which is meant as a guide to United States judges, " The Constitution, and laws and treaties in pursuance thereof." Article III., section 1.

        2. That which is meant as a guide to state judges, " The Constitution, and laws and treaties in pursuance thereof, shall be the supreme law of the land." Article VI.

4. The difficulties and consequences of a constructive introduction of the common law, viz. :

  1. The difficulties :

    1. Is it with or without the British statutes ?

    2. If with them, to what period ; the oldest or youngest colony, or a mean ?

    3. Is regard to be had to colonial modifications ? If so, which ? how ? &c.

  2. The consequences flowing from such construction.

    1. As to the several departments of the Federal Government : and therein as to,

      1. The legislative authority of the Union :

        1. If the common law be established by the *Constitution*,

          1. No part of it could be altered. Statutes mitigating its barbarous severities, including the sedition-law itself, would be void.

          2. The whole code, with all its incongruities, &c., would be inviolably saddled on the people.

        2. If the common law be supposed not fixed by the Constitution, but liable to alteration by Congress,

          It extends the authority of Congress to every subject of legislation, (for the common law embraces all,) and emancipates it from all limitations.

      2. The executive authority :

        1. The President's authority to execute, will be co-extensive with the legislative power to enact.

        2. The President's authority might be extended to the prerogatives which the common law confers on the crown.

      3. The judicial authority.:

        1. If the common law has a *constitutional* obligation, The judges would possess a discretion little short of legislative power, which would be permanent and uncontrollable.

        2. If it be of only *legal* obligation, subject to Congress :

          1. The dangerous discretion would exist, of determining what parts of the common law are adapted to the circumstances of the country.

          2. This discretion must continue until Congress could enact a full system of laws.

    2. As to the authority of the states :

      Their residuary sovereignty would be overwhelmed by this one construction.

2. Other arguments founded on various parts of the Constitution, viz. :

  1. On the preamble to the Constitution ; wherein consider,

    That this part of an instrument is never allowed to be set up in opposition to the plain meaning of the body thereof.

2. On the clause which gives Congress power to lay and collect taxes, &c., to pay the debts, and provide for the *common defence and general welfare*, &c.

The effect of this already considered, (ante, p. 179–80,) and supposed not to enlarge the enumerated powers of Congress.

3. On the clause which empowers Congress to make all laws necessary and proper to carry into effect the powers conferred by the Constitution ; wherein consider,

1. That this clause confers no new powers, but merely declares [what, at any rate, would have been implied], that the grant of a power shall include the means of its execution.

2. The mode of reasoning to be pursued under this clause.

1. To determine if the power to be exercised is expressed in the Constitution.

2. If not, to see if it is properly incident to any express power, and necessary to its execution.

3. The express power to which the enactment of a sedition law is supposed to be incident:

The power to *suppress* insurrections ; wherein consider,

1. That if a power to *suppress*, authorizes whatever *tends* to *prevent*, the power of Congress is unlimited.

2. That the contemporaneous construction, whilst the Constitution was under discussion, was *nem. con.*, that the incidental power must have to the principal the relation of *necessity*, and not of mere *tendency* to *promote*.

3. That such a construction frustrates an appeal to the judiciary, which can exert a judicial control if the relation of *necessity* is to exist, but not if a *tendency to promote* is enough.

2. The sedition-act exercises a power positively forbidden by one of the amendments to the Constitution; wherein consider,

1. That the freedom of the press is not to be determined by the meaning of the phrase at common law ; and therein consider,

1. That the sedition-act abridges the freedom of publication even by the common law of England.

2. That the common law idea of freedom of the press, viz., exemption from all *previous* restraint, is not the American idea ; because,

1. There is no material difference between a previous restraint, and a subsequent punishment of publications.

2. There is an essential difference between the government of Great Britain, and of America, requiring in the latter greater freedom of remark.

3. The object in the British government is to protect the press from the assaults of the executive. In America we desire to protect it, also, against the legislature.

4. That not only is freedom of the press secured by the Constitution in America, and in England merely by law, and not only does it extend in the former as well to subsequent penalties, as

previous restraint, but the actual freedom is greater in America than in England; wherein consider,

1. The difference in the governments, those of America being wholly elective and responsible.
2. The practice in England in respect to the elective and responsible members of the government.
3. The practice in the several states of the confederacy.
4. The good effects which have resulted from this free animadversion.
    1. In the world at large.
    2. As respects our Revolution, which was promoted by canvassing the measures of government.
    3. As respects the present Federal Constitution, which was substituted for the Articles of Confederation, in consequence of the latter's-defects being freely investigated.

3. That freedom of conscience and of religion are guaranteed by the same clause which relates to freedom of the press, and the former cannot be supposed to be limited by the common law meaning.

2. That the amendment in question positively denied to Congress *any* power over the press, and does not suppose such power to exist, with the qualification that its freedom shall not be abridged; because,

1. The provision was recommended by the ratifying conventions of several states with a view to exclude Congress from *all power over the subject.*
2. The amendment was introduced in order to quiet the apprehensions of those states.
3. It is more reasonable to deem the power withheld, than to suppose one so important left to vague construction.
4. The peculiar magnitude of some of the powers of the Federal Government, the duration of some of its offices, and the distance of many of the people from the seat of government, are reasons why it might have been the policy of the Federal Constitution to exempt the press from federal jurisdiction.

3. The exercise of this power over the press ought, more than any other, to produce universal alarm; and therein consider,

1. That the responsibility of officers of government cannot be secured without a free investigation of their conduct and motives.
2. That it is the right and duty of every citizen to make such investigation, and promulge the results.
3. That in the several elections, during the continuance of the sedition-act, it would tend to screen the incumbents of office from inquiry.
4. That it is no defence of the act that it allows the *truth* of the publication to be proved, and only punishes what is *false;* because,
    1. Formal legal proof, even of facts, in political disquisition, is extremely difficult.
    2. Opinions, inferences and conjectural observations, necessary concomitants of free inquiry, cannot generally be proved at all, in court.

5. That it is no defence of the act that the *intent* must be to defame, or bring into contempt, disrepute, or hatred, for such is ever the object of one who thinks he has discovered an error.

6. That the right of election (which depends on full information) is the essence of a free government, and is impaired by the sedition-act.

    1. Competitors against incumbents of office have not an equal chance, the latter being shielded by the act.

    2. The people cannot fully discuss and ascertain the relative merits of such competitors and incumbents.

6th Resolution. Refers to a declaration of the Virginia Convention which ratified the Federal Constitution, touching freedom of the press, and affirms that it would be a criminal degeneracy now to be indifferent to so palpable a violation thereof, &c. ; wherein of,

    1. The declaration of the Virginia Convention *in tot verbis.*

    2. Acquiescence in the violation of freedom of the press would yield a similar power over religion and conscience ; for,

        1. Neither power was delegated.

        2. Both were reserved by the same amendment, recommended and made at the same time.

        3. The common law measure applies to one, as well as to the other.

        4. A similar form of words is used to guarantee both.

7th Resolution. Professes sincere affection for the people of the other states, and anxiety to perpetuate the Union, and appeals to the other states to concur in declaring the alien and sedition-laws unconstitutional, and to take necessary and proper measures to maintain unimpaired the authorities, rights, and liberties reserved to the states respectively, or to the people ; wherein consider,

    1. That such declaration is no invasion of the functions of the judiciary, being a mere declaration of opinion.

    2. That the relations of the state legislatures to the Federal Government justified such a declaration ; for,

        1. They might address Congress to repeal the laws.

        2. They might instruct or request their own senators and representatives to vote to repeal the laws.

        3. They might originate an amendment to the Constitution.

    3. That neither the object (to maintain the Constitution, &c.) nor the means (such as were necessary and proper) could be objected to.

    4. That during the discussions on the ratification of the Federal Constitution, a vigilant supervision of the Federal Government by the state legislatures, was deemed a recommendation.

In view of all which the adoption of the following resolution is recommended.

Resolved, That the General Assembly, having carefully and respectfully attended to the proceedings of a number of the states, in answer to its resolutions of December 21, 1798, and having fully reconsidered the latter, find it to be its indispensable duty to adhere to the same, as founded in truth, as consonant with the Constitution, and as conducive to its preservation; and more especially to be its duty to renew, as it does hereby renew, its protest against "the alien and sedition acts," as palpable and alarming infractions of the Constitution.

REPORT OF 1799.

VIRGINIA.

HOUSE OF DELEGATES.

Report of the committee to whom were referred the communications of various states relative to the resolutions of the General Assembly of this state, concerning the Alien and Sedition-Laws.

WHATEVER room might be found in the proceedings of some of the states who have disapproved of the resolutions of the General Assembly of this commonwealth, passed on the 21st day of December, 1798, for painful remarks on the spirit and manner of those proceedings, it appears to the committee most consistent with the duty, as well as dignity of the General Assembly, to hasten an oblivion of every circumstance which might be construed into a diminution of mutual respect, confidence, and affection, among the members of the Union.

The committee have deemed it a more useful task, to revise, with a critical eye, the resolutions which have met with this disapprobation; to examine fully the several objections and arguments which have appeared against them; and to inquire whether there be any errors of fact, of principle, or of reasoning, which the candour of the General Assembly ought to acknowledge and correct.

The first of the resolutions is in the words following:

Resolved, That the General Assembly of Virginia doth unequivocally express a firm resolution to maintain and defend the Constitution of the United States, and the Constitution of this state, against every aggression, either foreign or domestic, and that they will support the government of the United States in all measures warranted by the former.

No unfavourable comment can have been made on the sentiments here expressed. To maintain and defend the Constitution of the United States, and of their own state, against every aggression, both foreign and domestic, and to support the government of the United States in all measures warranted by their Constitution, are duties which the General Assembly ought always to feel, and to which, on such an occasion, it was evidently proper to express its sincere and firm adherence.

In their next resolution—*The General Assembly most solemnly declares a warm attachment to the union of the states, to maintain which it pledges all its powers; and that, for this end, it is its duty to watch over and oppose every infraction of those principles, which constitute the only basis of that union, because a faithful observance of them can alone secure its existence and the public happiness.*

The observation just made is equally applicable to this solemn declaration, of warm attachment to the union, and this solemn pledge to maintain it; nor can any question arise among enlightened friends of the union, as to the duty of watching over and opposing every infraction of those principles which constitute its basis, and a faithful observance of which can alone secure its existence, and the public happiness thereon depending.

The third resolution is in the words following:

That this Assembly doth explicitly and peremptorily declare, that it views the powers of the Federal Government, as resulting from the compact, to which the states are parties, as limited by the plain sense and intention of the instrument constituting that compact; as no farther valid than they are authorized by the grants enumerated in that compact; and that in case of a deliberate, palpable and dangerous exercise of other powers, not granted by the said compact, the states who are parties thereto have the right, and are in duty bound, to interpose for arresting the progress of the evil, and for maintaining within their respective limits, the authorities, rights, and liberties appertaining to them.

On this resolution, the committee have bestowed all the attention which its importance merits; they have scanned it not merely with a strict, but with a severe eye; and they feel confidence in pronouncing, that, in its just and fair construction, it is unexceptionably true in its several positions, as well as constitutional and conclusive in its inferences.

The resolution declares, *first*, that " it views the powers of the Federal Government, as resulting from the compact to which the states are parties;" in other words, that the Federal powers are derived from the Constitution, and that the Constitution is a compact to which the states are parties.*

Clear as the position must seem, that the federal powers are derived from

---

* The position that the powers of the Federal Government result from a *compact* to which the states are parties, has been assailed as if it assumed that the idea of a Constitution was thereby excluded, and the government converted into a mere confederation. (1 Story's Comms. on Constitution, 287.) But the essential question to which the attention of the writer seems to have been directed, was not as to the nature of the Constitution, whether it were an instrument of confederation, or of government, but it was as to who are the parties thereto, the aggregate people of the whole Union, or the states in their highest sovereign capacity, not represented by their ordinary governments, but by delegates deputed for the sole purpose of expressing the will of the people of each state on the subject.

Whether or not it follows that because the states are parties to the Federal Government, they must, therefore, be the rightful judges in the *last resort* of alleged usurpations by that government, in any or all of its departments, is submitted to the reader upon the reasoning in the text. (See, also, 1 Tuck. Bl. App. 170.)

the Constitution, and from that alone, the committee are not unapprised of a late doctrine, which opens another source of federal powers, not less extensive and important, than it is new and unexpected.   The examination of this doctrine will be most conveniently connected with a review of a succeeding resolution.   The committee satisfy themselves here with briefly remarking, that in all the cotemporary discussions and comments which the Constitution underwent, it was constantly justified and recommended, on the ground, that the powers not given to the government, were withheld from it; and that, if any doubt could have existed on this subject, under the original text of the Constitution, it is removed, as far as words could remove it, by the 12th amendment, now a part of the Constitution, which expressly declares, " that the powers not delegated to the United States, by the Constitution, nor prohibited by it to the states, are reserved to the states respectively, or to the people."

   The other position involved in this branch of the resolution, namely, " that the states are parties to the Constitution or compact," is, in the judgment of the committee, equally free from objection.   It is indeed true, that the term " states," is sometimes used in a vague sense, and sometimes in different senses, according to the subject to which it is applied. Thus, it sometimes means the separate sections of territory occupied by the political societies within each; sometimes the particular governments, established by those societies ; sometimes those societies as organized into those particular governments; and, lastly, it means the people composing those political societies, in their highest sovereign capacity.   Although it might be wished that the perfection of language admitted less diversity in the signification of the same words, yet little inconveniency is produced by it, where the true sense can be collected with certainty from the different applications.   In the present instance, whatever different constructions of the term " states," in the resolution, may have been entertained, all will at least concur in that last mentioned ; because, in that sense, the Constitution was submitted to the " states:" in that sense the " states" ratified it : and, in that sense of the term " states," they are consequently parties to the compact, from which the powers of the federal government result.*

   The next position is, that the General Assembly views the powers of the federal government, " as limited by the plain sense and intention of the instrument constituting that compact," and " as no farther valid than they are authorized by the grants therein enumerated."   It does not seem possible, that any just objection can lie against either of these clauses. The first amounts merely to a declaration, that the compact ought to have

---

* This paragraph seems to have in view some observations of Mr. GEORGE KEITH TAYLOR, in the debate on the Resolutions in 1798, *ante*, pp. 122 to 126.   The Resolutions, as originally introduced into the House of Delegates, had the word "*alone*" following " *states*," so as to make that clause read thus :—" to which the states *alone* are parties."   Mr. *Taylor's* remarks, which are very ingenious, tended to show that the states,—which he interpreted to mean the ordinary governments of the states,—were not parties to the Federal Constitution, at all, much less, sole parties.   His argument so far prevailed as to induce Mr. GILES to move to strike out the word " *alone*," in which Mr. JOHN TAYLOR of Caroline, the mover of the resolutions, concurred, and it was stricken out accordingly.   (See *ante*, pp. 148 and 150.)

the interpretation plainly intended by the parties to it; the other to a declaration, that it ought to have the execution and effect intended by them. If the powers granted, be valid, it is solely because they are granted: and, if the granted powers are valid, because granted, all other powers not granted, must not be valid.

The resolution, having taken this view of the federal compact, proceeds to infer, "that, in case of a deliberate, palpable, and dangerous exercise of other powers, not granted by the said compact, the states, who are parties thereto, have the right and are in duty bound to interpose for arresting the progress of the evil, and for maintaining within their respective limits, the authorities, rights, and liberties appertaining to them."

It appears to your committee to be a plain principle, founded in common sense, illustrated by common practice, and essential to the nature of compacts, that, where resort can be had to no tribunal, superior to the authority of the parties, the parties themselves must be the rightful judges in the last resort, whether the bargain made has been pursued or violated. The Constitution of the United States was formed by the sanction of the states, given by each in its sovereign capacity. It adds to the stability and dignity, as well as to the authority of the Constitution, that it rests on this legitimate and solid foundation. The states, then, being the parties to the constitutional compact, and in their sovereign capacity, it follows of necessity, that there can be no tribunal above their authority, to decide in the last resort, whether the compact made by them be violated; and, consequently, that, as the parties to it, they must themselves decide, in the last resort, such questions as may be of sufficient magnitude to require their interposition.

It does not follow, however, that because the states, as sovereign parties to their constitutional compact, must ultimately decide whether it has been violated, that such a decision ought to be interposed, either in a hasty manner, or on doubtful and inferior occasions. Even in the case of ordinary conventions between different nations, where, by the strict rule of interpretation, a breach of a part may be deemed a breach of the whole, every part being deemed a condition of every other part and of the whole, it is always laid down that the breach must be both wilful and material to justify an application of the rule. But in the case of an intimate and constitutional union, like that of the United States, it is evident that the interposition of the parties, in their sovereign capacity, can be called for by occasions only, deeply and essentially affecting the vital principles of their political system.

The resolution has accordingly guarded against any misapprehension of its object, by expressly requiring for such an interposition, "the case of a *deliberate, palpable,* and *dangerous* breach of the Constitution, by the exercise of *powers not granted* by it. It must be a case, not of a light and transient nature, but of a nature *dangerous* to the great purposes for which the Constitution was established. It must be a case, moreover, not obscure or doubtful in its construction, but plain and *palpable.* Lastly, it must be a case not resulting from a partial consideration, or hasty determination; but a case stamped with a final consideration and *deliberate* adherence. It is not necessary, because the resolution does not require that the question should be discussed, how far the exercise of any particular power, ungranted by the Constitution, would justify the interposition of the parties to it. As cases might easily be stated, which none would contend ought to fall within that description ; cases, on the other hand, might, with ,equal ease, be stated, so flagrant and so fatal, as to unite every opinion in placing them within that description.*

---

* The cautious and moderate language of the text is worthy of observation. The cases proper for interposition by the states are said to be such *only* as involve *deliberate, palpable, and dangerous breaches of the Constitution, by the exercise of powers not granted.* The *objects* of interposition are merely to arrest the progress of the usurpation, and to maintain the authorities, rights, and liberties of the states, as parties to the Constitution.

Force, on this occasion, at least, appears to have been neither threatened nor contemplated. The moral influence of the sentiment of the states and of the people was relied upon. Not only does this appear from the declarations of Mr. Madison, in his letter to Ingersoll, *post,* p. 257, but it is abundantly manifested by the tenor of the debates on the resolutions, and by the report. Thus Mr. MERCER, replying to Mr. GEORGE K. TAYLOR, holds this language : " The gentleman from Prince George had told the committee that the resolutions introduced by the gentleman from Caroline were calculated to rouse the people to resistance, to excite the people of Virginia against the federal government. Mr. M. did not see how such consequences could result from their adoption. They contained nothing more than the sentiments which the people in many parts of the state had expressed, and which had been conveyed to the legislature in their memorials and resolutions, then lying upon the table." See *ante,* p. 41. Again : " The state believed some of its rights had been invaded by the late acts of the federal government, and proposed a remedy whereby to obtain a repeal of them. The plan contained in the resolutions appeared to Mr. M. the most advisable. Force was not thought of by any one." *Ante,* p. 42. Then, after citing some passages from the Federalist, to show that state interposition had been contemplated by the authors of that work, he argues that not only is the right of the states to communicate with each other defended by that authority, but that the adoption of a regular plan of opposition, in which they should combine all their resources, would also be justified by it. " But no such wish," says he, " is entertained by the friends of the resolutions; their object in addressing the states is to obtain a similar declaration of opinion," &c. *Ante,* p. 44.

Mr. BARBOUR observed, " that the gentleman from Prince George had remarked that these resolutions invited the people to insurrection and to arms. But, Mr. B. said, that if he could conceive the consequence foretold would grow out of the measure, he would become its bitterest enemy, for he deprecated intestine commotion, civil war, and bloodshed, as the most direful evils which could befall a country, except slavery. A resort to arms was the last appeal of an oppressed, an injured nation, and was never made but when public servants converted themselves, by usurpation, into masters, and destroyed rights once participated; and then it was justifiable." *Ante,* p. 54. Again : " The gentleman from Prince George was for the people's rising *en masse,* if the law was unconstitutional. For his part, he was for using no violence. It was the peculiar blessing of the American people to have redress within their reach by constitutional and peaceful means." *Ante,* p. 59.

Mr. JOHN TAYLOR, of Caroline, spoke of the threats of war, and the apprehension of civil commotion, towards which the resolutions were said to have a tendency. " Are the republicans," said he, " possessed of fleets and armies? If not, to what could they appeal for defence and support? To nothing, except public opinion. If that should be against them, they must yield." *Ante,* p. 113. And he is not less emphatic and distinct in a subsequent passage. *Ante,* pp. 114–15. See also the report, *post,* pp. 230–31.

It has been suggested, however, as proof that resistance by force was meditated, that Virginia prepared herself for the anticipated conflict by establishing arsenals, and

13

But the resolution has done more than guard against misconstruction, by expressly referring to cases of a *deliberate, palpable*, and *dangerous* nature. It specifies the object of the interposition which it contemplates, to be solely that of arresting the progress of the *evil* of usurpation, and of maintaining the authorities, rights, and liberties appertaining to the states, as parties to the Constitution.

From this view of the resolution, it would seem inconceivable that it

erecting armories. The fact standing alone, hardly warrants the inference under any conceivable circumstances, but especially does it not warrant it in the face of the declarations just cited of the prominent guides and advocates of the action of the state, at that period. But, in truth, the armory and arsenal bill was enacted 23d January, 1798, about six months before the alien and sedition-laws were passed, and three months, probably, before they were contemplated, at a time when Mr. Adams's administration, though certainly not popular in Virginia, was not particularly obnoxious. Can it be believed, indeed, that a party which could marshal so much talent and character, and so respectable an array of numbers against the less extreme measure of the resolutions of the succeeding session of 1798-9, when the provocation was infinitely greater, would have failed to penetrate the belligerent purpose of that bill, if any had existed, or that perceiving it, they would have hesitated to expose and denounce it?

This note, protracted, as it is, ought not to be concluded without referring to the temper of wise forbearance which, at this perilous crisis, was earnestly inculcated by Mr. JEFFERSON. In a letter to Mr. JOHN TAYLOR, in June, 1798, he says:

" Mr. New showed me your letter, which gave me an opportunity of observing what you said as to the effect with you, of public proceedings, and that it was not unwise now to estimate the separate mass of Virginia and North Carolina, with a view to their separate existence. It is true that we are completely under the saddle of Massachusetts and Connecticut, and that they ride us very hard, insulting our feelings, as well as exhausting our strength and substance. Their natural friends, the three other eastern states, join them from a sort of family pride, and they have the art to divide certain other parts of the Union, so as to make use of them to govern the whole." Then, after observing that this was not the natural state of things, and that time, of itself, would bring relief, which besides was likely to be hastened by impending events, he continues : " Be this as it may, in every free and deliberating society, there must, from the nature of man, be opposite parties, and violent dissension and discords ; and one of these, for the most part, must prevail over the other, for a longer or shorter time. Perhaps this party division is necessary to induce each to watch, and delate to the people the proceedings of the other. But if, on a temporary superiority of the one party, the other is to resort to a scission of the Union, no federal government can ever exist. If, to rid ourselves of the present rule of Massachusetts and Connecticut, we break the Union, will the evil stop there? Suppose the New England states alone cut off, will our natures be changed? Are we not men still, to the south of that, and with all the passions of men ? Immediately we shall see a Pennsylvania and a Virginia party arise in the residuary confederacy, and the public mind will be distracted with the same party-spirit. What a game, too, will the one party have in their hands, threatening the other that unless they do so and so, they will join their northern neighbours ! If we reduce our Union to Virginia and North Carolina, immediately the conflict will be established between the representatives of these two states, and they will end by breaking into their simple units. Seeing, therefore, that an association of men who will not quarrel with one another, is a thing which never yet existed, from the greatest confederacy of nations, down to a town-meeting, or a vestry ; seeing that we must have somebody to quarrel with, I would rather keep our New England associates for that purpose, than to see our bickerings transferred to others." " It is true that, in the mean time, we are suffering deeply in spirit, and incurring the horrors of a war, and long oppressions of enormous public debt. But who can say what would be the evils of a scission, and when and where they would end? Better keep together as we are, haul off from Europe as soon as we can, and from all attachments to any portion of it," &c. (3 Jeff. Mem., &c., 393.)

can incur any just disapprobation from those who, laying aside all momentary impressions, and recollecting the genuine source and object of the
Federal Constitution, shall candidly and accurately interpret the meaning
of the General Assembly. If the deliberate exercise of dangerous powers,
palpably withheld by the Constitution, could not justify the parties to it,
in interposing even so far as to arrest the progress of the evil, and thereby
to preserve the Constitution itself, as well as to provide for the safety of
the parties to it, there would be an end to all relief from usurped power,
and a direct subversion of the rights specified or recognised under all the
state constitutions, as well as a plain denial of the fundamental principle
on which our independence itself was declared.

But it is objected that the judicial authority is to be regarded as the sole
expositor of the Constitution, in the last resort; and it may be asked for
what reason, the declaration by the General Assembly, supposing it to be
theoretically true, could be required at the present day and in so solemn
a manner.

On this objection it might be observed, *first*, that there may be instances of usurped power, which the forms of the Constitution would never
draw within the control of the judicial department;* *secondly*, that
if the decision of the judiciary be raised above the authority of the

---

* Judge Story holds that each department of the government, and each member of
every department, is the interpreter of the Constitution for itself, in the first instance,
whenever called upon to act under it. If the question is not of a nature to be capable
of a judicial decision, he considers such determination by the department called on to
act,—whether it be the executive, or the legislative,—to be final. If it be capable of
judicial investigation, he regards the judicial power and the Supreme Court as the
head thereof, the final arbiter of the constitutionality of the act.

As to the second observation in the text, that the judicial department may also exercise or sanction dangerous powers, not granted by the Constitution, Judge Story
esteems it a case not to be supposed, or that, at all events, the people, in forming the
Constitution for the Union,—in like manner as in forming the state constitutions,—
have relied upon the judiciary as the ultimate barrier against usurpation, or the exercise
of unconstitutional power.

The difference between these views is certainly marked, but it is less considerable
than at first view may appear.

According to the text, if all the departments of government, including the judiciary
(where the question is of a nature to be submitted to it,) combine to commit or to sanction, a *deliberate, palpable, and dangerous violation* of the Constitution, the states, as
parties to the Constitution, may determine, in the last resort, whether the alleged violation has occurred, and may interpose to arrest the evil.

Judge Story allows of no interposition by the *states*, but insists that, in the case
supposed, when the evil has become no longer endurable, resort must be had, by the
people and not by the *states*, to the ultimate right of resistance.

Neither construction discards resistance to dangerous and palpable usurpation.
They only differ as to the means of ascertaining the usurpation in the *last resort*, and
of setting on foot the resistance, when ascertained. The one refers it to the states as
sovereign members of the confederacy; the other to the people exclusively. (See 1
Story's Com. on Const., 346 to 375.)

The *constitutional* remedies against the exercise of unconstitutional power, in Judge
Story's opinion, are:—if the Congress be the offendor, an appeal to the elective fran-
chise, and, if need be, an amendment of the Constitution; if the executive is guilty,
an impeachment, and a new election; if the judiciary, an impeachment, and an alteration, for the future, of the bad law as judicially expounded.

sovereign parties to the Constitution, the decisions of the other depart-ments, not carried by the forms of the Constitution before the judiciary, must be equally authoritative and final with the decisions of that de-partment. But the proper answer to the objection is, that the resolution of the General Assembly relates to those great and extraordinary cases, in which all the forms of the Constitution may prove ineffectual against infractions dangerous to the essential rights of the parties to it. The resolution supposes that dangerous powers, not delegated, may not only be usurped and executed by the other departments, but that the judi-cial department also may exercise or sanction dangerous powers beyond the grant of the Constitution; and, consequently, that the ultimate right of the parties to the Constitution, to judge whether the compact has been dangerously violated, must extend to violations by one delegated autho-rity, as well as by another; by the judiciary, as well as by the executive, or the legislature.

However true, therefore, it may be, that the judicial department, is, in all questions submitted to it by the forms of the Constitution, to decide in the last resort, this resort must necessarily be deemed the last in relation to the authorities of the other departments of the government; not in rela-tion to the rights of the parties to the constitutional compact, from which the judicial as well as the other departments hold their delegated trusts. On any other hypothesis, the delegation of judicial power would annul the authority delegating it; and the concurrence of this department with the others in usurped powers, might subvert for ever, and beyond the possible reach of any rightful remedy, the very Constitution which all were insti-tuted to preserve.

The truth declared in the resolution being established, the expediency of making the declaration at the present day, may safely be left to the temperate consideration and candid judgment of the American public. It will be remembered that a frequent recurrence to fundamental principles, is solemnly enjoined by most of the state constitutions, and particularly by our own, as a necessary safeguard against the danger of degeneracy to which republics are liable, as well as other governments, though in a less degree than others. And a fair comparison of the political doctrines not unfrequent at the present day, with those which characterized the epoch of our revolution, and which form the basis of our republican con-stitutions, will best determine whether the declaratory recurrence here made to those principles, ought to be viewed as unseasonable and improper, or as a vigilant discharge of an important duty. The authority of con-stitutions over governments, and of the sovereignty of the people over constitutions, are truths which are at all times necessary to be kept in mind; and at no time perhaps more necessary than at the present.

The fourth resolution stands as follows:

That the General Assembly doth also express its deep regret, that a spirit has in sundry instances, been manifested by the federal govern-ment, to enlarge its powers by forced constructions of the constitutional charter which defines them; and that indications have appeared of a design to expound certain general phrases, (which, having been copied

*from the very limited grant of powers in the former articles of confedera-
tion, were the less liable to be misconstrued,) so as to destroy the meaning
and effect of the particular enumeration which necessarily explains, and
limits the general phrases ; and so as to consolidate the states, by degrees,
into one sovereignty, the obvious tendency and inevitable result of which
would be, to transform the present republican system of the United States
into an absolute, or, at best, a mixed monarchy.*

The *first* question here to be considered is, whether a spirit has in
sundry instances been manifested by the Federal Government to enlarge
its powers by forced constructions of the constitutional charter.

The General Assembly having declared its opinion merely by re-
gretting in general terms that forced constructions for enlarging the federal powers have taken place, it does not appear to the committee necessary to go into a specification of every instance to which the resolution
may allude. The alien and sedition-acts being particularly named in a
succeeding resolution, are of course to be understood as included in the
allusion. Omitting others which have less occupied public attention, or
been less extensively regarded as unconstitutional, the resolution may be
presumed to refer particularly to the bank law,* which from the circum-

---

* The bank law referred to is that of 1791. Its constitutionality was the subject of
warm discussion in Congress. When it had finally passed both houses, and was submitted to the President, he requested the opinions of the members of the cabinet upon
the constitutional question. Mr. Hamilton deemed the law constitutional. An outline
of his argument may be seen in 2 Marshall's Washington, Notes, p. 5. Mr. Jefferson's
opinion, which he has himself preserved, was adverse to the power of Congress to in-
corporate a bank. (See 4 Jeff. Mem., 523.) The President, after considerable hesita-
tion, signed the bill. That charter having expired in 1811, Congress then refused, in
the Senate by the casting vote of Geo. Clinton, the Vice-President of the United States
and President of the Senate, to renew it. In 1815, a bank bill passed both houses of
Congress, but encountered the veto of President Madison, on the score of some objec-
tional provisions contained in it. But two years afterwards he gave his sanction to
another law for the incorporation of a bank, justifying his disregard of the constitutional objection, which in 1791 he had pressed in Congress with great vigour, upon the
ground that he felt himself obliged by the legislative and executive precedents, which
had occurred, affirming the constitutionality of such a law. (See his letter to Mr. Ingersoll, *post*, p. 257, and his veto message of 30th Jan., 1815.)

The question of the validity of the bank law of 1816 was soon brought before the
federal judiciary, and in 1819, in the great case of M'Culloch *v.* The State of Maryland, 4 Wheat., 316, the Supreme Court pronounced, by the mouth of C. J. Marshall,
an unanimous and decided opinion in favour of its constitutionality. The sentiment
upon the subject was not thereby quieted, however. Judge Roane, of Virginia, reviewed the judgment of the Supreme Court with freedom and ability, in a series of articles first published in the Richmond Enquirer, in June, 1819, under the signature of
" Hampden," and amongst the people, the dissentients were numerous and influential.
It was discussed also, along with several other constitutional questions, with his usual
acuteness, by Mr. John Taylor of Caroline, in a work called " Construction Construed,"
which deserves more readers than, by reason of its peculiarity of style, it has had, or is
likely to have.

In July, 1832, President Jackson vetoed a bill renewing the charter of the bank for
fifteen years from 1836, resting his objections in part upon constitutional grounds, and
in part upon the danger to the institutions of the country from so large a moneyed cor-
poration. A similar fate, at the hands of President Tyler, befell two other laws to in-
corporate a national bank in August and September, 1841.

stances of its passage, as well as the latitude of construction on which it is founded, strikes the attention with singular force; and the carriage tax,* distinguished also by circumstances in its history having a similar tendency. Those instances, alone, if resulting from forced construction and calculated to enlarge the powers of the Federal Government, as the committee cannot but conceive to be the case, sufficiently warrant this part of the resolution. The committee have not thought it incumbent on them to extend their attention to laws which have been objected to, rather as varying the constitutional distribution of powers in the Federal Government, than as an absolute enlargement of them; because instances of this sort, however important in their principles and tendencies, do not appear to fall strictly within the text under review.

The other questions presenting themselves, are—1. Whether indications have appeared of a design to expound certain general phrases copied from the "articles of confederation" so as to destroy the effect of the particular enumeration explaining and limiting their meaning. 2. Whether this exposition would by degrees consolidate the states into one sovereignty. 3. Whether the tendency and result of this consolidation would be to transform the republican system of the United States into a monarchy.

---

* The act of Congress, of 5th June, 1794, imposing a tax on carriages for the conveyance of persons, provoked a degree of opposition, especially in Virginia, the reason of which it is not, at this day, easy to understand. The complaint respecting it was that, although it was a direct tax, yet it was laid uniformly through the states, instead of being apportioned amongst the states, as the Constitution directs, according to population. One Hylton, in Virginia, in order to test the question, refused to enter certain carriages which he acknowled himself to possess, and an action having been instituted against him, in pursuance of the act, by the District Attorney, in the name of the United States, an agreed case was submitted to the Court, upon which a *pro forma* judgment was entered against the defendant, and thereupon he obtained a writ of error from the Supreme Court of the United States. That court pronounced the carriage tax not to be a direct tax, within the meaning of the Constitution, and that it was proper, therefore, to make it uniform. Congress, it was argued, possesses the power to tax all subjects of taxation, without limitation, with the exception of a duty on exports. There are two restrictions only, on the exercise of this authority :—1. All *direct* taxes must be apportioned; 2. All duties, imposts, and excises must be uniform. If the carriage tax were not a direct tax, within the meaning of the Constitution, nor a duty, impost, or excise, Congress was under no restriction as to the mode of laying it, in which case the tax ought to be uniform. But the Constitution could not have meant by a *direct* tax, which it orders to be apportioned, one which could not, with any regard to equality of burden, be apportioned, and if the tax on carriages could not be equally apportioned, it was, for that reason, not a direct tax. That it could not be so apportioned was manifest, since the number of carriages in the several states bore no relation to population, and consequently the tax on them might be $10 in one state, and $100 in another. The Court intimated an opinion that a direct tax, in the sense of the Constitution, could mean nothing but a tax on what is inseparably annexed to the soil, or otherwise capable of apportionment, under all circumstances, according to population, such as a tax on lands or persons, including slaves. (Hylton *v.* U. States, 3 Dall., 171.)

This view seems to have been acquiesced in, and when, in 1813, during the war with Great Britain, it was deemed expedient to resort to extraordinary taxation, a tax on carriages was again imposed according to the rule of uniformity. (4 Laws of United States, 570.)

I. The general phrases here meant must be those "of providing for the common defence and general welfare."

In the "articles of confederation," the phrases are used as follows, in Art. VIII. ' "All charges of war, and all other expenses that shall be incurred *for the common defence and general welfare*, and allowed by the United States in Congress assembled, shall be defrayed out of a common treasury, which shall be supplied by the several states, in proportion to the value of all land within each state, granted to, or surveyed for any person, as such land and the buildings and improvements thereon shall be estimated, according to such mode as the United States in Congress assembled shall from time to time direct and appoint."

In the existing Constitution, they make the following part of Sec. 8, "The Congress shall have power to lay and collect taxes, duties, imposts, and excises, to pay the debts, and to provide for the common defence and general welfare of the United States."

This similarity in the use of these phrases in the two great federal charters, might well be considered, as rendering their meaning less liable to be misconstrued in the latter; because it will scarcely be said, that in the former they were ever understood to be either a general grant of power, or to authorize the requisition or application of money by the old Congress to the common defence and general welfare, except in the cases afterwards enumerated, which explained and limited their meaning; and if such was the limited meaning attached to these phrases in the very instrument revised and remodelled by the present Constitution, it can never be supposed that when copied into this Constitution, a different meaning ought to be attached to them. '

That, notwithstanding this remarkable security against misconstruction, a design has been indicated to expound these phrases in the Constitution, so as to destroy the effect of the particular enumeration of powers by which it explains and limits them, must have fallen under the observation of those who have attended to the course of public transactions. Not to multiply proofs on this subject, it will suffice to refer to the debates of the federal legislature, in which arguments have on different occasions been drawn, with apparent effect, from these phrases, in their indefinite meaning.

To these indications might be added, without looking farther, the official report on manufactures, by the late Secretary of the Treasury, made on the 5th of December, 1791; and the report of a committee of Congress, in January, 1797, on the promotion of agriculture. In the first of these · it is expressly contended to belong " to the discretion of the national legislature to pronounce upon the objects which concern the *general welfare*, and for which, under that description, an appropriation of money is requisite and proper. And there seems to be no room for a doubt, that whatever concerns the general interests of LEARNING, of AGRICULTURE, of MANUFACTURES, and of COMMERCE, are within the sphere of the national councils, *as far as regards the application of money*."* The latter report

---

* This report on manufactures, by Mr. Hamilton, is an elaborate exposition of the protective · policy, in all its economical bearings, with reference especially to certain

assumes the same latitude of power in the national councils, and applies it to the encouragement of agriculture by means of a society to be established at the seat of government.* Although neither of these reports may have received the sanction of a law carrying it into effect, yet, on the other hand, the extraordinary doctrine contained in both, has passed without the slightest positive mark of disapprobation from the authority to which it was addressed.

Now, whether the phrases in question be construed to authorize every measure relating to the common defence and general welfare, as contended by some; or every measure only in which there might be an application of money, as suggested by the caution of others; the effect must substantially be the same, in destroying the import and force of the particular enumeration of powers which follow these general phrases in the Constitution. For it is evident that there is not a single power whatever, which may not have some reference to the common defence, or the general welfare; nor a power of any magnitude, which, in its exercise, does not involve or admit an application of money. The government, therefore, which possesses power in either one or other of these extents, is a government without the limitations formed by a particular enumeration of powers; and consequently, the meaning and effect of this particular enumeration is destroyed by the exposition given to these general phrases.

This conclusion will not be affected by an attempt to qualify the power over the "general welfare," by referring it to cases where the *general welfare* is beyond the reach of *separate* provisions by the *individual states;* and leaving to these their jurisdictions, in cases to which their separate provisions may be competent. For, as the authority of the individual states must in all cases be incompetent to general regulations

leading articles, such as fabrics of metals, of flax and hemp, of cotton, of wool, of silk, &c.

The constitutional power of the federal government to apply encouragement to manufactures, he disposes of very summarily, employing a process of reasoning not a little formidable to those who desire to maintain the organization of that government, as one of specific and limited powers. The sentence quoted in the text, however, is somewhat qualified by what follows. "The only qualification," Mr. Hamilton proceeds to observe, "of the generality of the phrase in question which seems to be admissible, is this, that the object to which an appropriation is to be made be *general* and not *local,* its operation extending in fact, or by possibility, throughout the Union, and not being confined to a particular spot. No objection ought to arise to this construction from a supposition that it would imply a power to do whatever else should appear to Congress conducive to the general welfare. A power to appropriate money, with this latitude, which is granted, too, in express terms, would not carry a power to do any other thing, not authorized by the Constitution, either expressly or by fair implication." (See the Report,—7 Amer. State Papers, 136.)

The constitutional question involved in protective duties is presented on both sides in 2 Story's Comm. on Const., 429, et seq., and 520, et seq. (See Construction Construed, 203, and Address of Phila. Free-trade Convention of 1831.)

* This report will be found 20 Am. State Papers, 154. It proposed to establish a society under the patronage of the general government, which should extend its influence through the whole country, and comprehend the extensive object of *national improvement,* but especially the promotion of agriculture. It was to have been a body corporate, capable of holding a limited amount of property, and was to be composed, in part, of the members of Congress, the judges of the Supreme Court, and the heads of departments.

operating through the whole, the authority of the United States would be extended to every object relating to the general welfare, which might, by any possibility, be provided for by the general authority. This qualifying construction, therefore, would have little, if any tendency, to circumscribe the power claimed under the latitude of the terms "general welfare."

'The true and fair construction of this expression, both in the original and existing federal compacts, appears to the committee too obvious to be mistaken. In both, the Congress is authorized to provide money for the common defence and *general welfare.* In both, is subjoined to this au- thority, an enumeration of the cases to which their powers shall extend. Money cannot be applied to the *general welfare* otherwise than by an application of it to some *particular* measures, conducive to the general welfare. Whenever, therefore, money has been raised by the general authority, and is to be applied to a particular measure, a question arises whether the particular measure be within the enumerated authorities vested in Congress. If it be, the money requisite for it may be applied to it ; if it be not, no such application can be made. This fair and obvious inter- pretation coincides with, and is enforced by the clause in the Constitution, which declares, that "no money shall be drawn from the treasury, but in consequence of appropriations by law." An appropriation of money to the general welfare would be deemed rather a mockery than an observance of this constitutional injunction.

2. Whether the exposition of the general phrases here combated would not, by degrees, consolidate the states into one sovereignty, is a question concerning which the committee can perceive little room for difference of opinion. To consolidate the states into one sovereignty, nothing more can be wanted, than to supersede their respective sovereignties in the cases reserved to them, by extending the sovereignty of the United States, to all cases of the "general welfare," that is to say, to *all cases whatever.*

3. That the obvious tendency and inevitable result of a consolidation of the states into one sovereignty, would be to transform the republican sys- tem of the United States into a monarchy, is a point which seems to have been sufficiently decided by the general sentiment of America. In almost every instance of discussion, relating to the consolidation in question, its certain tendency to pave the way to monarchy seems not to have been contested. The prospect of such a consolidation has formed the only topic of controversy. It would be unnecessary, therefore, for the commit- tee to dwell long on the reasons which support the position of the General Assembly. It may not be improper, however, to remark two conse- quences evidently flowing from an extension of the federal powers to every subject falling within the idea of the "general welfare."

One consequence must be, to enlarge the sphere of discretion allotted to the executive magistrate. Even within the legislative limits properly defined by the Constitution, the difficulty of accommodating legal regula- tions to a country so great in extent, and so various in its circumstances, has been much felt ; and has led to occasional investments of power in the executive, which involve perhaps as large a portion of discretion as can be deemed consistent with the nature of the executive trust. In propor- tion as the objects of legislative care might be multiplied, would the time allowed for each be diminished, and the difficulty of providing uniform and particular regulations for all be increased. From these sources would necessarily ensue a greater latitude to the agency of that department which is always in existence, and which could best mould regulations of a general nature, so as to suit them to the diversity of particular situations. And it is in this latitude, as a supplement to the deficiency of the laws, that the degree of executive prerogative materially consists.

The other consequence would be that of an excessive augmentation of the offices, honours, and emoluments depending on the executive will. Add to the present legitimate stock, all those of every description which a consolidation of the states would take from them, and turn over to the Federal Government, and the patronage of the executive would necessarily be as much swelled in this case, as its prerogative would be in the other.

This disproportionate increase of prerogative and patronage must, evidently, either enable the chief magistrate of the Union, by quiet means, to secure his re-election from time to time, and finally, to regulate the succession as he might please; or, by giving so transcendent an importance to the office, would render the elections to it so violent and corrupt, that the public voice itself might call for an hereditary, in place of an elective succession. Whichever of these events might follow, the transformation of the republican system of the United States into a monarchy, anticipated by the General Assembly from a consolidation of the states into one sovereignty, would be equally accomplished; and whether it would be into a mixed or an absolute monarchy, might depend on too many contingencies to admit of any certain foresight.

The resolution next in order, is contained in the following terms:

That the General Assembly doth particularly protest against the palpable and alarming infractions of the Constitution, in the two late cases of the "alien and sedition-acts," passed at the last session of Congress; the first of which exercises a power nowhere delegated to the Federal Government; and which, by uniting legislative and judicial powers to those of executive, subverts the general principles of a free Government, as well as the particular organization and positive provisions of the Federal Constitution; and the other of which acts exercises, in like manner, a power not delegated by the Constitution; but, on the contrary, expressly and positively forbidden by one of the amendments thereto: a power which, more than any other, ought to produce universal alarm; because it is levelled against that right of freely examining public characters and measures, and of free communication among the people thereon, which has ever been justly deemed the only effectual guardian of every other right.

The subject of this resolution having, it is presumed, more particularly led the General Assembly into the proceedings which they communicated to the other states, and being in itself of peculiar importance, it deserves the most critical and faithful investigation; for the length of which no other apology will be necessary.

The subject divides itself into *first*, "The alien-act," *secondly*, "The sedition-act."

I. Of the "alien-act," it is affirmed by the resolution, 1st. That it exercises a power nowhere delegated to the Federal Government. 2d. That it unites legislative and judicial powers to those of the executive. 3d. That this union of power subverts the general principles of free government. 4th. That it subverts the particular organization and positive provisions of the Federal Constitution.

In order to clear the way for a correct view of the first position, several observations will be premised.

In the first place, it is to be borne in mind, that it being a characteristic feature of the Federal Constitution, as it was originally ratified, and an amendment thereto having precisely declared, "That the powers not delegated to the United States by the Constitution, nor prohibited by it to the states, are reserved to the states respectively, or to the people," it is incumbent in this, as in every other exercise of power by the Federal Government, to prove from the Constitution, that it grants the particular power exercised.

The next observation to be made is, that much confusion and fallacy have been thrown into question, by blending the two cases of *aliens, members of a hostile nation ;* and *aliens, members of friendly nations.*" These two cases are so obviously and so essentially distinct, that it occasions no little surprise that the distinction should have been disregarded : and the surprise is so much the greater, as it appears that the two cases are actually distinguished by two separate acts of Congress, passed at the same session, and comprised in the same publication ; the one providing for the case of "alien enemies ;" the other " concerning aliens" indiscriminately ; and consequently extending to aliens of every nation in peace and amity with the United States. With respect to alien enemies, no doubt has been intimated as to the federal authority over them ; the Constitution having expressly delegated to Congress the power to declare war against any nation, and of course to treat it and all its members as enemies. With respect to aliens who are not enemies, but members of nations in peace and amity with the United States, the power assumed by the act of Congress is denied to be constitutional ; and it is accordingly against this act, that the protest of the General Assembly is expressly and exclusively directed.

A third observation is, that were it admitted, as is contended, that the "act concerning aliens" has for its object not a *penal,* but a *preventive* justice, it would still remain to be proved that it comes within the constitutional power of the federal legislature ; and if within its power, that the legislature has exercised it in a constitutional manner.

In the administration of preventive justice, the following principles have been held sacred: that some probable ground of suspicion be exhibited before some judicial authority ; that it be supported by oath or affirmation ; that the party may avoid being thrown into confinement, by finding pledges or sureties for his legal conduct sufficient in the judgment of some judicial authority ; that he may have the benefit of a writ of *habeas corpus,* and thus obtain his release, if wrongfully confined ; and that he may at any time be discharged from his recognizance, or his confinement, and restored to his former liberty and rights, on the order of the proper judicial authority, if it shall see sufficient cause.

All these principles of the only preventive justice known'to American jurisprudence are violated by the alien-act. The ground of suspicion is to be judged of, not by any judicial authority, but by the executive magistrate alone; no oath or affirmation is required; if the suspicion be held reasonable by the President, he may order the suspected alien to depart the territory of the United States, without the opportunity of avoiding the sentence, by finding pledges for his future good conduct ; as the President · may limit the time of departure as he pleases, the benefit of the writ of *habeas corpus* may be suspended with respect to the party, although the Constitution ordains, that it shall not be suspended, unless when the public safety may require it in case of rebellion or invasion, neither of which existed at the passage of the act ; and the party being under the sentence of the President, either removed from the United States, or being punished by imprisonment, or disqualification ever to become a citizen on conviction of not obeying the order of removal, he cannot be discharged from the proceedings against him, and restored to the benefits of his former situation, although the *highest judicial authority* should see the most sufficient cause for it.

But, in the last place, it can never be admitted, that the removal of aliens, authorized by the act, is to be considered, not as punishment for an offence, but as a measure of precaution and prevention. If the banishment of an alien from a country into which he has been invited, as the asylum most auspicious to his happiness ; a country where he may have formed the most tender of connexions, where he may have vested his entire property, and acquired property of the real and permanent, as well as the movable and temporary kind ; where he enjoys under the laws a greater share of the blessings of personal security and personal liberty than he can elsewhere hope for, and where he may have nearly completed his probationary title to citizenship ; if, moreover, in the execution of the sentence against him, he is to be exposed, not only to the ordinary dangers of the sea, but to the peculiar casualties incident to a crisis of war, and of unusual· licentiousness on that element, and possibly to vindictive purposes which his emigration itself may have provoked ; if a banishment of this sort be not a punishment, and among the severest of punishments, it will be difficult to imagine a doom to which the name can be applied. And if it be a punishment, it will remain to be inquired, whether it can be constitutionally inflicted, on mere suspicion, by the single will of the executive magistrate, on persons convicted of no personal offence.against the laws of the land, nor involved in any offence against the law of nations, charged on the foreign state of which they are members.

One argument offered in justification of this power exercised over aliens is, that the admission of them into the country being of favour, not of right, the favour is at all times revocable. ·

To this argument it might be answered, that allowing the truth of the inference, it would be no proof of what is required. A question would still occur, whether the Constitution had vested the discretionary power of admitting aliens in the federal government, or in the state governments.

But it cannot be a true inference, that because the admission of an alien is a favour, the favour may be revoked at pleasure. A grant of land to an individual may be of favour, not of right; but the moment the grant is made, the favour becomes a right, and must be forfeited before it can be taken away. To pardon a malefactor may be favour, but the pardon is not, on that account, the less irrevocable. To admit an alien to naturalization is as much à favour, as to admit him to reside in the country ; yet it cannot be pretended, that a person naturalized can be deprived of the benefit, any more than a native citizen can be disfranchised.*

Again, it is said, that aliens not being parties to the Constitution, the rights and privileges which it secures cannot be at all claimed by them.

To this reasoning, also, it might be answered, that although aliens are not parties to the Constitution, it does not follow that the Constitution has vested in Congress an absolute power over them. The parties to the Constitution may have granted, or retained, or modified the power over aliens, without regard to that particular consideration.

But a more direct reply is, that it does not follow, because aliens are not parties to the Constitution, as citizens are parties to it, that whilst they actually conform to it, they have no right to its protection. Aliens are not more parties to the laws, than they are parties to the Constitution; yet, it will not be disputed, that as they owe, on one hand, a temporary obedience, they are entitled in return to their protection and advantage.

If aliens had no rights under the Constitution, they might not only be banished, but even capitally punished, without a jury or the other incidents to a fair trial. But so far has a contrary principle been carried, in every part of the United States, that except on charges of treason, an alien has, besides all the common privileges, the special one of being tried by a jury, of which one-half may be also aliens.

It is said, further, that by the law and practice of nations, aliens may be removed at discretion, for offences against the law of nations; that Congress are authorized to define and punish such offences; and that to be dangerous to the peace of society is, in aliens, one of those offences.

The distinction between alien enemies and alien friends, is a clear and conclusive answer to this argument. Alien enemies are under the law of nations, and liable to be punished for offences against it. Alien friends, except in the single case of public ministers, are under the municipal law, and must be tried and punished according to that law only.

This argument also, by referring the alien-act to the power of Congress to define and *punish* offences against the law of nations, yields the point that the act is of a *penal*, not merely of a preventive operation. It must, in truth, be so considered. And if it be a penal act, the punishment it inflicts, must be justified by some offence that deserves it.

Offences for which aliens, within the jurisdiction of a country, are

---

* This argument, extending as it does, to governments of general, as well as to those of specified powers, is pressed too far. A state may prescribe what conditions it will to the admission of aliens, and amongst others, the condition which, indeed, may well be understood as implied, of dismissal when their presence becomes disagreeable. (Vattel, B. II. §§ 94, 100, and 101.) Whether the power to prescribe conditions has been conferred, in our system, upon the federal or the state governments, or upon neither, is a different question.

† As to aliens *domiciled* in a foreign country, see Vatt. B. I., § 213. As to aliens merely *sojourning* temporarily, see ib. B. II., § 102.

punishable, are first, offences committed by the nation of which they make a part, and in whose offences they are involved : Secondly, offences committed by themselves alone, without any charge against the nation to which they belong. The first is the case of alien enemies ; the second, the case of alien friends. In the first case, the offending nation can no otherwise be punished than by war, one of the laws of which authorizes the expulsion of such of its members, as may be found within the country, against which the offence has been committed. In the second case, the offence being committed by the individual, not by his nation, and against the municipal law, not against the law of nations, the individual only, and not the nation, is punishable; and the punishment must be conducted according to the municipal law, not according to the law of nations. Under this view of the subject, the act of Congress, for the removal of alien enemies, being conformable to the law of nations, is justified by the Constitution : and the " act," for the removal of alien friends, being repugnant to the constitutional principles of municipal law, is unjustifiable.

Nor is the act of Congress, for the removal of alien friends, more agreeable to the general practice of nations, than it is within the purview of the law of nations. The general practice of nations, distinguishes between alien friends and alien enemies. The latter it has proceeded against, according to the law of nations, by expelling them as enemies.* The former it has considered as under a local and temporary allegiance, and entitled to a correspondent protection. If contrary instances are to be found in barbarous countries, under undefined prerogatives, or amid revolutionary dangers, they will not be deemed fit precedents for the government of the United States, even if not beyond its constitutional authority.

It is said, that Congress may grant letters of marque and reprisal ; that reprisals may be made on persons, as well as property ; and that the removal of aliens may be considered as the exercise in an inferior degree, of the general power of reprisal on persons.

Without entering minutely into a question that does not seem to require it, it may be remarked, that reprisal is a seizure of foreign persons or property, with a view to obtain that justice for injuries done by one state or its members, to another state or its members, for which, a refusal of the aggressor requires such a resort to force under the law of nations. It must be considered as an abuse of words to call the removal of persons from a country, a seizure or reprisal on them: nor is the distinction to be overlooked between reprisals on persons within the country and under the faith of its laws, and on persons out of the country.†

But, laying aside these considerations, it is evidently impossible to bring

* Vatt. B. III., § 63.

† The idea that reprisals cannot lawfully be made upon persons, or property within the country, and under the faith of its laws, is plainly not necessary to the argument. The proposition that such reprisals are inadmissible is sustained by the authority of Vattel (B. II., § 344, and B. III., § 63,) and others, and is certainly conformable to the general usage of nations. If a state chooses, however, to adopt a less liberal policy, it cannot, for so doing, be reproached with the violation of any principle of international law. (See Martens' Summ. B. VIII., c. ii., § 5. The Boedes-Lust, 5 Rob. Adm'y Rep. 246. Brown v. United States, 8 Cranch, 121.)

the alien-act within the power of granting reprisals; since it does not allege or imply any injury received from any particular nation, for which this proceeding against its members was intended as a reparation.   The proceeding is authorized against aliens *of every nation;* of nations charged neither with any similar proceeding against American citizens, nor with any injuries for which justice might be sought, in the mode prescribed by the act.   Were it true, therefore, that good causes existed for reprisals against one or more foreign nations, and that neither persons nor property of its members, under the faith of our laws, could plead an exemption, the operation of the act ought to have been limited to the aliens among us, belonging to such nations.   To license reprisals against all nations, for aggressions charged on one only, would be a measure as contrary to every principle of justice and public law, as to a wise policy, and the universal practice of nations.

It is said, that the right of removing aliens is an incident to the power of war, vested in Congress by the Constitution.

This is a former argument in a new shape only; and is answered by repeating, that the removal of alien enemies is an incident to the power of war; that the removal of alien friends, is not an incident to the power of war.

It is said, that Congress are by the Constitution to protect each state against invasion; and that the means of *preventing* invasion are included in the power of protection against it.

The power of war in general, having been before granted by the Constitution, this clause must either be a mere specification for greater caution and certainty, of which there are other examples in the instrument, or be the injunction of a duty, superadded to a grant of the power.   Under either explanation, it cannot enlarge the powers of Congress on the subject.   The power and the duty to protect each state against an invading enemy, would be the same under the general power, if this regard to greater caution had been omitted.

Invasion is an operation of war.   To protect against invasion is an exercise of the power of war.   A power, therefore, not incident to war, cannot be incident to a particular modification of war.   And as the removal of alien friends, has appeared to be no incident to a general state of war, it cannot be incident to a partial state, or a particular modification of war.

Nor can it ever be granted, that a power to act on a case when it actually occurs, includes a power over all the means that may *tend to prevent* the occurrence of the case.   Such a latitude of construction would render unavailing every practicable definition of particular and limited powers.   Under the idea of preventing war in general, as well as invasion in particular, not only an indiscriminate removal of all aliens might be enforced, but a thousand other things still more remote from the operations and precautions appurtenant to war, might take place.   A bigoted or tyrannical nation might threaten us with war, unless certain religious or political regulations were adopted by us; yet it never could be inferred, if the regulations which would prevent war, were such as Congress had otherwise no power to make, that the power to make them would grow out of the purpose they were to answer.   Congress have power to suppress insurrections, yet it would not be allowed to follow, that they might employ all the means tending to prevent them ; of which a system of moral instruction for the ignorant, and of provident support for the poor, might be regarded as among the most efficacious.

One argument for the power of the general government to remove aliens, would have been passed in silence, if it had appeared under any authority inferior to that of a report, made during the last session of Congress, to the House of Representatives by a committee, and approved by the House.   The doctrine on which this argument is founded, is of so new and so extraordinary à character, and strikes so radically at the political system of America, that it is proper to state it in the very words of the report.

" The act [concerning aliens] is said to be unconstitutional, because to remove aliens is a direct breach of the Constitution, which provides, by the 9th section of the 1st article, that the migration or importation of such persons as any of the states shall think proper to admit, shall not be prohibited by the Congress, prior to the year 1808."

Among the answers given to this objection to the constitutionality of the act, the following very remarkable one is extracted :

" Thirdly, that as the Constitution has given to the states no power to remove aliens, during the period of the limitation under consideration, in the mean time, on the construction assumed, there would be no authority in the country, empowered to send away dangerous aliens, which cannot be admitted."*

The reasoning here used, would not in any view, be conclusive; because there are powers exercised by most other governments, which in the United States are withheld by the people, both from the general government, and from the state governments.   Of this sort are many of the powers prohibited by the declarations of right prefixed to the constitutions, or by the clauses in the constitutions, in the nature of such declarations. Nay, so far is the political system of the United States distinguishable from that of other countries, by the caution with which powers are delegated and defined, that in one very important case, even of commercial regulations and revenue, the power is absolutely locked up against the hands of both governments.   A tax on exports can be laid by no constitutional authority whatever.   Under a system thus peculiarly guarded, there could surely be no absurdity in supposing, that alien friends, who if guilty of treasonable machinations may be punished, or if suspected on probable grounds, may be secured by pledges or imprisonment, in like manner with permanent citizens, were never meant to be subjected to banishment by any arbitrary and unusual process, either under the one government or the other.

But, it is not the inconclusiveness of the general reasoning in this passage, which chiefly calls the attention to it.   It is the principle assumed by it, that the powers held by the states, are given to them by the Consti-

---

* The argument contained in the report here referred to, (which may be seen 20 Am. State Papers, 181), in vindication of the constitutionality of the alien and sedition laws, is condensed, but able.   It will repay the perusal of the diligent student, who desires audire et alteram partem.

tution of the United States; and the inference from this principle, that the powers supposed to be necessary which are not so given to state governments, must reside in the government of the United States.

The respect, which is felt for every portion of the constituted authorities, forbids some of the reflections which this singular paragraph might excite; and they are the more readily suppressed, as it may be presumed, with justice perhaps, as well as candour, that inadvertence may have had its share in the error. It would be an unjustifiable delicacy, nevertheless, to pass by so portentous a claim, proceeding from so high an authority, . without a monitory notice of the fatal tendencies with which it would be pregnant.

Lastly, it is said, that a law on the same subject with the alien-act, passed by this state originally in 1785, and re-enacted in 1792, is a proof that a summary removal of suspected aliens, was not heretofore regarded by the Virginia Legislature, as liable to the objections now urged against such a measure.

This charge against Virginia vanishes before the simple remark, that the law of Virginia relates to "suspicious persons being the subjects of any foreign power or state, who shall have *made a declaration of war*, or actually *commenced hostilities*, or from whom the President shall apprehend *hostile designs*;" whereas the act of Congress relates to aliens, being the subjects of foreign powers and states, who have *neither declared war, nor commenced hostilities, nor from whom hostile designs are apprehended.*

2. It is next affirmed of the alien act, that it unites legislative, judicial, and executive powers in the hands of the President.

However difficult it may be to mark, in every case, with clearness and certainty, the line which divides legislative power, from the other departments of power, all will agree, that the powers referred to these departments may be so general and undefined, as to be of a legislative, not of an executive or judicial nature; and may for that reason be unconstitutional. Details to a certain degree, are essential to the nature and character of a law; and on criminal subjects, it is proper, that details should leave as little as possible to the discretion of those who are to apply and to execute the law. If nothing more were required, in exercising a legislative trust, than a general conveyance of authority, without laying down any precise rules, by which the authority conveyed should be carried into effect; it would follow, that the whole power of legislation might be transferred by the legislature from itself, and proclamations might become substitutes for laws. A delegation of power in this latitude, would not be denied to be a union of the different powers.

To determine, then, whether the appropriate powers of the distinct departments are united by the act authorizing the executive to remove aliens, it must be inquired whether it contains such details, definitions and rules, as appertain to the true character of a law; especially, a law by which personal liberty is invaded, property deprived of its value to the owner, and life itself indirectly exposed to danger.

The alien-act declares, "that it shall be lawful for the President to order all such aliens as he shall judge *dangerous* to the peace and safety of the

United States, or shall have reasonable ground to *suspect*, are concerned in any treasonable, or *secret machinations*, against the government thereof, to depart," &c.

Could a power be well given in terms less definite, less particular, and less precise? To be *dangerous to the public safety;* to be *suspected of secret machinations* against the government : these can never be mistaken for legal rules or certain definitions. They leave everything to the President. His will is the law.

But, it is not a legislative power only, that is given to the President. He is to stand in the place of the judiciary also. His suspicion is the only evidence which is to convict : his order, the only judgment which is to be executed.

Thus, it is the President whose will is to designate the offensive conduct; it is his will that is to ascertain the individuals on whom it is charged; and it is his will, that is to cause the sentence to be executed. It is rightly affirmed, therefore, that the act unites legislative and judicial powers to those of the executive.

3. It is affirmed, that this union of power subverts the general principles of free government.

It has become an axiom in the science of government, that a separation of the legislative, executive, and judicial departments, is necessary to the preservation of public liberty.* Nowhere has this axiom been better understood in theory, or more carefully pursued in practice, than in the United States.

4. It is affirmed that such a union of powers subverts the particular organization and positive provisions of the Federal Constitution.

According to the particular organization of the Constitution, its legislative powers are vested in the Congress, its executive powers in the President, and its judicial powers in a supreme and inferior tribunals. The union of any two of these powers, and still more of all three, in any one of these departments, as has been shown to be done by the alien-act, must consequently subvert the constitutional organization of them.

That positive provisions, in the Constitution, securing to individuals the benefits of fair trial, are also violated by the union of powers in the alien-act, necessarily results from the two facts, that the act relates to alien friends, and that alien friends being under the municipal law only, are entitled to its protection.

II. The *second* object against which the resolution protests, is the sedition-act.

Of this act it is affirmed, 1. That it exercises in like manner a power not delegated by the Constitution. 2. That the power, on the contrary, is expressly and positively forbidden by one of the amendments to the Constitution. 3. That this is a power, which more than any other ought to produce universal alarm; because it is levelled against that right of freely examining public characters and measures, and of free communication thereon, which has ever been justly deemed the only effectual guardian of every other right.

---

* Montesq. Sp. Law. B. XI. c. 6.

1. That it exercises a power not delegated by the Constitution.

Here again, it will be proper to recollect, that the Federal Government being composed of powers specifically granted, with a reservation of all others to the states or to the people, the positive authority under which the sedition-act could be passed must be produced by those who assert its constitutionality. In what part of the Constitution, then, is this authority to be found?

Several attempts have been made to answer this question, which will be examined in their order. The committee will begin with one, which has filled them with equal astonishment and apprehension; and which, they cannot but persuade themselves, must have the same effect on all, who will consider it with coolness and impartiality, and with a reverence for our Constitution, in the true character in which it issued from the sovereign authority of the people. The committee refer to the doctrine lately advanced as a sanction to the sedition-act, "that the common or unwritten law," a law of vast extent and complexity, and embracing almost every possible subject of legislation, both civil and criminal, makes a part of the law of these states, in their united and national capacity.*

The novelty and, in the judgment of the committee, the extravagance of this pretension, would have consigned it to the silence in which they have passed by other arguments, which an extraordinary zeal for the act has drawn into the discussion: But the auspices under which this innovation presents itself, have constrained the committee to bestow on it an attention, which other considerations might have forbidden.

In executing the task, it may be of use to look back to the colonial state of this country, prior to the Revolution; to trace the effects of the Revolution which converted the colonies into independent states; to inquire into the import of the articles of confederation, the first instrument by which the union of the states was regularly established; and finally, to consult the Constitution of 1788, which is the oracle that must decide the important question.

In the state, prior to the Revolution, it is certain that the common law, under different limitations, made a part of the colonial codes. But whether it be understood that the original colonists brought the law with them, or made it their law by adoption; it is equally certain, that it was the separate law of each colony within its respective limits, and was unknown to them, as a law pervading and operating through the whole, as one society.

It could not possibly be otherwise. The common law was not the same in any two of the colonies; in some, the modifications were materially and extensively different. There was no common legislature, by which a common will could be expressed in the form of a law; nor any common magistracy, by which such a law could be carried into practice. The will of each colony, alone and separately, had its organs for these purposes.

---

* The argument that the sedition-act was justified by the common law, and that the common law is part of the law of the Federal Government, is stated at length by Mr. *George K. Taylor*, in the debate on the resolutions, *Ante*, p. 133, *et seq.* See, also, 1 Tuck. Bl. Part I. Appendix, p. 378, n. E.

This stage of our political history furnishes no foothold for the patrons of this new doctrine.

Did then the principle or operation of the great event which made the colonies independent states, imply or introduce the common law as a law of the Union?

The fundamental principle of the Revolution was, that the colonies were co-ordinate members with each other, and with Great Britain, of an empire, united by a common executive sovereign, but not united by any common legislative sovereign. The legislative power was maintained to be as. complete in each American parliament, as in the British parliament. And the royal prerogative was in force in each colony, by virtue of its acknowledging the king for its executive magistrate, as it was in Great Britain, by virtue of a like acknowledgment there. A denial of these principles by Great Britain, and the assertion of them by America, produced the Revolution.

There was a time, indeed, when an exception to the legislative separation of the several component and coequal parts of the empire obtained a degree of acquiescence. The British parliament was allowed to regulate the trade with foreign nations, and between the different parts of the empire. This was, however, mere practice without right, and contrary to the true theory of the Constitution. The conveniency of some regulations, in both those cases, was apparent; and as there was no legislature with power over the whole, nor any constitutional pre-eminence among the legislatures of the several parts, it was natural for the legislature of that particular part which was the eldest and the largest, to assume this function, and for the others to acquiesce in it. This tacit arrangement was the less criticised, as the regulations established by the British parliament operated in favour of that part of the empire which seemed to bear the principal share of the public burdens, and were regarded as an indemnification of its advances for the other parts. As long as this regulating power was confined to the two objects of conveniency and equity, it was not complained of, nor much inquired into. But, no sooner was it perverted to the selfish views of the party assuming it, than the injured parties began to feel and to reflect; and the moment the claim to a direct and indefinite power was ingrafted on the precedent of the regulating power, the whole charm was dissolved, and every eye opened to the usurpation. The assertion by Great Britain of a power to make laws for the other members of the empire *in all cases whatsoever*, ended in the discovery that she had a right to make laws for them *in no cases whatsoever*.

Such being the ground of our Revolution, no support nor colour can be drawn from it, for the doctrine that the common law is binding on these states as one society. The doctrine, on the contrary, is evidently repugnant to the fundamental principle of the Revolution.

The articles of confederation are the next source of information on this subject.

In the interval between the commencement of the Revolution and the final ratification of these articles, the nature and extent of the Union was determined by the circumstances of the crisis, rather than by any accurate delineation of the general authority. It will not be alleged, that the

" common law" could have had any legitimate birth as a law of the United States during that state of things. If it came, as such, into existence at all, the charter of confederation must have been its parent.

Here again, however, its pretensions are absolutely destitute of foundation. This instrument does not contain a sentence or syllable that can be tortured into a countenance of the idea, that the parties to it were, with respect to the objects of the common law, to form one community. No such law is named or implied, or alluded to as being in force, or as brought into force by that compact. No provision is made by which such a law could be carried into operation ; whilst, on the other hand, every such inference or pretext is absolutely precluded by Article 2d, which declares, " that each state retains its sovereignty, freedom, and independence, and every power, jurisdiction, and right, which is not by this confederation expressly delegated to the United States, in Congress assembled."

Thus far it appears that not a vestige of this extraordinary doctrine can be found in the origin or progress of American institutions. The evidence against it has, on the contrary, grown stronger at every step, till it has amounted to a formal and positive exclusion, by written articles of compact among the parties concerned.

Is this exclusion revoked, and the common law introduced as a national law, by the present Constitution of the United States? This is the final question to be examined.

It is readily admitted, that particular parts of the common law may have a sanction from the Constitution, so far as they are necessarily comprehended in the technical phrases which express the powers delegated to the government; and so far also, as such other parts may be adopted by Congress as necessary and proper for carrying into execution the powers expressly delegated. But, the question does not relate to either of these portions of the common law. It relates to the common law beyond these limitations.

The only part of the Constitution which seems to have been relied on in this case is the 2d Sect. of Art. III. " The judicial power shall extend to all cases *in law and equity*, arising *under this Constitution*, the laws of the United States, and treaties made or which shall be made under their authority."

It has been asked what cases, distinct from those arising under the laws and treaties of the United States; can arise under the Constitution, other than those arising under the common law ; and it is inferred, that the common law is accordingly adopted or recognised by the Constitution.

Never, perhaps, was so broad a construction applied to a text so clearly unsusceptible of it. If any colour for the inference could be found, it must be in the impossibility of finding any other cases in law and equity, within the provision of the Constitution, to satisfy the expression ; and rather than resort to a construction affecting so essentially the whole character of the government, it would perhaps be more rational to consider the expression as a mere pleonasm, or inadvertence. But, it is not necessary to decide on such a dilemma. The expression is fully satisfied, and its accuracy justified, by two descriptions of cases, to which the judicial authority is extended, and neither of which implies that the common law is the law of the United States. One of these descriptions comprehends the cases growing out of the restrictions on the legislative power of the states. For example, it is provided that "no state shall emit bills of credit," or "make anything but gold and silver coin a tender in payment of debts." Should this prohibition be violated, and a suit *between citizens of the same state* be the consequence, this would be a case arising under the Constitution, before the judicial power of the United States. A second description comprehends suits between citizens and foreigners, or citizens of different states, to be decided according to the state or foreign laws; but submitted by the Constitution to the judicial power of the United States; the judicial power being, in several instances, extended beyond the legislative power of the United States.

To this explanation of the text, the following observations may be added:

The expression, "cases in law and equity," is manifestly confined to cases of a civil nature; and would exclude cases of criminal jurisdiction. Criminal cases in law and equity would be a language unknown to the law.*

The succeeding paragraph of the same section is in harmony with this construction. It is in these words: "In all cases affecting ambassadors, other public ministers, and consuls, and those in which a state shall be a party, the Supreme Court shall have original jurisdiction. *In all* the other cases [including cases in law and equity arising under the Constitution] the Supreme Court shall have *appellate* jurisdiction both as to law and *fact;* with such exceptions, and under such regulations, as Congress shall make."

This paragraph, by expressly giving an *appellate* jurisdiction, in cases of law and equity arising under the Constitution, to *fact*, as well as to law, clearly excludes criminal cases, where the trial by jury is secured; because the fact, in such cases, is not a subject of appeal.† And, although the appeal is liable to such *exceptions* and regulations as Congress may adopt, yet it is not to be supposed that an *exception* of *all* criminal cases could be contemplated; as well because a discretion in Congress to make or omit the exception would be improper, as because

---

* The phrase "cases in law and equity" undoubtedly means cases in law, and cases in equity, and both were made cognizable by the federal judiciary. Whilst, then, there cannot be criminal cases in equity, as the text observes, there may be criminal cases at law, and so the expression in question would include such cases. The reasoning is not much aided by this observation of the text. It is fortunately strong enough without it.

† If this mode of argument were correct, it would in like manner exclude *all* cases at *law*, as well of a civil as a criminal nature, for the seventh amendment to the Constitution secures trial by jury in the former, as it had already been secured in the latter, and further declares, that no fact tried by a jury shall be otherwise reexamined in any court of the United States, than according to the rules of the common law. The general argument to prove that the common law is no part of the law of the Federal Government is irrefutable, but the conclusion is not helped by the inferences attempted to be drawn from the phrase "cases in law and equity."

it would have been unnecessary. The exception could as easily have been made by the Constitution itself, as referred to the Congress.

Once more; the amendment last added to the Constitution, deserves attention, as throwing light on this subject. " The judicial power of the United States shall not be construed to extend to any suit in *law* or *equity*, commenced or prosecuted against one of the United States, by citizens of another state, or by citizens or subjects of any foreign power." As it will not be pretended that any criminal proceeding could take place against a state, the terms *law* or *equity*, must be understood as appropriate to *civil*, in exclusion of *criminal* cases.

From these considerations, it is evident, that this part of the Constitution, even if it could be applied at all to the purpose for which it has been cited, would not include any cases whatever of a criminal nature ; and consequently, would not authorize the inference from it, that the judicial authority extends to *offences* against the common law, as offences arising under the Constitution.

It is further to be considered, that even if this part of the Constitution could be strained into an application to every common law case, criminal as well as civil, it could have no effect in justifying the sedition-act, which is an exercise of legislative, and not of judicial power : and it is the judicial power only, of which the extent is defined in this part of the Constitution.

There are two passages in the Constitution, in which a description of the law of the United States is found. The first is contained in Art. III. sect. 2, in the words following : " This Constitution, the laws of the United States, and treaties made, or which shall be made under their authority." The second is contained in the second paragraph of Art. VI. as follows : " This Constitution, and the laws of the United States which shall be made in pursuance thereof, and all treaties made, or which shall be made, under the authority of the United States, shall be the supreme law of the land." The first of these descriptions was meant as a guide to the judges of the United States ; the second, as a guide to the judges in the several states. Both of them consists of an enumeration, which was evidently meant to be precise and complete. If the common law had been understood to be a law of the United States, it is not possible to assign a satisfactory reason why it was not expressed in the enumeration.

In aid of these objections, the difficulties and confusion inseparable from a constructive introduction of the common law, would afford powerful reasons against it:

Is it to be the common law with or without the British statutes ?

If without the statutory amendments, the vices of the code would be insupportable.

If with these amendments, what period is to be fixed for limiting the British authority over our laws ?

Is it to be the date of the eldest or the youngest of the colonies ?

Or are the dates to be thrown together, and a medium deduced ?

Or is our independence to be taken for the date ?

Is, again, regard to be had to the various changes in the common law made by the local codes of America ?

Is regard to be had to such changes, subsequent, as well as prior, to the establishment of the Constitution?

Is regard to be had to future, as well as past changes?

Is the law to be different in every state, as differently modified by its code; or are the modifications of any particular state to be applied to all?

And on the latter supposition, which among the state codes would form the standard?

Questions of this sort might be multiplied with as much ease, as there would be difficulty in answering them.

The consequences flowing from the proposed construction, furnish other objections equally conclusive; unless the text were peremptory in its meaning, and consistent with other parts of the instrument.

These consequences may be in relation to the legislative authority of the United States; to the executive authority; to the judicial authority; and to the governments of the several states.

If it be understood, that the common law is established by the Constitution, it follows that no part of the law can be altered by the legislature; such of the statutes already passed, as may be repugnant thereto would be nullified; particularly the " sedition-act" itself, which boasts of being a melioration of the common law; and the whole code, with all its incongruities, barbarisms, and bloody maxims, would be inviolably saddled on the good people of the United States.

Should this consequence be rejected, and the common law be held, like other laws, liable to revision and alteration, by the authority of Congress, it then follows, that the authority of Congress is co-extensive with the objects of common law; that is to say, with every object of legislation: for to every such object does some branch or other of the common law extend.   The authority of Congress would, therefore, be no longer under the limitations marked out in the Constitution. They would be authorized to legislate in all cases whatsoever.

In the next place, as the President possesses the executive powers of the Constitution, and is to see that the laws be faithfully executed, his authority also must be coextensive with every branch of the common law.   The additions which this would make to his power, though not readily to be estimated, claim the most serious attention.

This is not all; it will merit the most profound consideration, how far an indefinite admission of the common law, with a latitude in construing it, equal to the construction by which it is deduced from the Constitution, might draw after it the various prerogatives making part of the unwritten law of England.   The English constitution itself is nothing more than a composition of unwritten laws and maxims.

In the third place, whether the common law be admitted as of legal or of constitutional obligation, it would confer on the judicial department a discretion little short of a legislative power.

On the supposition of its having a constitutional obligation, this power in the judges would be permanent and irremediable by the legislature. On the other supposition, the power would not expire, until the legislature should have introduced a full system of statutory provisions. Let it be observed, too, that besides all the uncertainties above enumerated, and which present an immense field for judicial discretion, it w,ould remain with the same department to decide what parts of the common law would, and what would not, be properly applicable to the circumstances of the United States.

A discretion of this sort has always been lamented as incongruous and dangerous, even in the colonial and state courts; although so much narrowed by positive provisions in the local codes on all the principal subjects embraced by the common law. Under the United States, where so few laws exist on those subjects, and where so great a lapse of time must happen before the vast chasm could be supplied, it is manifest that the power of the judges over the law would, in fact, erect them into legislators; and that, for a long time, it would be impossible for the citizens to conjecture, either what was, or would be law.

In the last place, the consequence of admitting the common law as the law of the United States, on the authority of the individual states, is as obvious as it would be fatal. As this law relates to every subject of legislation, and would be paramount to the constitutions and laws of the states, the admission of it would overwhelm the residuary sovereignty of the states, and by one constructive operation, new-model the whole political fabric of the country.

From the review thus taken of the situation of the American colonies prior to their independence; of the effect of this event on their situation; of the nature and import of the articles of confederation; of the true meaning of the passage in the existing Constitution from which the common law has been deduced; of the difficulties and uncertainties incident to the doctrine; and of its vast consequences in extending the powers of the Federal Government, and in superseding the authorities of the state governments; the committee feel the utmost confidence in concluding, that the common law never was, nor, by any fair construction, ever can be, deemed a law for the American people as one community; and they indulge the strongest expectation that the same conclusion will finally be drawn, by all candid and accurate inquirers into the subject. It is indeed distressing to reflect, that it ever should have been made a question, whether the Constitution, on the whole face of which is seen so much labour to enumerate and define the several objects of federal power, could intend to introduce in the lump, in an indirect manner, and by a forced construction of a few phrases, the vast and multifarious jurisdiction involved in the common law; a law filling so many ample volumes; a law overspreading the entire field of legislation; and a law that would sap the foundation of the Constitution as a system of limited and specified powers. A severer reproach could not, in the opinion of the committee, be thrown on the Constitution, on those who framed, or on those who established it, than such a supposition would throw on them.

The argument, then, drawn from the common law, on the ground of its being adopted or recognised by the Constitution, being inapplicable to the sedition-act, the committee will proceed to examine the other arguments which have been founded on the Constitution.

They will waste but little time on the attempt to cover the act by the preamble to the Constitution; it being contrary to every acknowledged rule of construction, to set up this part of an instrument, in opposition to the plain meaning expressed in the body of the instrument. A preamble usually contains the general motives or reasons, for the particular regulations or measures which follow it; and is always understood to be explained and limited by them. In the present instance, a contrary interpretation would have the inadmissible effect, of rendering nugatory or improper every part of the Constitution which succeeds the preamble.

The paragraph in Art. I. sect. 8, which contains the power to lay and collect taxes, duties, imposts, and excise; to pay the debts, and provide for the common defence and general welfare, having been already examined, will also require no particular attention in this place. It will have been seen that in its fair and consistent meaning, it cannot enlarge the enumerated powers vested in Congress.

The part of the Constitution which seems most to be recurred to, in defence of the " sedition-act," is the last clause of the above section, empowering Congress " to make all laws which shall be necessary and proper for carrying into execution the foregoing powers, and all other powers vested by this Constitution in the government of the United States, or in any department or officer thereof."

The plain import of this clause is, that Congress shall have all the incidental or instrumental powers necessary and proper for carrying into execution all the express powers; whether they be vested in the government of the United States, more collectively, or in the several departments or officers thereof. It is not a grant of new powers to Congress, but merely a declaration, for the removal of all uncertainty, that the means of carrying into execution, those otherwise granted, are included in the grant.

Whenever, therefore, a question arises concerning the constitutionality of a particular power, the first question is, whether the power be expressed in the Constitution. If it be, the question is decided. If it be not expressed, the next inquiry must be, whether it is properly an incident to an express power, and necessary to its execution. If it be, it may be exercised by Congress. If it be not, Congress cannot exercise it.

Let the question be asked, then, whether the power over the press, exercised in the " sedition-act," be found among the powers expressly vested in the Congress? This is not pretended.

Is there any express power, for executing which it is a necessary and proper power?

The power which has been selected, as least remote, in answer to this question, is that of " suppressing insurrections;" which is said to imply a power to *prevent* insurrections, by punishing whatever may *lead* or *tend* to them. But, it surely cannot, with the least plausibility, be said, that a regulation of the press, and a punishment of libels, are exercises of a power to suppress insurrections. The most that could be said, would be, that the punishment of libels, if it had the tendency ascribed to it, might prevent the occasion of passing or executing laws necessary and proper for the suppression of insurrections.

Has the Federal Government no power, then, to prevent as well as to punish resistance to the laws?

· They have the power, which the Constitution deemed most proper, in their hands for the purpose. The Congress has power before it happens, to pass laws for punishing it; and the executive and judiciary have power to enforce those laws when it does happen.

It must be recollected by many, and could be shown to the satisfaction of all, that the construction here put on the terms " necessary and proper," is precisely the construction which prevailed during the discussions and ratifications of the Constitution. It may be added, and cannot too often be repeated, that it is a construction absolutely necessary to maintain their consistency with the peculiar character of the government, as possessed of particular and defined powers only; not of the general and indefinite powers vested in ordinary governments. For, if the power to *suppress insurrection*, includes a power to *punish libels;* or if the power to *punish*, includes a power to *prevent*, by all the means that may have that *tendency;* such is the relation and influence among the most remote subjects of legislation, that a power over a very few, would carry with it a power over all. And it must be wholly immaterial, whether unlimited powers be exercised under the name of unlimited powers, or be exercised under the name of unlimited means of carrying into execution limited powers.

This branch of the subject will be closed with a reflection which must have weight with all; but more especially with those who place peculiar reliance on the judicial exposition of the Constitution, as the bulwark provided against undue extensions of the legislative power. If it be understood that the powers implied in the specified powers, have an immediate and appropriate relation to them, as means, necessary and proper for carrying them into execution, questions on the constitutionality of laws passed for this purpose, will be of a nature sufficiently precise and determinate for judicial cognizance and control! If, on the other hand, Congress are not limited in the choice of means by any such appropriate relation of them to the specified powers; but may employ all such means as they may deem fitted to *prevent*, as well as to *punish*, crimes subjected to their authority; such as may have a *tendency* only to *promote* an object for which they are authorized to provide; every one must perceive, that questions relating to means of this sort, must be questions of mere policy and expediency, on which legislative discretion alone can decide, and from which the judicial interposition and control are completely excluded.

2. The next point which the resolution requires to be proved, is, that the power over the press exercised by the sedition-act, is positively forbidden by one of the amendments to the Constitution.

The amendment stands in these words—" Congress shall make no law respecting an establishment of religion, or prohibiting the free exercise thereof, *or abridging the freedom of speech or of the press;* or the right of the people peaceably to assemble, and to petition the government for a redress of grievances."

In the attempts to vindicate the " sedition-act," it has been contended, 1. That the " freedom of the press" is to be determined by the meaning of these terms in the common law. 2. That the article supposes the power over the press to be in Congress, and prohibits them only from *abridging* the freedom allowed to it by the common law.

Although it will be shown, in examining the second of these positions, that the amendment is a denial to Congress of all power over the press, it may not be useless to make the following observations on the first of them.

It is deemed to be a sound opinion, that the sedition-act, in its definition of some of the crimes created, is an abridgment of the freedom of publication, recognised by principles of the common law in England.

The freedom of the press under the common law, is, in the defences of the sedition-act, made to consist in an exemption from all *previous* restraint on printed publications, by persons authorized to inspect and prohibit them. It appears to the committee, that this idea of the freedom of the press, can never be admitted to be the American idea of it: since a law inflicting penalties on printed publications, would have a similar effect with a law authorizing a previous restraint on them. It would seem a mockery to say, that no law should be passed, preventing publications from being made, but that laws might be passed for punishing them in case they should be made.

The essential difference between the British government, and the American constitutions, will place this subject in the clearest light.

In the British government, the danger of encroachments on the rights of the people, is understood to be confined to the executive magistrate. The representatives of the people in the legislature, are not only exempt themselves, from distrust, but are considered as sufficient guardians of the rights of their constituents against the danger from the executive. Hence it is a principle, that the parliament is unlimited in its power; or, in their own language, is omnipotent. Hence, too, all the ramparts for protecting the rights of the people, such as their magna charta, their bill of rights, &c., are not reared against the parliament, but against the royal prerogative. They are merely legislative precautions against executive usurpations. Under such a government as this, an exemption of the press from previous restraint by licensers appointed by the king, is all the freedom that can be secured to it.

In the United States, the case is altogether different. The people, not the government, possess the absolute sovereignty. The legislature, no less than the executive, is under limitations of power. Encroachments are regarded as possible from the one, as well as from the other. Hence, in the United States, the great and essential rights of the people are secured against legislative, as well as against executive ambition. They are secured, not by laws paramount to prerogative, but by constitutions paramount to laws. This security of the freedom of the press requires, that it should be exempt, not only from previous restraint by the executive, as in Great Britain, but from legislative restraint also; and this exemption, to be effectual, must be an exemption not only from the previous inspection of licensers, but from the subsequent penalty of laws.

The state of the press, therefore, under the common law, cannot, in this point of view, be the standard of its freedom in the United States.

But there is another view, under which·it may be necessary to consider· this subject. It may be alleged, that although the security for the freedom of the press, be different in Great Britain and in this country ; being a legal security only in the former, and a constitutional security in the latter ; and although there may be a further difference, in an extension of the freedom of the press here, beyond an exemption from previous restraint, to an exemption from subsequent penalties also ; yet that the actual legal freedom of the press, under the common law, must determine the degree of freedom which is meant by the terms, and which is constitutionally secured against both previous and subsequent restraints.

The committee are not unaware of the difficulty of all general questions, which may turn on the proper boundary between the liberty and licentiousness of the press. They will leave it therefore for consideration only, how far the difference between the nature of the British government, and the nature of the American governments, and the practice under the latter, may show the degree of rigour in the former to be inapplicable to, and not obligatory in the latter.

The nature of governments elective, limited, and responsible, in all their branches, may well be supposed to require a greater freedom of animadversion than might be tolerated by the genius of such a government as that of Great Britain. In the latter, it is a maxim, that the king, an hereditary, not a responsible magistrate, can do no wrong ; and that the legislature, which in two-thirds of its composition, is also hereditary, not responsible, can do what it pleases. In the United States, the executive magistrates are not held to be infallible, nor the legislatures to be omnipotent ; and both being elective, are both responsible. Is it not natural and necessary, under such different circumstances, that a different degree of freedom, in the use of the press, should be contemplated ?

Is not such an inference favoured by what is observable in Great Britain itself? Notwithstanding the general doctrine of the common law, on the subject of the press, and the occasional punishment of those who use it with a freedom offensive to the government ; it is well known, that with respect to the responsible members of the government, where the reasons operating here, become applicable there, the freedom exercised by the press, and protected by the public opinion, far exceeds the limits prescribed by the ordinary rules of law. · The ministry, who are responsible to impeachment, are at all times animadverted on, by the press, with peculiar freedom ; and during the elections for the House of Commons, the other responsible part of the government, the press is employed with as little reserve towards the candidates.

The practice in America must be entitled to much more respect. In every state, probably, in the Union, the press has exerted a freedom in canvassing the merits and measures of public men, of every description, which has not been confined to the strict limits of the common law. On this footing, the freedom of the press has stood ; on this footing it yet stands. And it will not be a breach, either of truth or of candour, to say, that no persons or presses are in the habit of more unrestrained animadversions on the proceedings and functionaries of the state governments, than the persons and presses most zealous in vindicating the act of Congress for punishing similar animadversions on the government of the United States.

The last remark will not be understood as claiming for the state governments an immunity greater than they have heretofore enjoyed. Some degree of abuse is inseparable from the proper use of everything; and in no instance is this more true, than in that of the press. It has accordingly been decided by the practice of the states, that it is better to leave a few of its noxious branches to their luxuriant growth, than by pruning them away, to injure the vigour of those yielding the proper fruits. And can the wisdom of this policy be doubted by any who reflect, that to the press alone, chequered as it is with abuses, the world is indebted for all the triumphs which have been gained by reason and humanity, over error and oppression; who reflect, that to the same beneficent source, the United States owe much of the lights which conducted them to the rank of a free and independent nation; and which have improved their political system into a shape so auspicious to their happiness. Had "sedition-acts," forbidding every publication that might bring the constituted agents into contempt or disrepute, or that might excite the hatred of the people against the authors of unjust or pernicious measures, been uniformly enforced against the press, might not the United States have been languishing at this day, under the infirmities of a sickly confederation? Might they not possibly be miserable colonies, groaning under a foreign yoke?

To these observations, one fact will be added, which demonstrates that the common law cannot be admitted as the *universal* expositor of American terms, which may be the same with those contained in that law. The freedom of conscience, and of religion, are found in the same instruments which assert the freedom of the press. It will never be admitted, that the meaning of the former, in the common law of England, is to limit their meaning in the United States.

Whatever weight may be allowed to these considerations, the committee do not, however, by any means intend to rest the question on them. They contend that the article of amendment, instead of supposing in Congress a power that might be exercised over the press, provided its freedom was not abridged, was meant as a positive denial to Congress, of any power whatever on the subject.

To demonstrate that this was the true object of the article, it will be sufficient to recall the circumstances which led to it, and to refer to the explanation accompanying the article.

When the Constitution was under the discussions which preceded its ratification, it is well known, that great apprehensions were expressed by many, lest the omission of some positive exception from the powers delegated, of certain rights, and of the freedom of the press particularly, might expose them to the danger of being drawn by construction within some of the powers vested in Congress; more especially of the power to make all laws necessary, and proper for carrying their other powers into execution. In reply to this objection, it was invariably urged to be a fundamental and characteristic principle of the Constitution, that all powers not given by it, were reserved; that no powers were given beyond those enumerated in the Constitution, and such as were fairly incident to them; that the power over the rights in question, and particularly over the press, was neither among the enumerated powers, nor incident to any of them; and consequently that an exercise of any such power, would be a manifest usurpation. It is painful to remark, how much the arguments now employed in behalf of the sedition-act, are at variance with the reasoning which then justified the Constitution, and invited its ratification.

From this posture of the subject, resulted the interesting question in so many of the conventions, whether the doubts and dangers ascribed to the Constitution, should be removed by any amendments previous to the ratification, or be postponed, in confidence that as far as they might be proper, they would be introduced in the form provided by the Constitution. The latter course was adopted; and in most of the states, the ratifications were followed by propositions and instructions for rendering the Constitution more explicit, and more safe to the rights not meant to be delegated by it. Among those rights, the freedom of the press, in most instances, is particularly and emphatically mentioned. The firm and very pointed manner, in which it is asserted in the proceedings of the convention of this state, will be hereafter seen.

In pursuance of the wishes thus expressed, the first Congress that assembled under the Constitution, proposed certain amendments which have since, by the necessary ratifications, been made a part of it; among which amendments, is the article containing, among other prohibitions on the Congress, an express declaration that they should make no law abridging the freedom of the press.

Without tracing farther the evidence on this subject, it would seem scarcely possible to doubt, that no power whatever over the press was supposed to be delegated by the Constitution, as it originally stood; and that the amendment was intended as a positive and absolute reservation of it.

But the evidence is still stronger. The proposition of amendment is made by Congress, is introduced in the following terms: " *The conventions of a number of the states having at the time of their adopting the Constitution expressed a desire, in order to prevent misconstructions or abuse of its powers, that further declaratory and restrictive clauses should be added; and as extending the ground of public confidence in the government, will best ensure the beneficent ends of its institutions.*"

Here is the most satisfactory and authentic proof, that the several amendments proposed, were to be considered as either declaratory or restrictive; and whether the one or the other, as corresponding with the desire expressed by a number of the states, and as extending the ground of public confidence in the government.

Under any other construction of the amendment relating to the press, than that it declared the press to be wholly exempt from the power of Congress, the amendment could neither be said to correspond with the desire expressed by a number of the states, nor be calculated to extend the ground of public confidence in the government.

Nay more; the construction employed to justify the " sedition-act," would exhibit a phenomenon, without a parallel in the political world. It would exhibit a number of respectable states, as denying first that any power over the press was delegated by the Constitution; as proposing next, that an amendment to it, should explicitly declare that no such power was delegated ; and finally, as concurring in an amendment actually re-cognising or delegating such a power.

Is then the federal government, it will be asked, destitute of every authority for restraining the licentiousness of the press, and for shielding itself against the libellous attacks which may be made on those who ad-minister it?

The Constitution alone can answer this question. If no such power be expressly delegated, and it be not both necessary and proper to carry into execution an express power; above all, if it be expressly forbidden by a declaratory amendment to the Constitution, the answer must be, that the federal government is destitute of all such authority.

And might it not be asked in turn, whether it is not more probable, under all the circumstances which have been reviewed, that the authority should be withheld by the Constitution, than that it should be left to a vague and violent construction; whilst so much pains were bestowed in enumerating other powers, and so many less important powers are in-cluded in the enumeration?

Might it not be likewise asked, whether the anxious circumspection which dictated so many *peculiar* limitations on the general authority, would be unlikely to exempt the press altogether from that authority? The peculiar magnitude of some of the powers necessarily committed to the federal government; the peculiar duration required for the functions of some of its departments; the peculiar distance of the seat of its proceed-ings from the great body of its constituents; and the peculiar difficulty of circulating an adequate knowledge of them through any other channel; will not these considerations, some or other of which produced other ex-ceptions from the powers of ordinary governments, all together, account for the policy of binding the hand of the federal government, from touch-ing the channel which alone can give efficacy to its responsibility to its constituents; and of leaving those who administer it, to a remedy for their their injured reputations, under the same laws, and in the same tribunals, which protect their lives, their liberties, and their properties?

But the question does not turn either on the wisdom of the Constitution, or on the policy which gave rise to its particular organization. It turns on the actual meaning of the instrument; by which it has appeared, that a power over the press is clearly excluded, from the number of powers delegated to the federal government.

3. And in the opinion of the committee, well may it be said, as the resolution concludes with saying, that the unconstitutional power exercised over the press by the "sedition-act," ought "more than any other, to pro-duce universal alarm; because it is levelled against that right of freely examining public characters and measures, and of free communication among the people thereon, which has ever been justly deemed the only effectual guardian of every other right."

Without scrutinizing minutely into all the provisions of the "sedition-act," it will be sufficient to cite so much of section 2, as follows: "And be it further enacted, that if any person shall write, print, utter, or publish, or shall cause or procure to be written, printed, uttered or published, or shall knowingly and willingly assist or aid in writing, printing, uttering or publishing any false, scandalous and malicious writing or writings against the government of the United States, or either house of the Congress of the United States, or the President of the United States, *with an intent to defame the said government, or either house of the said Congress, or the President, or to bring them, or either of them, into contempt or disrepute; or to excite against them, or either, or any of them, the hatred of the good people of the United States, &c. Then such person being thereof convicted before any court of the United States, having jurisdiction thereof, shall be punished by a fine not exceeding two thousand dollars, and by imprisonment not exceeding two years.*"

On this part of the act, the following observations present themselves :

1. The Constitution supposes that the President, the Congress, and each of its houses may not discharge their trusts, either from defect of judgment or other causes. Hence, they are all made responsible to their constituents, at the returning periods of election; and the President, who is singly entrusted with very great powers, is, as a further guard, subjected to an intermediate impeachment.

2. Should it happen, as the Constitution supposes it may happen, that either of these branches of the government may not have duly discharged its trust, it is natural and proper that, according to the cause and degree of their faults, they should be brought into contempt or disrepute, and incur the hatred of the people.

3. Whether it has, in any case, happened that the proceedings of either, or all of those branches, evince such a violation of duty as to justify a contempt, a disrepute or hatred among the people, can only be determined by a free examination thereof, and a free communication among the people thereon.

4. Whenever it may have actually happened, that proceedings of this sort are chargeable on all or either of the branches of the government, it is the duty as well as right of intelligent and faithful citizens, to discuss and promulge them freely, as well to control them by the censorship of the public opinion, as to promote a remedy according to the rules of the Constitution. And it cannot be avoided, that those who are to apply the remedy must feel, in some degree, a contempt or hatred against the transgressing party.

5. As the act was passed on July 14, 1798, and is to be in force until March 3, 1801, it was of course, that during its continuance, two elections of the entire House of Representatives, an election of a part of the Senate, and an election of a President, were to take place.

6. That consequently, during all these elections, intended by the Constitution to preserve the purity, or to purge the faults of the administration, the great remedial rights of the people were to be exercised, and the responsibility of their public agents to be screened, under the penalties of this act.

May it not be asked of every intelligent friend to the liberties of his country, whether the power exercised in such an act as this, ought not to produce great and universal alarm? Whether a rigid execution of such

15

an act, in time past, would not have repressed that information and communication among the people, which is indispensable to the just exercise
of their electoral rights? And whether such an act, if made perpetual,
and enforced with rigour, would not, in time to come, either destroy our
free system of government, or prepare a convulsion that might prove
equally fatal to it?

In answer to such questions, it has been pleaded that the writings and
publications forbidden by the act, are those only which are false and
malicious, and intended to defame; and merit is claimed for the privilege
allowed to authors to justify, by proving the truth of their publications,
and for the limitations to which the sentence of fine and imprisonment is
subjected.

To those who concurred in the act, under the extraordinary belief that
the option lay between the passing of such an act, and leaving in force
the common law of libels, which punishes truth equally with falsehood,
and submits the fine and imprisonment to 'the indefinite discretion of the
court, the merit of good intentions ought surely not to be refused. A like
merit may perhaps be due for the discontinuance of the *corporal punishment*, which the common law also leaves to the discretion of the court.
This merit of *intention*, however, would have been greater, if the several
mitigations had not been limited to so short a period; and the apparent
inconsistency would have been avoided, between justifying the act at one
time, by contrasting it with the rigors of the common law, otherwise in
force, and at another time by appealing to the nature of the crisis, as requiring the temporary rigour exerted by the act.

But, whatever may have been the meritorious intentions of all or any
who contributed to the sedition-act, a very few reflections will prove, that
its baneful tendency is little diminished by the privilege of giving in evidence the truth of the matter contained in political writings.

In the first place, where simple and naked facts alone are in question,
there is sufficient difficulty in some cases, and sufficient trouble and vexa-
tion in all, of meeting a prosecution from the government, with the full
and formal proof necessary in a court of law.

But in the next place, it must be obvious to the plainest minds, that
opinions, and inferences, and conjectural observations, are not only in
many cases inseparable from the facts, but may often be more the objects
of the prosecution than the facts themselves; or may even be altogether
abstracted from particular facts; and that opinions and inferences, and conjectural observations, cannot be subjects of that kind of proof which appertains to facts, before a court of law.

Again: It is no less obvious, that the *intent* to defame or bring into
contempt or disrepute, or hatred, which is made a condition of the offence
created by the act, cannot prevent its pernicious influence on the freedom
of the press. For, omitting the inquiry, how far the malice of the intent
is an inference of the law from the mere publication, it is manifestly impossible to punish the intent to bring those who administer the government
into disrepute or contempt, without striking at the right of freely discussing
public characters and measures: because those who engage in such discussions, must expect and *intend* to excite these unfavourable sentiments,

so far as they may be thought to be deserved. To prohibit, therefore, the intent to excite those unfavourable sentiments against those who administer the government, is equivalent to a prohibition of the actual excitement of them; and to prohibit the actual excitement of them, is equivalent to a prohibition of discussions having that tendency and effect; which, again, is equivalent to a protection of those who administer the government, if they should at any time deserve the contempt or hatred of the people, against being exposed to it, by free animadversions on their characters and conduct. Nor can there be a doubt, if those in public trust be shielded by penal laws from such strictures of the press, as may expose them to contempt or disrepute, or hatred, where they may deserve it, in exact proportion as they may deserve to be exposed, will be the certainty and criminality of the intent to expose them, and the vigilance of prosecuting and punishing it; nor a doubt, that a government thus intrenched in penal statutes, against the just and natural effects of a culpable administration, will easily evade the responsibility, which is essential to a faithful discharge of its duty.

Let it be recollected, lastly, that the right of electing the members of the government, constitutes more particularly the essence of a free and responsible government. The value and efficacy of this right, depends on the knowledge of the comparative merits and demerits of the candidates for public trust; and on the equal freedom, consequently, of examining and discussing these merits and demerits of the candidates respectively. It has been seen, that a number of important elections will take place whilst the act is in force, although it should not be continued beyond the term to which it is limited. Should there happen, then, as is extremely probable in relation to some or other of the branches of the government, to be competitions between those who are, and those who are not, members of the government, what will be the situations of the competitors? Not equal; because the characters of the former will be covered by the "sedition-act" from animadversions exposing them to disrepute among the people; whilst the latter may be exposed to the contempt and hatred of the people, without a violation of the act. What will be the situation of the people? Not free; because they will be compelled to make their election between competitors, whose pretensions they are not permitted, by the act, equally to examine, to discuss, and to ascertain. And from both these situations, will not those in power derive an undue advantage for continuing themselves in it; which by impairing the right of election, endangers the blessings of the government founded on it?

It is with justice, therefore, that the General Assembly have affirmed in the resolution, as well that the right of freely examining public characters and measures, and free communication thereon, is the only effectual guardian of every other right, as that this particular right is levelled at, by the power exercised in the "sedition-act."

The resolution next in order is as follows:

That this state having by its convention, which ratified the federal Constitution, expressly declared, that among other essential rights, "the liberty of conscience and of the press cannot be cancelled, abridged, restrained or modified by any authority of the United States," and from

its extreme anxiety to guard these rights from every possible attack of so-
phistry and ambition, having, with other states, recommended an amend-
ment for that purpose, which amendment was, in due time, annexed to
the Constitution, it would mark a reproachful inconsistency, and crimi-
nal degeneracy, if an indifference were now shown to the most palpable
violation of one of the rights thus declared and secured; and the establish-
ment of a precedent, which may be fatal to the other.

To place this resolution in its just light, it will be necessary to recur to
the act of ratification by Virginia, which stands in the ensuing form:

We, the delegates of the people of Virginia, duly elected in pursuance
of a recommendation from the General Assembly, and now met in conven-
tion, having fully and freely investigated and discussed the proceedings
of the federal convention, and being prepared as well as the most mature
deliberation hath enabled us to decide thereon, do, in the name and in
behalf of the people of Virginia, declare and make known, that the powers
granted under the Constitution, being derived from the people of the
United States, may be resumed by them, whensoever the same shall be
perverted to their injury or oppression; and that every power not granted
thereby, remains with them, and at their will. That, therefore, no right
of any denomination can be cancelled, abridged, restrained, or modified,
by the Congress, by the Senate, or House of Representatives, acting in
any capacity, by the President, or any department or officer of the United
States, except in those instances in which power is given by the Constitu-
tion for those purposes; and that, among other essential rights, the liberty
of conscience and of the press, cannot be cancelled, abridged, restrained,
or modified, by any authority of the United States.

Here is an express and solemn declaration by the convention of the
state, that they ratified the Constitution in the sense, that no right of any
denomination can be cancelled, abridged, restrained, or modified by the
government of the United States or any part of it; except in those instances in which power is given by the Constitution; and in the sense
particularly, " that among other essential rights, the liberty of conscience
and freedom of the press cannot be cancelled, abridged, restrained, or
modified, by any authority of the United States."

Words could not well express, in a fuller or more forcible manner, the
understanding of the convention, that the liberty of conscience and the
freedom of the press, were *equally* and *completely* exempted from all
authority whatever of the United States.

Under an anxiety to guard more effectually these rights against every
possible danger, the convention, after ratifying the Constitution, proceeded
to prefix to certain amendments proposed by them, a declaration of rights,
in which are two articles providing, the one for the liberty of conscience,
the other for the freedom of speech and of the press.

Similar recommendations having proceeded from a number of other
states, and Congress, as has been seen, having in consequence thereof,
and with a view to extend the ground of public confidence, proposed,
among other declaratory and restrictive clauses, a clause expressly
securing the liberty of conscience and of the press; and Virginia having
concurred in the ratifications which made them a part of the Constitution,

it will remain with a candid public to decide, whether it would not mark an inconsistency and degeneracy, if an indifference were now shown to a palpable violation of one of those rights, the freedom of the press; and to a precedent therein, which may be fatal to the other, the free exercise of religion.

That the precedent established by the violation of the former of these rights, may, as is affirmed by the resolution, be fatal to the latter, appears to be demonstrable, by a comparison of the grounds on which they respec- tively rest; and from the scope of reasoning, by which the power over the former has been vindicated.

First. Both of these rights, the liberty of conscience and of the press, rest equally on the original ground of not being delegated by the Consti- tution, and consequently withheld from the government. Any construc- tion, therefore, that would attack this original security for the one, must have the like effect on the other.

Secondly. They are both equally secured by the supplement to the Constitution; being both included in the same amendment, made at the same time, and by the same authority. Any construction or argument, then, which would turn the amendment into a grant or acknowledgment of power with respect to the press, might be equally applied to the free- dom of religion.

Thirdly. If it be admitted that the extent of the freedom of the press, secured by the amendment, is to be measured by the common law on this subject, the same authority may be resorted to, for the standard which is to fix the extent of the " free exercise of religion." It cannot be neces- sary to say what this standard would be; whether the common law be taken solely as the unwritten, or as varied by the written law of England.

Fourthly. If the words and phrases in the amendment, are to be con- sidered as chosen with a studied discrimination, which yields an argument for a power over the press, under the limitation that its freedom be not abridged, the same argument results from the same consideration, for a power over the exercise of religion, under the limitation that its freedom be not prohibited.

For, if Congress may regulate the freedom of the press, provided they do not abridge it, because it is said only " they shall not abridge it," and is not said, " they shall make no law respecting it," the analogy of reasoning is conclusive, that Congress may *regulate* and even *abridge* the free-exercise of religion, provided they do not *prohibit* it, because it is said only " they shall not prohibit it," and is *not* said, " they shall make no law *respecting*, or no law *abridging* it."

The General Assembly were governed by the clearest reason, then, in considering the " sedition-act," which legislates on the freedom of the press, as establishing a precedent that may be fatal to the liberty of con- science; and it will be the duty of all, in proportion as they value the security of the latter, to take the alarm at every encroachment on the former.

The two concluding resolutions only remain to be examined. They are in the words following:

That the good people of this commonwealth, having ever felt and con-

tinuing to feel the most sincere affection for their brethren of the other states ; the truest anxiety for establishing and perpetuating the union of all ; and the most scrupulous fidelity to that Constitution, which is the pledge of mutual friendship; and the instrument of mutual happiness; the General Assembly doth solemnly appeal to the like dispositions in the other states, in confidence that they will concur with this commonwealth in declaring, as it does hereby declare, that the acts aforesaid are unconstitutional ;* and, that the necessary and proper measures will be taken by each, for co-operating with this state, in maintaining unimpaired the authorities, rights, and liberties reserved to the states respectively, or to the people.

That the governor be desired to transmit a copy of the foregoing resolutions to the executive authority of each of the other states, with a request that the same may be communicated to the legislature thereof; and that a copy be furnished to each of the senators and representatives representing this state in the Congress of the United States.

The fairness and regularity of the course of proceeding here pursued, have not protected it against objections even from sources too respectable to be disregarded.

It has been said, that it belongs to the judiciary of the United States, and not the state legislatures, to declare the meaning of the Federal Constitution.

But a declaration that proceedings of the Federal Government are not warranted by the Constitution, is a novelty neither among the citizens, nor among the legislatures of the states; nor are the citizens or the legislature of Virginia, singular in the example of it.

Nor can the declarations of either, whether affirming or denying the constitutionality of measures of the Federal Government, or whether made before or after judicial decisions thereon, be deemed, in any point of view, an assumption of the office of the judge. The declarations, in such cases, are expressions of opinion, unaccompanied with any other effect than what they may produce on opinion, by exciting reflection. The expositions of the judiciary, on the other hand, are carried into immediate effect by force. The former may lead to a change in the legislative ex-

---

* In the original resolutions as submitted by Mr. John Taylor, there followed after the word "unconstitutional," the words "*and not law, but utterly null, void, and of no force or effect.*" In the course of the debate, they were stricken out upon motion of Mr. Taylor himself. (See *ante*, p. 150.) Mr. Madison's explanation of this fact, in his letter to Mr. Everett, (see *post*, Appendix, p. 256,) is, that although these words were, in fact, but synonymous with "unconstitutional," yet to guard against a misunderstanding of this phrase, as more than declaratory of opinion, the word "unconstitutional" was alone retained as not liable to that danger. This explanation is abundantly supported by the circumstances. Mr. John Taylor had contended that the resolution in question, merely expressed the *opinion* of the legislature, such as it was competent to it to express, as a necessary concomitant of an attempt to procure an amendment to the Constitution from the other states. (*Ante*, p. 112–13.) Mr. G. K. Taylor, on the other hand, insisted that the words used, imported not merely an opinion, but a *fact*, which discharged the people from any submission to the laws thus denounced (*ante*, p. 140); and then Mr. J. Taylor moved to strike out the words above mentioned.

pression of the general will; possibly to a change in the opinion of the judiciary; the latter enforces the general will, whilst that will and that opinion continue unchanged.

And if there be no impropriety in declaring the unconstitutionality of proceedings in the Federal Government, where can be the impropriety of communicating the declaration to other states, and inviting their concurrence in a like declaration? What is allowable for one, must be allowable for all; and a free communication among the states, where the Constitution imposes no restraint, is as allowable among the state governments as among other public bodies or private citizens. This consideration derives a weight, that cannot be denied to it, from the relation of the state legislatures to the federal legislature, as the immediate constituents of one of its branches.

The legislatures of the states have a right also to originate amendments to the Constitution, by a concurrence of two-thirds of the whole number, in applications to Congress for the purpose. When new states are to be formed by a junction of two or more states, or parts of states, the legislatures of the states concerned are, as well as Congress, to concur in the measure. The states have a right also to enter into agreements or compacts, with the consent of Congress. In all such cases, a communication among them results from the object which is common to them.

It is lastly to be seen, whether the confidence expressed by the resolution, that the *necessary and proper measures* would be taken by the other states for co-operating with Virginia in maintaining the rights reserved to the states, or to the people, be in any degree liable to the objections which have been raised against it.

If it be liable to objection, it must be because either the object or the means are objectionable.

The object being to maintain what the Constitution has ordained, is in itself a laudable object.

The means are expressed in the terms " the necessary and proper measures." A proper object was to be pursued, by means both necessary and proper.

To find an objection, then, it must be shown that some meaning was annexed to these general terms, which was not proper; and, for this purpose, either that the means used by the General Assembly were an example of improper means, or that there were no proper means to which the terms could refer.

In the example given by the state, of declaring the alien and sedition-acts to be unconstitutional, and of communicating the declaration to the other states, no trace of improper means has appeared. And if the other states had concurred in making a like declaration, supported, too, by the numerous applications flowing immediately from the people, it can scarcely be doubted, that these simple means would have been as sufficient, as they are unexceptionable.

It is no less certain that other means might have been employed, which are strictly within the limits of the Constitution. The legislatures of the states might have made a direct representation to Congress, with a view to obtain a rescinding of the two offensive acts; or, they might have represented to their respective senators in Congress their wish, that two-thirds thereof would propose an explanatory amendment to the Constitution; or two-thirds of themselves, if such had been their option, might, by an application to Congress, have obtained a convention for the same object.

These several means, though not equally eligible in themselves, nor probably, to the states, were all constitutionally open for consideration. And if the General Assembly, after declaring the two° acts to be unconstitutional, the first and most obvious proceeding on the subject, did not undertake to point out to the other states a choice among the farther measures that might become necessary and proper, the reserve will not be misconstrued by liberal minds into any culpable imputation.

These observations appear to form a satisfactory reply to every objection which is not founded on a misconception of the terms employed in the resolutions. There is one other, however, which may be of too much importance not to be added. It cannot be forgotten, that among the arguments addressed to those who apprehended danger to liberty from the establishment of the General Government over so great a country, the appeal was emphatically made to the intermediate existence of the state governments, between the people and that government, to the vigilance with which they would descry the first symptoms of usurpation, and to the promptitude with which they would sound the alarm to the public. This argument was probably not without its effect; and if it was a proper one then, to recommend the establishment of the Constitution, it must be a proper one now, to assist in its interpretation.

The only part of the two concluding resolutions that remains to be noticed, is the repetition in the first, of that warm affection to the union and its members, and of that scrupulous fidelity to the Constitution, which have been invariably felt by the people of this state. As the proceedings were introduced with these sentiments, they could not be more properly closed than in the same manner. Should there be any so far misled as to call in question the sincerity of these professions, whatever regret may be excited by the error, the General Assembly cannot descend into a discussion of it. Those, who have listened to the suggestion, can only be left to their own recollection of the part which this state has borne in the establishment of our national· independence, in the establishment of our national Constitution, and in maintaining under it the authority and laws of the Union, without a single exception of internal resistance or commotion. By recurring to these facts, they will be able to convince themselves, that the representatives of the people of Virginia, must be above the necessity of opposing any other shield to attacks on their national patriotism, than their own consciousness, and the justice of an enlightened public; who will perceive in the resolutions themselves, the strongest evidence of attachment both to the Constitution and to the Union, since it is only by maintaining the different governments and departments within their respective limits, that the blessings of either can be perpetuated.

The extensive view of the subject thus taken by the committee, has led them to report to the House, as the result of the whole, the following resolution:

Resolved, That the General Assembly, having carefully and respect-fully attended to the proceedings of a number of the states, in answer to its resolutions of December 21, 1798, and having accurately and fully re-examined and reconsidered the latter, finds it to be its indispensable duty to adhere to the same, as founded in truth, as consonant with the Constitution, and as conducive to its preservation; and more especially to be its duty to renew, as it does hereby renew, its protest against "the alien and sedition-acts," as palpable and alarming infractions of the Constitution.

The foregoing report was industriously circulated amongst the people by virtue of the following resolution.

IN THE HOUSE OF DELEGATES,

Monday, January 20, 1800.

Resolved, That five thousand copies of the report of the select com-mittee, to whom were referred the answers of several states upon the reso-lutions of the last legislature, the said answers, and, also, the instructions to the senators of this state, in the Congress of the United States, together with the names of those who voted on each of those subjects, be printed without delay; and that the executive be requested, as soon as may be, to distribute them equally, in such manner as it shall think best, among the good people of this commonwealth.

Attest,

WILLIAM WIRT, *C. H. D.*
H. BROOKE, *C. S.*

At the time of adopting this report, the General Assembly was com-posed of the following persons—the names of the Federalists being in *italics :*

HOUSE OF DELEGATES.

ACCOMAC.	ALBEMARLE.
John Wise,	Francis Walker,
Thos. M. Bailey.	Wm. Woods.
AMHERST.	**AMELIA.**
David S. Garland,	Wm. B. Giles,
Wm. B. Hare.	Joshua Chaffin.
AUGUSTA.	**BATH.**
Robt. Doake,	*Samuel Blackburn,*
Andrew Anderson.	Samuel Vance.

BEDFORD.
Samuel Hancock,
Isaac Otey.

BERKELEY.
Magnus Tate,
Alex. White.

BOTETOURT.
James Breckenridge,
John Miller,

BRUNSWICK.
James Fletcher,
Wm. Ruffin.

BUCKINGHAM.
Linnæus Bolling,
Charles Yancey.

BROOKE.
Robert Calwell,
Jno. G. Young.

CAMPBELL.
Thomas West,
John F. Powell.

CAROLINE.
John Taylor,
George Buckner.

CHARLOTTE.
Thos. Read,
Wm. Price.

CHARLES CITY.
Collier Harrison,
Samuel Tyler.

CHESTERFIELD.
Matthew Cheatham,
Thos. A. Taylor.

CUMBERLAND.
Wm. Daniel, Jr.,
James Deane.

CULPEPER.
John Roberts,
Moses Green.

DINWIDDIE.
Peterson Goodwin,
John Pegram, Jr.

ELIZABETH CITY.
George Booker,
W. Westwood.

ESSEX.
John Daingerfield,
James Garnett.

FAIRFAX.
Richard B. Lee,
Thomas Swann.

FAUQUIER.
William Clarkson,
Elias Edmonds.

FLUVANNA.
Joseph Haden,
James Payne.

FREDERICK.
Archibald Magill,
George Eskridge.

FRANKLIN.
Moses Greer,
Benjamin Cooke.

GREENESVILLE.
Nathaniel Rieves,
Braxton Robinson.

GLOUCESTER.
Wm. Hall,
Christopher Garland.

GOOCHLAND.
James Pleasants, Jr.,
Wm. Lee.

GREENBRIAR.
John Matthews,
Wm. H. Cavendish.

GRAYSON.
Philip Gaines.

HALIFAX.
John B. Scott,
Richard Howson.

HAMPSHIRE.
Fielding Calmes,
John Higgins.

HANOVER.
Thomas Starke,
Thomas White.

HARRISON.
John G. Jackson,
John Prunty.

HARDY.
Jacob Fisher,
Christian Simons.

HENRICO.
Miles Selden,
Wm. Price.

HENRY.
Joseph Martin,
John Redd.

ISLE OF WIGHT. ,
Dolphin'Driver,
James Johnston.

JAMES CITY.
Littleton W. Tazewell,
Wm. Lightfoot.

KING AND QUEEN.
Richard Corbin,
Larkin Smith.

KANAWHA.
Thomas Lewis,
David Ruffner.

KING GEORGE.
Gustavus B. Wallace,
Burdett Ashton.

KING WILLIAM.
Robert Pollard,
Nathaniel Burwell.

LANCASTER.
Joseph Carter,
James Ball.

LOUDOUN.
Joseph Lewis,
Wm. Noland.

LOUISA.
Wm. O. Callis,
Robt. Yancey.

LEE.
Charles Cocke,
David Chadwell.

LUNENBURG.
Francis Epes,
Wm. Cowan.

MATTHEWS.
Zadock Litchfield,
Joseph Billups, Jr.

MADISON.
Robert Roebuck,
Henry Hill.

MECKLENBURG.
Edward L. Tabb,
John Nelson.

MIDDLESEX.
Churchill Blakey,
Robt. B Daniel.

MONONGALIA.
John Evans,
Thomas Wilson.

MONTGOMERY.
James Craig,
Daniel Howe.

NANSEMOND.
Willis Riddick,
Wm. Sumner.

NEW KENT.
John D. Watkins,
James Taylor.

NORFOLK.
Thomas Matthews,
Robert Butt.

NORTHAMPTON.
Nathaniel Darby,
Wm. Satchell.

NORTHUMBERLAND.
Wm. Claughton,
Wm. Ball.

NOTTOWAY.
Freeman Epes,
Grief Green.

OHIO.
Benjamin Biggs,
Ebenezer Zane.

ORANGE.
James Madison,
James Barbour.

PITTSYLVANIA.
Theodoric B. M'Robert,
Thomas H. Wooding.

POWHATAN.
Wm. Moseley,
Frederick Woodson.

PRINCE EDWARD.
Peter Johnston,
Charles Scott.

PRINCE GEORGE.
James Cureton,
George K. Taylor.

PRINCE WILLIAM.
John Pope,
Thomas Mason.

PRINCESS ANNE.
James Robinson,
Thomas Lawson.

PENDLETON.
William M'Coy,
Jacob Hull.

PATRICK.
Joshua Rentfro,
Archelaus Hughes.

RANDOLPH.
William Wilson,
John Hadden.

RICHMOND.
Richard Barnes,
William M'Carty.

ROCKBRIDGE.
John Bowyer,
Andrew Moore.

ROCKINGHAM.
Benj. Harrison,
George Huston.

RUSSELL.
Simon Cockrell,
James M'Farlane.

SHENANDOAH.
John Gatewood,
Wm. H. Dulaney.

SOUTHAMPTON.
Wm. Blow,
Wm. Bailey.

SPOTTSYLVANIA.
John Mercer,
Larkin Stannard.

STAFFORD.
Nathaniel Fox,
Daniel C. Brent.

SURRY.
Canfield Seward,
Nicholas Sebrell.

SUSSEX.
John R. Mason,
Robert Smith.

WARWICK.
Richard Cary,
John Burnham.

WESTMORELAND.
Henry S. Turner,
George Garner.

WASHINGTON.
Samuel Meek,
James Dysart.

WYTHE.
Samuel Crockett,
John Evans.

YORK.
Samuel Shield,
Thomas Griffin.

RICHMOND CITY.
Charles Copland.

WILLIAMSBURG.
Benjamin C. Waller.

NORFOLK BOROUGH.
Robert B. Taylor.

SENATE.

The names of the senators will appear, so far as the·vote taken upon the report is concerned, from the *ayes* and *noes*, on the next page.

The vote upon the report, as proposed by the committee, was taken in the House of Delegates on the 7th of January, 1800, and in the Senate on the 18th.

The names of those who voted on·either side are as follows:

IN THE HOUSE OF DELEGATES.

In the affirmative.—Messrs. Smith (Speaker), Walker, Woods, Giles,

Chaffin, David S. Garland, Hare, Vance, Calwell, Young, Ruffin, Charles Yancey, Bolling, Buckner, Read, Price (of Charlotte), Collier Harrison, Tyler, Cheatham, Thomas A. Taylor, Roberts, Moses Green, William Daniel, Deane, Pegram, Goodwyn, Booker, Westwood, Daingerfield, Garnett, Haden, Payne, Greer, Cook, Hall, Christopher Garland, Pleasants, William Lee, Gaines, John B. Scott, Howson, Calmes, Higgins, Selden, Price (of Henrico), Starke, Thomas White, Jackson, Prunty, Martin, Redd, Driver, James Johnston, Lightfoot, Callis, Francis Epes, Hill, Roebuck, Billups, Litchfield, Blakey, Ro. B. Daniel, Craig, Howe, Riddick, Claughton, Ball, Freeman Epes, Grief Green, Madison, Barbour, M'Roberts, Moseley, Woodson, Peter Johnston, Pope, Thomas Mason, Rentfro, Haddan, Barnes, M'Carty, Bowyer, Moore, Benjamin Harrison, Huston, Cockrell, M'Farlane, Dulaney, Gatewood, Mercer, Stannard, Fox, Seward, Sebrell, Burnham, Meek, Dysart, John Evans, Shield, Waller.—100.

In the negative.—Messrs. Wise, Thomas Bailey, Doake, Anderson, Blackburn, Hancock, Otey, Tate, Alex. White, Breckenridge, Miller, West, Powell, Swann, Richard B. Lee, Clarkson, Edmonds, Magill, Eskridge, John Matthews, Cavendish, Braxton Robinson, Fisher, Simon, Thomas Lewis, Ruffner, Wallace, Ashton, Burwell, Ball, Joseph Lewis Jr., Noland, Cowan, Nelson, Tabb, John Evans, Jr., Thomas Wilson, Sumner, Watkins, James Taylor, Butt, Darby, Satchell, Biggs, Wooding, Charles Scott, George K. Taylor, Cureton, Lawson, James Robinson, M'Coy, Hull, Blow, William Bailey, Garner, Turner, Crockett, Griffin, Copland, Ro. B. Taylor.—60.

IN THE SENATE.

In the affirmative.—Messrs. Creed Taylor, Richard Kennon, Burwell Bassett, Thomas Royster, Nicholas Faulcon, Holden Hudgins, French Strother, Thomas Ridley, John Preston, John Hoomes, Benjamin Temple, Thomas Newton, Nicholas Cabell, George Penn, Robert Saunders.—15.

In the negative.—Messrs. John Tayloe, Francis Peyton, Charles Magill, Gideon Spencer, John Haymond, John Eyre.—6.

☞ The Senate then consisted of twenty-four members, so that three did not vote.

VI.

INSTRUCTIONS TO VIRGINIA SENATORS.

IN THE HOUSE OF DELEGATES,

Saturday, January 11, 1800.

THE House proceeded to consider the instructions from the General Assembly of Virginia, to STEPHENS THOMPSON MASON and WILSON CARY NICHOLAS, senators from the state of Virginia, in the Congress of the United States. The instructions are as follows :—

The General Assembly of the commonwealth of Virginia, though it entertains no doubt of your punctual performance of your duty, or of your faithful adherence to the great principles of constitutional law, and national policy, deems it incumbent on it to communicate its opinions, formed after the most mature deliberation, on certain subjects essentially connected, as it solemnly believes, with the dearest rights, and most important interests of the people.

The General Assembly of Virginia will not now enter into a minute detail of all the facts and reasonings which justify and require the instructions hereto subjoined. It cannot, however, forbear to remind you of some facts and observations, which it deems too expressive and important to be passed over in silence. It had indulged a hope, when there was a prospect of an accommodation of differences with the French republic, or, if even the existing mission should not terminate in that desirable event,* when all the belligerent nations of Europe are too much occupied

---

* The mission referred to was composed of Messrs. Oliver Ellsworth, of Connecticut, then Chief Justice of the United States, William R. Davie, of North Carolina, and William Vans Murray, of Maryland, then the United States minister at the Hague.

As soon as Talleyrand discovered the gross blunder he had committed in dismissing the American plenipotentiaries, in the manner related in the preface (see page xii.), and that the people of the United States would heartily support their government, he hastened to avert the gathering storm by instructing the French secretary of legation at the Hague to give Mr. Murray, our minister there, assurances, at first informal, but finally distinct and authoritative, that "whatever plenipotentiary the government of the United States might send to France, to put an end to the existing differences

with European concerns, to meditate an invasion of the United States, that the people would have been relieved from the evils and expenses incident to a military establishment, such as that authorized by the fifth Congress; but it has been with the most painful emotions, that it has seen, at the opening of the present session of Congress, a total disappointment in this just and pleasing expectation. The following intimation is contained in the speech of the President, and approved in the answers of the two houses of Congress. "The result of the mission to France is yet uncertain, but however it may terminate, a steady perseverance in a system of national defence, commensurate with our resources and the situation of the United States, is an obvious dictate of wisdom." This recommendation, if carried into practice, would materially lessen the advantages which would naturally result from an accommodation with the French republic, the most important of which would be a relief from the evils incident to a preparation for a rupture, and seems to establish a position never before officially advanced in the United States—that war in Europe is of itself a sufficient cause for raising a standing army here, equal at least to the present military establishment. The experience of all ages has shown that the respite from wars amongst the European nations is too short to justify disbanding an existing army, and raising another during the intervals of peace, as a preparation for the next rupture; and of course, if European wars be a sufficient cause for raising military establishments here, a perpetual standing army would be the certain consequence of the recommendation. It cannot have escaped your notice, that the present war in Europe has not hitherto been deemed a sufficient cause for increasing the military establishment of the United States. So far from it, that during the existence of the war, the former establishment was actually reduced. It is equally notorious that the only motive avowed for augmenting the military force, arose from the apprehension of an actual invasion from France; and the same law which gave rise to the army, contains a provision for disbanding it, upon an accommodation with that republic. It cannot therefore but produce much concern, that notwithstanding the existing prospect of accommodation, it should not only be considered as necessary to go on with the immense expense of such an establishment, but that it should be deemed expedient to persevere in a system of defence commensurate with the resources and situation of the United States, even in the event of a successful termination of the pacific mission and a restoration of that state

---

between the two countries, would be undoubtedly received with the respect due to the representative of a free, independent, and powerful nation,"—employing, it will be observed, the very terms which Mr. Adams had used in his message of 21st June, 1798, as expressive of the only condition on which he would again send a minister to France.

Mr. Murray, having acquainted his government with this overture, the President, on the 18th of February, 1799, nominated him to the Senate as minister plenipotentiary to the French republic. On the 25th, however, recalling that nomination, he presented the names of Messrs. Ellsworth, Henry, and Murray, who were confirmed. Mr. Henry having declined the appointment, it was subsequently conferred on Mr. Davie, who, together with Mr. Ellsworth, having joined Mr. Murray in Paris, in March, 1800, a convention was concluded, on the last day of the following September, which adjusted the principal differences between the two countries. (See 2 Am. St. Papers, 239, 240, and 295; 3 Jeff. Mem. 421–423.)

of things which preceded the crisis which was supposed by Congress to require so great an augmentation of the military force. Although the Constitution submits the right of raising armies to the discretion of Congress, yet, it evidently contemplated the militia as the great bulwark of national defence, as well, to use the language of the Constitution, *to repel invasions*, as to *execute the laws of the union and suppress insurrections*, and contemplated the right of raising armies for pressing and extraordinary emergencies. That the militia, except in such emergencies, is the only safe and adequate defence of the nation, is a political axiom hitherto held sacred in the United States. This is not only the obvious meaning of the Constitution, but is still more strongly evidenced by the practical construction thereof under the former administration, as will appear by reviewing its proceedings for several successive years after the government was put into operation. Shortly after that event, the first President in his speech on the 8th of January, 1790, called the attention of Congress, to the great business of providing for the national defence in the following words : " A free people ought not only to be armed, but disciplined, to which end an uniform and well-digested plan is requisite." Acting under the same impression in his speech on the 25th of October, 1791, he again reminded Congress of the militia, as the great depository of national force. Speaking of the several objects referred to the consideration of Congress, in referring to the militia, he observes : " The first is certainly an object of primary importance, whether viewed in reference to the national security, or to the satisfaction of the community, or to the preservation of order ; in connexion with this, the establishment of competent magazines and arsenals, and the fortifications naturally present themselves to consideration. The safety of the United States, under divine protection, ought to rest on the basis of systematic and solid arrangements, exposed as little as possible to the hazard of fortuitous circumstances."

These recommendations being considered as relating exclusively to the militia, gave rise to a law more effectually to provide for the national defence, by establishing an uniform militia throughout the United States. The President again recurring to the militia, as the safe and adequate defence of the nation, in his speech on the third of December, 1793, after speaking of the necessity of procuring arms and other military apparatus, emphatically observes :—" *Nor can such arrangements, with such objects, be exposed to the censure or jealousy of the warmest friends of republican government. They are incapable of abuse in the hands of a militia, who ought to possess a pride in being the depository of the force of the republic, and may be trained to a degree of energy equal to every military exigency of the United States. But it is an inquiry which cannot be too solemnly pursued, whether the act has organized them so as to produce their full effect.*" And again, after the militia had demonstrated their efficacy in promptly marching to suppress an opposition to the laws in Pennsylvania, on the 19th of November, 1794, in his speech the President observes : " The devising and establishing a well-regulated militia, would be a genuine source of legislative honour, and a perfect title to public gratitude. I therefore entertain a hope, that the present session will not pass, without carrying to its full energy the power of organizing, arming, and disciplining the militia, and thus providing in the language of the Constitution for calling them forth, to execute the laws of the Union, suppress insurrections, and repel invasions, as auxiliary to the state of our defence, to which Congress can never too frequently recur; they will not omit to inquire whether the fortifications which have been already licensed by law, be commensurate with our exigencies." These quotations require no illustration. They demonstrate the principle contended for by the General Assembly. Until the fifth Congress this principle appears to have been duly respected. It was then materially varied by the substitution of a military establishment, and by volunteer corps officered by the President and not by the states, as the Constitution requires that the militia should be, at the same time refusing to arm and equip any portion of the militia for the purposes of defence.

The solicitude of the Virginia Assembly for disbanding the army and reinstating the great constitutional principle of national defence, is greatly increased by referring to the enormous sums appropriated for supporting the army and navy. During the last year, whilst money was procured at eight per centum, the appropriations for the support of the army alone, amounted to 4,200,000 dollars; for fortifications, 700,000; for the navy, 4,350,000; amounting in the whole to 9,250,000, exclusively of a great and unascertained sum of voluntary subscriptions for building and equipping vessels of war for which the subscribers receive an interest at six per centum. Thus imposing an annual debt, or an annual tax upon the people of nearly two dollars for every individual throughout the United States, to say nothing of the moral and political evils incident to a standing army and some of which are already developing themselves in the United States. Considering the great distance of the United States from the powerful nations of Europe, the natural strength of the country, the spirit of the people, and the fate of one invading experiment made at a time and under circumstances infinitely unfavourable to the United States compared with their present situation, the General Assembly is persuaded that as long as the nations of Europe continue at war with each other, no formidable invasion is to be apprehended at all, nor a sudden and formidable invasion at any time. Under this prospect of things the General Assembly holds it as the dictate of true policy in the federal government to husband the public resources, to arrange and prepare the militia, and to cultivate harmony by removing as far as possible, causes of jealousy and disapprobation. With these advantages it cannot be doubted that the United States would be in a better posture for facing any danger that can be seriously apprehended, than can be given them by the present military establishment accompanied with the anticipation of resources and the accumulations of public debts and taxes inseparable therefrom.

In reviewing the measures adopted by the fifth Congress, the General Assembly cannot overlook the act suspending all commercial intercourse with the French dominions.* However ready the General Assembly and

---

* This policy was begun by act of 13th June, 1798, which took effect from 1st July following, and expired 3d March, 1799. It was renewed by act of 9th February, 1799, which expired 3d March, 1800. And was again renewed 27th February, 1800, until 3d March, 1801.

its constituents may be to bear with cheerfulness their full share of all necessary burdens, and to be among the foremost, in making all necessary sacrifices, they cannot be insensible to some of the effects of this measure, which press with peculiar weight on them, at the same time that they must be in some degree felt, by every part of the United States. The article of tobacco, as you well know, constitutes a principal staple in the exports of this state. For several years past it has been an increasing one. France and the markets supplied, or that could be supplied through her, consume a very great proportion of all the tobacco made in the United States. Great Britain is supposed to consume not more than ten or twelve thousand hogsheads. 'The consequence of passing this prohibitory act, cutting off one part of the continental market, in Europe, whilst the British' fleet under the pretext of blockades had cut off another, has been to throw almost the whole of this great and valuable staple into the ports of Great Britain; from which, as a belligerent country, re-exportation to other markets, must be made with great difficulty, risk, and charges, whilst the monopoly thus thrown into a single market has had the natural effect of reducing the price of the article far below its usual standard, at the very time when, within the prohibited markets, it would have sold at a rate still more above the usual prices. At the time of passing the law, the average price of tobacco in Virginia was about ten dollars—at present the price is not more than about three dollars and thirty-three cents, and although other circumstances may possibly in some degree have contributed to produce this immense difference, yet it cannot be doubted that the act in question has been the principal cause. From this state of things it necessarily happens, that the merchants who were engaged in this branch of trade have been most extensively injured; the planter receives not more than a third of the value of his labour bestowed on the article of tobacco; the ability to pay the requisite taxes, is proportionably diminished, and the revenue from imports likely to be reduced, by the reduction of the value of the exports. On this consideration we think it proper to instruct you, to solicit a revision of the act aforesaid, which we cannot, from any information known to the public, perceive to be in any manner conducive in its operation to the national interest. Nor do we perceive, that any inconvenience can result from such a measure, to the existing posture of things between the United States and the French republic. If it should have any influence on the negotiations depending, it will probably be of a conciliatory, rather than of a disadvantageous nature. And should the negotiations not issue in the desired accommodation, this branch of the arrangements, that may then become proper, will be subject to the same discretion which will decide on every other.

With respect to the navy, it may be proper to remind you that whatever may be the proposed object of its establishment, or whatever may be the prospect of temporary advantages resulting therefrom, it is demonstrated by the experience of all nations, who have ventured far into naval policy, that such prospect is ultimately delusive; and that a navy has ever in practice been known more as an instrument of power, a source of expense, and an occasion of collisions and wars with other nations, than as an instrument of defence, of economy, or of protection to commerce.

Nor is there any nation, in the judgment of the General Assembly, to whose circumstances this remark is more applicable than to the United States.

The General Assembly of Virginia would consider itself unfaithful to the trusts reposed in it, were it to remain silent, whilst a doctrine has been publicly advanced, novel in its principle, and tremendous in its consequences : That the common law of England is in force under the government of the United States! It is not at this time proposed to expose at large the monstrous pretensions resulting from the adoption of this principle.* It ought never, however, to be forgotten, and can never be too often repeated, that it opens a new tribunal for the trial of crimes never contemplated by the federal compact. It opens a new code of sanguinary criminal law, both obsolete and unknown, and either wholly rejected or essentially modified in almost all its parts by state institutions. It arrests or supersedes state jurisdiction, and innovates upon state laws. It subjects the citizen to punishment according to the judiciary will, when he is left in ignorance of what this law enjoins as a duty, or prohibits as a crime. It assumes a range of jurisdiction for the federal courts, which defies limitation or definition. In short, it is believed that the advocates for the principle would themselves be lost in an attempt to apply it to the existing institutions of federal and state courts, by separating with precision their judiciary rights, and thus preventing the constant and mischievous interference of rival jurisdiction.

With respect to the alien and sedition-laws, it is at present only deemed necessary to refer you to the various discussions upon those subjects which, in the opinion of the General Assembly of Virginia, clearly demonstrate the unconstitutionality of their principles; and experience has also sufficiently shown, the mischiefs of their operation.

The General Assembly of Virginia, confiding in your intelligence and zeal, trusts that these principles will be, on all proper occasions, illustrated and supported by you, with that candour, moderation and firmness, without which the friends of liberty and truth, however sincere, cannot render essential service to the cause in which they are engaged.

Deeply impressed with these opinions, the General Assembly of Virginia instructs the senators and requests the representatives from this state in Congress, to use their best efforts—

1. To procure a reduction of the army, within the narrowest limits compatible with the protection of the forts and the preservation of the arsenals maintained by the United States ; unless such a measure shall be forbidden by information not known to the public.

2. To prevent any augmentation of the navy, and to promote any proposition for reducing it, as circumstances will permit, within the narrowest limits compatible with the protection of the sea-coasts, ports, and harbours of the United States, and of consequence a proportionate reduction of the taxes.

3. To oppose the passing of any law founded on, or recognising the

---

* The consequences of this doctrine are exposed in the Virginia Report. See the argument there. *Ante*, p. 216 *et seq.*

principle lately advanced, "that the common law of England is in force under the government of the United States;" excepting from such opposition such particular parts of the common law as may have a sanction from the Constitution, so far as they are necessarily comprehended in the technical phrases which express the powers delegated to the government;—and excepting also such other parts thereof as may be adopted by Congress, as necessary and proper for carrying into execution the powers expressly delegated.

4. To procure a repeal of the acts of Congress commonly called the alien and sedition-acts.

IN THE HOUSE OF DELEGATES.

VOTES ON INSTRUCTIONS TO SENATORS.

Saturday, January 11, 1800.

The House, according to order, proceeded to consider the "instructions from the General Assembly of Virginia, to Stephens Thompson Mason and Wilson Cary Nicholas, senators from the state of Virginia, in the Senate of the United States;" and the first article of the said instructions being read, a motion was made to amend the same by adding thereto, "unless such a measure shall be forbidden by information not known to the public," and the same being read, a motion was made to amend the amendment, by substituting in lieu thereof, "as soon as an accommodation of the existing differences with the French republic may render such a reduction safe and expedient." And the question being put thereupon,

It passed in the negative.

On the motion of Mr. Richard B. Lee, seconded by Mr. George K. Taylor,

Ordered, That the names of the ayes and noes on the foregoing question be inserted in the journal.

The names of those who voted in the affirmative are—Messrs. Bailey, Doake, Anderson, Blackburn, Hancock, Tate, A. White, Breckenridge, Powell, R. B. Lee, Clarkson, Edmunds, Magill, Eskridge, J. Mathews, Cavendish, B. Robinson, Fisher, Simon, T. Lewis, Ruffner, Ashton, Burwell, Ball, J. Lewis, Noland, Cowan, Nelson, J. Evans, Jun., Sumner, J. Taylor, Darby, Satchell, Biggs, Geo. K. Taylor, Cureton, Lawson, J. Robinson, Blow, W. Bailey, Garner, Turner, Crockett, Griffin, Copland, R. B. Taylor.—46.

And the names of those who voted in the negative are—Messrs. Wise, Woods, Giles, Chaffin, David S. Garland, Hare, Vance, Calwell, Young, Otey, Fletcher, Charles Yancey, West, J. Taylor, Buckner, Reid, Tyler, Cheatham, T. A. Taylor, J. Roberts, M. Green, W. Daniel, Dean, Pegram,

Goodwyn, Booker, Westwood, Daingerfield, Garnett, Hayden, Payne, Greer, Cooke, Hall, C. Garland, Pleasants, William Lee, Gaines, John B. Scott, Calmes, Higgins, Selden, Price, (of Henrico,) Starke, T. White, Jackson, Prunty, Martin, Redd, Driver, James Johnston, Tazewell, Lightfoot, Wallace, Pollard, Cocke, Callis, Yancey, Francis Eppes, Hill, Roebuck, Billups, Blakey, Robert B. Daniel, Craig, Howe, Riddick, Watkins, Claughton, Ball, Freeman Eppes, Grief Green, Madison, Barbour, M'Roberts, Wooding, Moseley, Woodson, Peter Johnston, Charles Scott, Pope, Thomas Mason, M'Coy, Hull, Rentfro, Haddan, Barnes, M'Carty, Bowyer, Moore, B. Harrison, Huston, M'Farlane, Dulany, Gatewood, Mercer, Stannard, Fox, Seward, Sebrell, Smith, Burnham, Meek, Dysart, Evans, Shield, and Waller.—107.

The question being then put on the amendment first proposed,

It passed in the affirmative.

And then the question being put on the first article of the instructions, as amended,

It passed in the affirmative.

On the motion of Mr. Jackson, seconded by Mr. Geo. K. Taylor,

Ordered, That the names of the ayes and noes on the foregoing question be inserted in the journal.

The names of those who voted in the affirmative are—Messrs. Woods, Giles, Chaffin, David S. Garland, Hare, Vance, Calwell, Young, Hancock, Otey, Fletcher, C. Yancey, Bolling, West, James Taylor, Buckner, Reid, Price, (of Charlotte,) Tyler, Cheatham, T. A. Taylor, Roberts, M. Green, W. Daniel, Deane, Pegram, Goodwyn, Booker, Westwood, Daingerfield, Garnett, Hayden, Payne, Greer, Cooke, Hall, C. Garland, Pleasants, W. Lee, Gaines, J. B. Scott, Higgins, Selden, Price, (of Henrico,) Starke, T. White, Prunty, Fisher, Martin, Redd, Driver, J. Johnston, Tazewell, Jackson, Lightfoot, Pollard, Cocke, Callis, R. Yancey, Francis Eppes, Hill, Roebuck, Billups, Litchfield, Blakey, R. B. Daniel, Craig, Howe, Riddick, Watkins, Claughton, Ball, Freeman Eppes, G. Green, Madison, Barbour, M'Roberts, Wooding, Moseley, Woodson, Peter Johnston, C. Scott, Pope, T. Mason, M'Coy, Hull, Rentfro, Haddan, Barnes, M'Carty, Bowyer, Moore, B. Harrison, Huston, M'Farlane, Dulaney, Gatewood, Mercer, Stannard, Fox, Seward, Sebrell, Burnham, Meek, Dysart, John Evans, Shield, and Waller.—108.

And the names of those who voted in the negative are—Messrs. Wise, T. Bailey, Doake, Anderson, Blackburn, Tate, A. White, Breckenridge, Miller, J. F. Powell, R. B. Lee, Clarkson, Magill, Eskridge, Cavendish, Thomas Lewis, Ruffner, Wallace, Ashton, Burwell, Joseph Lewis, Noland, Cowan, Nelson, Evans, Jun., T. Wilson, Sumner, James Taylor, Darby, Satchell, Biggs, G. K. Taylor, Cureton, Lawson, J. Robinson, Blow, W. Bailey, Smith, Garner, Turner, Griffin, Copland, R. B. Taylor.—42.

The second article of the instructions being then read, a motion was made to amend the same, by striking out the whole of the said article from the third word, and substituting in lieu of the part so struck out, " unnecessary augmentation of the navy, and to promote any proposition for confining it within the narrowest limits compatible with the protection

of the sea-coasts, ports, and harbours, and of the commerce of the United
States ;" and the question being put thereon,

It passed in the negative.

On the motion of Mr. George K. Taylor, seconded by Mr. Cureton,

Ordered, That the names of the ayes and noes on the foregoing question be inserted in the journal.

The names of those who voted in the affirmative are—Messrs. Wise,
T. Bailey, Doake, Anderson, Blackburn, Hancock, Otey, Alexander White,
Tate, Breckenridge, Miller, West, J. F. Powell, Booker, Westwood, Richard B. Lee, Clarkson, Edmunds, Magill, Eskridge, John Matthews, Cavendish, B. Robinson, Fisher, Simon, T. Lewis, Ruffner, Wallace, Ashton,
Pollard, Burwell, Ball, Joseph Lewis, Jun., Noland, Cowan, Nelson, John
Evans, Jun., T. Wilson, Sumner, James Taylor, Darby, Satchell, Biggs,
George K. Taylor, Cureton, Lawson, James Robinson, Blow, William
Bailey, Garner, Turner, Griffin, Copland, and Robert B. Taylor.—54.

And the names of those who voted in the negative are—Messrs. Woods,
Giles, Chaffin, D. S. Garland, Hare, Vance, Calwell, Young, Fletcher,
C. Yancey, Bolling, John Taylor, Buckner, Price, (of Charlotte,) Tyler,
Cheatham, T. A. Taylor, Roberts, Green, W. Daniel, Deane, Pegram,
Goodwyn, Daingerfield, Garnett, Hayden, Payne, Greer, Hall, C. Garland, Pleasants, W. Lee, Gaines, J. B. Scott, Howson, Calmes, Higgins,
Selden, Price, (of Henrico,) Starke, T. White, Jackson, Prunty, Martin,
Redd, Driver, J. Johnston, Tazewell, Lightfoot, Cocke, Callis, R. Yancey,
F. Eppes, Hill, Roebuck, Billups, Litchfield, Blakey, R. B. Daniel, Craig,
Howe, Riddick, Watkins, Claughton, William Ball, Freeman Eppes, G.
Green, Madison, Barbour, M'Roberts, Woodings, Moseley, Woodson, Peter
Johnston, C. Scott, Pope, T. Mason, M'Coy, Hull, Rentfro, Haddan, Barnes,
M'Carty, Bowyer, Moore, B. Harrison, Huston, Cockrell, M'Farlane,
Dulaney, Gatewood, Mercer, Stannard, Fox, Seward, Sebrell, Smith, Burnham, Meek, Dysart, Evans, Shield, and Waller.—103.

A motion was then made to amend the said article, by inserting after
the word " it," in the first line, " as circumstances will permit."

It passed in the affirmative.

The third article of the instructions being then read, a motion was made
to amend it by the following addition : " excepting from such opposition
such particular parts of the common law as may have a sanction from the
Constitution, so far as they are necessarily comprehended in the technical
phrases, which express the powers delegated to the government : and excepting also, such other parts thereof as may be adopted as necessary and
proper for carrying into execution the powers expressly delegated." And
the question being put thereupon,

It passed in the affirmative.

On the motion of Mr. Cureton, seconded by Mr. Breckenridge,

Ordered, That the names of the ayes and noes on the foregoing question be inserted in the journal.

The names of those who voted in the affirmative are—Messrs. Wise,

T. Bailey, Woods, Giles, Chaffin, D. S. Garland, Hare, Doake, Anderson, Blackburn, Vance, Calwell, Young, Hancock, Otey, Tate, A. White, Breckenridge, Miller, Fletcher,'C. Yancey, Bolling, West, Powell, John Taylor, Buckner, Reid, Price, (of Charlotte,) Tyler, Cheatham, T. A. Taylor, Roberts, M. Green, W. Daniel, Deane, Pegram, Goodwyn, Booker, Westwood, Daingerfield, Garnett, R. B. Lee, Clarkson, Edmonds, J. Hayden, Payne, Magill, Eskridge, Greer, Cooke, Hall, C. Garland, Pleasants, W. Lee, Gaines, Cavendish, B. Robinson, J. B. Scott, Howson, Calmes, Higgins, Selden, Price, (of Henrico,) Starke, T. White, Prunty, Fisher, Simon, Martin, Redd, Driver, J. Johnston, Tazewell, Lightfoot, T. Lewis, Ruffner, Wallace, Ashton, Pollard, Burwell, Ball, J. Lewis, Noland, Callis, R. Yancey, Francis Eppes, Cowan, Nelson, Hill, Billups, Litchfield, Blakey, R. Daniel, Evans, Jr., T. Wilson, Craig, Howe, Riddick, Sumner, Watkins, James Taylor, Darby, Satchell, Claughton, Ball, Freeman, Eppes, G. Green, Biggs, Madison, M'Roberts, Wooding, Moseley, Woodson, C. Scott, Pope, G. K. Taylor, Cureton, T. Mason, Lawson, James Robinson, M'Koy, Hull, Rentfro, Barnes, M'Carty, Bowyer, Moore, B. Harrison, Huston, M'Farlane, Dulaney, Gatewood, Blow, William Bailey, Mercer, Stannard, Fox, Seward, Sebrell, Smith, Burnham, Garner, Turner, Meek, Dysart, Shield, Griffin, Waller, and R. B. Taylor.—149.

And the names of those who voted in the negative are——

And the question being then put on the article of instruction as amended,

It passed in the affirmative.

The fourth article of the instructions was then read, and the question being put upon the passage thereof,

It passed in the affirmative.

That part of the instructions which relates to the act of Congress concerning the suspension of intercourse with France and her dependencies was then read, and the question being put on the passage thereof,

, It passed in the affirmative.

The question being then put, that the instructions, as amended, do pass, They passed in the affirmative.

On the motion of Mr. Jackson, seconded by Mr. Bailey,

Ordered, That the names of the ayes and noes on the foregoing question be inserted in the journal.

The names of those who voted in the affirmative are—Messrs. Woods, Giles, Chaffin, David S. Garland, Hare, Vance, Calwell, Young, Fletcher, Charles Yancey, J. Taylor, Buckner, Reid, Price, (of Charlotte,) Tyler, Cheatham, Thomas A. Taylor, Roberts, Green, Wm. Daniel, Deane, Pegram, Goodwyn, Booker, Westwood, Daingerfield, Garnett, Hayden, Payne, Greer, Cooke, Hall, Christopher Garland, Pleasants, William Lee, Gaines, J. B. Scott, Howson, Calmes, Higgins, Selden; Price, (of Henrico,) Starke, Thos. White, Jackson, Prunty, Martin, Redd, Driver, James Johnston, Tazewell, Lightfoot, Cocke, Callis, R. Yancey, Francis Eppes, Hill, Roebuck, Billups, Litchfield, Blakey, Robert B. Daniel, Craig, Howe, Riddick, Watkins, Claughton, J. Ball, F. Eppes, G. Green, Madison, Barbour, M'Roberts, Wooding, Moseley, Woodson, Charles Scott, Pope, M'Coy,

Hull, Rentfro, Haddan, Barnes, M'Carty, Bowyer, Moore, B. Harrison, Huston, Cockrell, M'Farlane, Dulaney, Gatewood, Mercer, Stannard, Fox, Seward, Sebrell, Burnham, Meek, Dysart, Shield, and Waller.—102.

The names of those who voted in the negative are—Messrs. Wise, Thomas Bailey, Doake, Anderson, Blackburn, Hancock, Otey, Tate, A. White, Breckenridge, Miller, West, Powell, R. B. Lee, Clarkson, Edmonds, Magill, Eskridge, Cavendish, B. Robinson, Fisher, Simon, T. Lewis, Ruffner, Wallace, Ashton, N. Burwell, J. Ball, J. Lewis, Jun., Noland, Cowan, Evans, T. Wilson, Sumner, James Taylor, Darby, Satchell, Biggs, G. K. Taylor, Cureton, Lawson, J. Robinson, Blow, William Bailey, Garner, Turner, Griffin, Copland, and R. B. Taylor.—49.

VII.

APPENDIX.

MR. MADISON TO MR. EVERETT.

Montpelier, August, 1830.

DEAR SIR,—

I have duly received your letter, in which you refer to the "nullifying doctrine," advocated as a constitutional right, by some of our distinguished fellow-citizens, and to the proceedings of the Virginia Legislature in '98 and '99, as appealed to in behalf of that doctrine; and you express a wish for my ideas on those subjects.

I am aware of the delicacy of the task in some respects, and the difficulty in every respect, of doing full justice to it. But having in more than one instance complied with a like request from other friendly quarters, I do not decline a sketch of the views which I have been led to take of the doctrine in question, as well as some others connected with them; and of the grounds from which it appears, that the proceedings of Virginia have been misconceived by those who have appealed to them. In order to understand the true character of the Constitution of the United States, the error, not uncommon, must be avoided, of viewing it through the medium, either of a consolidated government, or of a confederated government, whilst it is neither the one nor the other, but a mixture of both. And having, in no model, the similitudes and analogies applicable to other systems of government, it must, more than any other, be its own interpreter, according to its text and *the facts of the case.*

From these it will be seen, that the characteristic peculiarities of the Constitution are, 1, the mode of its formation; 2, the division of the supreme powers of government between the states in their united capacity, and the states in their individual capacities.

1. It was formed, not by the governments of the component states, as the federal government for which it was substituted was formed. Nor was it formed by a majority of the people of the United States, as a single community, in the manner of a consolidated government.

It was formed by the states, that is, by the people in each of the states, acting in their highest sovereign capacity; and formed consequently by the same authority which formed the state constitutions.

Being thus derived from the same source as the constitutions of the states, it has, within each state, the same authority as the constitution of the state, and is as much a constitution in the strict sense of the term within its prescribed sphere, as the constitutions of the states are within their respective spheres; but with this obvious and essential difference, that being a compact among the states in their highest sovereign capacity, and constituting the people thereof one people for certain purposes, it cannot be altered or annulled at the will of the states individually, as the constitution of a state may be at its individual will.

2. And that it divides the supreme powers of government, between the government of the United States and the governments of the individual states, is stamped on the face of the instrument; the powers of war and of taxation, of commerce and of treaties, and other enumerated powers vested in the government of the United States, being of as high and sovereign a character as any of the powers reserved to the state governments.

Nor is the government of the United States, created by the Constitution, less a government in the strict sense of the term, within the sphere of its powers, than the governments created by the constitutions of the states are, within their several spheres. It is like them organized into legislative, executive, and judiciary departments. It operates, like them, directly on persons and things. And like them, it has at command a physical force for executing the powers committed to it. The concurrent operation, in certain cases, is one of the features marking the peculiarity of the system.

Between these different constitutional governments, the one operating in all the states, the others operating separately in each, with the aggregate powers of government divided between them, it could not escape attention, that controversies would arise concerning the boundaries of jurisdiction, and that some provision ought to be made for such occurrences. A political system that does not provide for a peaceable and authoritative termination of occurring controversies, would not be more than the shadow of a government; the object and end of a real government being, the substitution of law and order, for uncertainty, confusion, and violence.

That to have left a final decision, in such cases, to each of the states, then thirteen, and already twenty-four, could not fail to make the Constitution and laws of the United States different in different states, was obvious, and not less obvious that this diversity of independent decisions, must altogether distract the government of the Union, and speedily put an end to the Union itself. A uniform authority of the laws, is in itself a vital principle. Some of the most important laws could not be partially executed. They must be executed in all the states, or they could be duly executed in none. An impost, or an excise, for example, if not in force in some states, would be defeated in others. It is well known that this was among the lessons of experience, which had a primary influence in bringing about the existing Constitution. A loss of its general authority would moreover revive the exasperating questions between the states holding ports for foreign commerce, and the adjoining states without them; to which are now added all the inland states, necessarily carrying on their foreign commerce through other states.

To have made the decisions under the authority of the individual states, co-ordinate, in all cases, with decisions under the authority of the United States, would unavoidably produce collisions incompatible with the peace of society, and with that regular and efficient administration, which is of the essence of free governments. Scenes could not be avoided, in which a ministerial officer of the United States, and the correspondent officer of an individual state, would have rencounters in executing conflicting decrees; the result of which would depend on the comparative force of the local posses attending them; and that, a casualty depending on the political opinions and party feelings in different states.

To have referred every clashing decision, under the two authorities, for a final decision, to the states as parties to the Constitution, would be attended with delays, with inconveniences and with expenses, amounting to a prohibition of the expedient; not to mention its tendency to impair the salutary veneration for a system requiring such frequent interpositions, nor the delicate questions which might present themselves as to the form of stating the appeal, and as to the quorum for deciding it.

To have trusted to negotiation for adjusting disputes between the government of the United States and the state governments, as between independent and separate sovereignties, would have lost sight altogether of a Constitution and government for the Union, and opened a direct road, from a failure of that resort, to the *ultima ratio* between nations wholly independent of and alien to each other. If the idea had its origin in the process of adjustment, between separate branches of the same government, the analogy entirely fails. In the case of disputes between independent parts of the same government, neither part being able to consummate its will, nor the government to proceed without a concurrence of the parts, necessity brings about an accommodation. In disputes between a state government and the government of the United States, the case is practically as well as theoretically different; each party possessing all the departments of an organized government, legislative, executive, and judiciary, and having each a physical force to support its pretensions. Although the issue of negotiation might sometimes avoid this extremity, how often would it happen among so many states, that an unaccommodating spirit in some would render that resource unavailing? A contrary supposition would not accord with a knowledge of human nature, or the evidence of our own political history.

The Constitution, not relying on any of the preceding modifications for its safe and successful operation, has expressly declared, on the one hand, 1, "that the Constitution, and the laws made in pursuance thereof, and all treaties made under the authority of the United States, shall be the supreme law of the land; 2, that the judges of every state shall be bound thereby, anything in the Constitution and laws of any state to the contrary notwithstanding; 3, that the judicial power of the United States shall extend to all cases in law and equity arising under the Constitution, the laws of the United States, and treaties made under their authority," &c.

On the other hand, as a security of the rights and powers of the states, in their individual capacities, against an undue preponderance of the powers granted to the government over them in their united capacity, the Constitution has relied on, 1, the responsiblity of the senators and representatives in the Legislature of the United States to the legislatures and people of the states; 2, the responsibility of the President to the people of the United States; and 3, the liability of the executive and judicial functionaries of the United States to impeachment by the representatives of the people of the states in one branch of the Legislature of the United States, and trial by the representatives of the states, in the other·branch; the state functionaries, legislative, executive, and judicial, being, at the same time, in their appointment and responsibility, altogether independent of the agency or authority of the United States.

How far this structure of the government of the United States is adequate and safe for its objects, time alone can absolutely determine. Experience seems to have shown that, whatever may grow out of future stages of our national career, there is, as yet, a sufficient control, in the popular will, over the executive and legislative departments of the government. When the alien and sedition-laws were passed in contravention to the opinions and feelings of the community, the first elections that ensued put an end to them. And whatever may have been the character of other acts, in the judgment of many of us, it is but true, that they have generally accorded with the views of a majority of the states and of the people. At the present day it seems well understood, that the laws which have created most dissatisfaction, have had a like sanction without doors; and that, whether continued, varied, or repealed, a like proof will be given of the sympathy and responsibility of the representative body to the constituent body. Indeed, the great complaint now is, against the results of this sympathy and responsibility in the legislative policy of the nation.

With respect to the judicial power of the United States, and the authority of the Supreme Court in relation to the boundary of jurisdiction between the federal and the state governments, I may be permitted to refer to the thirty-ninth number of the "Federalist,"* for the light in which the subject was regarded by its writer, at the period when the Constitution was depending; and it is believed, that the same was the prevailing view then taken of it, that the same view has continued to prevail, and that it does so at this time, notwithstanding the eminent exceptions to it.

But it is perfectly consistent with the concession of this power to the Supreme Court in cases falling within the course of its functions, to

---

* No. 39. It is true, that in controversies relating to the boundary between the two jurisdictions, the tribunal which is ultimately to decide, is to be established under the general government. But this does not change the principle of the case. The decision is to be impartially made, according to the rules of the Constitution; and all the usual and most effectual precautions are taken to secure this impartiality. Some such tribunal is clearly essential to prevent an appeal to the sword, and a dissolution of the compact; and that it ought to be established under the general, rather than under the local governments; or, to speak more properly, that it could be safely established under the first alone, is a position not likely to be combatted. (Note by Mr. Madison.)

maintain that the power has not always been rightly exercised. To say nothing of the period, happily a short one, when judges in their seats did not abstain from intemperate and party harangues, equally at variance with their duty and their dignity, there have been occasional decisions from the bench which have incurred serious and extensive disapprobation. Still it would seem that, with but few exceptions, the course of the judiciary has been hitherto sustained by the predominant sense of the nation.

Those who have denied or doubted the supremacy of the judicial power of the United States, and denounce at the same time a nullifying power in a state, seem not to have sufficiently adverted to the utter inefficiency of a supremacy in a law of the land, without a supremacy in the exposition and execution of the law; nor to the destruction of all equipoise between the Federal Government and the state governments, if, whilst the functionaries of the Federal Government are directly or indirectly elected by and responsible to the states, and the functionaries of the states are in their appointment and responsibility wholly independent of the United States, no constitutional control of any sort belonged to the United States over the states. Under such an organization, it is evident that it would be in the power of the states, individually, to pass unauthorized laws, and to carry them into complete effect, anything in the Constitution and laws of the United States to the contrary notwithstanding. This would be a nullifying power in its plenary character; and whether it had its final effect, through the legislative, executive or judiciary organ of the state, would be equally fatal to the constituted relation between the two governments.

Should the provisions of the Constitution as here reviewed, be found not to secure the government and rights of the states, against usurpations and abuses on the part of the United States, the final resort within the purview of the Constitution, lies in an amendment of the Constitution, according to a process applicable by the states.

And in the event of a failure of every constitutional resort, and an accumulation of usurpations and abuses, rendering passive obedience and non-resistance a greater evil than resistance and revolution, there can remain but one resort, the last of all; an appeal from the cancelled obligations of the constitutional compact to original rights and the law of self-preservation. This is the *ultima ratio* under all governments, whether consolidated, confederated, or a compound of both; and it cannot be doubted that a single member of the Union, in the extremity supposed, but in that only, would have a right, as an extra and ultra-constitutional right, to make the appeal.

This brings us to the expedient lately advanced, which claims for a single state a right to appeal against an exercise of power by the government of the United States decided by the state to be unconstitutional, to the parties to the constitutional compact; the decision of the state to have the effect of nullifying the act of the government of the United States, unless the decision of the state be reversed by three-fourths of the parties.

The distinguished names and high authorities which appear to have asserted and given a practical scope to this doctrine, entitle it to a respect which it might be difficult otherwise to feel for it.

If the doctrine were to be understood as requiring the three-fourths of the states to sustain, instead of that proportion to reverse the decision of the appealing state, the decision to be without effect during the appeal, it would be sufficient to remark, that this extra-constitutional course might well give way to that marked out by the Constitution, which authorizes two-thirds of the states to institute and three-fourths to effectuate an amendment of the Constitution, establishing a permanent rule of the highest authority, in place of an irregular precedent of construction only.

But it is understood that the nullifying doctrine imports that the decision of the state is to be presumed valid, and that it overrules the law of the United States, unless overruled by three-fourths of the states.

Can more be necessary to demonstrate the inadmissibility of such a doctrine, than that it puts it in the power of the smallest fraction over one-fourth of the United States, that is, of seven states out of twenty-four, to give the law and even the Constitution to seventeen states, each of the seventeen having, as parties to the Constitution, an equal right with each of the seven, to expound it, and to insist on the exposition? That the seven might, in particular instances be right, and the seventeen wrong, is more than possible. But to establish a positive and permanent rule giving such a power, to such a minority, over such a majority, would overturn the first principle of free government, and in practice necessarily overturn the government itself.

It is to be recollected that the Constitution was proposed to the people of the states as *a whole*, and unanimously adopted by the states as *a whole*, it being a part of the Constitution that not less than three-fourths of the states should be competent to make any alteration in what had been unanimously agreed to. So great is the caution on this point, that in two cases where peculiar interests were at stake, a proportion even of three-fourths is distrusted, and unanimity required to make an alteration.

When the Constitution was adopted as a whole, it is certain that there were many parts, which, if separately proposed, would have been promptly rejected. It is far from impossible, that every part of a constitution might be rejected by a majority, and yet taken together as a whole be unanimously accepted. Free constitutions will rarely if ever be formed without reciprocal concessions; without articles conditioned on and balancing each other. Is there a constitution of a single state out of the twenty-four that would bear the experiment of having its component parts submitted to the people and separately decided on?

What the fate of the Constitution of the United States would be if a small proportion of the states could expunge parts of it particularly valued by a large majority, can have but one answer.

The difficulty is not removed by limiting the doctrine to cases of construction. How many cases of that sort, involving cardinal provisions of the Constitution have occurred? How many now exist? How many may hereafter spring up? How many might be ingeniously created, if entitled to the privilege of a decision in the mode proposed?

Is it certain that the principle of that mode would not reach further than is contemplated? If a single state can of right require three-fourths of its co-states to overrule its exposition of the Constitution, because that proportion is authorized to amend it, would the plea be less plausible that, as the Constitution was unanimously established, it ought to be unanimously expounded?

The reply to all such suggestions seems to be unavoidable and irresistible; that the Constitution is a compact; that its text is to be expounded according to the provision for expounding it—making a part of the compact; and that none of the parties can rightfully renounce the expounding provision more than any other part. When such a right accrues, as may accrue, it must grow out of the compact releasing the sufferers from their fealty to it.

In favour of the nullifying claim for the states, individually, it appears, as you observe, that the proceedings of the Legislature of Virginia, in '98 and '99, against the alien and sedition-acts, are much dwelt upon.

It may often happen, as experience proves, that erroneous constructions, not anticipated, may not be sufficiently guarded against, in the language used; and it is due to the distinguished individuals, who have misconceived the intention of those proceedings, to suppose that the meaning of the legislature, though well comprehended at the time, may not now be obvious to those unacquainted with the contemporary indications and impressions.

But it is believed that by keeping in view the distinction between the governments of the states, and the states in the sense in which they were parties to the Constitution; between the rights of the parties, in their concurrent and in their individual capacities; between the several modes and objects of interposition against the abuses of power, and especially between interpositions within the purview of the Constitution, and interpositions appealing from the Constitution to the rights of nature paramount to all constitutions; with an intention, always of explanatory use, to the views and arguments which were combatted, the resolutions of Virginia, as vindicated in the report on them, will be found entitled to an exposition, showing a consistency in their parts, and an inconsistency of the whole with the doctrine under consideration.

That the Legislature could not have intended to sanction such a doctrine, is to be inferred from the debates in the House of Delegates, and from the address of the two houses to their constituents, on the subject of the resolutions. The tenor of the debates, which were ably conducted, and are understood to have been revised for the press by most, if not all, of the speakers, discloses no reference whatever to a constitutional right in an individual state, to arrest by force the operation of a law of the United States.* Concert among the states for redress against the alien and sedition-laws, as acts of usurped power, was a leading sentiment; and the attainment of a concert, the immediate object of the course adopted

* Thus Mr. Mercer (*ante*, p. 42) says, "Force is not thought of by any one;" and Mr. Barbour (*ante*, p. 59) says, he was "for using no violence," but, "for giving Congress an opportunity of repealing those obnoxious laws." See also Mr. J. Taylor, (*ante*, p. 113, and *ante*, p. 193.)

by the legislature, which was that of inviting the other states " to *concur* in declaring the acts to be unconstitutional, and to *co-operate* by the necessary and proper measures in maintaining unimpaired the authorities, rights, and liberties reserved to the states respectively and to the people."* That by the necessary and proper measures to be *concurrently* and *co-operatively* taken, were meant measures known to the Constitution, particularly the ordinary control of the people and legislatures of the states, over the government of the United States, cannot be doubted; and the interposition of this control, as the event showed, was equal to the occasion.

It is worthy of remark, and explanatory of the intentions of the legislature, that the words " not law, but utterly null, void, and of no force or effect," which had followed, in one of the resolutions, the word " unconstitutional," were struck out by common consent. Though the words were in fact but synonymous with " unconstitutional ;" yet to guard against a misunderstanding of this phrase as more than declaratory of opinion, the word " unconstitutional" alone was retained, as not liable to that danger.

The published address of the legislature to the people, their constituents, affords another conclusive evidence of its views. The address warns them against the encroaching spirit of the general government, argues the unconstitutionality of the alien and sedition-acts, points to other instances in which the constitutional limits had been overleaped ; dwells upon the dangerous mode of deriving power by implication ; and in general presses the necessity of watching over the consolidating tendency of the federal policy. But nothing is said that can be understood to look to means of maintaining the rights of the states, beyond the regular ones, within the forms of the Constitution.

If any further lights on the subject could be needed, a very strong one is reflected in the answers to the resolutions, by the states which protested against them. The main objection of these, beyond a few general complaints of the inflammatory tendency of the resolutions, was directed against the assumed authority of a state legislature to declare a law of the United States unconstitutional, which they pronounced an unwarrantable interference with the exclusive jurisdiction of the Supreme Court of the United States. Had the resolutions been regarded as avowing and maintaining a right, in an individual state, to arrest, by force, the execution of a law of the United States, it must be presumed that it would have been a conspicuous object of their denunciation.

With cordial salutations,
JAMES MADISON.

---

* See the concluding resolution of 1798.

MR. MADISON TO MR. INGERSOLL.

Montpelier, Feb. 2, 1831.

DEAR SIR,—

I have received your letter of January 21, asking—

1. Is there any state power to make banks?

2. Is the federal power, as it has been exercised, or as proposed to be exercised by President Jackson, preferable?

· The evil which produced the prohibitory clause in the Constitution of the United States, was the practice of the states in making bills of credit, and in some instances appraised property, " a legal tender." If the notes of state banks, therefore, whether chartered or unchartered, be made a legal tender, they are prohibited; if not made a legal tender, they do not fall within the prohibitory clause. The number of the " Federalist" referred to, was written with that view of the subject; and this, with probably other cotemporary expositions, and the uninterrupted practice of the states in creating and permitting banks without making their notes a legal tender, would seem to be a bar to the question, if it were not inexpedient now to agitate it. ·

A virtual and incidental enforcement of the depreciated notes of state banks, by their crowding out a sound medium, though a great evil, was not foreseen; and if it had been apprehended, it is questionable whether the Constitution of the United States, which had so many obstacles to encounter, would have ventured to guard against it by an additional provision. A virtual, and it is hoped, an adequate remedy, may hereafter be found in the refusal of state paper when debased, in any of the federal transactions, and in the control of the federal bank, this being itself controlled from suspending its specie payments by the public authority.

On the other question, I readily decide against the project recommended by the President. Reasons more than sufficient appear to have been presented to the public, in the reviews and other comments which it has called forth. How far a hint for it may have been taken taken from Mr. Jefferson, I know not. The kindred ideas of the latter may be seen in his Memoirs, &c., vol. iv., pages 196, 207, 526, and his view of the state banks, vol. iv., pages 199, 220.

There are sundry statutes of Virginia prohibiting the circulation of notes payable to bearer, whether issued by individuals or unchartered banks.

These observations, little new or important as they may be, would have been promptly furnished, but for an indisposition in which your letter found me, and which has not yet entirely left me. I hope this will find you in good health, and you have my best wishes for its continuance, and the addition of every other blessing.

JAMES MADISON.

Charles J. Ingersoll, Esq., Harrisburg, Pa.

17

MR. MADISON TO MR. INGERSOLL.

Montpelier, June 25, 1831.
DEAR SIR,—

I have received your friendly letter of the 18th inst. The few lines which answered your former one of the 21st of January last, were written in haste and in bad health; but they expressed, though without the attention in some respects due to the occasion, a dissent from the views of the President, as to a bank of the United States and a substitute for it; to which I cannot but adhere. The objections to the latter have appeared to me to preponderate greatly over the advantages expected from it, and the constitutionality of the former I still regard as sustained by the considerations to which I yielded in giving my assent to the existing bank.

The charge of inconsistency between my objection to the constitutionality of such a bank in 1791, and my assent in 1817, turns on the question, how far legislative precedents, expounding the Constitution, ought to guide succeeding legislatures, and to overrule individual opinions.

Some obscurity has been thrown over the question, by confounding it with the respect due from one legislature to laws passed by preceding legislatures. But the two cases are essentially different. A constitution being derived from a superior authority, is to be expounded and obeyed, not controlled or varied by the subordinate authority of the legislature. A law, on the other hand, resting on no higher authority than that possessed by every successive legislature, its expediency as well as its meaning, is within the scope of the latter.

The case in question has its true analogy in the obligation arising from judicial expositions of the law on succeeding judges; the constitution being a law to the legislator, as the law is a rule of decision to the judge.

And why are judicial precedents, when formed on due discussion and consideration, and deliberately sanctioned by reviews and repetitions, regarded as of binding influence, or rather of authoritative force, in settling the meaning of a law? It must be answered: 1st. Because it is a reasonable and established axiom, that the good of society requires that the rules of conduct of its members should be certain and known, which would not be the case, if any judge, disregarding the decisions of his predecessors, should vary the rule of law according to his individual interpretation of it. *Misera est servitus ubi jus est aut vagum, aut incognitum.* 2d. Because an exposition of the law publicly made, and repeatedly confirmed by the constituted authority, carries with it, by fair inference, the sanction of those who, having made the law through their legislative organ, appear under such circumstances to have determined its meaning through their judiciary organ.

Can it be of less consequence that the meaning of a constitution should be fixed and known, than that the meaning of a law should be so? Can indeed a law be fixed in its meaning and operation, unless the constitution be so? On the contrary, if a particular legislature, differing in the con-

struction of the constitution, from a series of preceding constructions, proceed to act on that difference, they not only introduce uncertainty and in-
stability in the constitution, but in the laws themselves; inasmuch as all
laws preceding the new construction and inconsistent with it, are not only
annulled for the future, but virtually pronounced nullities from the beginning.

But it is said that the legislator, having sworn to support the constitution, must support it in his own construction of it, however different from
that put on it by his predecessors, or whatever be the consequences of the
construction. And is not the judge under the same oath to support the
law? yet has it ever been supposed that he was required, or at liberty to
disregard all precedents, however solemnly repeated and regularly observed; and, by giving effect to his own abstract and individual opinions,
to disturb the established course of practice in the business of the community? Has the wisest and most conscientious judge ever scrupled to
acquiesce in decisions in which he has been overruled by the mature
opinions of the majority of his colleagues, and subsequently to conform
himself thereto, as to authoritative expositions of the law? And is it not
reasonable that the same view of the official oath should be taken by a
legislator, acting under the constitution, which is his guide, as is taken by
a judge, acting under the law, which is his?

There is in fact and in common understanding, a necessity of regarding
a course of practice, as above characterized, in the light of a legal rule of
interpreting a law; and there is a like necessity of considering it a constitutional rule of interpreting a constitution.

That there may be extraordinary and peculiar circumstances controlling the rule in both cases, may be admitted: but with such exceptions,
the rule will force itself on the practical judgment of the most ardent
theorist. He will find it impossible to adhere to, and act officially upon,
his solitary opinions as to the meaning of the law or constitution, in opposition to a construction reduced to practice, during a reasonable period
of time; more especially where no prospect existed of a change of construction by the public or its agents. And if a reasonable period of time,
marked with the usual sanctions, would not bar the individual prerogative, there could be no limitation to its exercise, although the danger of
error must increase with the increasing oblivion of explanatory circumstances, and with the continual changes in the import of words and
phrases.

Let it then be left to the decision of every intelligent and candid judge,
which, on the whole, is most to be relied on for the true and safe construction of a constitution, that which has the uniform sanction of successive legislative bodies through a period of years, and under the varied
ascendency of parties; or that which depends upon the opinions of every
new legislature, heated as it may be by the spirit of party, eager in the
pursuit of some favourite object, or led astray by the eloquence and address of popular statesmen, themselves, perhaps, under the influence of
the same misleading causes.

It was in conformity with the view here taken of the respect due to
deliberate and reiterated precedents, that the Bank of the United States,

though on the original question held to be unconstitutional, received the executive signature in the year 1817.. The act originally establishing a bank had undergone ample discussions in its passage through the several branches of the government. It had been carried into execution throughout a period of twenty years with annual legislative recognitions; in one instance indeed, with a positive ramification of it into a new state; and with the entire acquiescence of all the local authorities, as well as of the nation at large, to all of which may be added, a decreasing prospect of any change in the public opinion adverse to the constitutionality of such an institution. A veto from the executive under these circumstances, with an admission of the expediency, and almost necessity of the measure, would have been a defiance of all the obligations derived from a course of precedents amounting to the requisite evidence of the national judgment and intention.

It has been contended that the authority of precedents was in that case invalidated by the consideration, that they proved only a respect for the stipulated duration of the bank, with a toleration of it until the law should expire, and by the casting vote given in the Senate by the Vice-President in the year 1811, against a bill for establishing a national bank, the vote being expressly given on the ground of unconstitutionality. But if the law itself was unconstitutional, the stipulation was void, and could not be constitutionally fulfilled or tolerated. And as to the negative of the Senate by the casting vote of the presiding officer, it is a fact well understood at the time, that it resulted not from an equality of opinions in that assembly on the power of Congress to establish a bank, but from a junction of those who admitted the power, but disapproved the plan, with those who denied the power. On a simple question of constitutionality, there was a decided majority in favour of it.

Mrs. Madison joins me in hoping that you will not fail to make the intended visit to Virginia, which promises us the pleasure of welcoming you to our domicile, and in a sincere return of all the good wishes you kindly express for us.

JAMES MADISON.

Mr. Ingersoll.

INDEX.

---

www.ingramcontent.com/pod-product-compliance
Lightning Source LLC
Chambersburg PA
CBHW020402100426

42812CB00001B/171